# Markets in Historical Contexts
## Ideas and Politics in the Modern World

*Markets in Historical Contexts* is the result of a dialogue between historians and social scientists thinking about markets in modern society. How should we approach markets after the collapse of Marxism? What alternative ways of thinking about markets can we recover from the past? The essays in this volume set out to challenge essentialist accounts of the market. Instead they suggest that markets are always embedded in distinctive traditions and practices that shape the ways in which they are conceived and the manner of their working. The essays range widely over European and non-European societies from the eighteenth century to the present, from the great transformation to globalisation. Rational peasants, republican economists, popular conservatives, guild theorists, early environmentalists, communitarians, progressives, consumers, Gandhi's descendants and others are all revived. The volume thus recovers alternative ways of thinking about markets, many of which are unduly neglected or marginalized in contemporary debates.

MARK BEVIR is Associate Professor of Political Science at the University of California, Berkeley. He is the author of *The Logic of the History of Ideas* (1999) and coauthor of *Interpreting British Governance* (2003).

FRANK TRENTMANN is Senior Lecturer in Modern History at Birkbeck College, University of London and Director of the ESRC- and AHRB-funded *Cultures of Consumption* Research Programme. He is the editor of *Paradoxes of Civil Society* (2000/2003).

# Markets in Historical Contexts

*Ideas and Politics in the Modern World*

*edited by*

Mark Bevir and Frank Trentmann

CAMBRIDGE
UNIVERSITY PRESS

CAMBRIDGE UNIVERSITY PRESS
Cambridge, New York, Melbourne, Madrid, Cape Town, Singapore, São Paulo

Cambridge University Press
The Edinburgh Building, Cambridge CB2 8RU, UK

Published in the United States of America by Cambridge University Press, New York

www.cambridge.org
Information on this title: www.cambridge.org/9780521833554

First published 2004
Reprinted 2005
This digitally printed version 2007

*A catalogue record for this publication is available from the British Library*

*Library of Congress Cataloguing in Publication data*
Markets in historical contexts : ideas and politics in the modern world / edited by
Mark Bevir and Frank Trentmann.
       p.     cm.
Includes bibliographical references and index.
ISBN 0 521 83355 8
1. Markets – History.   2. Markets.   I. Bevir, Mark.   II. Trentmann, Frank.
HF5471.M38   2004   380.1 – dc21   2003055052

ISBN 978-0-521-83355-4 hardback
ISBN 978-0-521-04451-6 paperback

# Contents

*Acknowledgements*                                                *page* vii
*List of contributors*                                                  viii

1  Markets in historical contexts: ideas, practices and
   governance                                                             1
   MARK BEVIR AND FRANK TRENTMANN

2  Improving justice: communities of norms in the Great
   Transformation                                                        25
   JAMES LIVESEY

3  The politics of political economy in France from
   Rousseau to Constant                                                  46
   RICHARD WHATMORE

4  Tories and markets: Britain 1800–1850                                 70
   DAVID EASTWOOD

5  Guild theory and guild organization in France and
   Germany during the nineteenth century                                90
   HEINZ-GERHARD HAUPT

6  Thinking green, nineteenth-century style: John Stuart
   Mill and John Ruskin                                                 105
   DONALD WINCH

7  Tönnies on 'community' and 'civil society': clarifying
   some cross-currents in post-Marxian political thought               129
   JOSE HARRIS

8  German historicism, progressive social thought, and
   the interventionist state in the United States since
   the 1880s                                                            145
   AXEL R. SCHÄFER

v

9   Civilizing markets: traditions of consumer politics in
    twentieth-century Britain, Japan and the United
    States                                                            170
    PATRICIA MACLACHLAN AND FRANK
    TRENTMANN

10  The ideologically embedded market: political
    legitimation and economic reform in India                         202
    ROB JENKINS

11  The locational and institutional embeddedness of
    electronic markets: the case of the global capital
    markets                                                           224
    SASKIA SASSEN

    *Index*                                                           247

# Acknowledgements

*Markets in Historical Contexts* is the result of a dialogue between historians and social scientists thinking about markets in modern society. How should we approach markets at the beginning of the twenty-first century? What alternative ways of thinking about markets can we recover from the past? Contributors were asked to explore the changing meaning and social contingency of markets in their particular subject area.

About half the chapters in this volume derive from a conference that we organized at Princeton University in September 2000. We should like to thank, for their generous support of the conference, the Davis Center, the President's Fund, the Center for International Studies, the Woodrow Wilson School, and the Committee for European Studies, all of Princeton University. We also thank Frank's former colleagues at Princeton's history department for their encouragement, and Pamela Long for administrative help. We are especially grateful to those who contributed so much to our discussions at the conference: Arun Agrawal, Terence Ball, Sheri Berman, Victoria de Grazia, Shel Garon, Eagle Glassheim, Molly Greene, John Hall, Harold James, Ellen Kennedy, Allan Megill, Dan Rodgers, Herman Schwartz, Gareth Stedman Jones and Shannon Stimson. We are also grateful to the anonymous readers and to Michael Watson of Cambridge University Press. Finally, we should like to thank Laura Bevir for her help with the index, and Joanne Hill for copy-editing the manuscript.

# Contributors

MARK BEVIR teaches political theory at the University of California at Berkeley. He is the author of *The Logic of the History of Ideas,* and coauthor (with Rod Rhodes) of *Interpreting British Governance.*

DAVID EASTWOOD is Vice-Chancellor of the University of East Anglia. He was formerly Fellow and Tutor in Modern History and Senior Tutor at Pembroke College, Oxford; and Professor of History at the University of Wales, Swansea. His books include *Governing Rural England* and (with Laurence Brockliss) *A Union of Multiple Identities: The British Isles 1750–1850.*

JOSE HARRIS is professor of history at Oxford. She is the author of *William Beveridge* and *Private Lives, Public Spirit: a Social History of Britain, 1870–1914,* and, most recently, the editor of a new English edition of F. Tönnies, *Community and Civil Society.*

HEINZ-GERHARD HAUPT is professor of history at the Universität Bielefeld. He is the author of many books on modern European social and political history, most recently *Konsum und Handel,* and (with Geoffrey Crossick) *Die Kleinbürger,* a study of the petite bourgeoisie in nineteenth-century Europe.

ROB JENKINS is professor of politics at Birkbeck College, University of London. He has published widely on post-colonial India and is the author of *Democratic Politics and Economic Reform in India* (Cambridge), and editor of *Regional Reflections: Comparing Politics Across India's States* (Oxford).

JAMES LIVESEY teaches modern history at Trinity College, Dublin, and has also taught at Harvard University. He is the author of *Making Democracy in the French Revolution.*

PATRICIA MACLACHLAN teaches comparative politics at the University of Texas at Austin and has published widely on Japanese politics and consumer movements. She is the author of *Consumer Politics in Post-War Japan*.

SASKIA SASSEN is the Ralph Lewis Professor of Sociology at the University of Chicago, and Centennial Visiting Professor at the London School of Economics. Her most recent books are *The Global City* and *Guests and Aliens*. She is currently completing her forthcoming book *Denationalization: Territory, Authority and Rights in a Global Digital Age*.

AXEL R. SCHÄFER teaches US history at Keele University. He has taught at the University of Washington, the Freie Universität Berlin, and Charles University, Prague. He is the author of *American Progressives and German Social Reform, 1875–1920*.

FRANK TRENTMANN teaches modern history at Birkbeck College, University of London, and has also taught at Princeton University and at the Universität Bielefeld. He is the editor of *Paradoxes of Civil Society* and is completing a monograph, *Food and Freedom: Consumption, Commerce, and Civil Society in Modern Britain*. He is director of the *Cultures of Consumption* research programme funded by ESRC and AHRB.

RICHARD WHATMORE is Senior Lecturer in Intellectual History at the University of Sussex. He is the author of *Republicanism and the French Revolution* (Oxford, 2000), and the editor (with Stefan Collini and Brian Young) of *Economy, Polity and Society* and of *History, Religion and Culture* (Cambridge, 2000).

DONALD WINCH is research professor at the graduate centre for humanities at the University of Sussex. His many publications include *Adam Smith's Politics* and *Riches and Poverty: An Intellectual History of Political Economy in Britain*.

# 1 Markets in historical contexts: ideas, practices and governance

*Mark Bevir and Frank Trentmann*

Social life requires co-ordination between individual actions. Co-ordination can arise intentionally or unintentionally and can take different forms. For much of the previous century, societies across the globe valorized two of forms of co-ordination – the market and state planning. All too often the market and the state appeared as polar opposites. Proponents of the market portrayed it as a natural and spontaneous form of order in which the free activities of individuals were co-ordinated for the public benefit by an invisible hand. Proponents of the state, meanwhile, portrayed hierarchical planning as a rational and just form of order in which humans took control of their own activity so as to overcome the irrationality and exploitation of unbridled capitalism. Today, in contrast, we witness increasing doubts not only about each of these visions, but also about the very dichotomy they seem to instantiate. Of course, there still remains a prominent – perhaps even a dominant – neo-liberal discourse that holds to an idealized vision of the market as a spontaneous co-ordinating mechanism that operates for the public good provided only that individuals are left to exchange freely with one another. Nonetheless, there is also a blossoming 'new political economy' that points to the superficialities and blindspots of this idealized account of the market. The new political economy draws on transactional, institutional and evolutionary economics to argue that all economic institutions, including markets, are necessarily established and transformed in the context of political, social and cultural authorities.[1] All economies have to be governed through complex patterns of rule that connect and regulate economic actors, organizations and interactions.

We should like to thank contributors for helpful comments and suggestions.
[1] For important statements of these overlapping strands of economics see respectively O. Williamson, 'Transaction-Cost Economics: The Governance of Contractural Relations', *Journal of Law and Economics* 22 (1979), pp. 223–61; A. Shonfeld, *Modern Capitalism: The Changing Balance of Public and Private Power* (Oxford, 1965); and R. Nelson and S. Winter, *An Evolutionary Theory of Economic Change* (Cambridge, MA, 1982). A recent philosophical critique of the rationality of the market system is J. O'Neill, *The Market: Ethics, Knowledge, and Politics* (London, 1998).

*Markets in Historical Contexts* is an interdisciplinary volume of essays that addresses questions that arise once we accept the embeddedness of markets. How have various forms of regulation and co-ordination been imagined and constructed at different times in different societies? How has the understanding of markets by thinkers and social movements been shaped by ideas of political order, social cohesion and ethics? In what ways have the unfolding and development of modern capitalisms been shaped by ideas and practices exogenous to markets or even critical of them? This volume of essays advances the debate about the embeddedness of markets by shifting attention beyond questions of institutional preconditions and trust to those of ideas, languages, and the alternative visions found within them.

In the first place, this volume is a project of retrieval. The dichotomies of state versus market, or culture versus market, that flourished during the twentieth century had the unfortunate legacy of burying beneath them a rich and fertile history of thought about the place of markets in modern societies. Instead of offering a convenient ideal-typical antagonism between pro-market and anti-market, this volume thus explores the ways in which liberals as well as radicals, conservatives and nationalists developed ambivalent understandings of the market – understandings that were shaped by intellectual traditions and social practices. To recover this rich, creative imagination, the volume offers original readings of canonical thinkers, like J. S. Mill, J. B. Say and F. Tönnies, while, at the same time, expanding our perspective beyond the canon to the ideas of groups who are all too easily neglected in the literature on markets, such as conservative elites or organized consumers.[2] To be sure, history is not a simple source of tools for solving current social and political problems. What it can do, however, is to reflect on earlier ideas and practices so as to alert us to different ways of framing markets, helping us to interrogate current wisdom and to broaden the debate about possible forms of governance. For those interested in reforming or civilizing markets, the new political economy has opened new avenues, such as the Third Way, that seek to avoid the binary of state versus market. As this volume shows, earlier ideas and practices too provide examples of alternatives to that very binary. The past offers a rich variety of ways of connecting civil society, markets and the state. Greater awareness of these can suggest dilemmas as well as opportunities for the agendas of present-day reformers.

Retrieving the embeddedness of markets in intellectual traditions and social practices opens up the space for the second contribution of this volume: reconsidering the role of agency in the development of modern

---

[2] For critical surveys of the canon of modern social thought, see R. J. Holton, *Economy and Society* (London, 1992), and D. Slater and F. Tonkiss, *Market Society: Markets and Modern Social Theory* (Cambridge, 2001).

capitalist societies. If the dichotomy between market and state, or market and culture, acted as one prominent frame of analysis, it was often complemented by another: that between modernity and tradition. A stylized version of the free market, which rendered it as a mode of impersonal co-ordination typical of modernity, encouraged an equally stylized picture of intimate communal relations that allegedly were characteristic of traditional societies. Such a picture, as anthropologists have observed, obscures both the cultural dynamics of modern markets and the market elements of 'traditional' communities.[3] It also assigns different social groups a priori positions of agency or passivity in the evolution of modern capitalisms. Peasants and rural elites all too easily became portrayed as bulwarks of resistance to the spirit of modernity, entrepreneurs its engine, liberal political economists its prophets. Even Werner Sombart – who explored the evolution of modern capitalism with a creative breadth and depth like no other – found it impossible to resist this sociological equation. While Sombart was keen to stress that economic life was part of cultural life, and while he wrote on the significance of the consumption of luxuries by elites in pre-modern Europe, his definition of modern capitalism as a system driven by a rational and calculating spirit and by hierarchical organization and decision-making still led him to locate agency with that group of actors who embodied just this spirit: entrepreneurs. 'If modern economic rationalism is like the mechanism of a clock', Sombart argued, then 'someone must be there to wind it up'.[4] Entrepreneurs spread the principles of economic rationality that gradually came to penetrate society in the age of *Hochkapitalismus* or 'full capitalism' (1760–1914): ' "the driving force" in modern capitalism is thus the capitalist entrepreneur and only he', for he is the 'only "productive", that is, creative force, . . . [since] labour and capital are dependent on him and only called to life through his creative action'.[5] In Sombart's account of the evolution of capitalism, other social groups thus played the role of passive human resources who were rearranged and organized to fit the demands of entrepreneurial rationalism.

Although Karl Polanyi's work approached modern capitalism from a very different theoretical perspective, and although it was equally critical

---

[3] A. Appadurai, 'Introduction: Commodities and the Politics of Value', in A. Appadurai, ed., *The Social Life of Things: Commodities in Cultural Perspective* (Cambridge, 1986), pp. 3–63.

[4] W. Sombart, 'Capitalism', in E. R. A. Seligman and A. Johnson, eds, *Encyclopedia of the Social Sciences*, vol. III (New York, 1930), p. 205.

[5] W. Sombart, *Der Moderne Kapitalismus: Historisch-Systematische Darstellung des gesamteuropäischen Wirtschaftslebens von seinen Anfängen bis zur Gegenwart*, vol. III: *Das Wirtschaftsleben im Zeitalter des Hochkapitalismus* (Munich, 1927), pt 1, p. 12; editors' translation. Of course, agency was not parcelled out equally amongst entrepreneurs. Only a few and diminishing group of businessmen had the creative genius to act as the 'Führer' of capitalism over time.

of Marxism's economistic fallacy and liberal narratives of the supposedly inevitable rise of markets, nonetheless it too illustrates the pervasiveness of an action-reaction model in the social sciences. In Polanyi's view, the dynamics of modern society derived from a 'double movement': the movement of an expanding market was met by a countermovement of social protection. Social movements and visions of social solidarity emerged to contain and reform market society, but they were not present at its birth, which was the result of mercantilist policies and liberal ideology. Here again, we thus find the conceptual separation of 'the principle of economic liberalism, aiming at the establishment of a self-regulating market, relying on the support of the trading classes' from 'the principle of social protection aiming at the conservation of man and nature',[6] relying primarily on the working and landed classes. This conceptual separation privileges an action-reaction account of causation in which markets and their sponsors come first, and concerns about social protection and their supporters come only later. While Polanyi's general outlook was holistic and highlighted the dominance of the social, in which the economy was embedded, his passionate dislike of market society led him to portray its development as a negative deviation, a process of disembedding, to which social protection was an organic countermovement.

There are problems with such a sociological division between ideas of social co-ordination. Liberals were not necessarily prophets of a 'modern' society in which a depersonalized market acted as the principal form of social co-ordination; rather, they could care about the conservation of man and nature. Likewise, peasants and rural elites were not necessarily bulwarks of tradition. Just as for liberal actors we can reclaim alternative visions of modernity, so for conservative elites and groups at the bottom of society. The question was, for all these groups, not simply one of support or resistance to markets but about how markets should be embedded within social and political contexts. Social groups and intellectual traditions that were ambivalent about markets also helped to shape the contours and dynamics of capitalist societies. Once we look beyond the market as an endogenous model of capitalist rationality, we quickly find other sources of modern rationality, such as science or communication, which were available to innumerable social groups, including peasants. Likewise, to shift our gaze from the early stages of modern capitalism to the end of the twentieth century, we should ask how inherited social infrastructures and cultural beliefs continue to shape – not just resist – the

---

[6] K. Polanyi, *The Great Transformation: The Political and Economic Origins of Our Time* (Boston, 1957), p. 130. See also F. Block and M. R. Somers, 'Beyond the Economistic Fallacy: The Holistic Social Science of Karl Polanyi', in T. Skocpol, ed., *Vision and Method in Historical Sociology* (Cambridge, MA, 1984), pp. 47–84.

dynamics of global capitalism, as this volume does in exploring consumer politics, responses to marketization in India in the 1980s and 90s, and the social connectivity that underlies the local centres of the global capital market today.

Together, the essays collected in this volume thus seek to re-embed markets as ideas and practices of social co-ordination within their political, social and cultural contexts. The essays contribute to a dialogue between historians and social scientists about how to recontextualize markets, past and present. While individual chapters show the strengths of particular disciplinary approaches, they also converge around related questions of embeddedness that point to a shared conceptual approach. They thereby shift our attention from questions about the good or evil nature of markets to questions about economic governance. In what follows, therefore, we want to cut a pathway through the historiographical and theoretical underpinnings of the turn to economic governance. Economic governance, we suggest, has arisen as an important interdisciplinary concern across the human sciences ranging from cultural historians and constructivist institutionalists to post-structuralists and democratic pluralists.[7] Several theoretical and substantive positions are shared by most of these varied approaches to economic governance: a concern with meanings or beliefs as constitutive of social and economic practices, an interest in the plurality of historical sites, an emphasis on contingency and context, and a recognition of the role of critique in the formation and development of modes of economic governance. The chapters in this volume offer historically informed explorations of these themes. One general implication that emerges is the centrality of agency. We want to suggest that a more satisfactory incorporation of human agency might strengthen yet further the study of economic governance. The concept of economic governance promotes, more generally, alternative narratives, modes of inquiry, and political practices to those that characterize neo-classical economics and its extensions in public choice theory.[8]

---

[7] The insights of the new political economy apply not only to the economy but also to individual firms. For studies in corporate governance – that is, firms in relation to legal and political authorities – see, among many, J. McCahery, P. Moerland, T. Raaijmakers and L. Renneboog, *Corporate Governance Regimes – Convergence and Diversity* (Oxford, 2002); and M. Roe, *Political Determinants of Corporate Governance* (Oxford, 2002). For bridges between corporate and economic governance see P. Hall and D. Soskice, eds, *Varieties of Capitalism: The Institutional Foundations of Comparative Advantage* (Oxford, 2001).

[8] Public choice theory is, of course, more varied than we can allow for here. Some public choice theorists are uncomfortable with universal assumptions about motivation, interests and rationality made outside particular sets of norms or beliefs, so they hope to

## The turn to governance

Political scientists, historians and theorists have turned to governance for several overlapping reasons. Political scientists turned to the concept to describe changes in the state.[9] Globalization, information technology and the end of communism, they argued, have inaugurated new times. Socio-economic processes have sped up the pace of change, made fluid what once were established boundaries within and between organizations, and increased reciprocal interdependence. The result has been a shift from government to governance or a hollowing out of the state. In this view, a new semi-sovereign type of state has emerged whose authority has been eroded internally and externally so that it can act only in conjunction with other organizations within interdependent networks. Hence, attention shifts from the formal institutions of the nation state to processes of governing or steering,[10] processes that often occur at the boundary between state and civil society, both at local and transnational levels. The resulting literature on governance has drawn on the sociological literature that conceptualizes networks as an alternative form of co-ordination to both hierarchies and markets.[11] Contemporary governance is characterized, in this view, by the state operating in and through networks. This

expand the theory to allow for contingency and contextualization of just that sort. See F. Kratochwil, *Rules, Norms, and Decisions* (Cambridge, 1989); W. Mitchell, 'The Shape of Public Choice to Come: Some Predictions and Advice', *Public Choice* 77 (1993), pp. 133–44; C. Vicchaeri, *Rationality and Co-ordination* (Cambridge, 1993), esp. pp. 221–41. On the limits of public choice theory, including these attempts to modify the theory, see D. Green and I. Shapiro, *Pathologies of Rational Choice Theory* (New Haven, 1994).

[9] On the turn to governance in political science see R. Mayntz, 'New Challenges to Governance Theory', in H. Bang, ed., *Governance, Governmentality, and Democracy* (Manchester, forthcoming, 2004). For further examples see J. Kooiman, ed., *Modern Governance* (London, 1993); J. Pierre, ed., *Debating Governance* (Oxford, 2000); R. Rhodes, *Understanding Governance: Policy Networks, Governance, Reflexivity and Accountability* (Buckingham, 1997); J. N. Rosenau and E.-O. Czempiel, eds, *Governance without Government: Order and Change in World Politics* (Cambridge, 1992); and L. Roubon, ed., *Citizens and the New Governance Beyond Public Management* (Amsterdam, 1999).

[10] We might question the novelty of this turn to ideas of steering and co-ordination. Many inter-war internationalists had developed a similar fascination with modes of co-ordination, following on from a critique of liberal ideas of sovereignty: see A. Salter, *Allied Shipping Control: An Experiment in International Administration* (Oxford, 1921); A. E. Zimmern, *The Prospects of Democracy and Other Essays* (London, 1929); and the discussion in F. Trentmann, 'Political Culture and Political Economy: The Erosion of Free Trade in Britain, c. 1897–1932' (Harvard PhD thesis, 1999), chs 5, 6.

[11] See J. Frances, R. Levacic, J. Mitchell and G. Thompson, eds, *Markets, Hierarchies, and Networks: The Co-ordination of Social Life* (London, 1991); and W. Powell, 'Neither Market nor Hierarchy: Network Forms of Organization', *Research in Organizational Behaviour* 12 (1990), pp. 295–336. M. Castells, *The Information Age: Economy, Society and Culture*, vol. I: *The Rise of the Network Society* (Oxford, 1996). See also the new journal *Global Networks*.

concern with governance as networks within civil society challenges too strict a dichotomy between state and market. Neither the state nor the market stands as a separate, self-defining institution. Rather, both are entangled in broader patterns of rule within civil society. And both arise as the intended and unintended consequences of collective choices in history.

Institutionalism and decentred theory have provided political scientists with ways of exploring patterns of governance conceived as historical products of collective choices. On the one hand, institutionalism highlights regional and historical variations in such choices and their legacies: it leads to an exploration of the different ways in which various markets are governed through hierarchies, networks, and other forms of power at the boundary of the state and civil society.[12] On the other hand, decentred theory provides political scientists with a means of relating the form and trajectory of institutions to micro-level accounts of individual beliefs, desires and actions.[13]

The revival of interest in civil society since the 1970s has also led democratic theorists to turn to governance as a way of breaking down the dichotomy between state and market. Civil society offered democratic pluralists a site for associations that could embody a richly textured social life while also constituting a buttress against hierarchic control from above, such as during the velvet revolutions in Eastern Europe.[14] More recently, the idea of a global civil society has sought to capture an expanding supranational network of governance in which social movements interact with business and government.[15] Finally here, there has been a debate about the extent to which the cultural components of civil society – sociability, toleration, civility, and even exclusiveness – exist in creative tension with the market.[16] Far from being a spontaneous type of order, liberal market economies arose as embedded within the context of

[12] S. Vogel, *Freer Markets, More Rules: Regulatory Reform in the Advanced Industrial Countries* (Ithaca, NY, 1996); N. Ziegler, *Governing Ideas: Strategies for Innovation in France and Germany* (Ithaca, NY, 1997); and J. Zysman, *Governments, Markets, and Growth: Finance and the Politics of Industrial Change* (Ithaca, NY, 1983).

[13] M. Bevir, 'Una Teoria Decentrata della "Governance" ', tr. L. Bellocchio, *Stato e Mercato* 66 (2002), pp. 467–92; and M. Bevir, R. Rhodes and P. Weller, eds, 'Traditions of Governance: History and Diversity', *Public Administration* 81/1 (2003).

[14] For overviews see J. Keane, *Civil Society: Old Images, New Visions* (Oxford, 1999); J. Hall, ed., *Civil Society: Theory, History, Comparison* (Cambridge, 1995); F. Trentmann, 'Paradoxes of Civil Society', in F. Trentmann, ed., *Paradoxes of Civil Society: New Perspectives on Modern German and British History* (New York, 2000/2003), pp. 3–46. A. Arato and J. Cohen, *Civil Society and Political Theory* (Cambridge, MA, 1992). Sudipta Kaviraj and Sunil Khilnani, eds, *Civil Society: History and Possibilities* (Cambridge, 2001).

[15] H. Anheier, M. Glasius and M. Kaldor, eds, *Global Civil Society 2001* (Oxford, 2001).

[16] Compare I. Hont and M. Ignatieff, *Wealth and Virtue: The Shaping of Political Economy in the Scottish Enlightenment* (Cambridge, 1983); and J. Pocock, *Virtue, Commerce, and*

particular types of civil society, which were themselves a contingent product of European history. Nonetheless, once market economies arose, the virtues, vices and habits they inculcated within people could pose a threat to the pluralistic culture of civil society. Here, too, then, governance provides a way of discussing the embeddedness of markets and the state in civil society.

The post-structuralist turn to governance and governmentality began through an interest in techniques of disciplining societies in the early modern period. Michel Foucault highlighted the exploration and deployment of specific rationalities applied to nations, families, populations, trade and prisons.[17] For Foucault, too, the activity of rule had no natural or spontaneous form; rather, it had to be invented and learnt through discourses and regimes of power. Post-structuralists since have gone on to explore the arts of governance in areas such as security, insurance, social economy, drainage and self-help.[18] These theorists too challenge the dichotomy between state and market. They highlight the technical character of liberal governmentality and point to its creation out of non-liberal practices of rule. Governance thus refers, once again, to a politics beyond the formal institutions of the modern nation state, a politics located at the boundaries of the state and civil society, a politics in which power operates in and through a vast network of organizations, actors and systems of knowledge.

Historians' interest in governance has grown from two principal sources: contextualism and culturalism. Contextualists, especially Quentin Skinner, did much to shift intellectual history from being concerned with the philosophical arguments of canonical texts to an interest in the discourses, concepts and ideologies that made possible social or political formations.[19] They recovered the historical contingency of

---

*History* (Cambridge, 1985). See also now Peter Burke, Brian Harrison and Paul Slack, eds, *Civil Histories, Essays Presented to Sir Keith Thomas* (Oxford, 2000).

[17] M. Foucault, *Discipline and Punish: The Birth of the Prison* (Harmondsworth, 1977); and M. Foucault, 'Governmentality', in G. Burchell, C. Gordon and P. Miller, eds, *The Foucault Effect: Studies in Governmentality* (London, 1991), pp. 87–104. For an explicit suggestion that the recent hollowing out of the state has created something akin to neomedieval or early modern governance see J. Zielonka, 'Should Europe Become a State? A Neo-Medieval Solution', in D. Leonard and M. Leonard, eds, *The Pro-European Reader* (Basingstoke, 2002), pp. 177–86.

[18] Burchell, Gordon, and Miller, eds, *Foucault Effect*; and A. Barry, T. Osborne and N. Rose, eds, *Foucault and Political Reason* (London, 1996); see also C. Otter, 'Making Liberalism Durable: Vision and Civility in the Late Victorian City', *Social History* 27 (2002), pp. 1–15.

[19] See especially Q. Skinner, *The Foundations of Modern Political Thought*, 2 vols (Cambridge, 1978). The parallels between Skinner and Foucault have been emphasized by J. Tully, 'The Agonic Freedom of Citizens', *Economy and Society* 28 (1999), pp. 161–82; and J. Tully, 'Political Philosophy as a Critical Activity', *Political Theory* 30 (2002), pp. 525–47.

the modern nation state as a form of governance that arose out of unconnected, fragmented debates about diverse practices of governance, often within civil society. The contextualists also recovered a republican tradition which argued that people could be free only as active citizens within a free state.[20] Whereas liberals equate freedom with the absence of constraint, whether in a democracy or a polity ruled by a benign dictator, republicans believe that liberty can exist only when people rule themselves and thereby avoid dependence on others. Although the contextualists are prone to suggest that republican concerns disappeared with the rise of liberalism, a more plausible view might be that these concerns have continued to echo in many of the radical and democratic struggles of the nineteenth and twentieth centuries – struggles to attain greater popular control over governing institutions in the economic and social spheres as much as the political one.[21] From this perspective, the republican tradition too points to elements of governance from below.

Social history has been more immediately affected by many of the changes lying behind the general turn to governance in the social sciences. The political successes of the new right and debates about globalization undermined the orthodox narrative of social history in which the working class arose inexorably out of the industrial revolution to attain influence over the relations and conditions of production through the state.[22] The search for a new narrative has led many social historians to a culturalism – an interest in language and meaning – that touches on questions of economic governance. Instead of a narrative of the emergence of class and welfare state, historians have retrieved non-class identities and visions and practices of social co-ordination and integration that looked outside

---

[20] J. Pocock, *The Machiavellian Moment: Florentine Political Thought and the Atlantic Republican Tradition* (Princeton, 1975); and Q. Skinner, *Liberty Before Liberalism* (Cambridge, 1998).

[21] For the shift from republicanism to modern radicalism see G. Claeys, 'The Origins of the Rights of Labour: Republicanism, Commerce, and the Construction of Modern Social Theory in Britain, 1796–1805', *Journal of Modern History* 66 (1994), pp. 249–90; G. Claeys, *Citizens and Saints: Politics and Anti-Politics in Early British Socialism* (Cambridge, 1989); G. Stedman Jones, 'Rethinking Chartism', in *Languages of Class: Studies in English Working-Class History, 1832–1982* (Cambridge, 1983), pp. 90–178; and M. Bevir, 'Republicanism, Socialism, and Democracy in Britain: The Origins of the Radical Left', *Journal of Social History* 34 (2000), pp. 351–68.

[22] We discuss the transformation of this narrative in M. Bevir and F. Trentmann, 'Critique within Capitalism: Historiographical Problems, Theoretical Perspectives', in M. Bevir and F. Trentmann, eds, *Critiques of Capital in Modern Britain and America: Transatlantic Changes 1800 to the Present Day* (Houndmills, Basingstoke, 2002), pp. 1–25; see also D. Feldman, 'Class', in P. Burke, ed., *History and Historians in the Twentieth Century* (Oxford, 2002), pp. 181–206; and M. Taylor, 'The Beginnings of Modern British Social History', *History Workshop*, 43 (1997), pp. 155–76.

the central state, such as idealist ideas about social relations or consumer politics anchored in civil society.[23] There has also been a recovery of alternative visions of modernity and capitalist development, often by groups who had previously been cast as atavistic survivors, such as peasants, gentry, guilds or evangelical Christians.[24] Finally, social and political historians have built on the rediscovery of 'republicanism' by intellectual historians and highlighted the continuing appeal of early modern ideas of governance and co-ordination in the modern period.[25]

Political scientists, theorists and historians have thus turned to governance from overlapping perspectives. Governance refers, in very general terms, to an account of social co-ordination in terms of the ways in which disparate actors within civil society come together in networks by means of dialogue and a sharing of resources. We might add that even when the resulting forms of co-ordination are a hierarchical state or market, they still should be examined as contingent historical products of just such a coming together. Indeed, how precisely any particular state or market operates will depend on how it is governed by a host of beliefs, discourses, practices and institutions. Interest in economic governance thus raises a set of distinctive questions which are taken up by the essays in this volume. These essays examine the embeddedness of capitalism in social networks, the role of political ideas in shaping economic governance, and the tensions between ideas of social co-ordination and markets.

## Embedded markets: networks, traditions and ideals

Should we think of the modern and contemporary period in terms of an increasingly autonomous, self-sustaining market? The chapters by James

[23] J. Harris, 'Political Thought and the Welfare State 1870–1940: An Intellectual Framework for British Social Policy', *Past and Present* 35 (1992), pp. 116–41; S. den Otter, *British Idealism and Social Explanation: A Study in Late Victorian Thought* (Oxford, 1996); F. Trentmann, 'Bread, Milk and Democracy: Consumption and Citizenship in Twentieth-Century Britain', in M. Daunton and M. Hilton, eds, *The Politics of Consumption: Material Culture in Europe and America* (Oxford, 2001), pp. 129–63; P. Gurney, *Co-operative Culture and the Politics of Consumption in England, c. 1870–1930* (Manchester, 1996).

[24] H.-G. Haupt, ed., *Das Ende der Zünfte: Ein Europäischer Vergleich* (Göttingen, 2002); L. Vardi, *The Land and the Loom: Peasants and Profits in Northern France, 1680–1800* (Durham, NC, 1993); B. Hilton, *The Age of Atonement: The Influence of Evangelicalism on Social and Economic Thought, 1795–1865* (Oxford, 1988); A. Vickery, *The Gentleman's Daughter: Women's Lives in Georgian England* (New Haven, 1998); for eighteenth-century local government, see D. Eastwood, *Governing Rural England: Tradition and Transformation in Local Government, 1780–1840* (Oxford, 1994).

[25] J. Livesey, 'Agrarian Ideology and Commercial Republicanism in the French Revolution', *Past and Present* 157 (1997), pp. 94–121; Stedman Jones, 'Rethinking Chartism'; E. Biagini and A. Reid, eds, *Currents of Radicalism* (Cambridge, 1991); E. Biagini, ed., *Citizenship and Community* (Cambridge, 1996).

Livesey and Saskia Sassen provide the bookends for the volume's exploration of how markets, as ideas and practices, have been socially embedded and continue to be so. Livesey, a historian, provides a fresh look at the social networks cultivating modern rationality during the crucial breakthrough of modern capitalist society in the eighteenth century. Sassen, a sociologist, asks to what degree globalization has led to a qualitatively different regime of markets and examines the social infrastructure that undergirds the global capital market today. While eighteenth-century Irish and French rural society is in many ways worlds apart from today's international financial elite moving between New York, Tokyo and London, it is possible to highlight common elements of social networks, cognition and knowledge-creation that condition capitalism during these two pivotal moments of its development.

If Livesey's chapter is a direct challenge to the dichotomy of modern market versus culture or tradition, its originality stems from rethinking the relationship between the two from the perspective of the latter. Rather than identifying the cultural workings of the market, he turns to eighteenth-century France, Scotland and Ireland to reveal the development of modern rationality out of the bosom of rural society. Instead of working with a standard divide between market economy and household economy, Livesey turns to alternative networks of socialization and knowledge-creation – the agricultural societies – to reveal how rural society became one source for the emergence of modern standards of rationality. Modernization depended on a 'subaltern knowledge' that was generated by farmer scientists and peasants who were interested in improving practices and in the new language of botany. Instead of viewing innovation and capitalist development as the outgrowth of an unfolding, increasingly autonomous, market, or reducing it to state action or bourgeois interest, Livesey argues for a more deep-seated cultural transformation in rural society that favoured a switch to modernity.

The role of social connectivity in the creation and maintenance of new technologies and practices of capitalist societies is a theme that also runs through Sassen's discussion of global capital markets at the present time. Global capital markets are, of course, nothing new.[26] Yet, as Sassen shows, the new information and communication technologies that have propelled the digitization of international finance have also created an altogether new type of market distinguished by material size and diversity (pension funds, hedge funds), global interconnectedness, and spatial organization. The interesting question is why, after a decade of deregulation,

[26] B. J. Eichengreen, *Globalizing Capital: A History of the International Monetary System* (Princeton, 1996).

the global financial sector has not dispersed but consolidated its activities in a limited number of centres, led by New York, Tokyo and London. Sassen's answer unpacks the social, cultural and institutional dimensions that have favoured this geographic concentration and in which global capital markets remain embedded. Far from being an increasingly disembedded global market, the financial industry depends on these global cities for a social infrastructure of human resources and interpretive knowledge, consolidated electronic networks, and a 'denationalized' cultural framework of interaction and sociability. Put differently, the technological transformation of capitalism through digitization has strengthened (not loosened) the social and geographic embeddedness of markets. It is precisely because of its global and electronic features that the market for capital today depends on the systems of trust and social networks contained within each financial centre to negotiate the speed and size of transactions: it might even seem that the more the electronic market for capital approximates the mode of the depersonalized market ruled by supply and demand forces, the more it becomes dependent on social networks and the thick environments of financial centres.

Such empirically grounded demonstrations of the embeddedness of markets are challenges to economistic reasoning and public choice theory and inevitably raise the question of how the market acquired its appeal as a mode of economic governance. How did people wrestling with questions of governance view the market as modern capitalisms expanded? The conventional answer is to draw a straight line between the evolution of the science of political economy and the liberal celebration of *laissez faire* in the nineteenth century. As the chapters by Whatmore, Eastwood and Schäfer show, such a perspective runs the risk of being teleological, reading backwards from latter-day ideas about markets to the historical development of political economy, thus obscuring the alternative ways in which historical actors approached markets. More than anything, it was political ideas and considerations of political governance that shaped the reception of markets.

Whatmore's chapter effectively rewrites the narrative of liberal political economy during and after the French Revolution. The hope pinned on markets as a policy and system of co-ordination, he shows, depended on contemporaries' understanding of politics, both in terms of what was meant by good government and what was seen to be the nature of geopolitics. Political economy did not emerge as the triumph of scientific reason over reactionary ideas. Instead of a presumed affinity between liberal politics and political economy, the new science was deeply divided by two rival conceptions of government: modern republicanism versus democratic republicanism. Benjamin Constant and Jean-Baptiste Say are reread by Whatmore to reveal the tensions between these two traditions, the first embracing a modern-day republic with a state defending equally the interests of its members, the second favouring a more democratic system in which the people would play a more active role in making laws and governing the economy. Political economy, and the discussion of markets, was part of a larger competition between rival projects of building republics. The sponsorship of *laissez faire* and free trade, then, has to be understood from within the democratic republican project. For Say, political economy, and its defence of markets and commerce, was not some timeless, universally valid, science about the creation of wealth; rather, it was attractive as a particular stage in the historical project of creating representative government. Democratizing the political sphere required democratizing the economy. Political economy would educate citizens. Without this education, Say feared, markets would be corrupted. As Whatmore observes, 'Say had no faith in the "hidden hand".'[27]

The merits of markets, moreover, were debated within a geopolitical context of power. Here the British model of development provided the litmus test. The different visions of government between Say and Constant were reinforced by opposite understandings of British society – for Constant it was a model republic, for Say it was an Empire where markets were dominated by the elite for the elite. For Say, markets in oligarchic Britain were necessarily a sham, but this did not undermine his populist belief that markets could moralize society. For Constant, by contrast, markets did not possess civic capital, and indeed could threaten the disinterested spirit of liberty with a selfish mentality; religious belief was a necessary antidote. Political economy thus ultimately remained divided in its assessment of markets because of opposite assessments of the democratic potential of human actors to govern their political and economic environment.

How political traditions construct alternative understandings of markets is also the theme of David Eastwood's discussion of a neglected chapter in the history of political economy in its formative phase in Britain in the first half of the nineteenth century. Rather than approaching the subject from the better-known centre of liberal economics, Eastwood proceeds from the margins, taking another look at Tory writers, who have all too easily been written off in Whiggish accounts as backward, romantic traditionalists incapable of grasping the rationality of the new science. High Tories, he shows, did not turn their back on economics and retreat into morals; rather, they worked out an increasingly sophisticated argument about the embeddedness of markets. Markets here were decentred,

[27] See below, p. 67.

not autonomous. Organic metaphors helped to subordinate markets to the service of moral and political ideals. Tories like Sadler and Southey contributed to the analysis of what came to be called 'market failure'. The High Tory argument emphasized, in particular, the imperial nature of markets and the social and constitutional dangers of privileging a free market model. Although this argument would lose in party politics once the Tories led by Peel accepted free trade in the 1840s, it anticipated in several ways future trends, not least by articulating an alternative monetary policy (bimetallism) and support for public work schemes.

The question of how markets are fitted into organic views of society and politics is broadened further by Schäfer's chapter, which explores the transnational transfer and reception of ideas between different societies and reform traditions. American progressivism drew heavily on German historical economics in the late nineteenth and early twentieth centuries. Yet it ultimately produced an original configuration of economics and ethics working from within an indigenous project of radical democracy. The German historical school, Schäfer shows, provided progressive thinkers in America with a substantive critique of classical liberal economics. Markets were historical not universal – a view that favoured an organic analysis of state and society and that downplayed a liberal rights-based view of individual citizens. Yet, instead of following the paternalist direction of their German teachers, American progressives connected this historicist and organic understanding of capitalist society to a democratic project of broadening public participation. Schäfer's essay offers a good illustration of the interpretive limitations of presuming a dichotomy between state and market. American social thinkers were attracted to urban reforms in the hope of expanding public arenas for democratic action. At the same time, Schäfer argues, the American translation of German historicism left progressivism with the difficult legacy of seeking to reconcile two quite different strategies for civilizing market society: participatory industrial democracy and distributive social welfare.

Throughout the twentieth century, organized consumers have often been at the forefront of attempts to civilize the market. As the chapter by Maclachlan and Trentmann on consumer politics in America, Japan and Britain shows, economic reform projects were developed within the context of particular traditions. Here the emphasis on the embeddedness of markets is connected, once again, to an argument about agency and a consequent scepticism toward economic essentialism and narratives of global convergence. Consumption and citizenship have often been intertwined projects, but these have been put together with different meanings in different political contexts, and thus with different policy implications. Maclachlan, a political scientist, and Trentmann, a historian, distinguish between the vision of free trade and civil society dominant in early twentieth-century British consumer movements, a labour-oriented vision of ethics and rights in America, and the national lifestyle culture of early Japanese movements. These traditions were not written in stone but mutated in dialogue with changes in political economy and political culture. In contrast to a narrative that presents contemporary consumer activism as a response to a global convergence around neo-liberalism, Maclachlan and Trentmann emphasize that consumer movements also contributed to the development of political economy and argue that their reform imagination remains rooted in different political discourses. Consumer politics was most influential where it was able to work with the grain of civic ideas. British Free Trade and the American New Deal are significant examples of this – organized consumers underwrote these political projects. In Japan, by contrast, the prominence of producer, nationalist, and state-oriented thinking made for a more subordinate role for consumer movements. The recent resurgence of consumer politics has been strongest where it has developed out of national debates over how best to strengthen citizenship and civil society, such as in Britain, where 'the consumer' in the 1980s and 1990s was re-energized in political debates about social services and civic participation.

How the success of neo-liberal reforms remains dependent on historically inherited popular understandings of the market is examined in greater detail in Rob Jenkins's discussion of political legitimation and economic reform in India in the 1980s and 1990s.[28] Complementing Maclachlan and Trentmann's attention to the shifting meanings of the consumer, Jenkins highlights how current understandings of 'the market' remain contested within divergent traditions of Indian politics. Jenkins, a political scientist, distinguishes between a first wave of neo-liberal policies and the long-term success of establishing a neo-liberal culture of the market. The neo-liberal image of the market had to compete with older associations of the market promulgated in movement politics, the Hindu temple movement (*Mandir*), and the subaltern politics of *Mandal*. These movements drew on the different ideas associated with *swadeshi* ('of one's own country') popularized by Gandhi at the beginning of the twentieth century. Attention to the ways in which the debate about markets remains embedded in inherited traditions has political implications and alerts us

[28] For how political elites in Britain and America developed a narrative of globalization in which markets are presented as insuperable forces of nature, see C. Hay, 'New Labour and "Third Way" Political Economy: Paving the European Road to Washington?', in Bevir and Trentmann, *Critiques of Capital*, pp. 195–219.

to the contingency of future neo-liberal policies. In the long run, the success of neo-liberal market politics, Jenkins concludes, will depend on who wins in the battle between competing versions of *swadeshi*. More generally, the Indian example illustrates how we can only understand the particular paths carved out by liberalization by situating global market politics firmly within local settings of traditions and practices which both compete with neo-liberalism and translate and mould the meanings of markets in political debate.

If the above discussion moves beyond a stark analytical dichotomy between market and state, thinking about governance also does well to interrogate any presumed dichotomy between economics and ethics, market versus culture, or *Gemeinschaft* and *Gesellschaft*. These polarizations have been an influential source of legitimation for many social projects and socialist reform traditions in the twentieth century, often linking them to other organic visions of political economy that incorporated ethical and social concerns. The chapters by Winch, Haupt and Harris recover three important earlier debates about subjects that continue to be of political significance today: the relationship between economic growth and environment; the relationship between markets and associations; and the relationship between community and civil society. As much of the current thinking about markets continues to employ idealized and simplified images of canonical ideas and their authors, a critical rereading of their thought is a step both to broaden the terms of contemporary debate and to alert us to dangerous cul-de-sacs.

Few contrasts have dominated images of political economy as much as that between J. S. Mill and John Ruskin, who are frequently paired to illustrate the widening gulf between the traditions of market and culture in the modern period. Yet, as the chapter by Donald Winch, the doyen of the history of economic ideas, reveals, such a contrast not only does injustice to Mill but also obscures the way in which a critique of the market continued to be generated from within the emergent science of economics, not just from its critics outside it. Reading against the established grain of the canon, Winch shows how Malthusian anxieties shaped Mill's thinking about growth and sustainability. Mill's view of the environmental limits of market societies was central to his vision of a stationary state or zero-growth society. In the generation after Mill, Alfred Marshall's ethicized liberal economics responded to Ruskin's romantic critique. Rather than being polar-opposites mutually sealed off from each other in rival universes of ideas and politics, liberal economists and their romantic critics in the Victorian period thus participated in a debate about the consequences of capitalism for the natural world and social relations. What changed in the course of professionalization at the turn of the twentieth century was the question. Instead of Mill's neo-Malthusianism and Wordsworthian outlook, welfare economics now turned to a cost-benefit analysis of environmental damages.

Throughout the modern period, discussion of the costs and benefits of markets has been inextricably entwined with the question of guilds as alternative models of social organization. The changing moral and political attraction of the guilds in nineteenth-century France and Germany is the focus of Heinz-Gerhard Haupt's chapter. Haupt explores an interesting paradox in the changing salience of guilds. In Enlightenment and revolutionary discourse, the guilds had been branded as bulwarks of tradition and backwardness. Their effective abolition in France and Germany during the revolutionary years was followed, however, by a renaissance of guild ideas during which guilds were presented as pillars of organic community, stability and religious order. Yet, as Haupt shows, the broad liberal support for guilds as a way of taming market forces was not a fixed component of national traditions. On the contrary, in the late nineteenth century, Emile Durkheim and Otto von Gierke developed ideas of corporation and association in different directions. For Durkheim guilds and corporations were not part of a reactionary project, as sometimes believed, but rather building blocks of modern democracy, generating social inclusion and feelings of mutual solidarity. Gierke, by contrast, broke with earlier German traditions and came to view guilds as stumbling blocks to the creation of a community that could overcome a dichotomy between the individual and the state. Here the critique of markets went hand in hand with a suspicion of guilds as limiting the free will of association and as relying too heavily on the state. As Haupt reminds us, it is too simplistic to write off these ideas of community and corporation because of their subsequent link with fascistic movements.

In the last two decades, 'civil society' and 'communitarianism' have re-emerged as two dominant languages of reform that seek to overcome the dichotomy between state and market, and the totalizing ideologies that came with it. At times, civil society and community have become fused. Yet, as Jose Harris's chapter makes clear, there are considerable dangers in losing a sense of the ideological differences between the two concepts. She returns to F. Tönnies's seminal work on *Gemeinschaft und Gesellschaft* both to reinsert some useful distinctions between civil society and community into the current debate and to issue warnings about their respective potentials as strategies for reforming market societies. Tönnies has been frequently used as if he discussed a chronological transition from traditional community to modern civil society. Instead, Harris shows that he was arguing in Kantian fashion for the simultaneous presence at all times of these formations, and their respective values, forms of consciousness, and will. While the balance between the forces favouring community and those favouring civil society shifted, it is a fallacy to equate the rise of markets with a turn away from 'archaic' community to 'modern' civil society. Harris's rereading of Tönnies's two systems of thought and social organization reveals the dangers of presuming an elective affinity between community and civil society, as do so many current discussions on both sides of the Atlantic. Rather, community and civil society stood in tension for Tönnies who stressed the different scope and quality of each. Community fostered intensive feelings of limited range; civil society fostered thinner emotions but with more universal range.[29] The first requires exclusion; the latter is more inclusive and tolerant. Mixing the two in social policies that fuse community and civil society may be counterproductive. What is more, to rely on either as a way of taming the globalization of markets might prove to be naïve since Tönnies's analysis suggests that community is too weak, and civil society is too complicit in market processes, for either to become a successful instrument of reform. These may be sobering conclusions for current advocates of community or civil society, but the reintroduction of such analytical and ideological distinctions will undoubtedly help to sharpen the present debate about what are effective ways of governing markets and their moral and social underpinnings and implications.

These explorations of the embeddedness of markets raise interesting questions about the changing power of the market as a mode of governance in the modern period. As any student of modern history will know, the market as an ideal and system of social co-ordination expanded with radically different speed and force in different societies, ranging from liberal societies to nationalist regimes and socialist groupings. Where markets were most successful in expanding this was not simply the result of some inexorable material force or because of the lack of some bulwark provided by some 'traditional' alternative system of social co-ordination. Markets needed a fertile soil of supporting traditions. Even (or perhaps especially) in more liberal societies, the success of the market, as an idea and as instrument of governance, depended on its ability to fit into traditions, such as radicalism. Markets were embraced and liberal political economy could be buttressed where historical thinkers and movements, like Say or the co-operative movement, could accommodate markets within broader visions of democracy and civil society. Markets, in other words, lacked the threat of social disintegration and anomie in settings where social and

---

[29] For the affinity of civil society with toleration (rather than with community or democracy), see also D. Colas, *Civil Society and Fanaticism: Conjoined Histories* (Stanford, 1997); and J. A. Hall, 'Reflections on the Making of Civility in Society', in Trentmann, ed., *Paradoxes of Civil Society*, pp. 47–57.

political beliefs predicted their full force would be tamed by alternative systems of co-ordination, such as civil society. Rather than seeing markets as the outgrowth of an advancing differentiation of social spheres, the emphasis thus falls here on their organic embeddedness in social networks and traditions among liberals and critics of liberalism alike. Here is an important contrast to the current dictum that the discipline of the market is inescapable. Even in the current climate of neo-liberalism, the persistence of social networks (as in global capital markets) and the persistence of national traditions (as in India with *swadeshi*) mean that the understanding of that 'discipline' and available strategies of managing markets are interpreted differently.

Attention to the role of beliefs and traditions in the way in which markets are supported, moulded and resisted raises questions about the unintended consequences of such beliefs and traditions for the evolution of modern capitalism. To invoke the contribution of traditions to the particular shape of political economy in different societies is not the same as to attribute historical responsibility. When organized consumers in Edwardian Britain stood up for free trade, this does not mean they should be held responsible for all the subsequent domestic and global consequences of free trade. What it does do, though, is to focus attention on the ways in which the different make-up of traditions favours particular strategies of governance over others, and can be more or less effective in moulding the path taken by modern capitalism. Thus, in the United States in the early twentieth century, for example, the internal make-up of a progressive tradition produced contradictory signals as to how to deal with consumer demand and industrial democracy and so ultimately disabled itself as a viable reform strategy.

### Theorizing economic governance

Governance draws our attention to the construction of economic orders out of various beliefs, discourses, practices and institutions. The chapters in this volume adopt what we might call an interpretive approach to governance. They focus on meaning and culture as embedded in actions, practices and the historical patterns of co-ordination that they generate. We want to turn now from the particular to the more general assumptions and perspectives of this interpretive approach to governance. While there are differences between them, the essays in this volume share a number of broad positions concerning meaning, the plurality of historical sites, and the contingency of social life. They, first, take seriously the beliefs or meanings that are embedded within forms of governance: Constant viewed markets through the lens of a particular republican tradition; the tradition of *swadeshi* informs Indian social movements' understanding of market reforms. Secondly, they see practices as arising out of actions, where we can adequately grasp actions only in terms of the beliefs or meanings that animate them: farmers and peasants were not pushed into modernity by external forces but entered by developing new forms of knowledge; consumers do not spring into political action because some innate material nerve is touched, but because of certain beliefs that interpret individual interests into collective notions of civil society, nation or fairness. Interpretive approaches thus follow the everyday practice of explaining actions by reference to the beliefs and desires of the actors. Indeed, what distinguishes interpretive approaches to governance is an insistence on bringing this everyday form of explanation into the human sciences. Positivist approaches often suggest that a certain institutional location or class membership defines the beliefs and desires that prompt people's actions. Interpretive approaches characteristically deny this on the grounds that there are no pure experiences so people's beliefs and desires cannot be derived from given facts about the world without any concern with how people construct these facts.[30]

Interpretivists share related emphases on the contingency of social life and the plurality of historical sites in which governance is created. A rejection of pure experience implies that people in the same situations could hold very different beliefs if only because their experiences of the situation could be laden with very different prior theories: we cannot assume that people in similar social situations will act in a uniform manner. Any abstract concept, such as a class or an institution, thus cannot properly explain people's beliefs, interests, or actions; rather, it can represent only an abstract stand-in for the multiple and complex beliefs and actions of the individuals we classify under it.[31]

---

[30] For an application of this argument see F. Trentmann, 'Political Culture and Political Economy', *Review of International Political Economy* 5 (1998), pp. 217–51. See also the literature on the sociology of knowledge in the early modern period, e.g., Peter Burke, *A Social History of Knowledge: From Gutenberg to Diderot* (Oxford, 2000); Steven Shapin, *A Social History of Truth: Civility and Science in Seventeenth-Century England* (Chicago, 1994).

[31] Even when constructivists postulate institutional unity, they typically conceive of it as an emergent property based on individual actions in the context of intersubjective norms, which, at least in principle, could be contested. Institutions are, in this view, constantly being recreated through a series of activities and processes. Clearly some institutionalists remain closer to positivism than an interpretive or constructivist position, though the boundary between the two is fuzzy. For attempts to distinguish a discursive or constructivist variety of institutionalism from rational-choice, historical and structural institutionalisms see J. Campbell and O. Pedersen, eds, *The Rise of Neoliberalism and Institutional Analysis* (Princeton, 2001); and J. Hoff, 'A Constructivist Bottom-up Approach to Governance', in Bang, ed., *Governance, Governmentality, and Democracy*. For an example

Once we accept that people in any given situation can interpret that situation and their interests in all sorts of ways, we are pressed also to accept that people's actions – how they respond to any given situation – are radically open. That is to say, no practice or institution can itself fix the ways in which its participants will act, let alone how they will innovate within it in response to novel circumstances. Hence, our norms and practices are contingent, lacking any fixed essence or logical path of development.

Through their sensitivity to meanings, the plurality of historical sites, and contingency, interpretivists can play an important role in historicizing economic governance. Positivists sometimes suggest that the emergence of networks is a new phenomenon characterizing a new epoch in which the state stands powerless before an interdependent global economy in contrast to earlier times when an all-powerful state undertook all governance.[32] Interpretivists, in contrast, treat hierarchies and markets as meaningful practices that are created and constantly recreated through contingent actions informed by diverse webs of belief. The allegedly new and special characteristics of networks are also present in hierarchies and markets. The establishment and operation of markets and free trade depend on contingent interactions of interdependent producers and consumers who rely on trust and dialogue as well as on economic rationality.[33] Likewise, the commands of a hierarchic bureaucracy do not have a fixed form but rather are constantly interpreted and made afresh through the creative activity of individuals. Once we stop reifying hierarchies and markets, we find that many of the allegedly unique characteristics of contemporary governance are ubiquitous aspects of social co-ordination, so we can explore governance in history as well as governance today.

Interpretivists highlight the diversity of the possible forms of economic governance. They are sceptical of claims about the uniformity or universality of particular modes of governance. Positivists sometimes portray governance as being composed of policies, such as marketization and the new public management, which are themselves allegedly

of how an interpretive approach can act as a critique of other forms of institutionalism see F. Trentmann, 'The British Sources of Social Power', in John Hall and Ralph Schroeder, eds, *The Anatomy of Power: The Historical Sociology of Michael Mann* (Cambridge, forthcoming).

[32] Aspects of this new times thesis appears in the work of many of the political scientists mentioned earlier. See J. Kooiman, 'Activation in Governance', in Bang, ed., *Governance, Governmentality, and Democracy*; and R. Rhodes, 'The New Governance: Governing without Government', in *Understanding Governance*, pp. 46–60.

[33] See the study of the governance of free trade by F. Trentmann, *Food and Freedom: Consumption, Commerce, and Civil Society in Britain, 1890s–1930s* (forthcoming).

the inexorable outcomes of global economic pressures. Interpretivists, in contrast, suggest that these pressures, far from being given as brute facts, are constructed differently in different traditions. They thereby infer that the policies and outcomes of governance can vary considerably even within allegedly monolithic contexts such as the new global economy. They are wary not only of any historical dichotomy between governance and earlier state formations, but also of any attempt to use the abstract idea of governance to account for particular developments in particular states. The relevance of an omnibus concept of governance depends upon empirical studies that explore the ways in which social co-ordination is achieved.

Finally, interpretivists highlight the contested nature of modes of governance, and the role of critique within their trajectory. Positivists often adopt an action-reaction model of governance and critique: having portrayed governance as an inexorable product of socio-economic forces, they reduce critique to a post-hoc reaction to it. Interpretivists, by contrast, regard social critiques and movements as constitutive elements of the clusters of actions and practices that constitute any given mode of governance as it operates in and through aspects of civil society. Governance and critique are not opposites; rather, they are interwoven processes, deeply implicated in the evolution of one another.

The essays collected here highlight the historicity, diversity and contestation of modes of economic governance. To understand modes of governance, they argue, we have to take seriously the constitutive role of meanings and beliefs, the diversity of historical sites and groups, and the contingency of social life. This shared framework, however, is a very broad one that leaves a number of questions unanswered.[34] Two theoretical issues stand out, namely, the composition of governance and the recentring of governance. It is arguable that post-structuralists have made almost all the running among interpretivists who are interested in addressing these theoretical issues. It is also arguable, however, that post-structuralist responses to these issues are at best ambiguous and at worst mistaken.

Interpretivists agree on the need to approach governance through a study of the meanings that inform it. Yet they are not always clear about the nature of these meanings. Sometimes the relevant meanings appear to exist as quasi-structures that possess an immanent logic or respond to random fluctuations of power.[35] At other times meanings are understood

---

[34] The theoretical perspective that follows extends that of M. Bevir, *The Logic of the History of Ideas* (Cambridge, 1999).

[35] See respectively M. Foucault, *The Order of Things: An Archaeology of the Human Sciences* (London, 1986); and the revised theory of the essays in M. Foucault, *Power/Knowledge: Selected Interviews and Other Writings 1972–1977* (Brighton, 1980).

in subjective terms as the intentions or beliefs of individuals, which suggests that the concept of a discourse or language refers only to inter-subjective conventions or understandings.[36] The question here is, should we conceive of people as agents or as passive constructs of social discourses? A sharper distinction between autonomy and agency is helpful. Autonomous subjects are able, at least in principle, to have experiences, reason, adopt beliefs, and act, outside of all social contexts. In contrast, although agents are able to reason and act in novel ways, they might be able to do so only against the background of social practices that influence them. Although interpretivists are increasingly wary of the idea of autonomy, then, they need not also reject agency. Rather, they could accept that people always set out against the background of a social inheritance, and still conceive of them as agents who can act and reason in novel ways so as to modify this background.

Interpretivists' curiosity about a plurality of historical sites encourages a focus on the multiplicity of conflicting actions and micro-practices that come together so as to create a contingent pattern of rule. Yet the more we emphasize the contingency and particularity of meanings and practices, the harder it seems to become to explain them by reference to a broader logic or social process. Interpretivists might usefully recentre their theories of governance by drawing on the contrast between agency and autonomy. To reject autonomy is to accept that subjects only experience the world in ways that reflect the influence upon them of a social background. Hence we need aggregate concepts that indicate how social influences permeate beliefs and actions even on those occasions when the speaker or actor does not recognize such influence. To allow for agency is, however, to imply that these aggregate concepts also need to allow that people possess the capacity to adopt beliefs and actions, even novel ones, for reasons of their own. We would suggest, therefore, that interpretivists might be well advised to think of the social context in terms of traditions rather than discourses: after all, the concept of a tradition implies that the relevant social structures are those in which subjects are born and which then act as the background to their beliefs and actions while also allowing for the possibility of their modifying, developing, and even rejecting much of their inheritance. As an explanatory concept, tradition has the advantage over discourse that it allows properly for agency and so provides a way of thinking about change.

Positivists often present a mode of economic governance as necessary; they imply that we are compelled to adopt or contemplate only a limited range of modes of governance by inexorable historical or social forces, the

---

[36] Q. Skinner, 'Motives, Intentions, and the Interpretation of Texts', in J. Tully, ed., *Meaning and Context: Quentin Skinner and His Critics* (Cambridge, 1988), pp. 68–78.

dictates of a universal reason, or even human nature itself. Globalization, for example, appears in many narratives as an inexorable social process that requires states to adopt liberal reforms.[37] In contrast, interpretivists think of modes of governance as products of agents modifying the traditions they inherit in response to problems.[38] Any mode of governance is contingent and contestable in that people from within other traditions might construct the problems differently, and in that there are no inherently correct responses to problems even when they are defined in the same way. When interpretivists portray modes of governance as contingent and contestable, they engage in a critical activity. In the first place, they challenge the self-understanding of those who expound such modes of governance; they reveal to them the contingent, historical conditions of their beliefs, thereby undercutting the notion that these beliefs are necessary. In the second place, they thus open up the possibility of alternative narratives, actions and practices; they give us, as a society, the opportunity to govern ourselves differently; they free us from the dominant modes of thinking and acting that define our current practices of governance. The following essays are a contribution to this project.

---

[37] For a critique of this view of globalization, with further references, see P. Hirst and G. Thompson, *Globalization in Question: The International Economy and the Possibilities of Governance* (Cambridge, 1996).

[38] They might even suggest that 'globalization' is often a purely rhetorical device that politicians or business elites use to justify policies or cost-cutting exercises that they want to adopt for other reasons. See Hay, 'New Labour and "Third Way" Political Economy'.

# 2    Improving justice: communities of norms in the Great Transformation

*James Livesey*

In 1775 William Pultenay suffered the loss of his childless English cousin and so acquired the charge of the estates and title of the Earl of Bath. On removing to England he left the management of his own estate of Solway Bank in his native Scotland in the hands of John Maxwell, a theoretical improver, whom he made factor. Their extensive correspondence reveals to us Maxwell's education into the nature of change in rural Scotland. He began his work with the assumption that the impediment to efficiency and economic rationality was the farmers:

Country people such as we have in this place in the world, constantly accustomed to enter farms exhausted by the unrestrained licence allowed their predecessors, and to labour only to the easiest and most immediate produce, cannot by any means be brought to raise their ideas to the advantages of entering to a well-conditioned farm, nor to look upon restraints to regular husbandry, such as your tacks [leases] preserve, in any other light than as so many drawbacks to their profit.[1]

His solution to this problem was one familiar to students of landlord–tenant relations and physiocratic economic theory; he proposed that leases should more exactly specify the methods farmers should use and the powers retained by the landlord and his agent over the farms: 'I am humbly of the opinion that the person employ'd should be daily going about the farms, observing the conduct of the tenants, and chequing abuses, which should be daily committed, or attempted to be committed.'[2] The effort was a disaster; the attempt to control the behaviour of the farmers drove them from the estate and the rent books fell.[3] As a consequence over the following two years Maxwell was re-educated to consider the farmers as agents of improvement rather than impediments to it. By 1777 he was writing of the estate at Highstoneriggs:

---

[1] Huntington Library LO 1582, John Maxwell to William Pultenay, 3 March 1775.
[2] Huntington Library LO 1586, John Maxwell to William Pultenay, 21 September 1775.
[3] Huntington Library PU 1597, John Maxwell to William Pultenay, 11 February 1776.

[I]n my present opinion they would make a sett of commodious farms, much more suitable to the circumstances of the country people in this part of the world than as they are at present, and fitter to draw offerers for them. I clearly see that in treating with different people about the farms their different humours and conceptions of things will lead them to insist upon various articles as conditions of their tacks, and I think a good tennant making a proper offer should not be lost for a small concession in that respect.[4]

Maxwell had come to think of his prospective tenants not as inadequately rational individuals, but as members of a community with their own ideas about what was rational and with structures of their own through which they could communicate those ideas. Anxious that his farms should be let and that prospective tenants should understand that his ambition to improve was an aid to their prospective profit rather than an impediment to it he set out to negotiate: 'I shall therefore send Clinkskills to the several smiths shops with commission to give each of the smiths a little ale to insure their good offices in promoting the continuation of the intelligence.'[5] Maxwell, an outsider to the community like ourselves but with more ready access to it, identifies the smithy, precisely the heart of the technological capacity of the community, as the strategic place where opinion was formed. Maxwell's attempt to instrumentalize the communicative networks of the community has the unwitting effect of revealing those structures to us. Through Maxwell's correspondence we can discern the lineaments of a rural community that was not the object of developmental process but the agent of it.

John Maxwell made the same discovery that has subsequently excited many contemporary agricultural historians; where he sought tradition and stubborn resistance to change he had instead found the 'rational peasant'.[6] Historians of the peasantry now take this particular rational actor for granted, and the older image of the farmer totally embedded in the cake of culture is now much harder to find in the literature.[7] Just how profound the consequent revolution in our understanding of the past will be

---

[4] Huntington Library PU 1115, John Maxwell to William Pultenay, 5 September 1777.

[5] Ibid.

[6] For two competing models of peasant agency and rationality see S. Popkin, *The Rational Peasant: The Political Economy of Rural Society in Vietnam* (Berkeley, 1979) and J. Scott, *Weapons of the Weak: Everyday Forms of Peasant Resistance* (New Haven, 1985). For a local account of the rational peasant see L. Vardi, *The Land and the Loom: Peasants and Profits in Northern France, 1680–1800* (Durham, NC, 1993).

[7] For some overviews of this historiographical departure see C. Zimmermann, 'Bäuerlicher Traditionalismus und agrarischer Fortschritt in der frühen Neuzeit', *Historische Zeitschrift*, 1995 Supplement, pp. 18, 219–38; G.-R. Ikni, 'Paysans et innovation à la veille de 1789 et pendant la Révolution française', *Historiens et Géographes* 327 (1990), pp. 247–54; C. B. Brettell, 'Moral economy or political economy? Property and credit markets in 19th century rural Portugal', *Journal of Historical Sociology* 12/1 (1999), pp. 1–28.

is not yet clear. The very concept of a market is disturbed by the collapse of a polarity that had given it meaning. No other area of historical explanation was more dependent on the idea of an essentialist, pure market as an instrument and explanation of social and economic change than modern agrarian history. Markets, by definition, were antithetical to peasant household economies. It was generally understood that the market disciplines which first in England, but later across Western Europe, allowed societies to escape the Malthusian limit on population in the eighteenth century and created the conditions for economies organized around continuous growth, had to be imposed on rural primary producers.[8] Polanyi, who coined the phrase 'the Great Transformation', argued the state imposed price discipline on rural producers, indeed he defined the Great Transformation as precisely the undermining of a household economy characteristic of a true peasantry in favour of a market economy.[9] The famous Brenner thesis argued that the coercion involved in imposing market norms on primary producers was that of a landlord class who eliminated family farms; in all accounts primary producers were the objects of historical process, that of either a state or a dominant class.[10] Capitalism was the project of an elite, either state or social, who induced rationality in a rural population by driving them into new institutional structures. The peasantry of Western Europe, in all these accounts, were indeed a sack of potatoes that had to be dragged or pushed to market.

When we assert that the peasantry actually performed the 'Great Transformation' and were not coerced into modernity, we transform our model of the peasantry, but even more importantly we transform the model of the transformation and of the rationality that characterizes it. In conditions of uncertainty, which by definition include all examples of structural change, culture, the assemblage of cognitive practices through which individuals orientate themselves in the world, cannot be taken as stable. Co-ordination in uncertainty is achieved by learning, by changes in culture. The evolution of new forms of commercial life, the Great Transformation, created such a situation of uncertainty and to understand the place of the rational peasant in that process we must investigate the institutions the peasants acted in but also the rationality that motivated them to do so. To understand the nature of cultural and economic change in

---

[8] Even Chayanov, who was sympathetic to peasant efforts at modernization, came to the conclusion that such efforts would simply have been irrational for the individual peasant, A. V. Chayanov, *The Theory of Peasant Economy*, tr. D. Thorner (Homewood, IL, 1966).

[9] K. Polanyi, *The Great Transformation: The Political and Economic Origins of our Time* (Boston, 1957), pp. 66–7.

[10] R. Brenner, 'Agrarian Class Structures and Economic Development in Pre-Industrial Europe', in *The Brenner Debate: Agrarian Class Structures and Economic Development in Pre-Industrial Europe* (Cambridge, 1985), p. 48.

the countryside of Western Europe we cannot rely on an endogenous account of market formation and commercialization. Rather, we have to find the 'development theory' of the eighteenth- and nineteenth-century European peasant, the set of understandings and expectations used by farmers to locate themselves in an open-ended time-frame that allowed for progressive growth and change. As Amartya Sen has explained, the dynamics that mobilize a population for development cannot be reduced to economic conditions, that is, price incentives.[11] This insight is now a standard assumption for the understanding of development outside Europe.[12] The hypothesis I would like to develop is that the cognitive skills necessary for market behaviour in Europe were also generated outside the market and then transferred. The corollary that I will develop is that the 'Great Transformation', the development of market norms as social principle, was a subsidiary phenomenon of a more general process of social learning. The institution of the market was not the instrument through which peasants made their particular region of the modern world.

## Making peasants modern: improvement and its practices in the eighteenth century

There is a consensus that there was a revolution in social epistemology, in the nature of knowing, by the eighteenth century at the latest.[13] After this point there is nothing but conflict on the nature, genealogy, meaning and significance of the shift. Weber famously simply defined modernity as purposive rationality, but as Ernest Gellner points out, the ambiguities and complexities within his idea of rationality make it almost impossible to tell what he meant by it.[14] Foucault's notion of 'classical' thought tried to capture exactly the transformation that concerns us, but his particular accounts within particular fields of knowledge are too empirically unreliable for his general thesis to retain its credibility.[15] The most empirically useful explorations of the idea of modern reason have been in the history of mathematics. Alexandre Koyré's title, *From the Closed World to the Infinite Universe*, captures the essential movement from the notion

---

[11] A. Sen, *Development as Freedom* (Oxford, 1999), p. 9.

[12] See R. Bates, *Beyond the Miracle of the Market: The Political Economy of Agrarian Development in Kenya* (Cambridge, 1989); R. Bates, 'Contra Contractarianism: Some Reflections on the New Institutionalism', *Politics and Society* 16 (1988), pp. 387–401.

[13] For a gallant effort to characterize the history of reason in a philosophical history see H. Blumenberg, *The Legitimacy of the Modern Age*, tr. R. M. Wallace (Cambridge, MA, 1983). This is also the project of J. Habermas, see *The Philosophical Discourse of Modernity*, tr. F. Lawrence (Cambridge, 1987).

[14] M. Weber, *The Protestant Ethic and the Spirit of Capitalism* (New York, 1958), p. 25; E. Gellner, *Nations and Nationalism* (Oxford, 1983), p. 20.

[15] For Foucault's definition of classical reason, see M. Foucault, *The Order of Things: An Archaeology of the Human Sciences* (London, 1970), p. 63.

of rationality as the possession of a series of apodectic dogmas to one of reason as a process of appropriation through reliable method that is, in principle, infinite.[16] To explore the consequences of even this limited description of the phenomenon would go far beyond the limitations of this chapter but a few must be pointed out to help interpret the specific cases that will be discussed. As Ian Hacking has argued, reasoning was now secure handling of signs through method, rather than the derivation of general causes.[17] This collapsed the divisions between the high and low sciences, between opinion and truth, and rendered all knowledge probabilistic. One of the most obvious effects was to create the possibility of a science of economics.[18] The new notion of reason also had some paradoxes within it. To be reasonable was to use the same method, analysis, in all contexts, in effect to decontextualize all local knowledge. This is a species of the 'disembedding' that Giddens and Gellner have both argued is a feature of modern life.[19] On the other hand the new idea of reason also relied on the idea of fact for its foundation, for ever more specific and local areas of competence. The modern idea of reason demanded communication of local and specific knowledge into disembedded, abstract structures. It created what Steven Shapin has identified as the problem of trust: '[M]undane reason is the space across which trust plays. It provides a set of presuppositions about self, others, and the world which embed trust and which permit both consensus and civil dissensus to occur. A world-known-in-common is built up through acts of trust and its properties are decided through the civil conversations of trusting individuals.'[20] The process of building that world in common generated specific cultures of rationality.

The agricultural societies were the most important instruments through which this kind of discussion was conducted in eighteenth-century rural Europe.[21] Agricultural societies began in Ireland and Scotland in the 1730s, spread to Brittany, and then from the 1760s

[16] A. Koyré, *From the Closed World to the Infinite Universe* (Baltimore, 1957). For a recent revision that emphasizes the specificity of the history of mathematics in the process, see M. Blay, *Reasoning with the Infinite: From the Closed World to the Mathematical Universe* (Chicago, 1998).

[17] I. Hacking, *The Emergence of Probability: A Philosophical Study of Early Ideas about Probability, Induction and Statistical Inference* (Cambridge, 1975), pp. 176–85.

[18] M. Poovey, *A History of the Modern Fact: Problems of Knowledge in the Sciences of Wealth and Society* (Chicago, 1998), pp. 236–49.

[19] A. Giddens, *The Consequences of Modernity* (Cambridge, 1991), p. 21; Gellner, *Nations and Nationalism*, pp. 21–4.

[20] S. Shapin, *A Social History of Truth: Civility and Science in Seventeenth-Century England* (Chicago, 1994), p. 30.

[21] Though it falls outside the scope of this paper it should not be forgotten that the agricultural society movement was very strong in England also. In 1830 there were 100 and by 1855 700 local societies: N. Goddard, 'Agricultural Societies', in G. E. Mingay, ed., *The Victorian Countryside* (London, 1981), 2 vols, vol. I, p. 246.

were promoted by the French state.[22] By its very nature, the network of agricultural reformers posed precisely the problems of reliable witness, communicability of experience, standards of evidence and others that were constitutive of the construction of a new model of reason.[23] The first correspondents to the original, Dublin, society, perfectly articulated their understanding that the function of the society was to create a culture of reliable witness, through which participants could pursue their self-interest on the basis of reliable knowledge; 'this general board, fixt in Dublin, ought to have corresponding members in each county, by way of clubs, to consider their wants, and what improvements are proper for the several counties'.[24] Objections to the creation of an agricultural society argued that the problem of trust was insurmountable, that 'he who sets himself to recommend the giving up a private advantage to the publick good, must expect to be laughed at'.[25] Reasoned trust was a particularly critical problem for agronomy, because the activity it concerned itself with was carried on by so many of the population and was of the first concern to their well-being. The problem of credibility imposed itself in a particularly radical way.

The programme developed by the original, Dublin, society, illustrates the manner in which the societies became the seed group for new cognitive values. The societies understood that they were innovative institutions and that their ideals implicitly conflicted with political norms. Proposing the foundation of such institutions in Ireland one of the founder members of the Dublin Society wrote:

I should humbly propose, that a school for husbandry were erected in every county, wherein an expert Master of the English methods shou'd teach at a fix'd yearly salary; and that Tusser's old Book of Husbandry shou'd be taught to the boys, instead of a primer or psalter, to read, to copy, and to get it by heart, to which end it might be reprinted and distributed, and let nobody object, that 'tis old English; we are not teaching words, but things: I am sure 'tis the very best English book of good husbandry and housewifery that ever was published, fitted for the use of mean men and farmers, and ordinary families.[26]

---

[22] A Mr Hope of Rankeilor is said to have founded the first in Scotland in 1723: see J. Sinclair, *Analysis of the Statistical Account of Scotland with a General View of the history of that country and discussion of some important branches of political economy* (Edinburgh, 1825), p. 303.

[23] L. Passy, *Histoire de la Société nationale d'agriculture de France: Tome premier 1761–1793* (Paris, 1912), p. 2.

[24] A. Dobbs, *An Essay on the Trade of Ireland Part II*, (Dublin, 1731), p. 98.

[25] Anonymous, *Some remarks occasion'd by the Revd Mr Madden's Scheme and Objections raised against it, by one that is no projector* (Dublin, 1732), p. 7.

[26] R. M. Molesworth, *Some Considerations for the Promoting of Agriculture and Employing the Poor* (Dublin, 1723), p. 30.

Nor was Molesworth content to abandon the nation as his normative horizon; religion also was differentiated from the ideal of improvement he had in mind:

In these schools, I wou'd not have any precepts, difference or distinction of religions taken notice of, and nothing taught, but only husbandry and good manners, and that the children should daily serve GOD according to their own religions, this school not being the proper place to make proselytes in: I doubt not but some such method as this wou'd make Husband-men, and prevent the increase of the Poor.[27]

Instruction in agriculture was ideally to release rural dwellers from the tutelage of politics and religion, and to introduce new secular criteria for the evaluation of the common good.

In France, as in Ireland, foundations of agricultural societies were deliberate efforts to inculcate new values. Bertin, effectively the Interior Minister under Louis XV and Louis XVI, took the opportunity of French reverses in the Seven Years War to promote agricultural societies as the seeds of the transformation of French society.[28] Agricultural societies would turn Frenchmen toward the arts of peace which would restore the pre-eminence lost through war. Preliminary work I have done on the membership lists of the later French foundations reveals that they represented elements of rural society that were absent from the more socially prestigious academies, a model they were at pains to distinguish themselves from. The society in Lyon explicitly stated in their draft constitution of 1762 'that we will not adopt any academic usages, that we will occupy ourselves with doing good rather than speaking well; to collect facts and to make them useful to society, that is our goal. The agricultural society ought to be considered as the depot for the observations of practical farmers (*cultivateurs*)'.[29] They provided a form of scientific sociability for curés, large farmers and junior civil servants, a rural knowledge elite rather than a fraction of the metropolitan world of the Enlightenment.[30] The societies were anxious to retain their utilitarian profile and not to become the cockpit for court or provincial politics. In 1762, for instance, the botanical section of the *Société royale des sciences* in Montpellier successfully fought off the attempt by the Archbishop of Narbonne to attach the society to the committee on taxation of the Estates of

---

[27] Ibid.

[28] *Arrest du conseil d'état du Roi qui ordonne l'établissement d'une société d'agriculture dans la généralité de Paris du 1er Mars 1761* (Paris, 1761).

[29] Archives Nationales H1 1510, *Projet de statuts pour l'établissement d'une chambre d'agriculture*, n.d.

[30] Daniel Roche, *Le siècle des lumières en province: académies et académiciens provinciaux, 1680–1789* (Paris, 1978), 2 vols.

Languedoc.[31] The agricultural societies were relatively open institutions seeking to concretize their utilitarian goals in practical projects and where the state or some other agency sought to co-opt them to its own ends the societies failed. In Scotland too the agricultural societies made possible forms of combination and action that would otherwise have been inconceivable. Agricultural societies opened up the possibility of enlightened actions for individuals who might otherwise lack the stimulus of communication:

As associations, by promoting a mutual communication, or interchange of ideas, and exciting a spirit of emulation, are found highly advantageous to the other arts, they certainly deserve encouragement, when directed to agriculture. Indeed farming, in some respects, requires such aid, more than other arts, because it is more of a solitary employment. The cultivator of the soil is in a manner insulated upon his own fields; while persons employed in the greater part of mechanical operations, carry on their work in company, and thence are therefore irresistibly led to see and profit by each other's ingenuity and skill. To make up for this disadvantage on the part of the husbandman, it seems necessary, that he should occasionally meet with his brethren, in order to communicate his observations, and in his turn, to receive the benefit of their experience.[32]

The agricultural survey for Clydesdale commented that the network of agricultural societies was so developed there that the members had set up a credit union among themselves.[33] The agricultural societies were remarkably open institutions which reflected and responded to the nature of social relations in the countryside.

The more profound education in new values was not experienced through the explicit confrontation with norms of politics and religion but in the unwitting innovations promoted in the process of communication. The context of what was originally thought of as gentlemanly science opened up even the most technical question to multiple horizons. Dr Stephens found that 'the design of this society, being to inquire into such foreign improvements as may be introduced here in order to lessen the value and quantity of our imports' turned his simple question of import substitution for blue dyes into one of 'a very large extent, and so indeed it is, comprehending many things, relating to manufactures, to the profession of physic, to our common food, and to many other uses of human life, more than I can propose to bring under consideration

---

[31] Archives Nationales H1 1511, M de Priest à M le Controleur Général, 22 February 1762.

[32] Sinclair, *Analysis*, p. 302.

[33] J. Naismith, *General View of the Agriculture of Clydesdale with observations of the means of its improvement drawn up for the consideration of the Board of Agriculture and Internal Improvement*, 2nd edn (Edinburgh, 1813), p. 169.

at present'.[34] Even simple questions of technique raised profound questions, especially concerning who was qualified to judge on these matters. The ideology of judgement was perfectly clear: 'gentlemen of fortune, conversant with books, cannot be at a loss for directions. They can peruse the discoveries of science and make experiments. The poorer sort, husbandmen and manufacturer, are the proper objects of instruction.'[35] Practice, however, tended to undermine this idyllic assumption that the social hierarchy and scientific insight reinforced one another. Much of the early programme of the society concerned itself with the promotion of improved agricultural machinery and to achieve this goal the 'poorer sort' had to be introduced as active participants, nor humble consumers of wisdom. In 1735, for example, the society had to advertise for a skilled ploughman whom they wished to employ to instruct the public on new techniques.[36] Later in the same year James Moore, a carpenter, was employed by the society to travel to Scotland to investigate a new model of threshing mill.[37] By the 1760s the gentleman amateur's authority was further undermined when the society employed a professional instrument maker, John Wynn Baker from Salford, to run the experiment grounds and instrument manufactory.[38] Baker was soon speaking to his audience, and potential customers, independently of the authority of the society and its members.[39] In fact he even began to complain that his own work was not being respected as gentlemanly science nor were the profits from it secure as a purely commercial venture. Instead he noted that the objects he manufactured were circulating in the world of emulation and craft, being copied and improved on:

And indeed, were it ever so compatible with my circumstances, I know not whether it would be altogether so prudent, to lay out a large sum of money, for carrying on a work, in which the public are much more interested, than I can possibly be as an individual; for I believe it a well-known fact, that many machines which are purchased of me, are intended only as patterns for others to work by.[40]

Baker's machines were part of subaltern science, a popular world in which the norms of reason lost their original mooring among gentlemen and became standards of evaluation and communication independent of social location. The original enthusiast for societies had envisaged them

[34] Royal Dublin Society, Minute Book 1, 14 October 1731, p. 12.
[35] RDS, Minute Book 1, 8 January 1737, p. 89.
[36] RDS, Minute Book 1, 13 February 1735, p. 18.
[37] RDS, Minute Book 1, 2 July 1735, p. 23.
[38] H. F. Berry, *A History of the Royal Dublin Society* (London, 1915), p. 136.
[39] J. W. Baker, *A Short Description and List with the Prices of the Instruments of Husbandry made in the Factory at Laughlinstown, near Celbridge, in the County of Kildare* (Dublin, 1967).
[40] Ibid., p. 5.

as something of a compromise between the gentlemanly and subaltern worlds of science:

There will be the more reason to hope for this blessed change, when we shall enjoy the advantage of seeing the best heads in the kingdom, assisted by hiring and employing the most skilful hands in agriculture, and enabled by an adequate fund to bear the charge of all kinds of unsuccessful experiments, that shall turn to no other account, but to set us right by their miscarriage; and as the great lord Bacon, the father of experimental philosophy expresses it, produce light, tho' no fruit to us.[41]

Agricultural societies opened up the question of norms for a wide population of rural Europeans.

The agricultural societies offered a location where the cultural superiority of the provincial might be asserted, without an appeal to tradition but by reference to science. It offered the ground of a rural, moralized, Enlightenment. The particular nature of rural scientific sociability as a communication between elite and subaltern worlds was illustrated in such rural hero figures as Jethro Tull, Parmentier and John Sinclair at the end of the century. The heroes of the British and French agricultural reform movements were provincial, enlightened and transformers of habits and ways of life that had been assumed to be immutable. They were the icons of a rural Enlightenment. The representation of the farmer scientist was however usually appropriated to landlords. As Thomas Robertson described it, only those who did not labour could gain the insight necessary to genuine progress:

Farming is a liberal art, and consists in appointing and in superintending labour; and in fact it is less laborious to do a thing, than to tell others what to do, how to do it, and to see it done. Were the farmer to see to his own plough, and perform the other menial exercises, he could not have time to make observations, to think, to read, to go to markets, to meet with his neighbours, to ride through the Parish and County, and neighbouring counties, to see better practices, and get information from all quarters. Farming is the most difficult of all the arts and nothing has retarded its advance so much as one farmer not knowing what another is doing at a distance from him . . .[42]

However Robertson was a Doctor of Divinity, a dignitary of the Scottish Presbyterian Church and a gentleman of science, asserting precisely the equation of gentility and scientific credibility that has been identified

---

[41] S. Madden, *A Letter to the Dublin Society on the Improving their Fund and the manufactures, tillage etc. in Ireland* (Dublin, 1739), p. 39.

[42] T. Robertson, *Outline of a General Report upon the Size of Farms and upon the Persons who cultivate Farms* (Edinburgh, 1796), p. 53.

by Steven Shapin.[43] Observers literally closer to the ground embraced the ideal of agricultural communication but argued that agricultural science had to be open, practical, and organized horizontally rather than hierarchically:

[M]en of all employments and capacities are included in the class of inventors, since by a particular turn of thinking, an accidental observation, a casual discovery, a lucky direction or hint taken hold of, varied, bent or applied; inventions and new lights leading to them, may be struck out, even by the meanest of the people. This taking in heads and hands of all sizes and forces, is of mighty importance, if duly employ'd and encourag'd, since none are too mean or too great for the labour, and nothing is above or below this enterprising Spirit that enlightens and enlarges the mind, encreasing the matter or method, the engines and instruments of redoubling our native powers to the service of God and Man, and the improvement of both the natural, artificial and moral world.[44]

The very capaciousness of the notion of development described here by Madden points to the transformative potential of the new value orientations sponsored by the agricultural societies. Rural knowledge elites appropriated new values through participation in the debates in agricultural societies but the nature of those debates meant that elites could not control the meaning and nature of the discussion. The plurality and multiplicity of the norms of reason that governed their activities provided the locus for cultural learning for these groups. Out of that speech situation grew the capacity for social and economic innovation.

It is difficult for us to discern the nature of rural rationality from beneath the ideology of peasant stupidity. The surface content of much commentary on farmers works on the assumption that peasants were ignorant and immobile by definition. 'The vast majority of our farmers, and unfortunately experience confirms this daily, are guided solely by blind routine, and because of prejudice are insensible to even their own interest,' wrote a rapporteur to the Conseil d'Etat in 1788, explaining that the peasantry were entirely ignorant of the methods and possibilities of empirical science.[45] The politics of enclosure in England particularly created a strong incentive to represent farmers and peasants as closed to all innovation. As an enthusiast for enclosures put it, 'Some persons, especially heretofore, have argued against enclosures, with a great deal of zeal, but with as much ignorance. As if it were not lawful, and necessary for the publick good, that all bad land should be made better. And that

---

[43] S. Shapin, *A Social History of Truth: Civility and Science in Seventeenth-Century England* (Chicago, 1994).

[44] Madden, *Letter to the Dublin Society*, p. 48.

[45] AN H[1] 1510, 'Observations sur la réunion de la société royale d'agriculture et du comité', MS 26 July 1788.

all the lazy lubbers, which live unprofitably upon the bad, and as so many thieves prey upon the good, should be made to work for their living.'[46] Other observers, even friends to the landlord such as John Sinclair, were less sure of the immobility of the peasant mentality.

It is pleasing also to remark, that, since the spirit for agricultural improvement has pervaded the country, farmers, who were formerly so obstinately attached to the practice of their forefathers, that they would not listen without a sneer, to any new plan of cultivation, have their prejudices now so completely removed, that they are eager to know, and anxious to understand, whatever experiments others are making, and even to adopt such methods as appear reasonable, though, at first, upon that cautious moderate scale, which prudence dictates.[47]

However, Sinclair, like many other observers, underlined that peasant innovation and curiosity was not the same as that of speculators and improvers, or even landlords. As a petition to the prefect of the Gard was to explain, peasants only needed to have the superiority of new methods shown to them, 'but for that they need facts, because the farmer wants concrete results. Speculative notions are not his area. A view out over a well fertilized field makes a greater impression on him than thousands of arguments.'[48] Peasant rationality was curiously concrete and its specificity had to be recognized. The best examples are those in which the official reason of the societies reveals its dependence on subaltern knowledge. In 1765 the Paris society proposed a prize for the best method of fertilizing land for grain.[49] In order to award the prize the society had to co-opt three farmers, 'Antoine Navarre laboureur a Compans, Pierre Sorty, laboureur a Villepinte, Claude Beuvin, laboureur a Mitry', all three of whom were known to be 'experienced in the art of agriculture', as they put it. The commissioners' anxiety about the competence of their fellow commissioners can be gauged by the fact that they required them to swear an oath 'to use all their knowledge to arrive at the goals of our commission'.[50] Elite actors did not feel competent to judge the ideas of subalterns without some reinforcing social discipline such as the oath, to help them. Peasants even represented themselves as having a specific scientificity. An anonymous entrant to the prize competition posed by the Société royale des sciences in Montpellier in 1773 wrote that 'I am persuaded that you do not desire a system of agriculture elaborated in the study, but a series

---

[46] Huntington Library, HM 1264, MS, *Means of a most ample encrease of the wealth and strength of England*, n.d., p. 23.

[47] Sinclair, *Analysis*, p. 235.

[48] AD Gard 7 M 101, Anonymous petition, 1 August 1838.

[49] AN H$^1$ 1501, Prizes proposed by the Société Royale d'Agriculture, 1764.

[50] AN H$^1$ 1501, Inspection of Farm of M Charlemagne, *laboureur* of Baubigny, winner of the 1765 prize, 21 March 1766.

of repeated experiments performed by an enlightened farmer. I take it as a duty to put the knowledge I have developed in the bosom of my family by twenty-five years of toil and careful work to the trial of your insight.'[51] The archives reveal a world of innovation and experiment just beyond the realm of the state and elites, though in contact with it. As late as 1845 the sub-prefect in Alais (modern Alès) was writing to his superior that he had discovered Jacques Pagès, a farmer who had invented an entirely new kind of plough.[52] While there were few rural rationalists as committed as Mouret of Saint-Jean de Bruel, who carried out a series of experiments on his own fields over ten years, there is ample evidence for significant evolution in peasant mentalities.[53]

The interaction of elite and subaltern worlds was particularly marked in one of the most important areas of activity of the societies: the promotion of new agricultural machinery. The first publication of the Dublin Society was a pirated edition of Jethro Tull's plans for horse-hoeing farming.[54] The society continued to promote new plough types, and sponsored ploughing matches as a pedagogical tool.[55] The introduction of new kinds of machines was potentially a transformative experience for peasant societies. Recent work in the history of technology by scholars such as Bruno Latour and Ken Alder has developed the idea that fashioned artefacts create worlds around themselves because they are, in M. Norton Wise's phrase, 'meeting grounds for diverse and conflicting interests, as well as instruments which mediate between the social and epistemological worlds'.[56] Alder for France and Merrit Roe Smith for the United States have argued that the most transformative form of technology in the eighteenth century was interchangeable parts manufacture.[57] These scholars have investigated efforts in military engineering to achieve the ideal of a system where tools and humans would be arranged in a regular process

---

[51] AD Hérault D 181, Entry number 10, 1773.

[52] AD Gard 7 M 434, Sub-prefect to Prefect, Alais, 15 January 1845.

[53] AD Hérault D 183, *Expériences d'agriculture et descriptions de plantes et d'insectes par M Mouret*, ten reports 1759–1769.

[54] J. Tull, *The new Horse-Houghing Husbandry, or, an Essay on the Principles of Tillage and Vegetation, wherein is shewn a method of introducing a sort of vineyard culture into the cornfields, in order to increase their product and diminish the common expense, by use of instruments lately invented* (Dublin, 1731).

[55] RDS, Minute Book 2, 22 December 1737, p. 62.

[56] M. Norton Wise, 'Meditations: Enlightenment Balancing Acts, or the Technologies of Rationalism', in *World Changes: Thomas Kuhn and the Nature of Science* (Cambridge, 1993), pp. 207–56; K. Alder, *Engineering the Revolution: Arms and the Enlightenment in France, 1763–1815* (Princeton, 1997); B. Latour, *We Have Never Been Modern* (Cambridge, MA, 1993); B. Latour, *Aramis, or the Love of Technology* (Cambridge, MA, 1996).

[57] M. Roe Smith, *Harper's Ferry Armoury and the New Technology: The Challenge of Change* (Ithaca, NY, 1987).

that would produce gun parts that were interchangeable. Little or no attention has been paid to the most achieved interchangeable part machine invented in the eighteenth century, James Small's swing plough.[58]

The transformations in the technology of farming introduced different agents into the world of rural Europe. Blacksmiths, land surveyors, projectors, and of course the improving landlords all played a role in persuading European farmers to invest in new technologies. The novelty cannot be overplayed. The basic plough type had remained unchanged in Europe from the tenth century to the eighteenth. The first true innovation was the Rotherham swing plough, developed in the 1730s. Small's plough perfected the swing plough and created a machine that demanded a new technological disposition on the part of those who would use it. It was quickly acknowledged as the new standard from which all subsequent ploughs would be derived.[59] Ploughboard technology, in particular, demanded of farmers that they acquire a technological view of the world, since the new ploughs were only efficient if constantly adjusted to changing soil types, but such adjustment had to be performed within parameters derived from a complex mathematics. The mathematics of the ploughboard, or moldboard, were not described until 1771 by Arbuthnot of Norfolk.[60] Small's major insight was to recognize that the optimal turn of the share and moldboard should carry the furrow through 130°. Ploughboards were a 'disembedded' technology, one that required the capacity to apply abstract rules in concrete situations. Farmers using these new instruments were drawn into a new world of technological discourse, as well as technological practice. This innovation dovetailed with the rural enlightenment inspired by the agricultural societies and created a ground for innovation in rural societies as a whole.

We can follow the effects of the introduction of the new ploughs by references to it in the agricultural surveys of the Scottish counties in the late eighteenth century. In Black Isle in the highlands the new plough type was new enough that using it was a marker of the improving attitudes.[61] In the more southerly and advanced Kincardineshire the basic plough had been appropriated and adapted to local needs.[62] In Clydesdale the community

---

[58] J. B. Passmore, *The English Plough* (Oxford, 1930), p. 18. Small was of course a Scot.

[59] L. le Villevielle, 'Rapport adressé à la société d'agriculture du département de l'Hérault sur les machines de Monsieur Fellenberg', *Bulletin de la société d'agriculture du département de l'Hérault* 2/14 (15 August 1808), p. 18.

[60] Passmore, *English Plough*, p. 16.

[61] J. Sinclair, *General View of the Agriculture of the Northern Counties and Islands of Scotland; including the Counties of Cromarty, Ross, Sutherland and Caithness, and the Islands of Orkney and Shetland* (Edinburgh, 1795), p. 21.

[62] G. Robertson, *A General View of the Agriculture of Kincardineshire or, the Mearns drawn up under the Direction of the Board of Agriculture*, 2nd edn (Edinburgh, 1813), p. 235.

of plough-users had completely accommodated itself to this new technological world and hybridized the implement at will. 'The improvements
which this ingenious mechanic made in the construction of the plough,
made it easier drawn, and it quickly obtained reputation, and was generally adopted. But it fell short of the perfection aimed, and has undergone
many modulations, almost every plough-wright having his own particular
cast of the mould-plate.'[63] Naismith's observation that it was the ploughboard that most attracted innovation is of course the most interesting
feature of his report. The kind of technological rationality demanded to
use these new capital goods efficiently was the same as that demanded by
inductive science, but it was now appropriated by the artisan rather than
the landlord or factor. Cognitive preference and technological demand
informed and reinforced one another. These negotiations of objects and
principles created the forms of rationality that were to allow for negotiations of different kinds of norms and objects: market principles and
commodities.

The open nature of the agricultural societies allowed them to foster new
ideas of rationality and practices of communication in provincial society.
The work of the societies implied two different ideas of rationality. The
more obvious was instrumental or practical. The societies were supposed
to promote new forms of agriculture which were more productive and
more profitable. They were explicitly designed to create a new kind of
economic consciousness which would accept the legitimacy of markets
even for subsistence goods, such as grain.[64] The scientific and technological innovations discussed already derived from this aspect of their work.
The second notion of reason that was implicated in their work was cognitive. The societies were founded at a revolutionary moment in the history of biology, indeed when the term itself was being coined. Linnaeus's
taxonomy and Buffon's pioneering work in natural history allowed the
life sciences to compete for the interest of educated Europeans with the
physical and medical sciences.[65] In 1766 the Dublin Society, which had
a botanical garden from 1731, sponsored a set of premiums to encourage
a set of natural histories of the Irish counties.[66] The progress in the life
sciences imposed new demands on local agronomists and botanists, however, primarily that their written and spoken communications accede to

---

[63] J. Naismith, *General View of the Agriculture of Clydesdale with observations of the means
of its improvement drawn up for the consideration of the Board of Agriculture and Internal
Improvement* (Edinburgh, 1813) 2nd ed., p. 94.
[64] For an account of the formation of the Scottish societies in precisely these terms, see
Sinclair, *Analysis*, p. 303.
[65] T. L. Hankins, *Science and the Enlightenment* (Cambridge, 1985), pp. 114–19.
[66] Berry, *Dublin Society*, pp. 69, 186.

the new standards of transparency and universality. This was particularly important because the life sciences were collaborative. Buffon's research, which was some of the most important of the era, was carried out with his network of correspondents in Europe and beyond. The accumulation of data that underpinned his monumental *Natural History* depended on his correspondents' control of norms of observation and communication. The activities of agricultural societies, such as evaluating the types of grain grown or species of animal raised in their regions, demanded the use of both notions of rationality. Correct taxonomy, proper modes of observation and profitable experiment were all, ideally, to converge in the person of the agronomist, the rural scientist.

The scientific sociability of the agricultural societies was inspired by notions of reason that were generated from the Enlightenment. The work of the societies did not simply generalize a consensual model of reason, though. Important debates over the relationship of cognitive and practical reason or, within the world of the life sciences, on the status and nature of taxonomies, were worked through in the agronomical and local botanical literature. In France, for instance, the investigation of nature was understood to have very specific ethical consequences. Jean-Jacques Rousseau argued that botanizing was a particularly ethical scientific behaviour, precisely because it was not instrumental.[67] Denis Diderot observed that a new taste for the life sciences went hand in hand with a renewed concern for ethical and political questions. Studying nature and working with it was widely understood to be an antidote to the abstract rationalism of the more mathematically informed sciences and a means of aligning modern social and economic life with simplicity. This kind of science was to morally improve its practitioners. One of the most obvious effects of this set of cultural assumptions was the construction of the identity of the life scientist. Linnaeus was portrayed as a provincial, ill-dressed and unsophisticated, guaranteeing the veracity of his research by the authenticity of his person.[68] It is therefore unsurprising that while Buffon dominated natural history in Paris, the provincial societies quickly committed themselves to Linnaeus's model of categorization.

The choice of the Linnean system implied more than simple identification with the assertion of cultural identity of the Swede. As Lisbet Koerner argues, the Linnean system of classification 'lowered the educational and financial entrance fee to the study of nature'.[69] The clarity and

---

[67] P. Saint-Amand, 'Rousseau contre les philosophes: l'exemple de la botanique dans les textes autobiographes', *Studies on Voltaire and the Eighteenth Century* 242 (1983), pp. 159–68.

[68] On Linnaeus's own primitivism see L. Koerner, *Linnaeus: Nature and Nation* (Cambridge, MA, 1999), pp. 56–81.

[69] L. Koerner, 'Carl Linnaeus in his time and place', in N. Jardine, J. A. Secord and E. C. Spary, eds, *Cultures of Natural History* (Cambridge, 1996), p. 145.

simplicity of Linnaeus's taxonomical system shattered the relationship between theory and practice. The programme in Natural History sponsored by Buffon depended on a strict distinction between observation and theorization.[70] Buffon's commitment to Lockean epistemology demanded that the categories under which phenomena were to be organized should only emerge after repeated observations. The local practitioners should not impose the expectations of a classificatory schema on the objects they observed, they should be experts only within defined contexts, local correspondents of a metropolitan reason they did not comprehend. Adanson, whose *Familles des Plantes* was the most explicit statement of Buffon's principles of classification in botany, even avoided Linnean nomenclature in order to guard local practitioners from a false sense of secure categorization.[71] The Linnean programme made exactly the opposite demand. Local observers were expected to master the explicit distinctions of the Linnean system in order to make their work communicable to other participants in biological research.[72] Linnaeus brought taxonomical order out of chaos with a rigorous system of telegram-style diagnoses, his development of an elaborate terminology of plant morphology, his standardization of synonymies and his invention of binomial nomenclature.[73] The very artificiality of Linnaeus's distinctions of Kingdom, Class, Order, Genus, Species and Variety underlined the distinction of concepts from experience.[74] Engagement with Linnaeus's programme of research in natural history carried with it an education in the capacity to operate in decontextualized arenas. The world of agronomical and botanical research was a template from which communities and individuals might learn the skills necessary to orientate themselves to other virtual frames of reference, such as society or the market. It opened up local practitioners to vastly expanded time horizons and to the conventional nature of norms. Simply being able properly to classify a wheat variety depended on control of exactly what a variety was and to do that demanded a whole array of cognitive skills.

Linnaeus was particularly important to the scientific institutions of the peasant societies of Ireland and southern France. The Dublin Society's botanical garden was laid out on Linnean grounds and it planned its *Flora Rustica Hibernica* on the organizational principles he promoted.[75]

---

[70] On Buffon see J. Roger, *Buffon: A Life in Natural History* (Ithaca, NY, 1997).

[71] A. G. Morton, *History of Botanical Science: An Account of the Development of Botany from Ancient Times to the Present Day* (London, 1981), p. 304.

[72] P. R. Sloan, 'The Buffon-Linnaeus Controversy', *Isis* 67/238 (September 1976), p. 366.

[73] E. Mayr, *The Growth of Biological Thought: Diversity, Evolution and Inheritance* (Cambridge, MA, 1982), p. 173.

[74] P. R. Sloan, 'Natural History, 1670–1802', in R. C. Olby, G. N. Cantor, J. R. R. Christie and M. J. S. Hodge, eds, *Companion to the History of Science* (London, 1990), p. 301.

[75] Berry, *Dublin Society*, p. 194.

Linnaeus was even more important to the Montpellier society. François Boissier de la Croix de Sauvages, a leading member of the Montpellier society, was the leading interpreter of Linnaeus in France and made Montpellier into the redoubt of Linnean science in the country.[76] Under his inspiration local collectors and botanists came to understand their activities as an education in the principles of taxonomy. A correspondent of the Montpellier academy of sciences, Blanquet lived in Mende in the Aveyron, then as now one of the most isolated and underpopulated parts of France. However, it was not as a local *érudit* but as a rural scientist that he contributed his memoir on the cultivation of new fruit species.[77] Blanquet admitted the difficulty of finding appropriate categories under which to organize observations: 'analogy is nothing but a false guide for weak and unquestioning minds, that reinforces their laziness and leads them astray'. However those with a more penetrating intellect can construct a chain of reasoning and 'generalize their ideas, and from many particular phenomena rise to general principles'. His sense of security in his cogitations was entirely derived from Linnaeus: 'sexual difference' was the fundamental principle that allowed categorization of plants and their hybridization. He was certain too that the sexual system which he admitted 'seemed in its time a revolting idea', but was Linnaeus's major contribution in botany, was reinforced by 'later observations, which lend it a degree of certainty that one can no longer doubt it'. Blanquet is the perfect example of someone whose participation in a world of scholarly communication created an inductive mentality.

Linnean botanizing created a distinct role for subaltern participants who had to have a secure grasp of classificatory principle. Women were particularly prominent practitioners in the field.[78] Their control of taxonomy made these women full collaborators in the development of the field, rather than just operating as collectors in a division of intellectual labour dominated by professional taxonomers. Botany, and the life sciences generally, depended on collaborators who were drawn from outside the world of gentlemanly science because they were built on a foundation of fieldwork.[79] On occasion the fieldworkers could completely destroy the social division of labour. In 1836 the Cuverian Society of Cork proposed

---

[76] P. Duris, *Linné et la France (1780–1850)* (Paris, 1993), pp. 39–44.

[77] A. D. Hérault D 181 f.185, Blanquet, 'Mémoire sur les moyens de se procurer des nouvelles espèces de fruit', 1781.

[78] A. B. Shteir, *Cultivating Women, Cultivating Science: Flora's Daughters and Botany in England 1760 to 1860* (Baltimore, 1996).

[79] M. J. S. Rudwick, *The Great Devonian Controversy: The Shaping of Scientific Knowledge among Gentlemanly Specialists* (Chicago, 1985), pp. 37–41.

the creation of a flora and fauna of the south of Ireland.[80] By 1842 the efforts of one participant were acknowledged to have exceeded anyone's expections:

Denis Murray of Ballinanought having from time to time communicated to the society his botanical discoveries by which an addition of twenty six plants within a short space of time has been made to the flora of the county of Cork in the society's possession, three of which are also new to that of Ireland, we deem it a duty as well as a pleasure to record our approval of his zeal and intelligence by presenting him a silver medal with a suitable inscription.[81]

However, Murray was not a member of the society but the gardener of one of the members. Murray's extended correspondence with the society in the end became something of an embarrassment to the gentlemen who comprised it since they could not recognize him as an equal but felt uncomfortable about rewarding him as a servant. The society eventually convened a special meeting to discuss 'the propriety of presenting Denis Murray the sum of 2 guineas as a compensation in part for the time and labour expended on his contribution to the "flora and fauna" '.[82] Denis Murray's control of botanical theory and practice made him a rational agent, the author of his own work and an independent participant in the collective project of the life sciences.

## Conclusion

The history of eighteenth-century rural Europe is characterized by conflict and struggle. In Scotland, Burgundy or Ireland landlords, tenants and labourers struggled to control resources and to appropriate profits.[83] This history of often violent confrontation, and of the cultural practices that accompanied it, is highly visible in the archives. It connotes a rural world of enforced transformation and dogged resistance. Polanyi's image of a world transformed by the imposition of a market and its disciplines from without derives its credibility from the evidence of confrontation. However, the archive also reveals another reality, of the collective transformation of values. Institutions of communication and scientific

[80] Boole Library, MS U221 A, Minute Book of the Cork Cuverian Society, 5 April 1936, p. 39.
[81] Boole Library, MS U221 A, Minute Book of the Cork Cuverian Society, 2 November 1842, p. 79.
[82] Boole Library, MS U221 A, Minute Book of the Cork Cuverian Society, 2 April 1845, p. 114.
[83] S. Clark and J. S. Donnelly, eds, *Irish Peasants: Violence and Rural Unrest 1780–1914* (Manchester, 1983); T. M. Devine, *The Transformation of Rural Scotland: Social Change and the Agrarian Economy, 1660–1815* (Edinburgh, 1994); H. L. Root, *Peasants and King in Burgundy: Agrarian Foundations of French Absolutism* (Berkeley, 1987).

activity fostered a model of improvement grounded in the idea of reason. Sporadic and spectacular violence, be it state or subaltern, is less evident here. Also missing in this process of transformation is the market, at least the market as a principle. Peasants clearly used markets, but the market was not a privileged site of transformation. Instead markets were embedded within a more capacious set of improving practices. The peasants of France, Scotland and Ireland were not beyond the reach of markets, but they developed their particular culture of modernity outside them.

The history of the rational peasant opens up questions that extend far beyond the local and specific context of the history of eighteenth-century rural Europe. The rationality of the rational peasant was not simple purposive rationality or utility maximization. That rationality was a complex cultural pattern learned and elaborated in a variety of practices. Crucially, the market was not the only institution within which practices of reason were learned. The agricultural societies, and the knowledge networks they sponsored, are examples of communicative institutions that allowed individuals to participate in cultures of reason. These two axes, of cultural content and institutional setting, are crucial to understanding the conditions within which the institution of the market worked and the manner in which it could attain legitimacy. For rural Europe, the market, and the political economy that animated it, could not have replaced a moral economy unless both were embedded in a more extensive process of modernization in which there were many opportunities for actors to appropriate new norms. Other studies of particular institutions, such as property rights, have allowed for subtle historical accounts of the interaction of economics and politics in the creation of particular economic configurations. Avner Grief's study of medieval Genoa and Jean-Laurent Rosenthal's work on the creation of water rights in the French Revolution both argue that political institutions created the conditions for economic growth.[84] Peasants become modern, for institutional economics, as they act politically and economically to create new incentive structures.[85] By restoring the relevance of the political strategies of economic actors this perspective has been particularly fruitful in re-establishing the logic of

---

[84] A. Greif, 'Self-enforcing political systems and economic growth: late medieval Genoa', in R. Bates, B. R. Weingast and A. Greif, eds, *Analytic Narratives* (Princeton, 1998), pp. 23–63; J.- L. Rosenthal, *The Fruits of Revolution: Property Rights, Litigation and French Agriculture, 1700–1860* (Cambridge, 1992).

[85] J. Livesey, *Making Democracy in the French Revolution* (Cambridge, MA, 2001), pp. 127–66; D. North and R. Thomas, 'The Rise and Fall of the Manorial System: A Theoretical Model', *Journal of Economic History* 31/4 (December 1971), pp. 777–803.

French economic development in the nineteenth century.[86] Institutional economics does not get us beyond markets, however; the essentialist market that was thrown out the door makes its reappearance through the rational-choice window. As Douglas North points out, public choice theory and institutional economics remain committed to the maximization assumption.[87] To further develop an interdisciplinary conversation on the creation and spread of markets it is precisely that assumption that we must overcome.

[86] See recently J. R. Lehning, *Peasant and French: Cultural Change in Rural France during the Nineteenth Century* (Cambridge, 1995); A. R. H. Baker, *Fraternity among the French Peasantry: Sociability and Voluntary Associations in the Loire Valley, 1814–1914* (Cambridge, 1999); J. A. Miller, *Mastering the Market: The State and the Grain Trade in Northern France 1700–1860* (Cambridge, 1999).

[87] D. C. North, 'What Do We Mean by Rationality?', *Public Choice* 77/1 (September 1993), p. 159.

# 3 The politics of political economy in France from Rousseau to Constant

*Richard Whatmore*

## The limits of the received story

Until Smith's work, the study of politics, properly speaking the science of government, had been confounded with political economy, which shows how wealth is created, distributed and consumed. This confusion stems perhaps solely from the unfortunate title given to researches of this kind . . . [in consequence] the demand has been made that political economy concern itself with all of the laws that regulate the domestic life of the political family.[1]

Jean-Baptiste Say's judgement can be seen to problematize the title of this essay: Say appeared to be turning his back on the politics of political economy. According to Say, political economy needed to be restricted to the empirically certain science of wealth; this, he said, was Adam Smith's achievement in the *Wealth of Nations*. Wealth was 'independent of forms of government'. A state could be prosperous, regardless of who governed it, 'if it is well administered'. Looking backwards from 1803, Say held Jean-Jacques Rousseau, along with François Quesnay's sect of 'économistes' or physiocrats, responsible for impeding the progress of political economy as a science. His rise to prominence during the Restoration did not alter this view.[2] Despite numerous changes made to Say's *Traité*, it was repeated in the editions of 1814, 1817 and 1826. When he published what he believed to be his magnum opus in 1828–9, the *Cours complet d'économie politique pratique*, he included an essay on the historical progress of political economy. This also condemned Rousseau's

Thanks to Manuela Albertone, Béla Kapossy, Donald Winch, Ruth Woodfield, Brian Young and the editors for comments on an earlier version of this chapter. A more general debt needs to be acknowledged to the work of Istvan Hont and Michael Sonenscher. The research was supported by grants from the British Academy, the Leverhulme Trust, and the School of Advanced Study at the University of London.

[1] J.-B. Say, 'Discours préliminaire', *Traité d'économie politique* (Paris, 1803), 2 vols, vol. I, pp. ii–iii.

[2] Say was appointed professor of *Économie industrielle* at the *Conservatoire* in 1819 and professor of *Économie politique* at the *Collège de France* in 1830.

continuing influence, but happily concluded 'there no longer remains a single partisan of Quesnay's doctrine'.[3]

Until his death in 1832 Say remained dogmatic in his hostility to any political economy that failed to respect the boundaries he was certain that Smith had erected. Even English disciples of Smith were considered to be at fault on this matter, as Say made clear in his *Lettres à Malthus* (1820). At first glance Say appeared to be echoing the view of David Hume and Smith that absolute monarchies were as capable of fostering commerce as mixed monarchies or republics. This explains Bonaparte's initial hope that the *Traité d'économie politique* might justify the Napoleonic regime.[4] On meeting the Emperor, Say made it clear that his intentions were altogether different. The resulting assumption has always been that only liberal politics were compatible with Say's political economy. The argument of this essay is that what Say meant was more contentious, with significant consequences for our view of political economy at this time and its relationship with politics, morals and religion.

The majority of historians have associated Say's work with the defence of a *laissez-faire* approach to markets in the context of legally entrenched civil liberties and limited government by representatives of the people.[5] Benjamin Constant was the source of this view. In writings between 1814 and 1820, quickly recognized to be definitive in the formation of French liberalism, Constant developed a perspective that was, on the surface, identical to Say's. Both argued that the post-revolutionary context made it imperative to couple plans for reform with a critique of historical writers who had misdirected French legislators in the past. For each writer, Rousseau was especially to be disparaged for causing France to decline economically. According to Constant, he had led the revolutionaries back to the politics of classical republicanism rather than accepting the necessity of embracing commercial society.[6] In Constant's opinion, France needed a new era of limited government along the lines of

---

[3] J.-B. Say, *Cours Complet d'économie politique pratique; ouvrage destiné à mettre sous les yeux des hommes d'état, des propriétaires fonciers et les capitalistes, des savans, des agriculteurs, des manufacturiers, des négocians, et en général de tous les citoyens, l'économie des sociétés* (Paris, 1837), pp. 560n, 568.

[4] For Say's description of his early relationship with Napoleon, and hatred of the Empire, see the letter to Charles Robert Prinsep, written from Paris in May 1821, in *Œuvres diverses de Jean-Baptiste Say*, ed. H. Say (Paris, 1848), pp. 429–38.

[5] G. de Ruggiero, *The History of European Liberalism* (Oxford, 1927), pp. 171–2; C. Welch, *Liberty and Utility: The French Ideologues and the Transformation of Liberalism* (New York, 1984), pp. 71–5; A. Jardin, *Histoire du libéralisme politique* (Paris, 1985), pp. 167, 187–8; A. Tiran, 'Jean-Baptiste Say: Manuscrits sur la monnaie, la banque, et la finance', in *Cahiers monnaie et financement* (Lyon, 1995), vol. X, pp. 1–229; E. L. Forget, *The Social Economics of Jean-Baptiste Say: Markets and Virtue* (London, 1999).

[6] B. Constant, *Traité de l'esprit de conquête et de l'usurpation* (Paris, 1814), ch. 7.

a reformed British constitution to repair the damage of the 1790s.[7] Commerce would then follow what Smith had famously called 'the Natural Progress of Opulence'. As Constant put it in his lecture to the *Athénée Royale* at Paris in 1819, 'Commerce has brought nations closer, it has given them customs and habits which are almost identical. The heads of states may be enemies: the peoples are compatriots.'[8] If politics and political economy were separated, and civil liberty recognized to be the most important political value, a new era of peaceful economic progress would begin.[9]

Constant successfully constructed a taxonomy of 'good' and 'bad' political economy, founded on a distinction between advocates and enemies of commerce. The former were necessarily liberals, moderns and scientists. Opponents of commerce were republicans, socialists, utopians and ancients. As political economy came to be seen as a distinct and intellectually successful science, 'whig' histories were written which ascribed the progress of liberal political economy to its 'scientific character'.[10] Smith was more often than not described as the founder of the subject, although some French histories began to pursue a more nationalistic line, emphasizing Smith's debt to the physiocrats in general and Turgot in particular. But the view that a distinctly liberal politics ought to accompany political economy dominated the historiography of the subject in France from the 1840s.[11] The view that the rise of political economy paralleled the triumph of reason over reactionary philosophies has directed most of the writings of twentieth-century historians of the subject.[12]

The aim of this essay is to challenge the orthodox story. Historians have underestimated the extent to which political economy was an insecure and divided discipline in the early nineteenth century, because of uncertainty about the consequences of Europe's turbulent recent past.

---

[7] B. Constant, *Principes de politique applicables à tous les gouvernements*, ed. E. Hofmann (Geneva, 1980 (orig. 1815)), pp. 25–41.

[8] B. Constant, 'The Liberty of the Ancients Compared with that of the Moderns', in *Political Writings*, ed. and tr. B. Fontana (Cambridge, 1988), pp. 324–5.

[9] B. Constant, *Commentaire sur l'ouvrage de Filangieri* (Paris, 1822), bk 1, ch. 1.

[10] H. Say, 'Notice sur la vie et les ouvrages de Jean-Baptiste Say', in J.-B. Say, *Traité d'économie politique*, 6th edn (Paris, 1838), pp. iii–iv; 'Introduction', in Say, *Œuvres diverses*; A. Walras, *De la Nature de la richesse et de l'origine de la valeur* (Paris, 1831); J.-A. Blanqui, *Histoire de l'économie politique en Europe, depuis les anciens jusqu'à nos jours*, 3rd edn (Paris, 1845), 2 vols, vol. I, ch. 36.

[11] For a nineteenth-century example see L. Say's *Turgot* (Paris, 1887). For a more recent view see Louis Dumont, *Homo Aequalis*, translated as *From Mandeville to Marx: The Genesis and Triumph of Economic Ideology* (Chicago, 1977). In Marxist literature there has been a similar outcome, in that politics is consigned to the ideological superstructure, with eighteenth-century authors accordingly derided for displaying feudal or bourgeois credentials.

[12] J. Schumpeter, *A History of Economic Analysis* (Oxford, 1954), pp. 491–2; T. Sowell, *Say's Law: An Historical Analysis* (Princeton, 1972), ch. 1.

The revolutionary attempt to transform a civilized monarchy into a commercial republic shattered assumptions about the relationship between the political and the economic. A state was created in France in 1789 dedicated to increasing commerce, yet founded on the sovereignty of a nation lacking hierarchical ranks and a recognizable religious establishment. Hitherto such conceptions of political rule and civil life had been associated with small states, such as the Swiss commercial republics, or uniquely fortunate conditions, such as the surplus of land enjoyed by the North American federal republic. Although the revolutionary state in France failed to maintain itself against internal assaults on its legitimacy, it successfully defeated a combined force of most of Europe's monarchies. In doing so it underlined the serious threat it posed to monarchical and aristocratic conceptions of sovereignty, and accordingly the accepted moral and social order. The question for the Napoleonic generation was how far the Empire or Restored Monarchy had vanquished commercial republicanism, or whether a form of republic could be found which coupled external military supremacy with internal order. Political economists disputed the meaning of the republican legacy. Advocates of free markets were divided over the fit between republican politics and commercial society; the particular position they adopted shaped what they meant by the liberty of trade.

Explaining how ideas about creating a stable republic influenced ideas about commerce and markets requires a reversal of the traditional lineage of eighteenth-century thinkers and their ideologies. In addition, a neglected distinction has to be reintroduced into historical analysis of this period: a distinction between 'modern republicans' and 'democratic republicans'. The choice of these terms is somewhat imprecise because of the difference between what is today meant by democracy and the altogether different definition adopted by eighteenth- and early nineteenth-century writers. A more accurate wording would be to employ the distinction made famous by Machiavelli, between the *governo largo*, or broad-based government, and the narrow or aristocratic *governo stretto*. The *governo largo* entailed neither popular sovereignty nor government by the people in the classic Athenian sense. Rather, following Aristotle, it combined a society of different orders of citizens with governance by the distinguished, who nevertheless accepted the legal equality of all members of the polity. For the sake of simplicity, but with their limitations in mind, this chapter will use the terms 'modern republican' and 'democratic republican'. Put schematically, the chapter will argue that Constant was a modern republican in a sense defined by Rousseau. Both of these thinkers advocated a republic in the sense of a state committed to defending equally the interests of all its members. But they were also fearful of the extremism that they expected to accompany popular rule.

Democracy in government, in the participatory sense, had to be curtailed. At the same time neither thinker had any faith in kings, aristocrats or merchants ruling in the place of the people. It was, therefore, necessary to create a source of authority that stood above all of the disparate elements of society. Rousseau, in the *Contrat Social*, called this authority the state or sovereign. Constant called it the *système représentatif*. In envisaging a republic in which sovereignty was held by an artificially created abstract being, they were depriving the people of political agency. Rousseau and Constant shared a scepticism about the capacity of human beings to act benevolently towards one another. For Constant, social hierarchy was essential to maintain public order. For each thinker, constitutional mechanisms were also vital. In the small state where political authority could be exercised legitimately, Rousseau argued that the state would assert itself by replacing governments that infringed popular liberty or failed to protect the citizens. By contrast, Constant held that political authority could be legitimately exercised in large commercial states, if the government represented the people in a carefully defined manner. Like the abbé Emmanuel Sieyès, Constant believed that politics ought to be conducted by experts, being analogous to the division of labour in the economic realm.

Say, alongside nearly all of his contemporaries, opposed democracy as a form of government; but he was a democratic republican because he believed that the *demos* or people had to be political agents in making law and in governing the economy. Say was not a modern republican because he believed that the people must ultimately rule themselves. He had more faith than Constant in the human capacity to be peacefully sociable. Creating political structures in government that were divorced from the people was, Say argued, politically deadly. By 'people' he meant the middle classes involved in the production of wealth, who could therefore be trusted because of their interest in public order. But he wanted as many individuals as possible, and ultimately every member of society, to be a productive agent. Say associated Constant's modern republicanism with Bonaparte's Empire and Britain's mixed monarchy. As Pierre-Samuel Dupont de Nemours recognized in a letter of 1815, Say remained a physiocrat in important respects despite his public castigation of physiocratic doctrine.[13] The physiocrats had argued that it was possible to educate people to behave rationally in political and economic life, by enlightening them about their self-interest and thereby calming the more socially dangerous natural passions. For Say, political economy had to do exactly this, and from a long-term perspective teach the people self-government.

---

[13] Letter to Say, 22 April 1815, Say, *Œuvres diverses*, p. 366.

Constant was wrong to see the political economy of his day as simply for or against commerce and the market. Ideas about markets that were superficially similar became very different when combined with the distinct moral and political philosophies of modern republicanism as opposed to democratic republicanism. After explaining what political economy meant to its readers in the eighteenth century, this essay follows work on Britain, the German states and France, which has revealed the complicated relationship between political economy and ideas about forms of government, national defence, religion and moral philosophy.[14] By focusing on the work of Rousseau and the physiocrats, the essay shows the extent to which political economy developed from controversies within Christian theology and the related issue of how to maintain peace in a world of competitive nation states. The essay then turns to the distinctive political economy of the revolutionary years in order to show the mistake historians have made in assuming continuity between the French Enlightenment and the Revolution. Rather than accepting the common verdict that the 1790s were characterized by utopian classical republicanism and Jacobin terrorism, it is argued that the revolutionaries were intellectual innovators in political economy, largely because of their interest in large-state republican politics. Having established an ideological context in place of the accepted framework, the essay concludes by reexamining Say and Constant's vehement disagreement about politics and political economy, putting to rest the ideological fraternity presumed by generations of commentators.

## The meaning of political economy before the Revolution

Writing in exile after the failed Genevan revolution of 1782, François D'Ivernois recalled the excitement generated by a celebrated compatriot's return in 1761:

[14] D. Winch, *Riches and Poverty: An Intellectual History of Political Economy in Britain, 1750–1834* (Cambridge, 1996); K. Tribe, *Governing Economy: The Reformation of German Economic Discourse, 1750–1840* (Cambridge, 1988); P. Steiner, 'Comment stabiliser l'ordre social moderne: J.-B. Say, l'économie politique et la revolution', in G. Faccarello and P. Steiner, eds, *La Pensée économique pendant la Révolution Française* (Grenoble, 1990), pp. 173–94; P. Steiner, 'Politique et économie politique chez Jean-Baptiste Say', *Revue française d'histoire des idées politiques* 5 (1997), pp. 23–58; P. Steiner, *La 'Science nouvelle' de l'économie politique* (Paris, 1998); P. Steiner, *Sociologie de la connaissance économique: Essai sur les rationalisations de la connaissance économique (1750–1850)* (Paris, 1998), pp. 187–248; I. Hont, 'The Permanent Crisis of a Divided Mankind: The Contemporary Crisis of the Nation State in Historical Perspective', *Political Studies* 42 (1994), pp. 166–231; M. Sonenscher, 'The Nation's Debt and the Birth of the Modern Republic: The French Fiscal Deficit and the Politics of the Revolution of 1789', *History of Political Thought*, 18 (1997), pp. 64–103, 267–325.

J.-J. Rousseau was come to Geneva to return to the protestant communion, from whence he had strayed through the folly of youthful days spent in romantic wandering. He studied in the constitution of his country those great principles of political economy, that he soon after displayed, and which encreased that celebrity so much lamented by him towards the close of his life.[15]

The principles of political economy 'soon after displayed' was a reference to the *Contrat Social*, published on 15 May 1762. For D'Ivernois, what Rousseau called *Économie politique* in his 1755 *Encyclopédie* article, 'the principles of political right' in the *Contrat Social*, and 'that great and useless science' in *Émile*, made political economy the study of the survival, stability and legitimacy of political societies, and especially small states such as their own Geneva. For the physiocrats too political economy had to be concerned with these issues if it was to be practically useful. The title of the collection of writings edited by Pierre-Samuel Dupont de Nemours in 1767 makes this abundantly clear: *Physiocratie, ou constitution naturelle du gouvernement le plus avantageux au genre humain* (1767). D'Ivernois's comment also underlines the extent to which political economy could not be divorced from religion. If Rousseau's political economy was, as D'Ivernois said, a panegyric on the Genevan constitution, this made it a defence of Calvinism to be contrasted with his earlier Catholicism ('the folly of youthful days spent in romantic wandering'). In fact, as Rousseau and the physiocrats acknowledged, they perceived their work to be theodicies: concerned with reconciling the existence of a just, all-seeing and all-powerful God with the ubiquity of evil. In the eighteenth-century context, exploring the possibility of moral action in a world marred by the Fall meant treating nation states like individuals: individuals equally subject to the corrosive passions.[16]

The association of political economy with this perspective on politics, and specifically with forms of government, would have been accepted as natural by contemporaries. The term 'political economy', and its synonym 'political arithmetic', had become popular with the intensification of competition between large monarchies in early modern Europe.[17] This was especially the case with respect to commerce, because commerce was widely recognized as the possible basis of a spectacular increase in national military power. Political economy, therefore, focused on the nature and

[15] F. D'Ivernois, *An Historical and Political View of the Constitution and Revolutions of Geneva in the Eighteenth Century*, tr. John Farell (London, 1784), pp. 160–1.

[16] See M. Sonenscher, 'Property, Community, and Citizenship', in M. Goldie and R. Wokler, eds, *The Cambridge History of Eighteenth-Century Political Thought*, forthcoming, and 'Physiocracy as a Theodicy', *History of Political Thought* 23 (2002), pp. 326–39.

[17] C. Larrère, *L'Invention de l'économie politique au XVIIIe siècle* (Paris, 1992); J.-Cl. Perrot, 'Économie politique', in *Une histoire intellectuelle de l'économie politique* (Paris, 1992), pp. 7–52.

characteristics of large commercial monarchies, and the manner by which their establishment affected the traditional survival strategies of smaller monarchies and republics. Writers such as Antoyne de Montchrétien, author of the *Traicté de l'œconomie politique* (1615), stated explicitly that political economy was an aid to princes in their battles for international supremacy, teaching them to maximize their natural and human resources to maintain their state. Such arguments have sometimes been called mercantilist, in order to make a contrast with later, presumably cosmopolitan, defences of economic liberty: exactly when mercantilist arguments were replaced by anti-mercantilist ones, however, remains uncertain.[18] Other than the abbé Charles-Irénée Castel de Saint-Pierre, who wrote just prior to and during the Regency, it is very difficult to find writers who believed that there was a short-term alternative to the internecine strife between states that had characterized European history, ancient and modern. Advocates of the liberty of the grain trade, such as the physiocrats themselves from the late 1750s, claimed that their policies would ultimately establish international peace; but they also openly admitted that this necessitated French hegemony, and, therefore, an end to the imperial ambitions of other European powers.[19]

If political economy was originally the study of how a state ought to defend itself against internal and external threats, by the eighteenth century it had tended to become a commentary on the relative strength of Britain and France. These states were important because of the rivalry between them, which manifested itself in diplomatic antagonism and, frequently, in military engagement. For most French writers of the middle decades of the eighteenth century, France was the supreme European power. It had an extensive population, ample natural resources, and enjoyed an advanced state of civilization. Nevertheless, Britain, inferior in all these respects, had defeated France in war at the beginning of the century and affirmed its military superiority during the Seven Years War of 1757–63. Britain's success appeared to defy the natural order. Accordingly, political economy became concerned with the merits of mixed monarchy as opposed to other forms, the contrast between commercial practices among Protestant and Catholic peoples, and the possibility of fighting wars by reliance upon public credit. It also studied how practical it was

[18] E. F. Heckscher, *Mercantilism*, tr. M. Shapiro (London, 1935), 2 vols, vol. II, pt v; the best critical commentary is by D. C. Coleman, 'Eli Heckscher and the Idea of Mercantilism', in *Revisions in Mercantilism* (London, 1969), pp. 92–117; and D. C. Coleman, 'Mercantilism Revisited', *Historical Journal* 23 (1980), pp. 773–91.

[19] M. Sonenscher, 'French Economists and Bernese Agrarians: The Marquis de Mirabeau and the Economic Society of Berne', unpublished paper at the conference *Republican Political Economy and Enlightenment: The Patriotic and Economic Societies of Berne in European Context* (Lausanne, 2000).

to transform the *mœurs* or manners of a nation, to make its people more attuned to certain kinds of commerce compatible with moral or political virtue. By addressing such issues the French reading public expected its political economists to discover the secret of Britain's phenomenal rise, and apply the lessons to French circumstances. Alternatively, because the rise of Britain had been so unexpected and precipitous, they could reassure them that Britain's power and prosperity rested on shaky foundations. Looking back on over a hundred years of intermittent war, and the third major defeat of France by Britain, Restoration writers attacked the physiocrats and Rousseau for being political enthusiasts whose ideas were among the causes of the economic disaster that the French Revolution was deemed to have been. When seen as more direct contemporaries saw them, from the pressing perspective of the debate about Britain, a different picture emerges.

## Rousseau's modern republicanism for small states

In the case of Rousseau the antagonism of the Restoration writers was understandable. A cult of Rousseau had developed from the late 1760s, centring as much on his personal life as his philosophical paradoxes. Most of his books were publishing successes, including, it is now clear, the *Contrat Social*.[20] More often they were publishing sensations. When the first part of Rousseau's *Confessions* appeared posthumously, in 1781, this cult intensified. The extent of the cult in revolutionary France has been well documented, particularly the moment when Rousseau's ashes were transferred to the *Panthéon*, accompanied by a series of commemorative public *fêtes*.[21] The Jacobins who turned to judicial murder in the belief that it would save the state from destruction identified Rousseau as the archetypal *homme révolutionnaire*.[22] A view of Rousseau articulated in the early years of the Revolution by its critics, such as Jacques Mallet Dupan and Jean-Joseph Mounier, came to hold sway, namely that Rousseau had contributed more than any other author to national instability.[23] Rousseau's

[20] R. A. Leigh, 'The impact of Rousseau's "Contrat Social" in eighteenth-century France: Mornet's private libraries revisited', in J. T. A. Leigh, ed., *Unsolved Problems in the Bibliography of J.-J. Rousseau* (Cambridge, 1990), pp. 1–23.

[21] See R. Barny, *L'Eclatement révolutionnaire du rousseauisme* (Paris, 1988).

[22] L. A. L. F. de Saint-Just, 'Rapport fait au nom du comité de salut public sur la nécessité de déclarer le gouvernement révolutionnaire jusqu'à la paix' and 'Rapport au nom du Comité de salut public et du comité de sureté général, sur la justice, le commerce, la législation et les crimes des factions', in *Œuvres complètes* (Paris, 1984), pp. 520–30, 806–10.

[23] J.-J. Mounier, *Recherches sur les causes qui ont empeché les François de devenir libres, et sur les moyens qui leur restent pour acquérir la liberté* (Geneva, 1792); J. Mallet du Pan,

politics were described as those of an 'ancient', a seeker after classical republican notions of virtue; such an aspiration was considered by these writers to be a world away from the problems of modern societies and, therefore, politically deadly.[24] In his political economy, Rousseau was described simply as an arch-opponent of commerce. But when a distinction is made between Rousseau the political icon and Rousseau the political author the necessary link with revolutions and political radicalism disappears. This was what Pierre-Louis Rœderer recognized when he reminded his listeners, in a series of public lectures in the spring of 1793, that Rousseau 'would have believed it impossible to create a constitution at such a time as this. He believed that governments founded in times of upheaval will ultimately destroy the State.'[25] In short, to use Rousseau in the revolutionary context it was necessary to find a republican kernel within an anti-republican shell.

Rousseau's 'Économie politique' of 1755 attracted attention for the statement that only free states could defend and maintain themselves in modern conditions. None of the leading monarchies of Europe, and very few of the minor republics and monarchies, were considered by Rousseau to be free or capable of establishing liberty as he defined it. All violated the division between sovereignty (the making of law) and government (the execution of law) which, he explained, was the key to liberty in modern states.[26] Political economy had to find means of creating free states in which citizens were genuinely independent, living under laws that were just and enjoying liberties that defined the best life possible given the power of the passions over every human soul. Rousseau warned that such a state had to be small, agrarian, probably mountainous, and sparsely populated, with inhabitants whose manners were dominated by an artificially created civil religion, which placed patriotism and the practice of social duties above other activities. In addition to the distinction between sovereignty and government, only a state that respected the civil

---

*Considérations sur la nature de la Révolution en France, et sur les causes qui en prolongent la durée* (London, 1793). See also Mounier's *De l'influence attribuée aux philosophes, aux franc-maçons et aux illuminés sur la Révolution de France* (Tübingen, 1801).

[24] A sense of the opposition to Rousseau can be gleaned from the *supplément* published to the *Œuvres de Rousseau* (Paris, 1820) containing a series of critical responses to 'sa personne et ses ouvrages'. For an overview see R. Derathé, 'Les Réfutations du "Contrat Social" en France dans la première moitié du dix-neuvième siècle', in S. Harvey, M. Hobson, D. J. Kelley and S. S. B. Taylor, eds, *Reappraisals of Rousseau: Studies in Honour of R. A. Leigh* (Manchester, 1980), pp. 90–110.

[25] P.-L. Rœderer, *Cours d'organisation sociale* (1793), in *Œuvres de Rœderer*, ed. A.-M. Rœderer (Paris, 1853–6), 8 vols, vol. VIII, pp. 261–2.

[26] J.-J. Rousseau, 'Discours sur l'économie politique', in *Du Contrat Social*, ed. R. Derathé (Paris, 1964), p. 66. The *Encyclopédie* article 'Économie politique' of 1755 was reprinted as the *Discours* at Geneva in 1758.

liberty of its citizens could be truly said to be free. This meant that acts of government had to be as constrained as possible: in Rousseau's parlance, they should deal only with 'particular acts'. Acts of law had to be general, in that they were rules in the interest of every member of the community; as they were made by the political community as a whole this union of public good and law could be guaranteed. The incapacity of humanity for virtue, however, made it necessary for this restricted notion of government to be combined with legislators who sought to *former les hommes*: by public instruction, by religion, and by public and private example. Forms of government were of minimal relevance. Although Rousseau preferred an aristocracy of the wise, he was arguing that distinctions between monarchies and republics did little to help establish free states. What *did* do so was the calibre of the laws:

> I call Republic any State ruled by laws, whatever may be the form of administration: for then the public interest alone governs, and the public thing counts for something. Every legitimate Government is republican. By this word I understand not only an Aristocracy or Democracy, but in general any government guided by the general will, which is the law. To be legitimate, the Government must not be confused with the Sovereign, but be its minister: Then monarchy itself is a republic.[27]

Like so many of his contemporaries, Rousseau expressed the view that Britain would decline as a great power. He agreed with Hume's 'Of Liberty and Despotism' (1741) that Britons enjoyed no more liberty than the French.[28] Against Hume, he believed that neither were free states and were consequently unstable political entities. This was mainly because he believed that Britain, abetted by France, was undermining the balance of power between nation states through useless wars for trade; this at a time when the barbarians were once again at the edge of the continent. He predicted in the ninth chapter of the second book of the *Contrat Social* that '[t]he Russian Empire will try to subjugate Europe, and will itself be subjugated. The Tartars, its subjects or neighbours, will become its masters and ours: This revolution seems to me inevitable. All the Kings of Europe are working in concert to hasten it.'

Taking steps to avoid such an outcome meant adopting Rousseau's small-state solution. Rousseau was therefore not seeking to return Europe to a classical past of expansive republican empire. He made this clear in the seventh letter of the *Lettres écrites de la montagne*, explaining that 'the

---

[27] Rousseau, *Contrat Social*, bk III, ch. 6. Translations are from V. Gourevitch's edition (Cambridge, 1997).
[28] For commentary see J. G. A. Pocock, 'Hume and the American Revolution: The dying thoughts of a North Briton', in *Virtue, Commerce and History* (Cambridge, 1985), pp. 125–42.

ancients cannot be a model for the moderns [because] they are so foreign to us in every respect'. Rousseau *was* seeking to prove that small anti-commercial states were the most stable political structures. The most innovative aspect of his study would have been to show how such states could defend themselves and not be subjugated by commercial monarchies. Unfortunately, although he promised to show 'how the external power of a great People can be combined with the simple administration and good order of a small State', the second part of the *Contrat Social*, completing his *Institutions politiques*, was never written.[29] In failing to show how Poland, Corsica and Geneva could challenge larger states, Rousseau passed on such problems to the next generation.

Rousseau was a sceptic in politics and an arch-critic of the existing order. This was the verdict of Albrecht von Haller when he likened Rousseau's ideas to those of the ancient sceptic Carneades.[30] In terms of political economy, Rousseau warned that its practitioners had to be attentive to justice, the most important of all human values. Justice, he believed, was being destroyed by *amour propre*, the egoism that accompanied unfettered commerce. Humanity could do something about this because of their free will. In making this argument Rousseau surprised many of his Calvinist compatriots because he was rejecting Protestant accounts of Providence. To Rousseau the problem was that because of their enslavement to unnatural passions and inability to reason men had made a hell on earth. If only small and commercially simple states were capable of sustaining the artificial morality most akin to natural justice, it had to be accepted that redemption was unlikely, if not impossible. But an equally important message for subsequent writers was that such issues could not be distinguished from political economy proper.

## Physiocracy as a Christian critique of modernity

The extent of Rousseau's pessimism led contemporaries to try and work out whether a more positive politics could be developed from his books. One person who tried was Victor Riquetti, the Marquis de Mirabeau. Mirabeau had been converted to Quesnay's physiocracy in July 1757, while revising *L'Ami des hommes*, the book which shared Rousseau's aim of restoring justice by addressing the worst ills of commerce, and particularly the tendency of commercial states to fight wars. In his view, Rousseau's work could be read as that of an unorthodox Christian who associated

---

[29] Rousseau, *Contrat Social*, bk III, ch. 15.
[30] On Swiss Protestant readings of Rousseau see B. Kapossy, 'The Sociable Patriot: Isaak Iselin's Protestant Reading of Jean-Jacques Rousseau', *History of European Ideas* 27 (2001), pp. 153–70.

excessive commerce with moral laxity: a Christian critique of modernity, like physiocracy itself. Mirabeau wrote to Rousseau in 1767, sending him a copy of Mercier de la Rivière's *De l'Ordre naturel et essentiel des sociétés politiques*. Rousseau responded that, although he shared the aim of finding a form of government that might place laws above corrupt humankind, he could see 'no middle ground between the most austere democracy and the most perfect Hobbism, for the conflict between men and laws, which makes for a perpetual unresolved war in the State, is the worst of all political states'.[31]

Mirabeau replied in turn that Rousseau had misunderstood the physiocrats' intentions, which were simply to return humanity to 'the primary notions of nature and instinct'.[32] These were first outlined during the crisis of public credit caused by the Seven Years War, when *anglomanes* were demanding that the nobility follow the British example and embrace commerce.[33] The physiocrats came to prominence with the writing of the *Théorie de l'impôt* in 1760, which promised to reform the French monarchy, and restore French fortunes in the process, without major constitutional upheaval. The popularity of such ideas in court circles was aided by Quesnay's links as Royal Physician to Mme de Pompadour and her opponents, the nobles of the houses of Noailles and Villeroy.[34]

Physiocracy has, like many eighteenth-century ideas, largely been viewed from a nineteenth-century perspective. It has emerged as a proto-positivist philosophy, and more recently as proto-Marxist.[35] Commentators have usually described it as flawed because of the assertion of the primacy of agriculture, which could be refuted by reference to the self-evident effects of industry. Physiocracy was not in fact opposed to commerce per se; it was rather one of the most confident and complex responses to the progress of commerce and civilization (a term coined by Mirabeau in *L'Ami des hommes*). The physiocrats sought to develop kinds of commerce that were compatible with Christian virtue, by establishing a political and legal framework within which the harmful passions would be curbed and a natural morality reasserted. As such it amounted to theodicy, explaining how God created evil in order to ensure human redemption. The resulting moral philosophy entailed a particular theory

---

[31] Rousseau to Mirabeau, 27 July 1767, *Correspondance complète de Rousseau*, ed. R. A. Leigh (Oxford, 1965–98), 51 vols, vol. XXXIII, p. 240.

[32] Mirabeau to Rousseau, 30 July 1767, *Correspondance complète de Rousseau*, vol. XXXIII, p. 256.

[33] Abbé Coyer, *La noblesse commerçante* (London and Paris, 1757), p. 112; J. Grieder, *Anglomania in France, 1740–1789* (Geneva, 1985), chs 1, 4.

[34] Sonenscher, 'The Nation's Debt', pp. 89–95.

[35] R. L. Meek, *The Economics of Physiocracy* (London, 1962); R. L. Meek, *Social Science and the Ignoble Savage* (Cambridge, 1976).

of sovereignty and of government.[36] The final aspect of physiocracy was a set of policies intended to guide French legislators in restoring the natural order. By focusing exclusively on the latter transition programme historians have neglected its broader concerns.

Quesnay, following Malebranche, came to the conclusion that the Fall could be combated because God gave humans the physical ability to maintain themselves despite the corruption of their moral faculties. The origin of human societies lay not in any innate sociability, or in the formation of a contract between wary individuals, but in the meeting of physical needs by the natural establishment of certain conventions and practices (such as benevolent relationships between men and women, the protection of children, etc.). Physical feelings had a cognitive content because of the divinely created universal spirit that all creatures imbibed when breathing. This divine framework had been corrupted when more complex societies were created by violence stimulated by the lust for power and property. Such amoral social developments had led to the establishment of the 'unnatural and retrograde order' of modern commercial societies. But God had ensured that foundational physical sensations continued to direct humans to make positive moral choices. This 'Grace of Christ' made redemption possible by linking self-love and self-preservation to such sensations. A better world could be created by returning to such a natural order, requiring the use of the kinds of commercial capital that were themselves the product of corruption and egoism. Evil therefore served a purpose and could be reconciled with Providence. Removing antagonism between the classes of commercial society meant using the surplus generated by agriculture above the satisfaction of basic needs to support the institutions responsible for justice. The 'net product' of agriculture was to be the sole source of public revenues, and set at a level that ensured that the agricultural sector maintained itself. The resulting high productivity of agriculture, abetted by freeing trade, would ensure that manufactured goods were competitive.[37] An economy would gradually be created that was self-sufficient, with a commercial sector incapable of doing moral harm to the populace or financial damage to the political order. In the international arena such a transformed state would have no incentive to coerce or pillage the commerce of other states. It would play the role of peacemaker, secure on its

---

[36] This section follows Sonenscher, 'Physiocracy as a Theodicy' and I. Hont, 'The Political Economy of the "Unnatural and Retrograde" Order: Adam Smith and Natural Liberty', in M. Barzen, ed., *Französische Revolution und Politische Ökonomie* (Trier, 1989), pp. 122–49.

[37] F. Quesnay, 'Maximes de gouvernement économique', in *François Quesnay et la physiocratie* (Paris, 1958), 2 vols, vol. II, pp. 496–510.

remarkable economic foundation. With its natural resources, and social groups critical of commerce, France was held to be a prime candidate for physiocratic experiment.[38]

According to the physiocrats, economic justice could only be established if the political system rested on the distinction between the making of laws and their execution. The most efficient and wise method of making law was by a single individual, the sovereign monarch.[39] Armed with knowledge of the natural order, and with an interest in defending the interests of his subjects, such a monarch would in effect be a legal despot, ruling subject to the natural laws described by the physiocrats. The execution of law would be carried out by separate institutions; to this end the physiocrats called for the restoration of the provincial estates of France as administrative and executive bodies. Although aristocratic and democratic republics were legitimate, the best form of rule was that of a hereditary monarch, because it was impossible in practice for a single man to both make and execute the law. The problem with alternative forms of government was their tendency to be corrupted by the confusion of legislative and executive powers. If uncertainty existed about the roles of the different elements of the state, faction would result. Such a perspective was the basis for the physiocratic critique of the British constitution.[40]

The physiocrats believed the kinds of commerce characteristic of the Dutch and British states to be particularly unstable. Overly dependent on the sale of manufactured goods, they had to ensure that these goods were competitive. This necessitated the low price of labour and made the state seek markets for its products, which sometimes required military action. In order to ensure high profits, which provided revenues to support the political system, the supply of goods had to be restricted. Most physiocratic writings expressed horror at the tendency of British and Dutch merchants to abandon their cargoes in order to maintain buoyant profits. It was clear, they argued, that the assumed prosperity of the British poor was a myth because such states could only support meagre domestic markets, being dependent on low labour costs. As Mirabeau wrote, such states 'gather up the flowers of the economic tree and suppress its fruit'.[41] The constitutional analogue to a commercial system dependent on merchants was a division of sovereignty between the mercantile and

---

[38] V. Riqueti, Marquis de Mirabeau and F. Quesnay, *Traité de la monarchie (1757–59)*, ed. G. Longhitano (Paris, 1999).

[39] F. Quesnay, 'Droit naturel', in *François Quesnay et la physiocratie*, vol. II, p. 740.

[40] P.-S. Dupont de Nemours, *De l'origine et progrès d'une science nouvelle* (London, 1768), pp. 25–30.

[41] V. Riqueti, Marquis de Mirabeau, *Philosophie rurale, ou économie générale et politique de l'agriculture, reduite à l'ordre immuable des lois physiques & morales qui assurent la prospérité des empires* (Amsterdam, 1764), 3 vols, vol. III, p. 317.

landed interests. A mixed system of government, in which legislative and executive functions were necessarily enmeshed, amounted to a recipe for civil war. As Quesnay put it in his *Despotisme de la Chine* (1767), 'All the different ranks of the State can contribute in a mixed government to the ruin of the nation, through the discordance between private interests that divide and corrupt the tutelary authority, causing it to degenerate into political intrigues and abuses deadly to society.'[42]

Several conclusions can be drawn from this brief survey. The first is the extent to which modern divisions between subject areas cannot be applied to eighteenth-century ideas. The second is the anglophobe character of French political economy, which refused to believe that Britain would long defy the natural order without collapsing either through bankruptcy or civil war. The third is that attitudes to markets were not simply positive or negative. Both Rousseau and the physiocrats accepted that commerce was vital to meeting needs. In different ways they were trying to define forms of commerce compatible with social stability and their version of social morality. Their perceived enemy, itself largely mythical, was the Mandevillean amoral approach to markets associated with existing British and Dutch commerce. In forming their arguments, Rousseau and the physiocrats were foreshadowing the liberal and socialist critics who have been described as innovators in the early nineteenth century. Although Rousseau questioned whether it could be done in practice, both he and the physiocrats shared the belief that laws and institutions designed to combat tendencies to corruption in the political world had of necessity to be applied to the economic realm. Defences of *laissez faire*, such as the physiocrats' own, become more complicated when the Christian framework of this idea is taken into account: a framework with moral and political connotations.

## The innovative political economy of the 1790s

In 1789 the revolutionaries abolished the ancient constitution and replaced monarchical sovereignty with the sovereignty of the nation. The three estates of society were condemned in law. French society was henceforth to have distinct ranks based on different kinds of labour, with no rank superior to another. The revolutionaries promised a more cosmopolitan approach to commerce. One of the reasons that Smith's *Wealth of Nations*

---

[42] *François Quesnay et la physiocratie*, vol. II, p. 919. See also Nicolas Badeau, *Première introduction à la philosophie économique ou analyse des états policés* (Paris, 1767), pp. 385–406; P.-P.-F.-J.-H. Le Mercier de la Rivière, *L'Ordre naturel et essentiel des sociétés politiques* (London, 1767), pp. 139–50.

was reprinted in France at this time was his critique of Britain's mercantile system, which suited French aspirations.[43] Priests of the Catholic Church in France were forced to take an oath of allegiance to the new order, accepting the primacy of their loyalty to France and their role as servants of the civil state. In 1789 the King retained a constitutional function as chief magistrate. When this failed the revolutionaries abolished monarchy, declaring the first French Republic in September 1792. In undertaking these acts they made a sharp break with the politics of the Enlightenment authors they venerated. Rousseau, Voltaire, the physiocrats and Montesquieu would have questioned the assertion of national sovereignty. They had also believed the creation of a republic in a large state to be impossible. It was an accepted fact of political discussion that republicanism was incompatible with the existence of a diverse political culture, and particularly one that had until recently been characterized by social hierarchy and clerical control over education. The luxury-based forms of commerce that Montesquieu had said were the bedrock of the French economy in *De L'Esprit des lois* were also deemed to be corrosive of a republican state. Republicanism in France was therefore distinct from that of the North American Founding Fathers. North America was blessed by being a new state, predominantly agricultural, and with seemingly infinite amounts of land. It was altogether more challenging to create a republic at the centre of Europe in the face of the opposition of kings, priests and aristocrats. As Rœderer said, it was necessary 'to expose the futility of historical reasoning on this subject'.[44]

From 1792 the Revolution was continuous in its aim of maintaining Europe's first large commercial republic. This meant that the revolutionaries perceived themselves to be innovators in politics, defending a new kind of state. In such conditions they turned to philosophers ancient and modern: more editions of classic books on politics appeared, alongside the collected works of major authors, than in any other decade of the century.[45] The political economists who had been concerned with the regeneration of France under the Old Regime were forced to adapt themselves to these circumstances. The response of the remaining physiocrats is significant because it reveals how a group united before 1789 quickly became divided. Nicolas Badeau was an early opponent of the Revolution. By contrast, Dupont de Nemours attempted to make physiocracy compatible with revolutionary needs, advising legislators 'not to exhaust

---

[43] R. Whatmore, 'Adam Smith's Role in the French Revolution', *Past and Present* 175 (2002), pp. 65–89.

[44] P.-L. Rœderer, 'Entretien de plusieurs philosophes célèbres, sur les Gouvernments Républicains et Monarchiques' in *Œuvres*, vol. VII, pp. 61–71.

[45] For an overview see R. Darnton and D. Roche, eds, *Revolution in Print: The press in France, 1775–1800* (Berkeley, 1989), pt three.

themselves by seeking models in history, of which there is not one'.[46] Initially Dupont argued that the class of landed proprietors ought to be responsible for making law, and therefore form political assemblies as representatives of the nation.[47] Once the debate over the new constitution was complete, Dupont sought to make physiocracy a force for education and popular moral change. In the aftermath of his imprisonment during the Terror, he turned to the new religion of Theophilanthropy as the latest means to promote ideas he continued to describe as physiocratic.[48] Condorcet, like Dupont, argued in 1789 that the class of landed proprietors ought to be given a prominent role in any new constitution.[49] After the King's flight to Varennes, however, he underwent a conversion to the doctrine of large-state republicanism. With Thomas Paine and the Brissotins, he campaigned for a new republican constitution, education system and economy. While in hiding prior to his suicide, he wrote the *Esquisse d'un tableau historique de l'espèce humain*, which described revolutionary republicanism as the ninth stage of intellectual progress. Although superior to Enlightenment politics, it foreshadowed the transformation of human nature that would be the end-point of the Revolution.

The promotion of the new republicanism became the goal of French political economy. J.-A. Creuzé-Latouche stated in the Convention in 1794 that political economy was 'the unique means of restoring abundance and making it compatible with liberty'.[50] In the same speech he called for the inauguration of the first chair of political economy in France; it was established at the *École normale de Paris* later in the year and held by the mathematician Alexandre Vandermonde. Other revolutionaries rejected the term political economy because of its historic association with physiocracy, and preferred to use other terms, such as the 'social art' (although it had been coined by Badeau), the 'science of the social organization', or 'social science'. When the Directory set up the Moral and Political Sciences branch of the *Institut National*, all of these terms, in addition to political economy, were used to describe what was essentially the same project.[51] Political economy had a dual goal. The first was to work

---

[46] P.-S. Dupont de Nemours, *De la périodicité des assemblées nationales* (Paris, 1789), p. 4.

[47] P.-S. Dupont de Nemours, *Examen du gouvernement de l'Angleterre, comparé aux institutions des États-Unis* (London, 1789), p. 186.

[48] P.-S. Dupont de Nemours, *Philosophie de l'univers* (Paris, an IV [1796]), pp. 102–4.

[49] M. J. A. N. Caritat, Marquis de Condorcet, *Essai sur la constitution et les fonctions des assemblées provinciales* (Paris, 1788); *Œuvres de Condorcet*, ed. A. Condorcet O'Connor (Paris, 1847–9), 12 vols, vol. VIII, p. 126.

[50] J.-A. Creuzé-Latouche, *Discours sur la nécessité d'ajouter à l'école normale un professeur d'économie politique* (Paris, 1794), p. 10.

[51] Abbé Grégoire, 'Réflexions extraites d'un ouvrage sur les moyens de perfectionner les sciences politiques', in *Mémoires de l'Institut National, Classe des Sciences Morales et Politiques* (Paris, 1796–1803), 5 vols, vol. I, pp. 556–66. On the *Institut* see M. Staum, *Minerva's Message: Stabilizing the French Revolution* (Montreal and Kingston, 1996).

out means of creating a republican constitution that would be popular but stable. Numerous journals, speeches and books across the spectrum of republican opinion made clear the extent to which political economy had become inter-linked with this aspect of revolutionary politics. When Algernon Sidney's *Discourses on Government* was translated in 1793 it is significant that it was reviewed under the heading political economy.[52]

Given that France was at war with European monarchies financed by Britain, it was unsurprising that one of the intellectual continuities before and after the Revolution was the extent of national anglophobia.[53] The politics of republican political economy was irrepressibly opposed to the British constitutional model. The second objective came to the fore as the republican constitutions continued to meet civil opposition. Political faction and antagonism were blamed on the political culture of the Old Regime. It became accepted that if a stable republic could be created in France a new and homogeneous political culture would have to be established, and established in every rank of the nation. Political economy became concerned with this issue: as one of the public essay questions set by the *Institut national* in 1797 asked, *Quelles sont les institutions les plus propres à fonder la morale d'un peuple?* Throughout the 1790s, paper money projects, public instruction, terrorism, and ultimately religion itself were employed to tie the people to the Revolution. After the Consular constitution of 1799 failed, Bonaparte's inauguration of the First French Empire set the scene for a thorough review of the republican experiment. This is the context in which to understand Say's utterance about politics and political economy.

## 'Modern' versus 'democratic' republicanism

In separating the 'science of government' from political economy Say was turning his back on the experiments in building republican constitutions of the 1790s. In itself this was unsurprising. The constitutions of 1793, 1795 and 1799 had each been undermined by political divisions and had failed to maintain civil peace. Identifying Rousseau as a source of the problem was equally common among enemies of Jacobinism. In the 1790s Say would have been well aware of Rousseau's use by Robespierre and Saint-Just, and his writings condemned both Rousseau and the Terror. In 1787 Say had commenced an apprenticeship in the life assurance business by serving as the Genevan financier Etienne Clavière's secretary.

[52] *La Décade philosophique, politique, et littéraire* (Paris, 1794–1807), 42 vols, vol. III, pp. 537–44.
[53] For an overview see N. Hampson, *The Perfidy of Albion: French Perceptions of England During the Revolution* (Basingstoke, 1998).

It was Clavière who first allowed Say to read his copy of the *Wealth of Nations*.[54] Clavière had been involved in radical politics in Geneva, France, and in Ireland for decades: associating with him led Say to work on the journal *Courier de Provence* in the early 1790s. The journal was in theory the mouthpiece of the revolutionary orator Gabriel Honoré Riquetti de Mirabeau, the son of the great physiocrat Victor Riquetti. In practice it was written by Clavière and three other Genevans, Jacques-Antoine Du Roveray, Etienne Dumont, and Pierre-Saloman Reybaz. These men became known as the *Atelier de Mirabeau*.[55] It is worth noting that, as Genevan radicals, none of the *Atelier* was particularly sympathetic to Rousseau's politics: they believed that Rousseau had betrayed the small-state reformist cause in the late 1760s.[56]

That Say embraced the politics of the Mirabeau circle is evident from his earliest writing. It is also clear that he followed Clavière in becoming a large-state republican: he was probably still serving as Clavière's secretary when he became the last minister of finance under the monarchy and the first of the French Republic.[57] While Clavière, alongside Brissot, Condorcet, Paine and Roland, supported the Girondin faction in the Legislative Assembly, Say had volunteered to serve in the revolutionary army in 1793. He therefore missed the beginning of the Terror and the death of Clavière and many of the other Girondins. On his return he was involved in the establishment of a republican journal antagonistic to the Jacobins, *La Décade philosophique, politique et littéraire*. Opposition to Rousseau could therefore have come from Genevan sources or from his support for the Gironde. As the political correspondent for his journal in the late 1790s, Say continued his close relationship with Parisian political life. His opposition to the physiocrats is equally traceable to this fact. Say knew both Condorcet and Dupont de Nemours through Clavière and would have seen at first hand their involvement in republican constitutionalism. Dupont de Nemours also submitted articles for inclusion in *La Décade*. It was natural for Say to associate the physiocrats with the Mirabeau circle and with the republicanism that had so manifestly failed when Napoleon came to power.

Many historians aware of Say's revolutionary republicanism have assumed that with the publication of the *Traité* he made a seamless transition

---

[54] J.-B. Say, draft *Mémoires* (1818), Say papers, Bibliothèque Nationale, microfilm 6739, pp. 151–212.

[55] J. Bénétruy, *L'Atelier de Mirabeau: quatre proscrits Genevois dans la tourmente révolutionnaire* (Geneva, 1962).

[56] For Rousseau's opposition to revolution see his letters to the Genevan constitutional reformers (1767–8) in *Correspondance complète*, vol. XXXV, pp. 92–3, 101.

[57] J.-B. Say, *De la liberté de la presse* (Paris, 1789); J.-B. Say, *La Science du bonhomme Richard de Benjamin Franklin* (Paris, 1794).

to liberalism. This is not the case. He continued to describe himself as a republican, as his friends later testified.[58] He also saw himself as a revolutionary, by which he meant someone who valued the liberties gained in 1789 and sought means of maintaining them. For Say, liberty could only exist once aristocracy had been extinguished. Continued vigilance was necessary to ensure that no new nobility arose, as he believed had occurred under Bonaparte. Say also associated liberty with opposition to organized religion, especially on a national basis. Although he believed Calvinism to be less dangerous than Catholicism, he was certain that religion had done little good in society. He believed the origins of the Terror to lie in Roman-Gallican fanaticism. During the Revolution Say's was accordingly among the most virulently anti-clerical and anti-Christian voices among the writers for *La Décade*, an attitude exemplified by his view of, and love for, Gibbon's work.[59] At some point after 1815 he planned to write a book that would show the damage done to humanity by religious belief. One of his notes states that 'religions will be replaced by industry as a centrifugal force in society'.[60] Like many anti-clericals, however, he considered himself to be an austere moralist. Making a society that was virtuous was the project that had failed during the Revolution: Say continued to believe that it ought to be resurrected.[61] By virtue Say meant a society characterized by frugality and industry, respect for the liberties of others, and the adherence to a moral code that eschewed luxury and was dedicated to the public good. The problem was how to moralize society given the failure of constitutionalism, civic instruction, and Clavière's own paper money project.

Say believed that the work of making society virtuous would take generations. Once some form of representative government was established, aristocracy outlawed, and clerical influence over education minimized, he argued that commerce would operate in a different manner from the way that it operated in other forms of society. Government involvement

---

[58] Charles Dunoyer, review of the *Traité* (3rd edn.), in *Le Censeur Européen, ou Examen de diverses questions de droit public, et diverses ouvrages littéraires et scientifiques, considérés dans leurs rapports avec les progrès de la civilisation* (1817), vol. I, pp. 159–227, vol. II, pp. 169–221; Charles Comte, 'Notice historique sur la vie et les ouvrages de J.-B. Say', in *Cours complet* (Paris, 1837), pp. v–xiii; Theodor Fix, 'De l'économie politique: quels en sont le but, les principes et les lois', in *Revue Mensuelle d'Économie Politique* (Paris, 1833–7), 4 vols, vol. I, pp. 4–8; John Stuart Mill, *Autobiography* (Boston, 1969), pp. 38–9; Augustin Pyrhamus de Candolle, *Mémoires et souvenirs* (Paris, 1862), pp. 123–4.

[59] Say called the Bible 'one of the most scandalous books ever written': 'Obituary of Gibbon', *La Décade*, 54 (30 Vendémaire, an IV), pp. 147–52. For commentary see R. Whatmore, *Republicanism and the French Revolution: An Intellectual History of Jean-Baptiste Say's Political Economy* (Oxford, 2000), pp. 120–5.

[60] Say papers, Bibliothèque Nationale, microfilm 9096, p. 174; 6739, pp. 214–16.

[61] Say, *Traité* (1803), vol. I, pp. 81–2n, 262–4.

in the economy had to be limited because of the temptation to corruption that no political officer could resist in the existing moral climate. But this did not mean that markets could be relied upon to be a force for morality by their independent action alone. Say had no faith in the 'hidden hand'.[62] In a simple society, such as the one which Say identified in certain North American states, the very lack of government, noblemen and priests, combined with an abundance of natural resources, allowed commerce to co-exist with virtuous morals.[63] But in France it was necessary to use more direct means to influence the market. People from all of the productive groups of society had to be taught that self-interest corresponded with a life lived according to the precepts of virtue. When they embraced this creed they would recognize its benefits, and lead others to behave similarly. A moral revolution would gradually be achieved by such means.[64] After such change a return could be made to republican constitutionalism. Say admitted this in his final writings, arguing that once political economy had civilized nations 'pure politics and constitutional organization' would again come to the fore.[65] In the hope of preparing future generations for this eventuality, Say wrote a *Traité de politique pratique* to accompany his books on political economy. It was never completed, but the surviving manuscripts show that he continued to try to resolve the eighteenth-century conundrum of how to create a large state that was commercial yet just towards the poor.[66] Say therefore remained a republican committed to democratizing the political realm. But the prior need was to 'democratize' the economic arena, by reducing inequality, extinguishing luxury, and promoting social virtues that would prevent new aristocracies from developing.

The role of political economy was to provide the education that would direct individuals in the economic realm. Without such a moral education markets would be corrupted. If inequalities continued to grow morality would gradually be extinguished. This was why it was so important to remind the French to avoid the British example. Say remained a dedicated anglophobe during the Restoration. He attacked the inequalities evident in Britain, which he traced to the existence of aristocracy and a national church. He also developed friendships with those whose view of politics

---

[62] Ibid., vol. I, p. 96, vol. II, p. 345.

[63] J.-B. Say, 'Cours à l'Athénée' (1819), in *Cours d'économie*, ed. P. Steiner (Paris, 1997), pp. 83–6.

[64] J.-B. Say, 'Discours d'ouverture du cours d'économie industrielle', in *Œuvres diverses*, pp. 145–7.

[65] J.-B. Say, 'Discours d'ouverture d'Économie politique, de l'année scolaire 1831–2', in *Œuvres diverses*, pp. 162–5; J.-B. Say, 'Discours d'ouverture au Collège de France' (1831), Bibliothèque Nationale, microfilm 6648, pp. 12–13.

[66] Say Papers, Bibliothèque Nationale, microfilm 9095, pp. 33–4, 270–329.

and morals he believed he shared, and described those of Jeremy Bentham as being superior to any other writer of the post-revolutionary era.[67] In describing a more egalitarian commercial society in which labour was fairly rewarded, thereby reducing the extremes of riches and dearth, Say relied on Book III of the *Wealth of Nations*, in which Smith sketched the natural progress of opulence and the reasons for its corruption in British economic history. It is significant that Say's view of politics, and particularly his view of Britain's constitution, had little in common with Smith's own view.[68] Smith was attractive because he fitted the French republican perspective on immoral commerce. Say's central claim, that it was pointless experimenting with a republican constitution if social *mores* were already corrupted, was an idea made commonplace by the influence of Rousseau's writings. For each writer, the nature of political culture, and its link with popular *mœurs*, was always a pressing concern of political economy.

Say's opposition to Constant can now be clarified. It stemmed from their differing assessments of the nature and prospects of the British state. The revolutionary years had taken Britain to the very edge of military catastrophe, national bankruptcy and civil rebellion. Yet the state had not only survived, but, by 1814, it had further entrenched itself as the leading European power. One consequence was that *anglomanie*, rather than being an obsession with the *mores* of Britain's commercially minded nobility, began to take the form of a more general interest in Britain's political history and peculiar constitutional structure.[69] The possibility of creating a constitution in France directly modelled on that of Britain ceased to be an impractical fusing of antagonistic political cultures, or a dangerous experiment that would probably have resulted in the collapse of either state. Constant was in the vanguard of this movement, considering Britain to be a model modern republic. Say hated the prominent aristocracy that fostered luxury-based commerce. The economic liberty associated with Britain's commerce was a sham, Say claimed, because the aristocracy manipulated markets for their own personal gain. Partial liberty in the context of the mercantile control of trade was no freedom at all. Britain was, to Say, a modern republic in the same sense as Bonaparte's Empire: leaders ruled in the name of the people, but in

---

[67] See Say's review of Bentham's 'Plan of Parliamentary Reform', *Le Censeur Européen* 5 (1817), pp. 105–27.

[68] See D. Winch, 'A Great Deal of Ruin in a Nation', in P. Clarke and C. Trebilcock, eds, *Understanding Decline: Perceptions and Realities of British Economic Performance* (Cambridge, 1997).

[69] For an example see Guizot's revealingly entitled *The History of England . . . for a rising generation*, tr. M. Thomas (London, 1882), 3 vols, vol. III, p. 410.

practice *against* the interests of the people. The people lacked political agency in Britain and in France. Say believed that the Catholic Church especially, but in fact all established churches, were modern republics because they behaved in exactly the same way. They governed the people rather than teaching them self-rule. By contrast, for Constant religion was another tool for legislators to use against the popular tendency to violence and disorder.[70] In his ideas about political economy, Constant was well aware that markets were shaped by political and religious frameworks. But he rejected Say's view that markets could themselves be used to moralize society, once a republican social structure had been formed. At root, they espoused opposed moral philosophies. Say remained the disciple of Helvétius and Bentham in believing that self-interest could be enlightened. To Constant such ideas were false and dangerous because they ultimately fostered the kinds of egoism that their exponents labelled benevolence. Disinterested support for liberty had of necessity to rely on religious belief and practice.[71]

Such disagreement between liberals complicates the historical record for those who continue to espouse a 'black and white' approach to the intellectual history of markets. Scrutiny of Say's and Constant's ideas restores Rousseau to prominence as a political economist, and the French Revolution as an independent intellectual event. Furthermore, debates about the nature of republicanism in large commercial states become a significant force in early nineteenth-century life. Constant won the battle of ideas in justifying a modern republic and a political economy whose legitimacy we would now accept. But Say's belief that modern republics actually deprive the people of political and economic agency is a recurring theme in contemporary political culture.

---

[70] B. Constant, *De la Religion considérée dans sa source, ses formes et ses développements*, ed. T. Todorov and E. Hofmann (Tübingen, 1999), bk 1, ch. 4, pp. 61–2.

[71] B. Constant, *Du Polythéisme romain*, ed. M. J. Matter (Paris, 1833), 2 vols, bk 12, ch. 2.

# 4    Tories and markets: Britain 1800–1850

*David Eastwood*

One of the peculiarities of the British political tradition was the Conservatives' emergence as the party of the market and, more ambivalently, the party of free trade. Like much in the British political tradition, the origins both of Conservatism and the Conservative Party are deep, ambiguous and contested. The modalities of the constitutional crises of the 1680s and 1690s gave birth to a fiercely bi-polar politics, whose convulsions were only stilled by the political improvisations of Sir Robert Walpole who, after 1720, imposed a powerful and persistent Whig ascendancy. What emerged was a political culture quite different from that anywhere else in Europe. This was a political culture in which a still predominantly landed polity embraced mercantile and commercial dynamism, and thereby created the political and cultural preconditions for prodigious economic growth.[1] The confidence, and the first British Empire, on which this prosperity was predicated might have been decisively punctured by the trauma of defeat in the American War of Independence. In the event, though, Britain's trading and manufacturing ascendancy proved reliant, and between 1783 and 1789 its young Prime Minister, William Pitt, embarked on a bold reconstructing of Britain's fiscal system designed to enhance its economic position. The American War, the French Revolution

The argument of this chapter owes much to discussions with colleagues over the years. I have particularly benefited from discussions with Harry Dickinson, Peter Ghosh, Joanna Innes, Paul Langford, Peter Mandler, Patrick O'Brien and Noel Thompson. My greatest debt on this occasion is to Anna Gambles, whose Oxford D.Phil. I supervised and whose work on Tory political economy was profoundly important. Her illness has robbed nineteenth-century British history of one of its most original and intellectually powerful voices. She should have contributed this chapter, and it would have been so much better, in so many ways, if she had been able to.

[1] The literature on British politics and political culture in 'the long eighteenth century' is now extensive. Among the more important and suggestive recent works are J. Hoppit, *A Land of Liberty? England, 1689–1727* (Oxford, 2000); P. Langford, *A Polite and Commercial People: England, 1727–1783* (Oxford, 1989); J. Brewer, *The Sinews of Power: War, Money, and the English State, 1688–1783* (London, 1989); H. T. Dickinson, *Liberty and Property: Political Ideology in Eighteenth-Century Britain* (London, 1977); J. A. W. Gunn, *Beyond Liberty and Property: The Process of Self-Recognition in Eighteenth-Century Political Thought* (Kingston and Montreal, 1983).

and Pittite politics conspired to transform the British political system, and from this crucible new party alignments and new party ideologies were forged. This too was a complex and ambiguous process. Pitt always called himself a Whig, but in the early nineteenth century would come to be venerated as a conservative. Most of Pitt's followers would become the vanguard of the Conservative Party that kept Lord Liverpool in office from 1812 to 1827.[2] By the 1830s, aided by the 1832 Reform Act, a recognizably 'modern' party political system had taken shape, with a Conservative party privileging the constitution and more restrictive modes of political participation, and rooted in landed and old wealth; whilst Whiggism transformed itself into the Liberal Party, promoting a more broadly based polity, a new partnership with new manufacturing wealth, and a more religiously pluralistic politics.[3]

In this story political economy played a curious part. In the early years of the nineteenth century political ideologies seemed to be reinforced by antagonistic political economies. In 1815 a Corn Law was passed avowedly to protect the interests of land and farming. Economic policy thus seemed to be the handmaiden of political or constitutional priorities. Protection might be the instrument of constitutional defence of the old landed order against the new: protection would arrest the development of the British 'party of movement'. Actually, in the first half of the nineteenth century, an odd thing happened: the Conservative Party became a party of free trade, and protectionism and the protectionists became marginalized within it, banished to the backbenches, believing an old faith but unable to articulate it in terms which resonated with the increasingly technical discourses of political economy.[4] Thus an emergent political tradition which in the later eighteenth century tended instinctively

[2] For William Pitt, Lord Liverpool, and the early origins of the Conservative Party see M. Duffy, *The Younger Pitt* (Harlow, 2000); J. Ehrman's 3-volume life of Pitt, *The Years of Acclaim* (London, 1969), *The Reluctant Transition* (London, 1983), and *The Consuming Struggle* (London, 1996); J. E. D. Binney, *British Public Finance and Administration, 1774–1792* (Oxford, 1958); R. Stewart, *The Foundations of the Conservative Party, 1830–1867* (London, 1978), esp. pp. 2–107; and N. Gash, *Lord Liverpool* (London, 1984).

[3] Among the more suggestive works here are Jonathan Parry, *The Rise and Fall of Liberal Government in Victorian Britain* (New Haven and London, 1993); P. Mandler, *Aristocratic Government in the Age of Reform: Whigs and Liberals, 1830–1852* (Oxford, 1990); S. Collini, D. Winch and J. Burrow, *The Noble Science of Politics: A Study in Nineteenth-Century Intellectual History* (Cambridge, 1983); R. Brent, *Liberal Anglican Politics: Whiggery, Religion, and Reform, 1830–1841* (Oxford, 1987); I. Newbould, *Whiggery and Reform, 1830–41* (Houndmills, Basingstoke, 1990).

[4] The realities behind what became known to historians as 'liberal Toryism' are authoritatively explored in B. Hilton's brilliant study, *Corn, Cash, Commerce: The Economics of the Tory Governments, 1815–1830* (Oxford, 1977). See also W. R. Brock, *Lord Liverpool and Liberal Toryism, 1820 to 1827* (London, 1941); and cf. M. Bentley, 'Liberal Toryism in the Twentieth Century', *Transactions of the Royal Historical Society* 6/4 (1995), pp. 177–201.

to embrace protection within the domestic market and imperial preference beyond had, by the 1850s, abandoned protection and, within limits,
was moving towards embracing the internationalism of free trade. The
party which had hallowed the 1815 Corn Law and resisted legal privileging of enterprise and speculation was, by the 1850s, reconciled to the
ending of sectoral protection within the economy and to the essential
protection of capitalistic enterprise afforded by limited liability legislation.[5] Voices which had proclaimed that protection was the only economic strategy consonant with constitutional priorities were stilled, and
Tories who had deprecated the market for its debasing of social relations
and its ruthless displacement of Christian moral principles by capitalistic moral imperatives now passed out with the oldest of the old guards.
The political significance of this transformation of Conservatism was oc-
cluded in the later nineteenth century by Liberalism's doctrinal commitment to the market and to the small state. In the twentieth century,
though, when Liberalism became distributionist, and Labour variously
corporatist, welfarist, and isolationist, Conservatism could trumpet its
market credentials largely unchallenged until the 1990s. The nearly orthodox narrative of the Conservative Party in the nineteenth century is
a narrative of the party's transition from the party of land to the party
of capital.[6]

But Toryism has never been wholly comfortable with the market and its
meanings. Indeed the most convulsive crises in British Conservatism –
over the Corn Laws in the 1840s, over Tariff Reform after 1903, and
over the European single market and single currency after 1985 – have all
been rooted in Conservatism's ambivalence about the political meanings
of free trade and market economics.[7] In each case, being the party of the
nation and the party of free trade and free markets proved painfully dis-
sonant. For politicians, as for consumers, markets compel choices, and
these choices did not always sit easily within the Conservative tradition.
The Conservative Party's reputation as the party of the market is rooted

[5] Sir S. Northcote, *Twenty Years of Financial Policy* (London, 1862); B. Hilton, *The Age
of Atonement: The Influence of Evangelicalism on Social and Economic Thought, 1785–1865*
(Oxford, 1988), esp. pp. 203–97; P. R. Ghosh, 'Disraelian Conservatism: A Financial
Approach', *English Historical Review* 99 (1984), pp. 268–96; H. C. G. Matthew, 'Gladstone, Disraeli, and the Politics of Mid-Victorian Budgets', *Historical Journal* 22 (1979),
pp. 615–43.

[6] B. Coleman, *Conservatism and the Conservative Party in Nineteenth-Century Britain*
(London, 1988), pp. 200–8.

[7] R. Stewart, *The Politics of Protection: Lord Derby and the Protectionist Party, 1841–1852*
(Cambridge, 1971); B. Disraeli, *Lord George Bentinck: A Political Biography* (London,
1852); E. H. H. Green, *The Crisis of Conservatism: The Politics, Economics, and Ideology of
the Conservative Party, 1880–1914* (London, 1994); J. Ramsden, *An Appetite for Power: A
History of the Conservative Party Since 1830* (London, 1998).

not in the party's Tory inheritance, but rather in its very particular, some would say peculiar, relationship to Liberalism in the nineteenth century and neo-Liberalism in the later twentieth century. These later transformations are beyond the immediate scope of this chapter. Nevertheless, what happened in the early nineteenth century did much to determine what became Conservative political economy. Tories may have moved hesitantly and even reluctantly to embrace the market, but as with many such relationships the public passion of the eventual consummation was all the more euphoric.

In the Manichean world beloved of many historians the advent of political economy inaugurated a short struggle between the new science of economics and a doomed nostalgia for a traditionally ordered world. While classical economics forged an increasingly technical language to describe and order the world of material production and exchange, siren voices, deaf to these new harmonies, still sang old songs of providential dispensations and a beauteous old order. The fact that many of the critics of political economy were poets has perpetuated this simple picture of a dialectical struggle between modernists and traditionalists. 'Tory romantics, including literary men like Southey, Wordsworth and Coleridge, were *instinctively* opposed to anything that seemed to them to a destruction of traditional society by the godless and ugly worship of industrial mammon.'[8] The difficulty with this kind of characterization, with its juxtaposition of intellectual sophistication and Christian-humanitarian sentimentality, is less its inaccuracy than its insufficiency.[9] Many Tories and most Tory romantics did repudiate classical political economy. Two leading poets, and radicals turned Tory thinkers, can stand proxy here for a wider tradition. Robert Southey, poet laureate and a leading economic writer for the widely circulating Tory *Quarterly Review*, did tend to juxtapose 'Moral versus political economy'.[10] For Southey, political economy was a profoundly demoralized social discourse. Samuel Taylor Coleridge inveighed against the pernicious sensibility wrought by 'the commercial

---

[8] N. Gash, *Aristocracy and People: Britain, 1815–1865* (London, 1979), p. 194; my ital.

[9] Much the most suggestive recent accounts are D. Winch, *Riches and Poverty: An Intellectual History of Political Economy in Britain, 1750–1834* (Cambridge, 1996); and Hilton, *Age of Atonement*. See also A. M. C. Waterman, *Revolution, Economics and Religion: Christian Political Economy, 1798–1833* (Cambridge, 1991); and I. Hont and M. Ignatieff, eds, *Wealth and Virtue: The Shaping of Political Economy in the Scottish Enlightenment* (Cambridge, 1983).

[10] J. W. Water, ed., *Southey's Common-Place Book*, 4th ser. (London, 1850), p. 702; R. Southey, 'On the Corn Laws', *Quarterly Review* 51 (1834), p. 276; R. Southey, *Sir Thomas More: Or, Colloquies on the Progress and Future Prospects of Society* (London, 1829), 2 vols, vol. II, pp. 172–3. For Robert Southey's economic thought see D. Eastwood, 'Robert Southey and the Intellectual Origins of Romantic Conservatism', *English Historical Review* 104 (1989), pp. 308–31; and Winch, *Riches And Poverty*, pp. 288–405.

spirit'.[11] Until well beyond the 1832 Reform Act the imagery of High Toryism remained infused with notions of a 'great chain of being' and a highly particularized form of Christian providentialism. Key texts of High Tory economic thinking, from Coleridge's *Lay Sermons* (1817), Southey's *Colloquies on the Progress and Future Prospects of Society* (1829), Michael Sadler's *The Law of Population* (1830), to myriad pamphlets indicting the factory system in the 1830s, all inclined towards a counterpoint between the natural order and the baleful artificiality of commercial marketized society.

There is no doubt that High Tories could privilege political and poetic discourses over economic theory. Certainly modes of thinking emerged in which the primacy of politics was absolute, and the lyrical or the indignant became the characteristic languages of social description.[12] But none of this was *instinctive*; rather, it created the framework for an alternative political economy. Tories did not repudiate economics as science, but rejected the priorities and methods enshrined in political economy in its Smithian, Malthusian, Ricardian and Millite forms. Against both Ricardian orthodoxy and Malthusian demographic determinism, High Tories elaborated alternative political economies that did not repudiate the idea of a technical language of economic analysis but re-engineered this to serve quite different priorities. At times this appeared as a de-centring of the market. In fact High Tories characterized markets quite differently and, crucially, denied the market an autonomous or hegemonic role. Theirs was an economics in which the state, constitutional ideals, certain moral imperatives, and even concerns about social allocation were to the fore. By the 1840s High Tory critics of marketized economics had lost, the protectionist vision had faded, and the Conservative Party moved decisively towards becoming the party of free trade and a largely self-regulating market.

It was not for nothing that High Tory economic thinking embraced poets and the poetic. A fundamental point of difference concerned what

---

[11] For Coleridge's position see especially his second 'Lay Sermon' of 1817, S. T. Coleridge, *Lay Sermons*, ed. R. J. White (Princeton, 1972); W. F. Kennedy, *Humanist versus Economist: The Economic Thought of Samuel Taylor Coleridge* (Berkeley, 1958). R. Holmes, *Coleridge: Darker Reflections* (London, 1998), pp. 447–51 is good on the context for the second Lay Sermon.

[12] This was the case made by Thomas Babington Macaulay against Southey in particular and romantic socio-economic thinking in general, see 'Southey's Colloquies on Society', published in the *Edinburgh Review* in 1830 but most accessible in Lord Macaulay, *Critical and Historical Essays* (London, 1878), 3 vols, vol. I, pp. 217–69. See also B. Fontana, *Rethinking the Politics of Commercial Society: The 'Edinburgh Review', 1802–1832* (Cambridge, 1985); J. Clive, *Thomas Babington Macaulay: The Shaping of a Historian* (London, 1973), pp. 96–141; W. Thomas, *The Philosophic Radicals: Nine Studies in Theory and Practice, 1817–1841* (Oxford, 1979), pp. 147–205; W. A. Speck, 'Robert Southey, Lord Macaulay and the Standard of Living Controversy', *History* 86 (2001), pp. 467–77.

might be termed the imaginary language of economics. For High Tory critics, the market was a metaphor for patterns of economic activity and economic exchange. No one who had read the *Wealth of Nations* – and most High Tory economic writers had immersed themselves in Smith's great text – could doubt that Smith too saw the market as a metaphor. Why else offer us images of butchers and the social benevolence of self-interested exchanges?[13] In terms of the nature of its language, as in so much else, British political economy was transformed by Ricardo, whose *Principles* took economics to different domains of technical language and philosophic sensibility from those inhabited by Smith.[14] The crucial difference between orthodox classical political economy and its Tory critics was that, whereas classical political economy offered a picture of market relations as efficient mechanisms for distribution and allocation and advocated a policy of deregulating market controls, their High Tory opponents offered pictures of market failures and advocated protectionist interventions to subordinate market operations to moral and political priorities.[15]

In describing the effects of market capitalism, High Tory writers first highlighted its tendency to exaggerate inequalities in the distribution of wealth and inefficiencies in the allocation of capital. Later they came to associate these market inefficiencies with the miseries of the trade cycle. Thus in 1807 Robert Southey, commenting on Manchester and the manufacturing system, anticipated what was to become the stock-in-trade of Tory critiques.

In no other country can such riches be acquired by commerce, but it is the one which grows rich by the labour of the hundred . . . Wealth flows into the country, but how does it circulate there? Not equally and healthfully through the whole system; it sprouts into wens and tumours, and collects in aneurisms which starve and palsy the extremities.[16]

Two decades later, in the *Colloquies on the Progress and Prospects of Society*, Southey returned to the theme and to the same metaphorical language.

You have prided yourselves upon this system; you have used every means for extending it; you have made it the measure of your national prosperity. It is a wen, a fungous excrescence from the body politic . . . now it has acquired so

---

[13] A. Smith, *An Inquiry into the Nature and Causes of the Wealth of Nations*, ed. Edwin Cannan (London, 1904), 2 vols, bk I, ch. 2, pp. 15–18.

[14] D. Ricardo, *Principles of Political Economy* (London, 1817). Ricardo's models, and more austere and economically introspective language, made poetic and constitutional engagement with Ricardian economics altogether different and more distant.

[15] D. Eastwood, 'Ruinous Prosperity: Robert Southey's Critique of the Commercial System', *The Wordsworth Circle* 25 (1994), pp. 72–6.

[16] [R. Southey], *Letters From England* (1807), pp. 209–10.

great a bulk, its nerves have branched so widely, and the vessels of the tumour are so inosculated [sic] into some of the principal veins and arteries of the natural system, that to remove it by absorption is impossible, and excision would be fatal.[17]

These kinds of organicist metaphors, of the economy as a palsied body rather than a benign market, were characteristic. Of course classical economic theory did not deny market inefficiencies but offered a model that suggested they would not persist. By contrast Tory critics offered a picture of Britain's current economic state as cancerous, unstable and socially unsustainable. Nor was such alternative imagery confined to High Tory circles. Radical critics of orthodox political economy elaborated a not dissimilar critique of market excess, economic instability and commercial unsustainability.[18] Thomas Carlyle's indictment of the market, free trade and *laissez faire* in 'Signs of the Times' (1929) and *Chartism* (1839) recognizably and avowedly owed a good deal to what he called the 'Toryisms' of Southey, Coleridge and the High Tories of *Blackwood's Edinburgh Magazine*.[19] The radical political economy of Thomas Hodgskin, developed most fully in his *Popular Political Economy* (1827), had a different lineage, in the natural theology of William Paley and even a radicalized reading of Lockean notions of property. Nevertheless Hodgskin too characterized the market's failings in ways which recalled High Tory critics, although his radically anti-statist solutions were far removed from their attempts to develop a refined protectionism.[20]

The kinds of organicist metaphors that High Tory economic writers used to describe economic relations and activities embodied a political preference for an organicist social vision. What most alienated High Tory critics from orthodox political economy was its celebration of individualism. Whether in the form of Smith's self-interested butcher or, far more perniciously from their point of view, Malthus's demographically driven model of individuals competing for diminishing resources, High Tories held the moral consequences of market economics to be profoundly

[17] Southey, *Colloquies*, vol. I, p. 171.
[18] N. Thompson, *The People's Science: The Popular Political Economy of Exploitation and Crisis, 1816–1834* (Cambridge, 1984); N. Thompson, *The Market and Its Critics: Social Political Economy in Nineteenth-Century Britain* (London, 1988); W. Stafford, *Socialism, Radicalism and Nostalgia: Social Criticism in Britain, 1770–1830* (Cambridge, 1987); G. Claeys, *Money, Machinery and the Millennium: From Moral Economy to Economic Socialism, 1815–1860* (London, 1987).
[19] [T. Carlyle], 'Signs of the Times', *Edinburgh Review* 49 (1829); T. Carlyle, *Chartism* (London, 1839); T. Carlyle, *Past and Present* (London, 1842); T. Carlyle, *Reminiscences*, ed. J. A. Froude (London, 1881), 2 vols, vol. II, pp. 309–29.
[20] T. Hodgskin, *Labour Defended against the Claims of Capital . . .* (London, 1825); T. Hodgskin, *Popular Political Economy* (London, 1827); T. Hodgskin, *The Natural and Artificial Rights of Property Contrasted* (London, 1832); D. Stack, *Nature and Artifice: The Life and Thought of Thomas Hodgskin, 1787–1869* (Woodbridge, 1998).

pernicious. Malthus's crude excursion into self-consciously metaphorical language, with his image of 'Nature's Feast' in the 1803 version of the *Essay on the Principle of Population*, at once appalled and gratified his Tory opponents.[21] Both Southey and Coleridge thought the metaphor 'garbage', and Southey's stinging review in the 1803 *Annual Review* fused his own moral indignation with Coleridge's poetic repudiation and John Rickman's statistical contempt.[22] By 1806 Malthus had withdrawn the section on 'Nature's Feast', but the combination of his demographic mechanics and Ricardo's highly abstracted economic language continued to be seen by High Tories as the essential features of the new political economy. Southey framed the argument, which others deployed and developed. Smith's *Wealth of Nations* 'considers man as a manufacturing animal . . . it estimates his importance, not by the sum of goodness or knowledge which he possesses . . . but by the gain which can be extracted from him'. Malthus's system absolves the rich of social obligations: transferring wealth to alleviate the poverty is presented as economically counterproductive and therefore morally objectionable. Thus Malthus's *Principle of Population* had become 'the bible of the rich, the selfish, and the sensual'.[23] This repudiation of the mechanization of social relations was developed further in the *Colloquies on the Progress and Prospects of Society* in 1829, and again the similarities between Southey's social vision and Carlyle's 'Signs of the Times' published in the same year were striking. Both rejected the market as the main or characteristic mechanism for social interaction, both repudiated a science of economics that conceived of and measured man as an instrument of production. Both, in short, wanted to marginalize or mitigate market modes of thinking.

Precisely the same tendencies are apparent in Michael Sadler's massive anti-Malthusian *Law of Population*. 'It is', Sadler suggested, 'the purpose of the new school to treat and regard men as animated machines.' In its Malthusian form, political economy had converted a natural system of

---

[21] On this and what followed see P. James, *Population Malthus: His Life and Times* (London, 1979), pp. 79–159; K. Curry, 'A Note of Coleridge's Copy of Malthus', *Publications of the Modern Languages Association of North America* 54 (1939), pp. 613–15; T. R. Malthus, *Principles of Population* (1803 edn), ed. and intro. T. H. Hollingsworth (London, 1973), pp. 531–2; E. A. Wrigley, 'Malthus and the Prospects for the Laboring Poor', *Historical Journal* 31 (1988), pp. 813–29.

[22] John Rickman is a notable and interesting figure in Tory economic thinking. He was the government statistician who was responsible for the first four censuses (1801–41), statistics on poverty, crime and public expenditure that informed government and public policy. Rickman provided the statistical data and statistical arguments that informed Southey's economic articles in the *Quarterly Review* from 1811 to the early 1820s. The idea that Tory alternatives to political economy were bereft of statistical underpinnings needs therefore to be radically qualified. Rickman lacks a modern study, but see O. Williams, *Life and Letters of John Rickman* (London, 1912).

[23] R. Southey, *Essays, Moral and Political* (London, 1832), 2 vols, vol. I, pp. 92, 111–12; *Annual Review* 2 (1803), pp. 292–301.

cooperation and plenty into a theoretically driven nightmare of competition and diminishing returns.

> They [political economists] have written . . . about the market for labour, as it is called, and yet they seem not to know, or, at all events, frequently to forget, that mankind are reciprocally producers and consumers; that, under proper regulations, they are equally necessary to each other, whatever be their numbers; that mutual wants are so balanced and connected in the mechanism of the social system, of which necessity is the main spring, as to produce that perpetual motion, the harmonious movements of which nothing but the interference of such philosophers can disturb or destroy.[24]

In passages such as this, the power of theory is acknowledged. The competitive individualism that characterizes market relations was promoted by theorists and apologists for a marketized society. On other occasions, of course, it is patterns of production rather than paradigm shifts in economic theory that are accorded principal responsibility for reshaping social relations. Factory owners, capitalistic producers of new wealth, now command and dehumanize labour. Southey in the *Colloquies* suggested that the manufacturer 'uses his fellow-creatures as bodily machines for producing wealth'.[25] This easy elision of the manufacturer and the political economist was far from inadvertent. To High Tory critics, theorizing manufacturing capitalism in terms of classical political economy both intensified and legitimized their analysis of its social and moral tendencies. The language of classical political economy in general, and the image of the market in particular, was presented by High Tories not as a language of economic description or analysis but as a language of moral apologia, even moral advocacy. This was what Coleridge tried to capture when he inveighed against 'the commercial spirit'. This commercial spirit was constituted from real patterns of production and exchange *and* from the modes of thinking and imagining promoted by classical political economy.[26]

Although it now seems perverse to accord poets a pivotal role in political economy, I have dwelt on Southey because his was one of the profounder influences on the development of High Tory economic thinking in the early nineteenth century. In particular, his anti-Malthusianism

---

[24] M. T. Sadler, *The Law Of Population* . . . (London, 1830), 2 vols, vol. I, pp. 10–11. Sadler (1780–1835) was MP for Newark 1829–31 and Aldborough 1831–2. He unsuccessfully contested Leeds in 1832 and Huddersfield in 1834.

[25] Southey, *Colloquies*, vol. I, p. 170.

[26] J. Morrow, *Coleridge's Political Thought: Property, Morality and the Limits of Traditional Discourse* (Houndmills, Basingstoke, 1990); J. Morrow, ed., *Coleridge's Writings*, vol. I: *On Politics and Society* (Houndmills, Basingstoke, 1990); J. Colmer, *Coleridge: Critic of Society* (Oxford, 1959).

was a powerful creative, or, if you prefer, limiting condition for the development of Tory economic thought. Southey counterposed a poetic or-
ganicism against Malthus's Euclidean economics. Both, of course, were
abstractions; both employed statistics but never allowed empiricism to
disturb theorized certainties; and both despised each other. Southey's
secular faith, like that of many leading High Tories, rested in an active
state and the demonstrated utility of public works and the distributionist
energy of the national debt.[27] If Malthus wrote for anything, he wrote to
persuade that there were modes of state social intervention in the market
which must be nullified. In particular Malthus preached the pernicious
economic heresy of the poor laws. Malthus's commitment to poor law
abolition, which he bequeathed to David Ricardo, Nassau Senior, and
every orthodox political who came to matter, made him to many High
Tories the most quintessential and the most pernicious of the political
economists.[28] In post-war Britain, the future of the poor laws became a
battleground not just for the future of welfare but also for configuring
the relationship between the state and the market. The Tories claimed
that Malthus had pronounced absolution over the rich. Smith might have
assured them that self-interested market behaviour would be rendered socially beneficial through the mechanism of the market, but Malthus went
further, telling them that their statutory commitment to public welfare
through the poor laws intensified the very problems of poverty the poor
laws purported to mitigate. Steeling yourself against the importunities of
the poor was now promoted as economically prudent and morally prefer-
able. As with its attack on the poor laws, so with its assault on protection,
political economy was depriving the state of the instruments it might use
to regulate the market as an agency both for the social distribution of
wealth and the economic allocation of capital.[29]

For these reasons, Southey blocked the possibility of Malthus's becoming a major economic writer for the highly influential *Quarterly Review*.

[27] Southey, *Colloquies*, vol. I, pp. 182–9, 193–4; cf. S. T. Coleridge, 'On the Vulgar Error
respecting Taxes and Taxation', *The Friend* (1818), ed. B. E. Rooke (Princeton, 1969),
2 vols, vol. I, pp. 228–44.

[28] Ricardo, *Principles of Political Economy*, p. 107; N. Senior, *Three Lectures on Wages*
(London, 1830); N. Senior, *Letters on the Factory Act* (London, 1837); N. Senior, *Remarks
on the Opposition to the Poor Law Amendment Bill* . . . (London, 1841); S. Leon Levy,
*Nassau Senior, 1790–1864* (Newton Abbot, 1970).

[29] For the debate on poverty and the poor laws see Winch, *Riches And Poverty*;
J. R. Poynter, *Society and Pauperism: English Ideas on Poor Relief, 1795–1834* (London,
1969); R. G. Cowherd, *The Political Economists and the English Poor Laws* (Athens, OH,
1977); G. Himmelfarb, *The Idea of Poverty* (New York, 1984); L. H. Lees, *The Solidar-
ities of Strangers: The English Poor Laws and the People, 1700–1948* (Cambridge, 1998),
pp. 82–229; P. Mandler, 'The Making of the New Poor Law *Redivivus*', *Past and Present*
117 (1987), pp. 131–57; D. Eastwood, 'Rethinking the Debates on the Poor Law in
Early-Nineteenth Century Britain', *Utilitas* 6 (1994), pp. 97–116.

From around 1810 editors of the *Quarterly* regarded Southey as its 'sheet anchor' and he was a major contributor on economic as well as on political, literary and historical topics.[30] Malthus did contribute briefly in 1823–4, when Southey was writing much less for the *Quarterly*, but the possibility of the *Quarterly* developing a distinctive and coherent economic position based on Malthus's agrarianism had passed.[31] As Donald Winch has argued, Malthus's particular importance in the history of political economy lies in his accommodating of the tenets of political economy to wartime conditions, and his elaborating an essentially dynamic concept of economic development.[32] In so doing, and in constructing a tight relationship between population and the means of subsistence, Malthus accorded agriculture a privileged position within the market denied by his Smithian and Ricardian opponents. The best case for the Corn Laws and agrarian protection was the case advanced by Malthus between 1815 and 1820.[33] Viewed from the High Tory perspective, were it not for his having been anathematized by his assault on the poor laws, Malthus would have provided a compelling case for agricultural protection and for the state's taking a view of the sectoral balance within the economy and then taking legislative instruments to promote that balance. The energy invested in burying Malthus is one of the most striking features of the debate on public policy in Britain in the first half of the nineteenth century. Ricardo understood Malthus, and in confronting Malthus's protectionist and interventionist preferences knew what he was doing, and why he was doing it.[34] Similarly, Edwin Chadwick and the social reformers of the mid-nineteenth century tramped on Malthus's grave to create the foundations for their experiments in activist social policy.[35] Malthus's Tory critics knew Malthus less well, and failed to see what they were losing by

---

[30] R. B. Clark, *William Gifford: Tory Satirist, Critic, and Editor* (New York, 1930), p. 227; J. O. Hayden, *The Romantic Reviews 1802–1824* (London, 1969); J. Shattock, *Politics and Reviews: The 'Edinburgh' and the 'Quarterly' in the Early-Victorian Age* (Leicester, 1989); Southey to Grosvenor Bedford, 18 October 1822, in *Selections from the Letters of Robert Southey*, ed. J. W. Water (London, 1856), 4 vols, vol. III, pp. 33–4, 336–7, 343, 445.

[31] F. W. Fetter, 'The Economic Articles in the "Quarterly Review" and their Authors', *Journal of Political Economy* 64 (1958), pp. 45–64; F. W. Fetter, 'The Economic Articles in the "Quarterly Review": Articles, Authors and Sources', ibid., pp. 150–70.

[32] Winch, *Riches and Poverty*.

[33] T. R. Malthus, *Observations on the Effects of the Corn Laws* (London, 1814); T. R. Malthus, *Grounds of an Opinion on the Policy of Restricting the Importation of Foreign Corn* (London, 1815); T. R. Malthus, *The Nature and Progress of Rent* (London, 1815); T. R. Malthus, *Principles of Political Economy* (London, 1820).

[34] P. Saffra, ed., *The Works and Correspondence of David Ricardo*, vol. II: *Notes on Malthus's Principles of Political Economy* (Cambridge, 1957); J. Bonar, ed., *Letters of David Ricardo to Thomas Robert Malthus, 1810–1823* (Oxford, 1887).

[35] E. Chadwick, *Report on the Sanitary Condition of the Labouring Population of Great Britain* (1842), ed. M. W. Flinn (Edinburgh, 1965); C. Hamlin, *Public Health and Social Justice in the Age of Chadwick: Britain, 1800–1854* (Cambridge, 1998); S. E. Finer, *The Life and Times of Sir Edwin Chadwick* (London, 1952).

their uncompromising rejection of Malthusian economics in its entirety. Although High Tory economics developed without any Malthusian scaffolding, it does not follow that it developed without technical sophistication. Indeed, one of the more interesting features of recent scholarship has been its reconstruction of a Tory economic discourse which did engage with orthodox political economy, but which conceived of the market in different ways and defended strategies for market intervention in terms of the constitution, the quest for economic stability, and the imperative of thinking in terms of imperial rather than local markets.[36] In the process the differences between High Tory economic discourse and classical political economy became clearly etched into the political and policy-making landscape. More importantly still, in political terms at least, Sir Robert Peel's refashioned liberal Conservatism embraced political economy in its most canonical forms.

By the 1820s, the influence of political economy within parliament was powerful, and, in some areas of policy and market regulation, even dominant.[37] There is no clearer example of Ricardo's influence on policy than the development of monetary policy in and after 1819. Britain's abandonment of convertibility in 1797 was a remarkable gamble by Pitt. Driven by wartime exigencies, and faced with the example of the crippling depreciation of France's paper currency after 1790, Pitt's measure was a massive statement of trust in the inherent strength both of the British economy and of British financial institutions. Viewed historically, this experiment in paper currency was a huge success. There was no major inflationary crisis in wartime Britain, the majority of wartime spending was met from current taxation, and an expanded national debt created economically beneficial capital flows between fundholders and economic enterprise. In the process, state intervention in the economy reached new levels of intensity.[38] The strength of the British state and the stability of the British economy were inseparably linked by wartime circumstances. In the

---

[36] Here the work of Anna Gambles has been of fundamental importance, especially *Protection and Politics: Conservative Economic Discourse, 1815–1852* (Woodbridge, Suffolk, 1999); and 'Rethinking the Politics of Protection: Conservatism and the Corn Laws, 1830–1852', *English Historical Review* 113 (1998), pp. 928–52. See also A. Macintyre, 'Lord George Bentinck and the Protectionists: A Lost Cause?', *Transactions of the Royal Historical Society* 5/39 (1989), pp. 141–65; S. Rashid, 'David Robinson and the Tory Macroeconomics of "Blackwood's Edinburgh Magazine"', *History of Political Economy* 10 (1978), pp. 258–70; H. Perkin, *The Origins of Modern English Society, 1780–1880* (London, 1969), esp. pp. 237–52.

[37] B. Gordon, *Political Economy in Parliament, 1819–1823* (London, 1976); B. Gordon, *Economic Doctrine and Tory Liberalism, 1824–1830* (London, 1979).

[38] For the history of fiscal and monetary policy between 1787 and 1821 see Hilton, *Corn, Cash, Commerce*, pp. 31–97; W. Smart, *Economic Annals of the Nineteenth Century, 1801–1820* (London, 1912); A. Feaveryear, *The Pound Sterling: A History of English Money*, 2nd edition, rev. E. V. Morgan (Oxford, 1963), pp. 173–230.

post-war era, political economists and their political allies set about dismantling the wartime economic settlement. A relentless drive for economy, an attack on patronage and 'old corruption', and a dreary pressure to cut establishments, were designed to reduce taxation and cut the national debt.[39] Had political economists carried the day, these retrenchments in central government expenditure would have been completed by a slashing of local government expenditure through poor law abolitionism. Above all, the mildly inflationary effects of a paper currency were eliminated. The Bullion Committee of 1810–11 had raised the spectre of a depreciating paper currency and adverse foreign exchanges. Ricardo trumpeted the case for resuming convertibility, Robert Peel, who chaired the key parliamentary committee in 1819, accepted the case for a restoration of the gold standard and cash payments, and by 1821 Britain had experienced the deflationary pain and was back on the gold standard.[40]

To Ricardo and Peel, the attraction of convertibility, like the attraction to Peel of the centralization of note issue in the 1844 Bank Charter Act, was not only that it provided an anti-inflationary discipline whilst seeking to sustain confidence in paper issues, but also that it constituted a self-acting check on note issue.[41] It linked the currency to a known and simple measure of value and ensured that this crucial aspect of monetary policy was a function neither of government policy nor of bankers' discretion. In linking note issue to bullion reserves and in privileging the position of the Bank of England, advocates of convertibility proceeded from a rather centralized and integrated vision of the market. Tory critics of the policy held a quite different view of the operation of a paper currency and the localism of many markets. When the debate over the issue of small notes raged, both Walter Scott in well-publicized open letters, and David Robinson, in *Blackwood's Edinburgh Magazine*, developed sophisticated critiques of the 'metallization' of currency policy.[42] Scott argued that paper currency, issued by country banks, facilitated the operation of local

---

[39] Philip Harling, *The Waning of 'Old Corruption': The Politics of Economical Reform in Britain, 1779–1846* (Oxford, 1996), esp. pp. 89–196.

[40] *The Paper Pound of 1797–1821: The Bullion Report*, 2nd edn, ed. E. Cannan (London, 1925); F. W. Fetter, *The Development of British Monetary Orthodoxy, 1797–1875* (Cambridge, MA, 1965).

[41] The 1844 Bank Charter Act, and the debate that preceded it, involved highly technical debate which, as with small note issue in 1825–6, carried strong constitutional overtones. Much the most perceptive account is in B. Hilton, 'Peel: A Reappraisal', *Historical Journal* 22 (1979), pp. 585–614.

[42] M. Malagrowther [Walter Scott], *Thoughts on the proposed Change of Currency etc.* (Edinburgh, 1826); Rashid, 'David Robinson and the Tory Macroeconomics of "Blackwood's"'; F. W. Fetter, 'The Economic Articles in "Blackwood's Edinburgh Magazine" and the Authors', *Scottish Journal of Political Economy* 7 (1960), pp. 85–107, 213–31.

markets, and provided forms of credit and exchange in markets where Bank of England notes hardly reached. David Robinson argued that paper currency as a form of credit was adequately regulated by local economic activity. Limiting the availability of paper money would, he argued, have deleterious economic and social effects, reducing wages and employment by restricting necessary credit and capital. These kinds of Tory argument had a clear economic location, and they closely paralleled the pro-paper arguments of the later anti-Ricardian 'Banking School'.[43] They also had a constitutional dimension, suspicious of the centralization of currency policy in and through the Bank of England, and insisting that policy should recognize what was distinctive in local economies. This preference for local banking liberties, and for local economic functions being performed through local, independent institutions, was wholly characteristic of Tory economic thought. In these ways, not only did Tories offer an alternative monetary policy, they also infused both monetary policy and market analysis with prior constitutional concerns.[44]

High Tory thinking on small note issue was part of a much broader indictment of monetary policy after 1819. If the direction of government policy was broadly Ricardian (in the sense of a quest for a largely self-regulating system of market self-limitations), Tory critics pointed to the casualties of these policies. Viewed from a Ricardian or Peelite perspective, the effects of the 1819 return to cash payments, the banking and joint stock legislation of 1825–6, and the Bank Charter Act of 1844 was to establish confidence in paper issue. If the price of this was limiting credit in the form of note advances from country banks and the Bank of England, this was a price worth paying. High Tory critics from the 1820s onwards were pointing to the sectoral consequences of the ways in which strict convertibility limited credit. Agriculture in particular found its requirement for seasonal credit tightly squeezed and rural areas experienced shortage of specie and notes. The fact that more sophisticated credit instruments were available to the commercial and industrial economy did not mitigate these local credit bottlenecks and, for Tory critics, simply highlighted the extent to which monetary policy was being driven by the priorities of the commercial and industrial sectors. Tory critics responded partly by emphasizing that continued agricultural protection was imperative, and partly by developing an alternative monetary policy. Throughout the 1820s Tory economic thinkers such as David Robinson struck a resolutely anti-Ricardian position, and argued

---

[43] For a useful summary see A. Arnon, *Thomas Tooke: Pioneer of Monetary Theory* (Ann Arbor, 1991); M. Collins, *Money and Banking in the UK : A History* (London, 1988).

[44] This case is powerfully developed in Gambles, *Protection and Politics*, pp. 89–115; see also Hilton, *Corn, Cash, Commerce*, pp. 202–31.

for a move away from strict convertibility with gold. A bimetallic standard was widely favoured, along with considerable discretion to country banks in note and capital advances. This critique was developed still more fully by the 1840s and Peelism faced a coherent, if ultimately unavailing, critique.[45]

Archibald Alison's interventions in the house journal of High Tory political economy, *Blackwood's Edinburgh Magazine*, capture the tone and sophistication of High Tory economic thinking and well illustrate its preoccupation with a looser monetary policy and with diminishing the distances between the economic experiences of the rich and poor, and taking some measures to dampen the frenzied speculation that fuelled the trade cycle and thus gave rise to the longer misery of economic recession. Like most High Tories, Alison was sensitive both to the scale of economic change in the early nineteenth century and the ways in which its costs and benefits had been distributed.

No one can have considered the state of the British empire during the last half century, without being convinced that some great and unprecedented causes have been at work in producing the prodigious fluctuations by which its domestic history has in that time been distinguished. Nothing similar to it ever occurred without external disaster, or the actual overthrow of society by the ravages of war, since the beginning of the world . . . [These changes] have exhibited a combination of prosperity and adversity, of strength and weakness, of riches and poverty, of progress and decline, of grandeur and debility, of joy and sorrow, unparalleled in any former ages of the world, and which, in future times, instructed by our errors, and warned by our sufferings, will probably never again occur.[46]

The parliamentary 'blue books' told a story of anguish induced by trade cycles.

The blue folios of the houses of parliament teem with authentic and decisive evidence of the vast increase during the last thirty years of crime and frequent destitution among the working classes in all parts of the empire. Every four or five years a brief feverish period of gambling, extravagance, and commercial prosperity is succeeded by a long and dreary season of anxiety, distress, and depression.[47]

Alison's indictment of the social injustice of market allocations is as searing as Engels's: '[W]hat we do say is unparalleled in the history of the

---

[45] J. S. Mill, *Principles of Political Economy* (1848), new edn (London, 1888), bk III, pp. 264–420; F. W. Fetter, *The Economist in Parliament, 1780–1868* (Durham, NC, 1980), pp. 88–135; Feaveryear, *Pound Sterling*, pp. 231–75; E. Wood, *English Theories of Central Banking Control, 1819–58* (Cambridge, MA, 1939); N. Gash, *Sir Robert Peel*, 2nd edn (London, 1986), pp. 431–8, 623–31; Fetter, *Development of British Monetary Orthodoxy*.

[46] A. Alison, *England in 1815 and 1845; or, a Sufficient and a Contracted Currency* (Edinburgh, 1845), p. 1.

[47] Ibid., p. 13.

word, is the *co-existence* of so much suffering in one portion of the people, with so much prosperity in another; of unbounded private wealth, with unceasing public misery'. The speculative booms of 1824–5 and 1835–6 amounted to 'a perilous plethora of exuberant prosperity'.[48] Here, a generation later and in a more restrained register, are Southey's 'wens and tumours'.

Like Southey, Alison refused to accept this misallocation of social resources as a necessary consequence of economic development. Like so many Alison took Malthus to be arguing that misery was a function of the pressure of population on the means of subsistence. Alison dismissed Malthusian fears in a series of statistical flourishes. If Malthus was right, the price of grain would be steadily rising and food imports would be increasing. Neither of these trends was evident. The 'distressing' differences in wage earnings within the working classes suggested that misery was induced by regional and sectoral differences within the economy rather than by any overarching Malthusian crisis. Rather, the explanation of Britain's social distress must lie in market failures and the effects of economic policy. Alison insisted, 'Capital exists, and to profusion, amply sufficient to give full and profitable employment to the whole community.'[49]

Typically, Alison laid the blame for these failures at the door of Peelite monetary policy: '[T]he contraction of the currency, which was unnecessarily made to accompany the resumption of cash payments by the bill of 1819 . . . has been the chief cause of all these effects.' Resumption between 1819 and 1821 was severely deflationary and thereafter policy had continued to diminish currency in proportion to 'national transactions'. Based on the position in 1819, had note issue kept pace with the growth in exports it would now have stood at £120m, parity with imports would have raised note issue to £96m, and parity with population to £72m. In fact note issue was just £56m. This both constrained and distorted economic growth. It could, of course, be objected that Alison and other High Tory critics ignored the role of non-currency credit instruments, but then so did Peelite orthodoxy. Moreover, Alison argued that much of Britain's social misery and periodic unemployment was a consequence of the commercial crises of 1824–5 and 1835–6. Both these crises, he argued, were attributable directly to monetary policy. Both could have been 'prevented, or in a great degree alleviated, by . . . an increased issue of paper, in the absence of gold'.[50] Such pleas for a loosening of monetary policy were an axiom of the High Tory alternative to orthodox political economy as practised by Huskisson and Peel. Whatever its validity as an alternative economic strategy, High Tory economic policy was hardly the

[48] Ibid., pp. 15, 32.   [49] Ibid., pp. 18, 21, 27–8.   [50] Ibid., pp. 35–9, 61–5, 93.

product of a technically unsophisticated economics or of an unwillingness to take markets seriously.

Monetary policy was thus taken intensely seriously by the more technically minded Tory critics of the icy eminence now enjoyed by classical political economy. For those who had ears to hear, there was a real debate to be had here. There was a debate, too, over empire. Before Britain discovered that free trade carried its own imperialist charge, High Tories sought to promote economy strategies which recognized Britain's imperial interests. As with their commitment to country banks and protecting agriculture, their economics of empire was grounded in constitutional priorities. Here again taking empire seriously meant resisting the onward rush towards free trade. Reluctantly, slavery was conceded in 1833, but imperial preference was promoted all the more fiercely thereafter, with imperial protection presented as compensating for the price of free labour. The interests of West Indian producers were not to be easily sacrificed to optimizing capital accumulation or maximizing Britain's comparative advantage. More serious, by the 1840s at least, was the challenge to Britain's imperial economy of free labour posed by slave-produced coffee and sugar.[51] Hence the fierce debates within the Conservative Party over tariff reductions between 1842 and 1845. Whether in its 1820s Huskissonian form or its 1840s Peelite guise, the tariff reforming movement was objectionable when it elevated doctrinal purity or even short-term economic advantage over imperial stability.

Ultimately the touchstone of this debate was protection. Much has been written on Britain's transition from protection to free trade, most of it teleological, and much of it overly simplistic.[52] The orthodox account runs something like this: on the question of free trade classical economists, with the notable exception of Malthus, sang from the same hymn sheet. From Pitt in the 1780s, through William Huskisson in the 1820s, to Peel in the 1840s and Gladstone in the 1850s, a liberal political tradition developed which steered Britain into the safe modern haven of free trade. Protection was damned from 1776 and politically dead from the 1820s. Peel would pronounce the last rites and Gladstone erect the funerary monument to protectionist folly. As Anthony Howe has shown, much of this is a misreading.[53] What happened in 1845–6 marked a sudden and, in its way, very particular transition to *unilateral* free trade.

---

[51] B. Semmel, *The Rise of Free Trade Imperialism* (Cambridge, 1970).

[52] The classic accounts are D. G. Barnes, *A History of the Corn Laws from 1660–1846* (London, 1930); C. R. Fay, *The Corn Laws and Social England* (Cambridge, 1932). Richard Price has recently offered an interestingly synoptically cast variation in *British Society, 1680–1880* (Cambridge, 1999), pp. 88–122.

[53] A. Howe, *Free Trade and Liberal England, 1846–1946* (Oxford, 1997).

Hitherto the move to free trade had been gradual and often (particularly in the 1820s) bilaterally or multilaterally negotiated.[54] Moreover, and importantly, those retrospectively hailed as the architects of free trade thought of themselves not as free traders but as tariff reformers. Now is not the time to rehearse the argument, but I have argued elsewhere that Peel in his great budget of 1842 was thinking within the theoretical paradigms of protection, pushing tariff reform to the limit, but retaining the notion that fiscal instruments – whether tariffs or direct taxation – should be used to preserve sectoral balance within the economy. Thus fiscal policy was to be used in part to preserve balanced economic growth and to balance the interests of labour and capital.[55]

Put like this, what had been at issue in the increasingly strident debates between High and liberal Tories over economic policy since the 1820s was the degree of protection, and the extent to which agriculture should enjoy a privileged status. Moreover, as Anna Gambles has demonstrated, High Tory economic discourse was more emphatic in investing the politics of protection with a strongly constitutionalist strain.[56] The degree of national dependence on new wealth was troubling. They shared Edmund Burke's belief that agriculture was structurally immune from speculative frenzy and represented real, solid and enduring wealth. Thus Coleridge, *Blackwood's Edinburgh Magazine*, David Robinson, Disraeli, and the majority in Peel's party that opposed him, retained a professed belief that the national interest was best served by privileging agriculture and limited capitalistic speculation. Similarly, through Lord Ashley and Richard Oastler, High Tories held to a moral economy that directly echoed Southey's indictment of the factory system.[57] National prosperity could be purchased too dearly, and the market (especially when the Whigs had done so much to crush trade union power in the 1830s) provided no real check on manufacturing capital's tendency to exploit labour. Thus for Ashley the solution must be state intervention to control both the conditions and hours of labour. It would be wrong to see High Tory economic

---

[54] A. Brady, *William Huskisson and Liberal Reform* (London, 1928); Hilton, *Corn, Cash, Commerce*, esp. pp. 173–202, 269–301; L. Brown, *The Board of Trade and the Free Trade Movement, 1830–42* (Oxford, 1958).

[55] D. Eastwood, 'The Age of Uncertainty: Britain in the Early-Nineteenth Century', *Transactions of the Royal Historical Society* 6/3 (1998), pp. 91–115; D. Eastwood, ' "Recasting our Lot": Peel, the Nation, and the Politics of Interest', in L. Brockliss and D. Eastwood, eds, *A Union of Multiple Identities: The British Isles, c.1750–c.1850* (Manchester, 1997), pp. 29–43.

[56] Gambles, *Protection and Politics*; and 'Rethinking the Politics of Protection'.

[57] E. Hodder, *The Life and Work of the Seventh Earl of Shaftsbury*, new edn (London, 1888), esp. pp. 50–379; J. T. Ward, *The Factory Movement, 1830–1855* (London, 1962); C. Driver, *Tory Radical: The Life of Richard Oastler* (New York, 1946); G. B. A. M. Finlayson, *The Seventh Earl of Shaftsbury, 1801–1885* (London, 1981), esp. pp. 57–270.

thought between 1815 and 1850 as neo-mercantilist, and there are dangers in giving romantic Conservative discourse a socialist tincture. Nevertheless, one cannot understand High Tory economic thinking in post-war Britain without appreciating the extent to which it was committed to an active state. They did not want to resurrect the panoply of controls that Smith believed to have checked economic growth. As I have already argued, in many ways their position on fiscal and monetary policy, and on public works and social relations, was strikingly ambitious. Imagining markets differently, and remaining committed to a more constitutionalist economics, gave their systems of thought a degree of coherence.

The circumstances of Peel's remaking of fiscal and economic policy between 1842 and 1846 profoundly altered the trajectory of Tory development. Liberal Tory economic thought, which had dominated the executive but not the Tory party since 1812, delivered a blow to High Tory discourse which was more politically shattering than anything which had been mustered by the *Edinburgh Review* or the *Westminster Review*. By breaking from tariff reform in favour of unilateral free trade, and then, quite brilliantly, appealing over the head of parliament to the people in 1846, Peel began that strikingly British association of prosperity with free trade and freed markets.[58] Peel's populist rhetoric, presenting Corn Law appeal as giving the labouring man 'cheap bread', associated his Conservative Party with the Anti-Corn Law League's rather disingenuous imagery. The image of the large loaf sustained British free trade through the tariff reform crisis of 1903–10. This was a measure of the political and ideological reconfigurations of the 1840s. The significance of Peel's great speech of 29 June 1846, three days after the Repeal of the Corn Laws, has not always been fully appreciated.

I shall surrender power severely censured . . . by others, who from no interested motives, adhere to the principles of protection, considering the maintenance of it to be essential to the welfare and interests of the country; I shall leave a name execrated by every monopolist who, from less honourable motives, clamours for protection because it conduces to his own individual benefit; but it may be that I shall leave a name sometimes remembered with expressions of good will in the abodes of those whose lot is to labour, and to earn their daily bread by the sweat of their brow, when they shall recruit their exhausted strength with abundant and untaxed food, the sweeter because it is no longer leavened by a sense of injustice.[59]

In a brilliant *coup de théâtre* Peel had intruded a populist note into parliamentary politics. The crowds cheered Peel home and remained outside

---

[58] D. Read, *Peel and the Victorians* (Oxford, 1987), pp. 158–241.
[59] *Speeches of the late Rt. Hon. Sir Robert Peel delivered in the House of Commons* (London, 1831), 4 vols, vol. IV, pp. 716–17.

his house cheering long after. Many friends and political allies thought the speech as a whole, and especially its great peroration, quite gratuitous.[60] Historians have dubbed this the 'Cobden eulogy'. To the extent that Peel named and lauded Richard Cobden, the leader of the Anti-Corn Law League, it was.[61] But Peel did nothing that was not calculated, and the great peroration was about his protectionist opponents in the Conservative Party rather than his former enemies in the Anti-Corn Law League. In stridently populist language, Peel was seeking to bury the Tory protectionist agenda. True they may be 'disinterested', they may genuinely believe that protection is conducive to the national interest, but prosperity and distributive economic justice now lie in free trade. The apologetics of High Tory economic discourse are dismissed. Although the text carefully distinguishes them and Peel does not say that Tory protectionists are monopolists, he does juxtapose the two in a way which would leave those who read the speech in no doubt that protectionism was sustained by monopolistic *reflexes*. Most compellingly, the concern with labour and poverty that had animated High Tory critics of market individualism from Southey through the *Blackwood's* circle to Lord Ashley, was here annexed to free trading market capitalism. In holding out the prospect of abundant and untaxed food, no longer leavened with a sense of injustice, Peel demonstrated that he spoke more eloquently than Ricardo wrote, but he also confirmed that Ricardo had not written in vain. Free trade, free markets, and market-distributed entitlements all came together. In the process the attempt to develop a distinctively Tory political economy, and with it to subordinate the market to the constitution, was drawing to a close, and this particular attempt to make poets the acknowledged legislators of the economic world faded into the realms of fancy.

[60] Read, *Peel*, pp. 236–41.
[61] And was understood as such by Cobden, see J. Morley, *The Life of Richard Cobden*, new edn (London, 1903), pp. 390–402.

# 5    Guild theory and guild organization in France and Germany during the nineteenth century

*Heinz-Gerhard Haupt*

Hardly any institution of old Europe called the principles of the free market into question to such an extent as the guilds. In most early modern European cities and rural areas alike, master artisans and retail traders associated in order to control the quality, quantity and exchange of commodities, and in order to limit access to the labour market to a select circle of persons who were either specially trained or provided with special certificates. The guilds produced a balance between the guarantee of income and 'food' for the master artisans and the needs of the population for sufficient provision, which was often precarious. Consequently, the access to the urban market of producers and service providers was limited to guild members, who rarely yielded to the pressure of municipal authorities or admitted outsiders into their ranks. Their most important goals were the protection against commodities produced outside the guilds, which were stopped at the gates of the city, and the maintenance of the social exclusivity and monopoly of the master artisans and principals of the guilds. These influential persons controlled both the market of commodities and the labour market. They limited the number of journeymen and apprentices, and subjected these groups to strict qualification standards and a particular *cursus honorum*, which, if the professional training was successful, culminated in the degree of 'master'. Based on similar concepts of honour and a system of mutual respect and dependence, the labour market was withdrawn from the free interplay of supply and demand and subjected to guild patterns. Just as journeymen and apprentices could not move freely, master artisans, too, were bound to certain rules. They were subjected to the regulations of the guilds, which were partly of an economic and partly of a moral nature; in case of a violation of these regulations, they were liable to the jurisdiction of the guilds. A tendency towards monopolization (instead of a free interplay of supply and demand) and a tendency towards heavy regulation (instead of individual freedom) were, thus, the two main characteristics of the guilds of early modern Europe.[1]

Already in the course of the eighteenth century, the guild system came under huge pressure. The development of a market economy and the industrial putting out system, together with the rise of the modern territorial state, destroyed corporate structures in several parts of Europe and was replacing them with the principle of free enterprise. At the same time, economic writers and intellectuals were attacking the guilds as old-fashioned and outdated structures, bodies which were not only out of tune with the spirit of modern society but which hindered the development of liberal institutions.[2] Interestingly, however, those political theorists who were defending the principles of personal freedom and juridical equality did not refrain from using the guilds as instruments of their own political reform project. In certain conjunctures during the nineteenth century, guild ideas were revived and defended by liberal authors. This chapter explores this historical paradox by focusing on two authors, Otto von Gierke in Germany and Emile Durkheim in France. Both were concerned with the polarization of society and the power of the modern state and both turned in different ways to the guild system to balance the structures of modern society.

The French Revolution, with the decrees of Allard (2 May 1791) and Le Chapelier (14 June 1791), abolished the guilds and severely reduced the freedom of coalition.[3] All over Europe these changes unleashed a series of discursive changes as well as institutional transformations. If in the past liberalism had been synonymous with a critique of the guild system, counter-revolutionary thinking now turned to a defence of guild principles. Here guilds were celebrated for their link with the past, representing an organic community which, in accordance with the laws of the nature and of history, was hierarchically organized and linked to religious functions. The restoration of the Ancien Régime, according to counter-revolutionary thinking, should be accompanied by the restoration of the guild system where it had been abolished (in France, Belgium, and parts of Italy and Germany) and its defence where it had managed to survive (in Central and Eastern Europe, the Netherlands, Austria, and southern Germany). During the revolutionary and Napoleonic periods, the attitude towards guilds was a litmus test of political allegiance. The more intellectuals were committed to the aims and principles of the French

---

[1] H.-G. Haupt, ed., *Das Ende der Zünfte: Ein europäischer Vergleich* (Göttingen, 2002).
[2] A. Black, *Guilds and Civil Society in Europe. Political Thought from the 12th Century to the Present* (Ithaca/New York, 1984).
[3] A. Plessis, ed., *Naissance des libertés économiques. Le décret d'Allard et la loi Le Chapelier, leurs conséquences 1791 – fin XIXe siècle* (Paris, 1993).

Revolution, the more they would be critical of the guilds. The more they were critical of the French Revolution, its programme and its outcome, the more they would defend guild organizations in Europe.[4] To what degree this stark contrast is correct can be examined by way of comparing intellectual developments in nineteenth-century Germany and France, and especially by focusing on those who defended the principles of the French Revolution in the two societies: the liberals.

Against the background of these legal and institutional developments, a series of debates took place in Germany and France in the course of the nineteenth century about the future role of the guilds, and, more broadly, about the regulation of commercial life and the solution of 'the social question'. Even in France, the early abolition of the guilds did not only provoke enthusiasm. Already in the course of the French Revolution, the big merchants of the northern French city Lille voiced their concerns about the revolutionary decrees. They demanded a substitute institution that would provide them with an adequate representative body, and that could guarantee a sensible control of the quality of products and the standards of the training of the apprentices.[5] In early nineteenth-century debates about the order of commercial life and solutions of the social question, many ascribed positive functions to the guilds. The conservative Comte de Villeneuve-Bargemont, for instance, wrote in his *Économie politique chrétienne* that he could not imagine a full restoration of the guilds to their traditional functions and privileges, but that he could envisage them as a desirable form of organization for labourers. An organization similar to that of the old guilds should be established to issue apprenticeship certificates and, at the same time, serve as a relief fund, working on the principle of mutuality: 'The institutional guild of workers which would not limit industry and which would not have the bad consequences of the old guilds, would encourage the spirit of association and mutual help, give guarantees of instruction and good behaviour and replace the bad institutions of artisanal workers.'[6]

From a different political angle, Sismond de Sismondi rejected a restoration of any institutions of the Ancien Régime, but nonetheless regarded corporations as useful bodies to control the mechanization of

[4] Black, *Guilds*, pp. 198–203.

[5] J.-P. Hirsch, 'L'effet Le Chapelier dans la pratique et les discours des entrepreneurs français, 1760–1860', in Plessis, ed., *Naissance*, pp. 159–66; J.-P. Hirsch, *Les deux rêves du commerce, entreprise et institution dans la région lilloise (1760–1860)* (Paris, 1991).

[6] Comte de Villeneuve-Bargemont, *Économie politique chrétienne* (Paris, 1834), 3 vols, vol. II, p.146: 'L'institution des corporations d'ouvriers qui sans gêner l'industrie et sans avoir les fâcheuses conséquences des anciens maîtrises et jurandes, favoriseraient l'esprit d'association et de secours mutuels, donnerait des garanties d'instruction et de bonnes conduites être, implacerait la déplorable institution du compagnonnage.'

work and to avoid unemployment and pauperism.[7] Although both authors came from different ends of the political spectrum, they shared
doubts about the free interplay of market forces. Although not envisaging a complete restoration of the guilds, they were clearly attracted to the
guilds as a means of taming the destructive powers of the market and
of curtailing its dangerous social dynamics. Such anxieties about excessive liberalization were shared by numerous contemporaries. It forms a
leitmotif in contemporary accounts. The founder of the *Ecole spéciale de
commerce de Paris*, Legret, for instance, observed in November 1826 that
'from the Revolution on nobody has discovered a just milieu between
one liberty which I call licence and the old units of the guilds in order to
establish wise limits onto industry without limiting its development. We
should not limit liberties, but not encourage licence either.'[8]

Some institutions were created to establish a greater balance, such
as the chambers of commerce, which had already been founded during the French Revolution, and the court of commerce – *le Conseil des
Prud'hommes* –, which the *Empire* had founded for the silk industry of
Lyon, with the aim of observing and controlling market forces. First and
foremost, however, French liberals between 1830 and 1870 tried to tame
markets and integrate them into the framework of French society by appealing to the state for the protection of small enterprises and by
cautioning against an all too swift expansion of big industry. For this
purpose, economists like Adolphe Blanqui, Ambroise Clément and Louis
Wolinski did not demand the restoration of the guilds but the limita-
tion of the expansion of big industry – even if that necessitated state
intervention. They feared that if large enterprises had their way France
would be threatened by overproduction, unemployment, and revolution.
Social polarization became the common writing on the wall. Blanqui's
prophecy was that 'the great number of workers earning four and six
Francs per day and small entrepreneurs with a certain wealth would
be replaced by a few big businessmen earning millions of Francs and
a great multitude of starving workers. The big would eat the small . . .
society will be in trouble.'[9] Not surprisingly, then, they were opposed
both to the monopolies which already existed in some branches such as

---

[7] S. de Sismondi, *Mouvements principes d'économie politique* (Paris, 1834), p. 156.
[8] F. Demier, 'L'impossible retour au régime des corporations dans la France de la Restau-
ration, 1814–1830', in Plessis, ed., *Naissance*, p. 137: 'Depuis la Révolution on n'a point
découvert de milieu entre une liberté indéfinie que j'appelle licence et les anciennes
chaînes des corporations, pour contenir l'industrie dans de sages limites sans nuire à son
essor. Ne gênons point la liberté mais ne favoriserons pas la licence'.
[9] A. Blanqui, *Cours d'économie industrielle (1838–1839)* (Paris, 1840), p. 211; cf. F. Demier,
'A. Blanqui, Un économiste libéral face à la Révolution industrielle 1794–1854' (Thèse
3e cycle, Paris X, 1979): 'Au lieu d'un grand nombre d'ouvriers à 4 F et 6 F par jour, et

the production of coal or steel and to legislation which tried to replace limited partnerships with joint-stock companies in order to introduce a legal form of commercial organization which favoured the emergence of big enterprises. According to the liberal credo, a political strategy which paid more attention to the interests of small enterprises and avoided any preferential treatment of big business was well suited to keep both small and big enterprises afloat and, thus, to slow down the expansion of the market and to assimilate it to the structural conditions of French society. For Blanqui, for instance, 'it is clear that big industry should live beside the small'.[10]

Debates among German liberals in the first half of the nineteenth century demonstrate that similar worries about the consequences of freedom of trade and the industrial system were widespread. In contrast to their French counterparts, however, German liberals favoured a middleclass model rather than a model of a balance between small and big business. In the apt words of the historian Lothar Gall, their ideal was that of 'a classless civil society of the middling sort' (or, if one wants to describe it retrospectively, of a pre-industrial middling rank society organized along professional lines and based on patriarchical principles).[11] This model was a far cry from Manchesterism and an unconditional trust in the self-regulating powers of the market (or Adam Smith's famous 'invisible hand'), since it demanded intervention and assistance by the state in order to realize and guarantee this middling-sort civil society. In the eyes of the Baden liberal Karl von Rotteck, this aim was perfectly compatible with a guild system – as long as these guilds were freely accessible. Rotteck flatly rejected the idea of unlimited freedom of trade and the free interplay of economic powers as a 'war of all against all'. According to Rotteck, this would mean 'an end to the quiet homely feeling, which was based on modesty, but at the same time on the consciousness of a guaranteed state of being fed'.[12] Like French liberals, southern German liberals were afraid of social polarization – a fear which they tried to counter with

---

de petits entrepreneurs dans l'aisance, on verra quelques chefs de maison milliardaires et des ouvriers à quelques sous. Les gros mangeront les petits . . . la société sera ébranlée.'

[10] Demier, 'Blanqui', p. 533: 'C'est un fait accompli, la grande industrie doit vivre à côté de la petite'; cf. H.-G. Haupt, 'Die französische Handwerkerdiskussion des 19. Jahrhunderts', in F. Lenger, ed., *Handwerk, Hausindustrie und die historische Schule der Nationalökonomie. Wissenschafts- und gewerbegeschichtliche Perspektiven* (Bielefeld, 1998), pp. 132–43.

[11] 'Klassenlose Bürgergesellschaft "mittlerer Existenzen"'; L. Gall, 'Liberalismus und "bürgerliche Gesellschaft". Zu Charakter und Entwicklung der liberalen Bewegung in Deutschland', in L. Gall, ed., *Liberalismus* (Cologne, 1976), p. 176.

[12] 'Krieg Aller gegen Alle'; 'Es sei aus mit dem stillen hauslichen Gemüte, gegründet auf Mäßigkeit, aber zugleich auch auf das Bewußtsein eines gesicherten Nahrungszustandes', cit. in H. Sedatis, *Liberalismus und Handwerk in Südwestdeutschland* (Stuttgart,

their model of a society which was stabilized by a strong middle class. Rotteck expressed the fear that 'the class of producers is divided into smart, happy, and greedy entrepreneurs on the one hand and permanently anxious working people who are exposed to poverty and can never enjoy their life, on the other'.[13] It was this future against which the liberals set themselves. It is true that both the critique of corporate society and the rejection of modern class society were integral parts of the liberal tradition, but that did not prevent liberals from employing institutions of the Ancien Régime, like the guilds, as instruments for regulating and moderating market society.

It was only among Rheinland liberals that the fear of markets declined as confidence increased that a new middle class 'of well-reputed merchants and entrepreneurs' would put German society on a new foundation.[14] Therefore, they rejected any reference to traditional institutions such as guilds, although that did not mean they were prepared to do without a vision of economic order providing a harmonious relationship between trade, agriculture and industry.

In contrast to France, the guilds – if in a reformed shape – played an important role in German liberal discourse as an instrument for taming and regulating market forces and for maintaining social harmony in civil society. French and German liberals expected beneficial social developments from state interventions. Yet, whereas French liberals pinned their hope on a balance between small and big business, the majority of German liberals focused on a partial restoration of the guilds.

In this attitude they were partly able to draw on G. W. F. Hegel's conception of the guilds. Hegel stressed the importance of guilds (*Korporationen*) in his *Elements of the Philosophy of Right* (*Grundlinien der Philosophie des Rechts*). Next to the family they were one of the roots of civil society and indispensable for the organization of industry. He conceived of them as institutions of self-defence and of professional socialization. In Hegel's opposition between the general and the particular, guilds were part of the general pattern of civil society. The individual, in this perspective, had to be a member of a guild, otherwise he would lose the sense of honour attached to his rank (*Stand*) and be reduced to a selfish material occupation. Against the tendency of the modern state to abolish guilds, Hegel

---

1979), pp. 44, 51; cf. F. Lenger, *Sozialgeschichte des deutschen Handwerks seit 1800* (Frankfurt/Main, 1988), pp. 36–9, 88–9.

[13] D. Langewiesche, *Liberalismus in Deutschland* (Frankfurt/Main, 1988), pp. 30–3. See also the chapters in F. Trentmann, ed., *Paradoxes of Civil Society: New Perspectives on Modern German and British History* (New York and Oxford, 2000/2003).

[14] Langewiesche, *Liberalismus*, p. 31; R. Walther, 'Wirtschaftlicher Liberalismus', in O. Brunner et al., eds, *Geschichtliche Grundbegriffe* (Stuttgart, 1982), 8 vols, vol. III, pp. 787–815.

stressed their important function in offering a general mentality and specific help to the citizen. Hegel emphasized that 'it is necessary to provide ethical man with a universal activity in addition to his private end. This universal [activity], which the modern state does not always offer him, can be found in the corporation.'[15] Guilds or corporations contributed in Hegel's sense to the schooling of ethical life (*Sittlichkeit*), thus helping to overcome particularism and materialism, laying, instead, the foundations of a civil society. In his defence of the guilds, Hegel has an elective affinity with some conservative ideas. At the same time, however, Hegel shared liberals' hostility towards closed guilds for limiting their role in civil society. He thus appealed to the state to guarantee the openness of the corporate structure and its integration into the value system of civil society.

Moving beyond the inclusion of corporate elements in the theories of counter-revolutionary authors, an interesting paradox emerged in the second half of the nineteenth century. While the German lawyer Otto von Gierke refrained from taking up the idea of corporations, the republican sociologist Emile Durkheim fell back upon it. Their critiques of the market resulted in clearly divergent ideas. In the course of developing their ideas under the influence of the social question, both authors broke with the national patterns of the socio-political debate of the first half of the nineteenth century discussed so far. If Gierke had argued in accordance with the liberal orthodoxy, he might have seized on the guilds as one means of reforming society, while the republican Durkheim, at the end of the nineteenth century, might easily have thought of other means of social reform. Neither followed this pattern.

How to explain the departure of these two thinkers from the main currents of their indigenous intellectual traditions? When Gierke turned his attention towards associations, he was in part following major changes in the political landscape in Germany where guilds had been abolished and replaced by voluntary associations. The revolution of 1848 marked a turning point in the debate between rival organizational models for reforming society. Associations, rather than guilds, were now seen in accordance with the vision of a reformed economy and society. As the historian Hans Jäger has argued, 'by the late 1860s, economic liberalism and the idea of free trade had become dominant forces. Nobody any longer thought about the restoration of guilds.'[16] For the liberal Lujo Brentano, factory

---

[15] '[e]s ist aber notwendig, den sittlichen Menschen außer seinem Privatzwecke eine allgemeine Tätigkeit zu gewähren. Dieses Allgemeine, das ihm der moderne Staat nicht immer reicht, findet er in der Korporation', G. W. F. Hegel, *Grundlinien der Philosophie des Rechts*, ed. Bernhard Ladebrink (Stuttgart, 1970), p. 385; Engl. tr. *Elements of the Philosophy of Right*, ed. A. W. Wood, tr. H. B. Nisbet (Cambridge, 1991), § 255, p. 273.
[16] 'In der Praxis schien sich der wirtschaftliche Liberalismus und insbesondere der Freihandelsgedanke Ende der sechziger Jahre in Deutschland endgültig durchgesetzt zu haben.

laws were an indignant abandonment of civil liberties and trade unions a return to the guild system. Finally, mercantilism appeared to have been overcome.[17] The distance between Gierke and the surrounding intellectual climate was not as obvious as it seemed to be. The insistence of Durkheim upon guilds may be seen as the result of his intellectual experience in Germany where he acknowledged the restoration of guild structures among artisans during the 1880s. His reception of guild theory did not follow in the tracks of counter-revolutionary ideas, but developed from his own experience in Germany.[18]

Like other liberal authors after 1870, Otto von Gierke, the representative of the historical school of Germanic law, set out from a critical analysis of the destructive powers of the market and their contribution to social polarization and the oppression of workers. In his *Deutsches Genossenschaftsrecht* he wrote in 1868 that '[f]rom the atoms of the old, dismantled economic society new economic organisms [have developed] as all-powerful forms which have an inherent inclination to continue to grow in power and for which financial capital represents both the basis and the master, while labour is but a dependent tool. These organisms are the capitalist enterprises of all kinds.'[19] In the course of this development, according to Gierke, the original patriarchical labour relations within enterprises had deteriorated. 'With the overwhelming power of financial capital, the personal and human relationship between the master and the worker has changed, as the impersonal power of capital has increasingly segregated both.' 'Thanks to this', Gierke continued, 'the situation of the worker has fundamentally changed, since he is not a full-blown citizen, but a subject of the economic association which shapes and rules his life.'[20] Against this form of rule, Gierke favoured the principle of association, which he did not perceive only as a means of the disadvantaged to realize their aims, but also as 'a better, moral community, in which the

---

Niemand dachte mehr an eine Wiederbelebung der Innungen.' H. Jäger, *Geschichte der Wirtschaftsordnung in Deutschland* (Frankfurt/Main, 1988).

[17] 'Fabrikgesetzgebung galt als eine empörende Preisgebung der staatsbürgerlichen Freiheit . . . Gewerkvereine als eine Rückkehr zum Zunftwesen . . . Der Merkantilismus schien endgültig überwunden.' L. Brentano, *Mein Leben im Kampf um die soziale Entwicklung Deutschlands* (Jena, 1931), p. 73.

[18] E. Durkheim, 'Sources et modèles, l'influence allemande', in *Textes*, ed. V. Karady (Paris, 1975), ch. III; B. Lacroix, *Emile Durkheim et la politique* (Paris, 1981).

[19] Otto Gierke, *Rechtsgeschichte der deutschen Genossenschaft* (Berlin, 1868), p. 1036; cf. in English, A. Black, ed., *Community in Historical Perspective* (Cambridge, 1990), pp. 46–220; G. Dilcher, 'Genossenschaftstheorie und Sozialrecht; Ein "Juristensozialismus" O. v. Gierkes?', in *Quaderni Fiorentini* 3–4 (1974/5), pp. 319–65.

[20] Black, *Community*, p. 221; cf. O. G. Oexle, 'O. von Gierkes Rechtsgeschichte der deutschen Genossenschaft. Ein Versuch wissenschaftsgeschichtlicher Rekapitulation', in Volker Hammerstein, ed., *Deutsche Geschichtswissenschaft um 1900* (Stuttgart, 1980), pp. 193–217.

individual [has given up] a part – and a significant part, for that matter – of his personality for the sake of the whole'. Nonetheless, Gierke excluded any compulsory character of associating, as he believed all associations should be based on the principle of 'associating by the free will of the associated'.[21] Thus, his critique was directed at the purely capitalist market, which subjugated workers, at the individualism of enlightened philosophy and market society, which encouraged egoism and isolation, and, finally, at the *étatisme* of the state. Gierke believed that the association as 'any body of Germanic law based on associating, i.e. an organization with an independent legal personality' did not only integrate the individual into society and allow for resistance against the state and socio-economic developments: the association also kept the actions of the state within reasonable limits. Gierke has thus been claimed as one of the fathers of the idea of association in Germany, since he was convinced that the present and future of Germany were dependent on the realization of this idea.

Yet Gierke did not only argue prospectively, but derived his ideas from a historical analysis. The final victory of the association had to be viewed in the framework of a world historical struggle between the two principles of association and individualism, between unity and freedom, and between association and power respectively. 'The struggle of these two great principles determines one of the most powerful movements in history.'[22] This conflict was complicated by the fact that – apart from individualism which dissolved association – the state endeavoured to keep associations in direct dependence. Gierke distinguished among the following stages of development. About 800 years ago, political power defeated the model of associations, while the middle ages were characterized by the success of 'free union' which was able to check both individual tendencies of gaining independence and power strategies of the state. Until 1800, a 'state of subordination' prevailed, according to Gierke, which pushed associations into dependence. By contrast, the nineteenth century appeared as the period during which associations would develop to the point of integrating the individual and successfully defying the arbitrary power of the state.[23] Between the market and *étatisme*, according to Gierke, the system of free associations 'had already produced great things [and] was bound to produce even greater things in both the near and the far-off future'.[24]

Gierke tried to escape the dichotomy between the state and the individual in nineteenth-century German political thought. He was afraid of

---

[21] Gierke, *Rechtsgeschichte*, p. 11; he is talking about associations as institutions 'von keiner ständischen Fessel mehr gebunden, von keiner Ausschließlichkeit eingeengt'.

[22] Ibid., p. 2.

[23] Ibid., p. 10; cf. W. Hardtwig, *Genossenschaft, Sekte, Verein in Deutschland. I: Vom Spätmittelalter bis zur Französischen Revolution* (Munich, 1997), 2 vols, vol. I, pp. 25–33.

[24] Gierke, *Rechtsgeschichte*.

a development that would leave behind a weak individual clashing with a powerful state: 'as if only the free and equal individual and the omnipotent, mechanistic state would be left on the battlefield – an individual released from all communal relations facing a community of people that has been emptied into the vacuous space of a general public'.[25] Against the strict individualism of the Enlightenment he was emphasizing the need for co-operation between individuals.

Man owes what he is to union with his fellow man. The possibility of forming associations [*Associationen*], which not only increase the power of those alive at the time, but also – and most importantly, because the existence of the association outspans that of the individual personality – unite past generations with those to come, gave us the possibility of evolution, of history.[26]

This trust in evolution, based on associational ideas, would eventually unite all of mankind, in Gierke's view. Not competition between producers, but their co-operation is at the heart of Gierke's vision of history. It is not surprising, therefore, that producers' associations (for workers as well as capitalists) were deemed the finest instruments of organization and progress.

Against the state and its power, Gierke developed his idea of the *Gemeinde* or community. He criticized French ideas of uniformity and mechanic principles, and insisted on the Germanic roots of German self-government. Rather than strengthening the state, he was turning to urban liberties, the rights to develop an urban public opinion and to strengthen the self-government of burghers at the same time as extending their responsibility in their community. The state is seen not as an entity distinct from the association, but continuous with the structures and abilities developed in the community.[27]

---

[25] '[A]ls sollten . . . nur das freie und gleiche Individuum und der omnipotente mechanische Staat, der jeder Gemeinschaft entledigte Einzelne und die aus der Gemeinschaft der Menschen in den leeren Raum emporgehobene Allgemeinheit auf dem Kampfplatz bleiben', O. Gierke, *Die soziale Aufgabe des Privatrechts. Vortrag gehalten am 5. April 1889 in der Juristischen Gesellschaft zu Wien* (Berlin, 1889), p. 7; tr. by the editors.

[26] 'Was der Mensch ist, verdankt er der Vereinigung von Mensch und Mensch. Die Möglichkeit, Associationen hervorzubringen, die nicht nur die Kraft der gleichzeitig Lebenden erhöhen, sondern vor allem durch ihren die Persönlichkeit des Einzelnen überdauernden Bestand die vergangenen Geschlechter mit den kommenden verbinden, gab uns die Möglichkeit der Entwicklung, der Geschichte.' Gierke, *Rechtsgeschichte*, p. 1; A. Black, ed., *Community in Historical Perspective. A translation of selections from Das Deutsche Genossenschaftsrecht (The German Law of Fellowship) by Otto Gierke* (Cambridge, 2002), p. 2; cf. Gierke, *Rechtsgeschichte*, p. 11: 'Ausschließliche Schöpferin ist sie für eine alle Gebiete des öffentlichen und privaten Lebens ergreifendes und neugestaltendes Vereinswesen, das, so Großes es schon hervorgebracht hat, Größeres noch in näherer und ferner Zukunft wirken wird.'

[27] Gierke, *Rechtsgeschichte*, p. 1; cf. M. Peters, *Die Genossenschaftstheorie Otto v. Gierkes (1841–1921)* (Göttingen, 2001).

Gierke has been seen as the champion of competing values. On the one hand, some authors have attacked him as an intellectual who supported industrial cartels and Germanic interest groups; this characterization goes back to his understanding of German law and his idea that Germany was uniquely suited to realize the associational ideal. On the other hand, Gierke has been viewed as the lawyer who developed the idea of local self-government; Hugo Preuss, one of the founding fathers of the Weimar constitution, could be seen in his footsteps. It is true that Gierke remained attached to a kind of thinking which was critical of the Enlightenment and the liberal heritage. It is also true that he referred to elements of the liberal critique of capitalism and the market. Yet, at the same time, he did not revert to a corporatist model. Two reasons may be given to explain this deviation. On the one hand, guilds did not guarantee the free will of associating, which was regarded as an indispensable condition in Gierke's model; they represented compulsory associations instead. In this respect, Gierke followed the liberal critique. On the other hand, corporations needed the support of the state, which Gierke, in his early writings, wanted to see pushed back. Like the eulogy on the system of associations, this represented a genuinely liberal thought. But at the end of the nineteenth century Gierke moved to a more organic vision of society and stressed more the power of community. Here he came close to Tönnies.[28]

In contrast to Gierke, the republican sociologist Emile Durkheim did indeed revert to the guild system, if in a modified form. He dedicated a long passage of the foreword to the second edition of his work *La division sociale du travail* (1902) to this topic.[29] However, Durkheim's objective was not a critique of individualism which he welcomed as much as the Enlightenment or the French Revolution. His critique of the liberal model of the market concentrated on the free interplay of economic forces, where, according to Durkheim, no public moral existed. For Durkheim, the egoism of the economically active individual did not create any cohesion from which discipline could emerge, so that it was not surprising that anomie ruled and social conflicts broke out. To overcome this state of affairs, he suggested the establishment of a regulative system. This could only emerge in an organized and self-contained group. Without a moral basis, he maintained, there could be neither social peace nor society: 'A society which consists of a multitude of unorganized individuals and which a hyper state attempts to tame and limit is truly a sociological

---

[28] See the chapter by Jose Harris in this volume, below, pp. 129–44.

[29] E. Durkheim, *La division du travail sociale* (Paris, 1902); cf. F. H. Tenbruck, 'Emile Durkheim oder die Geburt der Gesellschaft aus dem Geist der Soziologie', *Zeitschrift für Soziologie* 10 (1981), pp. 333–50, esp. 340.

monster.'[30] Durkheim was concerned with the organization of a '*groupement professionel*', which would produce moral cohesion, and lay a moral foundation of economic life, which a market society could not produce. '[I]t is necessary that a regulative power plays the same role for the moral necessities than the organization is playing for physical necessities. That is to say that this power could only be moral.'[31]

Durkheim did not find a form of organization suited for this purpose in the unions of employers and employees, since they only represented private associations without any legal authority or power of regulation. Besides, these unions only organized interests, not the profession. Therefore, as a whole, Durkheim did not believe in Gierke's associations as an appropriate panacea for the ills of a market society. Instead, he reverted to the idea of corporations, whose inflexibility and monopoly-like character he nonetheless criticized. He saw in these corporations an opportunity to create institutions specific and helpful for nineteenth-century conditions, bodies that were accepted by the state and at the same time capable of infusing enough discipline to organize a profession on all levels and to establish a professional ethos. From his historical analysis, which took him to antiquity (not unlike Gierke), he concluded that institutions which had a long history reflected societal needs and, therefore, could not be arbitrary or coincidental in character. He especially emphasized their moral effect, which was mirrored in the religious character, the feasts and parades of the guilds, and which, he felt, had to be preserved. In a reformed version, guilds could develop 'the moral strength to tame individual egotisms, to maintain a stronger feeling of mutual solidarity in the hearts of the workers, and to prevent the law of the jungle from influencing the trade and exchange relations to such a brutal extent'.[32] Yet Durkheim had even more comprehensive plans for the *groupements professionels*. In the process of the nationalization and the globalization of the market, they would grow beyond the local domain and thus abstain from the parochial politics which had turned out to be disastrous in the past. In addition, they could become institutions of education and social welfare. 'A gigantic system of professional organizations active on a nation-wide scale' certainly did not represent a panacea in Durkheim's eyes, but it was an indispensable part of any national organization. After all, '[a] nation can only support itself if it inserts a whole series of secondary groups between the state and its citizens – groups, which are sufficiently close to

---

[30] Durkheim, *Division*, p. 68.
[31] Durkheim, *Le Suicide: étude du sociologie* (Paris, 1969): 'Il faut qu'une puissance régulatrice joue pour les besoins moraux le même role que l'organisation pour les besoins physiques. C'est dire que cette puissance ne peut être que morale.'
[32] Durkheim, *Division*, p. 49.

the individuals to be able to catch them within their compass of action and to carry them along in the general torrent of social life.'[33]

Starting from his criticism of the anomic character of a market society that expressed itself in the law of the jungle and the lack of solidarity among the economic subjects, Durkheim developed an organization of economic and political life which was founded on his *groupements professionels*. These would develop a professional ethos, integrate the individual, and infuse morals into economic life in general. In the course of developing this idea, Durkheim doubtlessly took over certain elements of the guild system, although – as he himself noted self-critically – he seemed to 'swim against the current of history'. Corporatist elements, then, played an important role in Durkheim's thinking at the turn of the twentieth century, which can be explained by an effort to re-animate those intermediary institutions between state and society that had been removed by the French Revolution – a thesis which has been put forward by Robert Nisbet for French sociology in general.[34]

Durkheim distanced himself from current visions of corporation in France developed by traditionalist authors like René de la Tour du Pin La Charce. For la Tour du Pin, the corporations were key elements of his criticism of liberalism in religion, economy and politics. He stressed the importance for all members of a society to be part of corporations that include the owners and directors of enterprises as well as their workers. These organizations should exclude conflicts and struggles for power as well as concurrence by the fact that proletarians became partial owners of the means of production. Membership inside the corporation would protect individuals more than their political rights like the right to vote, which la Tour du Pin wanted to abolish. This early vision of corporatist structures, realized in fascist Italy, was based on a critique of market economy and especially of the egoistic tendencies of the French bourgeoisie. Especially the Jewish element of this bourgeoisie was attacked by la Tour du Pin, and later by Edouard Drumont.[35] This reactionary and anti-Semitic connotation of the guild idea may explain why it was astonishing that a republican and laicist author like Emile Durkheim was attracted to the guilds and gave them an important part in his social reform project. However, he was a member of those intellectuals who tried

---

[33] Cf. the contradictory positions in the articles of Oexle and Dilcher.
[34] R. A. Nisbet, *Durkheim* (Englewood Cliffs, NJ, 1965); R. A. Nisbet, 'The French Revolution and the Rise of Sociology in France', in E. A. Toryakian, ed., *The Phenomenon of Sociology* (New York, 1971).
[35] René de la Tour du Pin, *Vers un ordre social chrétien (Jalons de route 1882–1907)*, Paris n.d. vol. VII, pp. 92, 350. R. Byrnes, *Antisemitism in Modern France* (New Brunswick, 1950).

to overcome the radical division in republican theory between the democratically legitimized state and the isolated individuals and to rethink this relationship – an enterprise considered dangerous after Tocqueville. The debate about the necessity to recreate the *corps intermédiaires* (intermediate corporations) was at the heart of French social thought at the end of the nineteenth century. Léon Duguit, doyen of the faculty of law at Bordeaux, developed the ideas of Léon Bourgeois and tried to recreate by political means 'solidarity' inside society. Durkheim, too, was concerned to study society by scientific means and to change its moral structure. In his view corporations were adequate means for protecting the citizen against the power of the idea that the modern democracy was reacting against the 'individualist doctrines of the Revolution'. Some years later, he was writing about the success of this campaign that they had been witness

during the last 20 years to a singular spectacle: while our politicians reaffirm the greatness of the accomplishment of the Revolution, all the nation, consciously or unconsciously, is trying to remake and to adopt to the new conditions the institutions which the Revolution has destroyed . . . The individualism was everywhere in the legislation of the Revolution. Today, the association is everywhere in the manners, in the objectives and in the laws.[36]

Strange as the ideas of Durkheim may appear and different as he seems to be from the republican mainstream, he was nonetheless part of a critical re-examination of the republican heritage and very much concerned with the social situation in France. Placed within the discussion about the importance of intermediate bodies in modern democracy in a post-Tocquevillean tradition, his ideas about guilds and their restoration are losing any connotation of reactionary thinking. They were part of a strategy to build modern democracy on a more moral and institutional basis which could develop – as Léon Bourgeois called it – solidarity in despite of struggle and concurrence. Institutions like the guilds were not seen as antinomical to the democratic and parliamentary basis of the French state, but as a necessary complement in order to educate the leading classes about the needs of the lower ones and to instruct the lower classes in order to help them understand the logic of state action. 'The professional group might well satisfy all the conditions we have laid down,' wrote Durkheim in his work 'Le Socialisme'. 'On the one hand, it will not weigh heavily on industry, it is sufficiently close to the interests it will have to regulate not to repress them excessively. Furthermore, like every group formed of individuals, it is capable of being a moral force for its

---

[36] J. E. S. Hayward, 'Solidarist Syndicalism: Durkheim and Duguit', in P. Hamilton, ed., *Emile Durkheim: critical assessments* (London, 1990), 4 vols, vol. IV, p. 137.

members.' On the other hand, the state should delegate some rights and duties to the guilds, which 'through the rapprochement between the work of all' would ensure social stability and economic progress.[37]

In 1939, Svend Ranulf wrote an article on the 'scholarly forerunners of fascism'.

The believers in the superiority of 'Gemeinschaft' to 'Gesellschaft' in Germany and the followers of Durkheim in France . . . have – for the most part unintentionally and unconsciously – served to prepare the soil for fascism by their propagation of the view that the society in which they were living was headed for disaster because of its individualism and liberalism and that a new solidarity was badly needed.[38]

This vision of intellectual history was not only finalistic because it overstressed the relationship between criticism of liberalism and fascist movements. It also overestimated the link between research of new solidaristic ties and fascist movements.

In nineteenth-century liberal thinking, guild ideas reveal distinct strands of a critique of the market. The market stands accused of polarizing society socially, of creating a structural inequality between entrepreneurs and workers, of contributing to social conflicts, and of undermining a 'moral economy'. In this context, guilds were perceived to have the purpose not of annulling the mechanisms of the market, but rather of diminishing and moralizing their effects.

[37] Ibid., p. 142.
[38] S. Ranulf, 'Scholarly Forerunners of Fascism' (1939), in Hamilton, ed., *Assessments*, vol. I, p. 35.

# 6 Thinking green, nineteenth-century style: John Stuart Mill and John Ruskin

*Donald Winch*

Neither Mill nor Ruskin can be treated as representative Victorian figures, but they do have qualifications – some self-acquired, some imposed on them in retrospect – to act as standard bearers for two warring styles of thought, with irreversible damage to the natural environment, presumptively at least, serving as one of the significant battlefields. Whatever qualifications might be added to Mill's credentials as some kind of radical liberal, he could not possibly emerge as 'a violent Tory of the old school', Ruskin's description of his own political credo.[1] In the long aftermath of his initial attack on political economy in *Unto This Last* (1860), Ruskin did his best to position himself before the Victorian public as the humane alternative to everything for which he took Mill to stand. This included secular modernism, liberalism, utilitarianism, and acting as the chief exponent of a *soi-disant* science that Ruskin regarded as responsible for almost everything that had gone wrong in the headlong pursuit of Mammon in nineteenth-century Britain. To Ruskin – not much given to understatement – Mill was literally 'the root of nearly all immediate evil among us in England'; he was also the embodiment of a science that was 'the most cretinous, speechless, paralysing plague that has yet touched the brains of mankind'.[2]

By the time Ruskin died in 1900 he had acquired a reputation as one of the leaders of the 'romantic' protest against Victorian capitalism. In retrospect he could be viewed as an essential link in a 'romantic' tradition that led from Samuel Taylor Coleridge and Thomas Carlyle at one end to William Morris and a sequence of socialist critics at the other. The pursuit of wealth through market imperatives had created alienated forms of

[1] The opening sentence of Ruskin's autobiography, *Praeterita*, as reprinted in *The Works of John Ruskin*, ed. E. T. Cook and A. Wedderburn (London, 1902–12), 39 vols, vol. XXVII, pp. 14–15. All references to Ruskin's *Works* will be to this edition.
[2] See letter to Henry Acland, 10 February, 1877, in *Works*, XXXIV, p. 528; letter to Norton, 12 September, 1869, in *The Correspondence of John Ruskin and Charles Eliot Norton*, ed. J. L. Bradley and I. Ousby (Cambridge, 1987), p. 172; and a letter to J. Brown, August 1862, cited in *Works*, XVII, p. lxxxii.

labour and reliance upon science-based technologies that were responsible not merely for cultural and moral decay, but for the despoliation of the natural and built environment as well. Hence Ruskin's prominent role in the 'culture-and-society' tradition constructed by Raymond Williams in the mid-twentieth century, building to some extent on foundations laid by F. R. Leavis.[3] For Leavis, the problem was a quasi-Ruskinian one of rescuing 'a culture independent of any economic, technical or social system' from the pressures of industrialism and mass civilization.[4] Williams, on the other hand, while accepting the catastrophist view of the industrial revolution and of the results of capitalism more generally, rejected the elitist and reactionary features of Leavis's cultural pessimism. Repossessing (and often tendentiously repositioning) a tradition of social criticism, of which Ruskin was an example, became part of a larger ambition to sustain a holistic critique of the bourgeois (anti-collectivist) foundations of contemporary culture. Ruskin later featured in Williams's related tradition of 'socialist ecology', if only as Morris's mentor in such matters.[5] In more recent attempts to create a genealogy for 'romantic ecology', however, Ruskin's credentials are being turned, so to speak, from red to green.[6] Ruskin features as the inspiration for the founders of the National Trust, Octavia Hill and Canon Rawnsley, with protection of the Lake District from the encroachments of modern industrial and urban pressures as their first major goal.[7] Failure to mention Ruskin in this British context would be equivalent to ignoring Henry David Thoreau, Ralph Waldo Emerson and John Muir when talking about the American conservation and wilderness movement.

Mill's qualifications as a green thinker are less well known, which is why they receive most attention here. He is sometimes granted a walk-on part in the 'culture-and-society' tradition, chiefly by virtue of his essays on Bentham and Coleridge. In this respect he becomes a flawed or failed romantic, capable only of appreciating the private consolations of literature.[8] He will feature here more as the author of the *Principles of Political Economy, with Some of their Applications to Social Philosophy*, a work that

[3] R. Williams, *Culture and Society, 1780–1950* (London, 1958; Harmondsworth, 1961). The Leavis connections are spelled out in my essay on 'Mr Gradgrind and Jerusalem', in S. Collini, R. Whatmore and B. Young, eds, *Economy, Polity, and Society: British Intellectual History 1750–1950* (Cambridge, 2000), pp. 243–66.

[4] F. R. Leavis, *For Continuity* (Cambridge, 1933), p. 168.

[5] See R. Williams, 'Socialism and Ecology', in G. Gable, ed., *Resources of Hope* (London, 1989), pp. 210–24.

[6] See J. Bate, *Romantic Ecology: Wordsworth and the Environmental Tradition* (London, 1991); and M. Wheeler, ed., *Ruskin and Environment: The Storm Cloud of the Nineteenth Century* (Manchester, 1995).

[7] See the literature cited in note 22 below.

[8] The role assigned to him in Williams, *Culture and Society*, ch. 3.

became the bible for all serious students of the science from its first appearance in 1848 up to Mill's death in 1873. Those prepared to take on the rigours of Mill's exposition of the laws of production, distribution and exchange were rewarded with a fourth book on the 'influence of the progress of society on production and distribution', and a fifth on the 'influence of government' in which the exceptions to *laissez faire* were analysed. Mill's environmentalist concerns figure in Book IV alongside a chapter on 'the probable futurity of the labouring classes'. Mill provides a prominent example of how a critique of economic growth could be mounted from within a tradition normally thought to be wedded solely to an exploration of the internal logic of market-led development. The contrast with Ruskin shows some unexpected convergences, while at the same time confirming important differences between the underlying environmentalist ethic endorsed by these two spokesmen, respectively, for the 'romantic' and 'utilitarian' positions. Moreover, by adding, in a brief final section of this chapter, a third dimension to the contrast, that represented by Alfred Marshall, the leading neo-classical economist of his day, we can observe how a highly ethicized late-Victorian version of economics responded to Ruskinian charges that the science was insensitive to the kinds of problems associated with rampant forms of capitalist economic development and urbanization.

## Mill's neo-Malthusian environmentalism

Paradoxical though it might seem to those who continue to be influenced by 'culture-and-society' perspectives, Mill's environmentalism is strongly connected with that central element in 'classical' political economy which led Carlyle and others to condemn it as the 'dismal science': his acceptance of the basic Malthusian propositions concerning the relationship between population growth and the costs associated with an expansion in the supply of subsistence goods. The Malthusian theory and its partner, the law of diminishing returns in agriculture and other activities involving the use of natural resources, remained an article of faith with Mill from his earliest debates with Owenite and Tory 'sentimentalist' critics of political economy in the 1820s to his engagements with radicals and socialists in the final decades of his life. Half a century after he had been arrested for distributing birth control literature as a seventeen-year-old youth, Mill continued to believe that restraining the Malthusian devil was essential to any prospect for raising working-class living standards, or for realizing the full potential for raising wages made possible by technological and other moral improvements.

Neo-Malthusianism underlies a number of characteristic opinions that Mill entertained throughout his life. For example, he was convinced that systematic, state-supported emigration to 'new' British colonies was still necessary in the 1860s, long after the Irish famine had led to massive resort to this option in one part of the United Kingdom. Cheaper transport and better information about colonial opportunities had aided the process of voluntary emigration, but Mill held that state aid might still be needed 'to keep the communication open between hands needing work in England, and the work which needs hands elsewhere'.[9] In that sustained attack on the 'tyranny of mass opinion', his essay *On Liberty* (1859), Mill had argued that the full weight of public disapproval should be brought to bear on irresponsible parents, those who had placed the future of fellow wage-earners in jeopardy by having more children than they could support or educate properly. He was even prepared to countenance legislation 'to forbid marriage unless the parties can show that they have the means of supporting a family'.[10] Mill's support for peasant proprietorship and for some experiments in co-operative socialism, though it belongs to a later period in his development, derived strength from his belief that parental irresponsibility would be more clearly perceived and hence controlled under those arrangements. Removing the burden of large families was an integral part of his feminism too. Since he regarded sexual intercourse chiefly as an 'animal' demand made on women by their husbands, it followed that working-class wives could not be held responsible for having large families. Feminism was linked with environmentalism because Mill, departing from his usual concern in the *Subjection of Women* (1869) to deny that we knew what attributes were essential to woman's 'nature', was convinced that 'as in so many other things . . . women will be much more unwilling than men to submit to the expulsion of all beauty from common life'.[11]

Neo-Malthusianism also accounts for Mill's dubious qualifications for membership of what Ruskin was later to describe and dismiss as the 'steam-whistle party', those who celebrated industrial and scientific progress and entertained optimistic visions of the prospects held out by further technological innovation.[12] Mill's optimism was hedged around with qualifications, chief among them being those connected with population.

[9] See *Principles* in *The Collected Works of John Stuart Mill*, general editor J. M. Robson (Toronto, 1965–91), 33 vols, vol. III, pp. 963, 967. All Mill references are to this edition and will simply be designated from here on as CW, followed by volume number and page.

[10] CW, II, p. 371.

[11] Letter to Charles W. Wilkinson, 24 October 1869, in CW, XVII, p. 1659.

[12] Ruskin's phrase was originally applied to Dickens; see letter of 19 June 1870, in *Works*, XXXVII, p. 7.

Hitherto it is questionable if all the mechanical inventions yet made have lightened the day's toil of any human being. They have enabled a greater population to live the same life of drudgery and imprisonment, and an increased number of manufacturers and others to make fortunes. They have increased the comforts of the middle classes. But they have not yet begun to effect those great changes in human destiny, which it is in their nature and in their futurity to accomplish. Only when, in addition to just institutions, the increase of mankind shall be under the deliberate guidance of judicious foresight, can the conquests made from the powers of nature by the intellect and energy of scientific discoverers, become the common property of the species, and the means of improving and elevating the universal lot.[13]

On this subject one could say that the public moralist was at war with the political economist in Mill, though it would be more accurate to cite this as a case where the abstract 'science' had no authority over the 'art' of public policy and the choice of the ultimate ends of social existence. As he said of these in the *Principles*:

I confess that I am not charmed with the ideal of life held out by those who think that the normal state of human beings is that of struggling to get on; that the trampling, crushing, elbowing and treading on each other's heels, which form the existing type of social life, are the more desirable lot of human kind, or anything but the disagreeable symptoms of one of the phases of industrial progress.[14]

Worship of the 'idol' of production, that 'disposition to sacrifice every thing to accumulation' and the 'exclusive and engrossing selfishness which accompanies it', was one of Mill's earliest strictures on the mentality and culture of his fellow countrymen. He was particularly keen to make such remarks when writing to St Simonian friends who were disposed to admire British economic successes.[15] He added the 'dollar-hunting' habits of Americans later, and classified America alongside Britain as the two chief examples of the 'industrial' mentality, where this refers to the pursuit of economic gain rather than to manufacturing. Mill's Francophilia and the ascetic intellectual stance that was part of his penchant for looking to the 'intelligent classes', the non-mercantile and non-aristocratic classes, as the leaders of enlightened opinion play their part here. But the underlying Malthusian assumptions of his political economy, together with a distinctly post-Ricardian emphasis on the ways in which a capital-rich country like Britain could now afford to shift its priorities from private accumulation to public investment and redistribution, provide the economic rationale.[16]

---

[13] *Principles* in CW, III, pp. 755–6.    [14] Ibid., p. 754.

[15] See letters to Gustave D'Eichtal, 15 May and 8 October 1829, in CW, XII, pp. 31, 37.

[16] For Mill's formal withdrawal of earlier Ricardian fears about capital accumulation see *Principles*, bk IV, ch. IV.

E. A. Wrigley's writings on the classical economists and the industrial revolution provide a useful way of characterizing the techno-scepticism of the leading economists within the classical camp.[17] Wrigley does so by means of a distinction between organic or pre-industrial economies and those in which inorganic industrial processes prevail. Organic economies are those in which the ability to obtain food and raw materials from land, the fixed factor, create a bottleneck. The trajectory of growth in such societies was, in consequence, treated as asymptotic, confined within limits, rather than exponential or open ended, with control over nuptiality being required to ensure the maintenance of rising living standards. By contrast, inorganic or industrial economies are those that escape the bottleneck by discovering and applying technologies that enable inorganic materials and processes to act as substitutes for those based on natural resources. The importance Mill attached to the law of diminishing returns, despite recognizing the ways in which its operation had been suspended, place him among those who thought of the typical growth path in 'old' countries as asymptotic.

Consciously or unconsciously, steam-whistlers took the opposite view. There is a well-known statement by Thomas Babington Macaulay that helps to bring the difference of opinion into closer focus. In responding to Robert Southey's gloomy diagnosis of the state of British society in 1830, Macaulay had asserted that he was 'unable to find any satisfactory record of any great nation, past or present, in which the working classes have been in a more comfortable situation than in England during the last thirty years'. He prophesied that a century hence the English would have a population of 50 million, 'better fed, clad, and lodged than the English of our time', with cultivation 'rich as that of a flower-garden' being 'carried up to the very tops of Ben Nevis and Helvellyn'.[18] These were the very places – especially Helvellyn, a Lakeland fell standing over Thirlmere, the first (and last) of the lakes to be taken over by Manchester to supply its water needs – that acquired emblematic significance to nineteenth-century environmentalists.

Neo-Malthusianism has played a role in modern environmentalist thinking, with the pressures exerted on non-renewable energy resources by population growth taking centre stage in any account of the limits to growth.[19] Mill must have been one of the earliest political economists

[17] E. A. Wrigley, *Continuity, Chance and Change; The Character of the Industrial Revolution in England* (Cambridge, 1988), and *People, Cities, and Wealth* (Oxford, 1989).

[18] See his review of Southey's *Colloquies* in *Lord Macaulay's Essays* (London, 1900), p. 120.

[19] The *locus classicus* of this position can be found in D. H. Meadows et al., *The Limits of Growth: A Report for the Club of Rome's Project on the Predicament of Mankind* (New York, 1972).

to stress environmental limits when enthusing about the possibilities of embracing a stationary state in which all future improvements in technology could be redirected towards redistribution and the quality of life rather than an increase in the quantities associated with aggregate growth. Mill's stationary state was to be a virtuous version of an idea that had been used by his mentors as a bogeyman to support those measures, such as free trade and the reduction of public expenditure, that would maintain capital accumulation and widen, if not remove, the organic bottleneck to further capital accumulation and growth. One lengthy quotation from Mill's defence of a zero-growth society conveys the substance of his environmentalist concerns.

There is room in the world, no doubt, and even in old countries for a great increase of population, supposing the arts of life to go on improving, and capital to increase. But even if innocuous, I confess I see little reason for desiring it. The density of population necessary to enable mankind to obtain, in the greatest degree, all the advantages both of co-operation and of social intercourse, has, in all the most populous countries, been attained. A population may be too crowded, though all be amply supplied with food and raiment. It is not good for man to be kept perforce at all times in the presence of his species. A world from which solitude is extirpated, is a very poor ideal. Solitude, in the sense of being often alone, is essential to any depth of meditation or of character; and solitude in the presence of natural beauty and grandeur, is the cradle of thoughts and aspirations which are not only good for the individual, but which society could ill do without. Nor is there much satisfaction in contemplating the world with nothing left to the spontaneous activity of nature; with every rood of land brought into cultivation, which is capable of growing food for human beings; every flowery waste or natural pasture ploughed up, all quadrupeds or birds which are not domesticated for man's use exterminated as his rivals for food, every hedgerow or superfluous tree rooted out, and scarcely a place left where a wild shrub or flower could grow without being eradicated as a weed in the name of improved agriculture. If the earth must lose that great portion of its pleasantness which it owes to things that the unlimited increase of wealth and population would extirpate from it, for the mere purpose of enabling it to support a larger, but not a better or a happier population, I sincerely hope, for the sake of posterity that they will be content to be stationary, long before necessity compels it.[20]

## Romantic environmentalism

The final remark about 'necessity' suggests a grim Malthusian asymptote, but the rest of the passage has little or no connection with what one would normally associate with an economic analysis of optimal population size – judged, as Mill was also prepared to judge it, mainly in terms of trends

[20] *Principles* in CW, III, p. 756.

in real wages. It is also worth bearing in mind that when Mill first wrote this passage, the population of England, Scotland and Wales – though it had increased faster than ever before (or since) during the first decades of the nineteenth century – was still no more than 18 million. The language is clearly a 'romantic' one, and the emphasis on the 'spontaneous activity of nature' and of 'solitude in the presence of natural beauty and grandeur' mark it as a Wordsworthian evaluation of the benefits of communing with nature. Mill was bringing neo-Malthusianism to bear on a Wordsworthian insight in a manner that lies outside the confines of the 'culture-and-society' tradition and goes well beyond the cultivation of personal feelings. Once more, Macaulay provides the contrasting steam-whistler view: he could find little to praise in Wordsworth's posthumously published *Prelude*; it was merely a repetition of the 'old raptures about mountain scenery and cataracts; the old flimsy philosophy about the effect of scenery on the mind; the old crazy, mystical metaphysics'.[21] Mill was prepared to share the raptures while giving, as we shall see, the mystical metaphysics a more solid basis of his own construction – one that consorted better with utilitarian ethics, his interest in the natural and moral sciences, and his hopes for a secular religion of humanity.

At this juncture then we encounter a dimension of Mill's concern for the environment that was shared by many Victorian admirers of Wordsworth's nature poetry, with its evocation of the beauty and sublimity of Lakeland scenery. Fellow-admirers, most of whom would probably have disdained any connection with political economy, included Ruskin and those like-minded members of the Wordsworth Society who were to take part in campaigns against the extension of railways into the Lake District and the take-over by Manchester of Thirlmere, thereby laying the foundations for the movement that eventually led to the creation of the National Trust.[22] But it is important to note that whatever part Wordsworth's poetry played in Mill's personal history, the environmental interests predate its influence. Wordsworth gave poetic form to what Mill described as 'one of the strongest of my pleasurable susceptibilities – the love of rural objects and natural scenery', especially that to be found

---

[21] See G. O. Trevelyan, ed., *Life and Letters of Lord Macaulay* (London, 1901), p. 614.

[22] See J. D. Marshall and J. K. Walton, *The Lake Counties from 1830 to the Mid-Twentieth Century: A Study in Regional Change* (Manchester, 1981), ch. 9; G. Murphy, *Founders of the National Trust*, (London, 1987); J. Gaze, *Figures in a Landscape: A History of the National Trust* (London, 1988). On the practical conservationist activities of Wordsworthians see the final chapter in S. Gill, *Wordsworth and the Victorians* (Oxford, 1998). For Ruskin's part in this see Wheeler, ed., *Ruskin and Environment*, especially the essays by J. K. Walton and T. Gifford. For an excellent recent study of Victorian environmentalism see James Winter, *Secure from Rash Assault: Sustaining the Victorian Environment*, (Berkeley, 1999).

among mountains. Mill acquired these tastes as a fourteen-year-old while living in France, where he learned the pleasures of Pyrenean scenery and was introduced to his life-long passion for botany. The long botanizing walks Mill undertook, partly as a cure for tuberculosis, the disease he thought would kill him in the 1850s, enabled him to become an amateur expert on the flora of Britain and several other European countries.[23] Hence too Mill's indignation when faced with Auguste Comte's 'overweening presumption' in proposing that all animals and plants that could not be justified for existing human use should be eliminated.

As if any one could presume to assert that the smallest weed may not, as knowledge advances, be found to have some property serviceable to man. When we consider that the united power of the whole human race cannot reproduce a species once eradicated – that is what is once done, in the extirpation of races, can never be repaired; one can only be thankful that amidst all which the past rulers of mankind have to answer for, they have never come to the measure of the great regenerator of Humanity; mankind have not yet been under the rule of one who assumes that he knows all there is to be known, and that when he has put himself at the head of humanity, the book of human knowledge may be closed.[24]

Mill's acknowledgement of the therapeutic role played by Wordsworth's poetry in lifting him from depression in 1827–8, by impressing on him the enduring rewards attached to the active pursuit of the 'culture of the feelings', is amply documented in his *Autobiography*.[25] The pilgrimage he made in 1831 to meet Wordsworth amid his native mountains and lakes, and experience their picturesque qualities for himself, followed naturally. The journey was undertaken with vivid recollections of Wordsworth's earlier and shorter poems in mind, and with Wordsworth's *Description of the Scenery of the Lakes in the North of England* in hand.[26] The visit had both passing and permanent significance to Mill's development. One surprising permanent element should be mentioned immediately: Mill's willingness to cite Wordsworth as an authority on land tenure in his *Principles*. The brief paean to the 'perfect Republic of Shepherds and Agriculturists' in the *Description* appears at the beginning of Mill's lengthy discussion

---

[23] For the records of Mill's botanical interests see CW, XXXI. As his friend, Alexander Bain, pointed out: 'Plant hunting was to him what sports are to other persons'; see *John Stuart Mill: A Criticism* (London, 1882), p. 152.

[24] *Auguste Comte and Positivism* in *CW*, X, pp. 357–8.

[25] *Autobiography* in *CW*, I, pp. 148–53.

[26] For the journal Mill kept while in the Lake District see CW, XXVII. The best accounts of the episode can be found in the introduction to this volume and Anna J. Mill, 'John Stuart Mill's Visit to Wordsworth, 1831', *Modern Language Review* 44 (1949), pp. 341–50. The same author was also the first to examine the aesthetic that accompanied Mill's interest in Wordsworth; see 'John Stuart Mill and the Picturesque', *Victorian Studies* 14 (1970), pp. 151–63.

of the benefits of peasant proprietorship.[27] The Lakeland 'statesmen' showed what could have been achieved elsewhere if the yeoman ideal had not given way to English prejudices in favour of *grande culture* as the best means of feeding her rising population. If anything, Mill exceeds Wordsworth in his enthusiasm on this subject. Whereas Wordsworth was elegiacally describing the situation as it existed sixty years before, Mill takes it as a fair representation of the existing state of affairs: 'No other agricultural population in England could have furnished the originals of Wordsworth's peasantry.' The memory of his visit in 1831, when he had recorded that 'no penury' was visible among the peasantry, remained with him when marshalling evidence in favour of peasant proprietorship on a pan-European scale in the 1840s.

Of more temporary biographical significance is the fact that the visit enabled Mill to renew his acquaintance with Wordsworth and Southey at a time when his interest in their 'speculative Toryism' was at its height. He had already shown interest in the work of the third member of the Lakeland trio of poets, Coleridge, as a result of his friendship with John Sterling and F. D. Maurice. The glowing account of his meeting with Wordsworth that he gave to Sterling sealed their friendship and marked a break in his relations with some philosophic radicals, notably John Arthur Roebuck, against whom Mill championed the claims of Wordsworth as a poet against those of Byron.[28] Within a few years Mill had reflected sufficiently on his reactions to romantic poetry to formulate his own aesthetic theory, connecting it with his long-established interests in associationist psychology, while abandoning the positions on the beautiful and the sublime that he had learned from his father's *Analysis of the Phenomena of the Human Mind*. The encounter with Wordsworth's poetry, and his subsequent reading of Wordsworth's prose writings on aesthetics, were crucial in forming his position.[29]

The recollection of the entire episode given in the *Autobiography*, first drafted in 1854, is cooler. It does not alter the main lineaments of the account given to Sterling, but by then Mill was in a position to put the 'romantic' influence into the broader context of his mature opinions. Thus whereas the letter to Sterling minimizes the differences between himself and a 'philosophic Tory' such as Wordsworth ('our principles

---

[27] *Principles* in CW, II, pp. 252–3.

[28] See letter to Sterling, 20 October 1831, in CW, XII, pp. 74–88.

[29] See the essays on poetry in CW, I, and J. M. Robson, 'J. S. Mill's Theory of Poetry', *University of Toronto Quarterly* 29/4 (1960), pp. 420–38. In passing, too, it should be noted that Ruskin's juxtaposition of Wordsworth's poetry alongside Turner's landscapes in *Modern Painters* also played a part in Mill's formulation of his views on beauty, though not in a way that Ruskin would have approved; see Mill's commentary on the *Analysis* in CW, XXXI, pp. 224–6.

would be the same, and we should be like two travellers pursuing the same course on the opposite banks of a river'), the *Autobiography* inserts a blunt hint that amid the grand imagery to be found in *The Ode: Intimations of Immortality* there is also 'bad philosophy'.[30] We get a more explicit statement of this in the early draft. Speaking of the Coleridgeans, Mill says: 'But if I agreed with them much more than with Bentham on poetry and general culture, I was as much opposed to them as ever on religion, political philosophy, ethics and metaphysics.'[31] This is a fairly comprehensive list, suggesting that the river had come to seem a good deal wider during the intervening years.

### A non-Christian environmentalist ethic

Although the 'romantic' influence contributed an important aesthetic dimension to Mill's thinking, it came as a supplementary revelation to the central tenets of his utilitarian upbringing. This conclusion is of some importance to an understanding of the environmentalist ethic that Mill drew from his encounter with the Lake poets because it differentiates the style if not the content of his position from that of Ruskin as well as Wordsworth. The key terms in Mill's list of differences are ethics and religion. It would be impossible to envisage a Wordsworthian or Ruskinian environmentalist ethic that did not include a profound belief in a Christian deity. Indeed, charges that his poetry was guilty of pantheism led Wordsworth to modify his earlier poems to ensure that a more orthodox Anglican message could not be missed.[32] The case of Ruskin is more complex, chiefly due to his 'un-conversion' in 1858. But if Ruskin severed his sectarian connections with Evangelicalism then, requiring modification to his position as an art critic and as an impassioned defender of the natural environment, he certainly cannot be described as having parted company with transcendentalism. The bible on which he had been reared became more important as a major source, among others of classical provenance, of mythical symbolism.

We have no direct evidence of Wordsworth's reaction to his meetings with his youthful utilitarian admirer. Although Mill had not yet made his reputation as a political economist, his connections with Benthamism would have been well known to Wordsworth. A few weeks before Mill arrived in the Lake District, Wordsworth had been condemning the influence of Malthus on current Poor Law debates, a position he was to expound more fully in a postscript to the 1835 edition of his poems,

---

[30] See CW, I, p. 153.    [31] Ibid., p. 162.
[32] S. Gill, *William Wordsworth: A Life* (Oxford, 1989), pp. 344, 398–9, 416–19.

where the malign connection between political economy and the Poor Law Amendment Act was noted, and the virtues of 'a christian government standing *in loco parentis* towards all its subjects' extolled.[33] Mill was to deliver a withering judgement on the inadequacies of the 'theory of dependence' in his *Principles*.[34] It needed no modification to serve as an answer to Ruskin's paternalist version of the science of political economy first published a decade later, which may be one reason why Mill never bothered to answer any of Ruskin's attacks upon political economy or himself.

Opposition to Malthusianism in any form was an enduring feature of the Lake poets' views on politics and morals.[35] Malthus's depiction of the laws of nature as requiring constant exertion to avoid misery and vice proved especially challenging to Wordsworth's more benevolent view of Nature's healing qualities.[36] Like Ruskin later, and Coleridge and Southey before him, Wordsworth associated much that he disliked about the modern world with utilitarianism and political economy. When opposing the extension of the railway into the heart of the Lake District in 1844, for example, he employed the conventional charge that 'Utilitarianism' served 'as a mask for cupidity and gambling speculations' – a charge that was to become central to Ruskin's denunciations of capitalism. He also expressed the hope that since man did not live by bread alone, political economy would not be allowed to decide whether the Lake District would be violated by working-class day-trippers from Manchester in search of cheap amusements.[37]

Mill's support for the Commons Preservation Society that was formed in 1865, with Henry Fawcett, his disciple in all economic matters, as a leading light, may suggest a different set of priorities from those espoused by Wordsworth. Preserving the rights of all people to enjoy common or waste land in and around London from the economic activities of urban landowners and developers brought Mill's environmentalist concerns and anti-landlord antagonisms together. But Wordsworth too hoped that Manchester's operatives could learn to appreciate natural beauty closer

---

[33] See letter to Lady Beaumont, 8 July 1831, in *The Letters of William and Dorothy Wordsworth*, ed. A. G. Hill (Oxford, 1978–88), 8 vols, vol. V, pp. 405–6; and *The Prose Works of William Wordsworth*, ed. W. J. B. Owen and J. W. Smythe (Oxford, 1974), 3 vols, vol. III, pp. 240–8.

[34] In the famous chapter 'On the Probable Futurity of the Labouring Classes', CW, III, pp. 758–98.

[35] See my *Riches and Poverty: An Intellectual History of Political Economy in Britain, 1750–1834* (Cambridge, 1996), especially ch. 11 and 12.

[36] For a detailed examination of the ambiguities of Wordsworth's relationship with Malthus see the excellent study by Philip Connell, *Romanticism, Economics and the Question of 'Culture'* (Oxford, 2001), ch. 1.

[37] See *The Prose Works*, vol. III, p. 352.

to home, in their 'neighbouring fields'. As an economist, Mill was always in favour of strict parliamentary regulation of the monopoly powers of the railway companies. This included the choice of routes, with what would now be known as their environmental impact on sites of natural beauty and botanical interest forming one of the criteria.[38]

Mill followed his father's advice in concealing his lack of orthodox religious belief in his writings. But this did not apply to his dealings with friends, even temporary ones. Southey had no hesitation in branding Mill an 'atheist' after their meeting in the Lake District, claiming that Mill had confessed to this. His reported reaction to this revelation is very much what one might expect of an ultra-Tory:

> I can live in charity with all men, but I should seem to act as absurdly in taking the opinion of any person who is dogmatically a disbeliever in God and in a future state of reward and punishment, upon any of the vital interests of society, as if I were to take that of a man born blind upon optics. The foundation of my system of opinion is Christian faith.[39]

As far as the appreciation of natural beauty is concerned, Mill provides standing (or better still, walking) disproof of Ruskin's sweeping generalization that 'supposing all circumstances otherwise the same with respect to two individuals, the one who loves nature most will be *always* found to have more *faith* in God than the other'.[40]

The Christian legacy to environmental ethics is a divided one. Biblical injunctions legitimating the dominion of humankind over the animal kingdom jostle with others stressing wise stewardship of what Ruskin was to call 'the great entail'.[41] But the latter interpretation gained force during the nineteenth century, not least through the example and efforts of Wordsworth and Ruskin. If we leave the inherited and retrospectively applied ideological categories aside, it should also be possible to add the names of Mill and Fawcett to this list, despite their supposed membership of that enlarged category labelled representatives of *laissez-faire* liberalism or bourgeois individualism.[42] In their case too, as their activities as

---

[38] For example, Mill opposed one of the London-to-Brighton routes that would have passed through the vale of Norbury, a district known to him through residence and botanizing trips in the North Downs; see CW, V, p. 328.

[39] Letter cited in A. J. Mill, 'J. S. Mill's Visit to Wordsworth', p. 344n.

[40] *Works*, XVII, p. 32

[41] 'God has lent us the earth for our life; it is a great entail. It belongs as much to those who come after us, and those whose names are already written in the book of creation as to us; and we have no right by anything that we do or neglect, to involve them in unnecessary penalties, or deprive them of benefits which it was in our power to bequeath.' *Works* VIII, p. 233.

[42] This is still the role assigned to Mill in a recent work that represents one of the latest attempts to extend the culture-and-society tradition; see D. A. Kaiser, *Romanticism, Aesthetics, and Nationalism* (Cambridge, 1999), pp. 14, 26, 72–3, 76–81, 90, 112.

members of the Commons Preservation Society reveal, far from seeking to defend the separation of private and public spheres, they made good use of their standing as Members of Parliament to make the private enjoyment of nature a public good.[43] Epping Forest, Wimbledon Common, and the Banstead Downs may not have quite the same sublime connotations as the Lake District, but their preservation as public spaces was as much of a public achievement as many of those associated with the National Trust.

As a secular utilitarian who was opposed to claims of knowledge based on intuition, untested by reference to inductive proof, Mill's pre-Darwinian environmentalism shunned providentialist interpretations of Nature, leaving his environmental ethic deprived of any idea of divine sanction. Being thoroughly acquainted with the conventional objections to utilitarianism as a narrow selfish ethic, Mill was keen to demonstrate that his version of the doctrine provided equivalent, usually superior, answers to questions that involved our concern for others, including past and future generations. One way in which he accomplished this can be found in his essay on *Utilitarianism* (1861), in which Christ's teachings of love are portrayed as 'the ideal perfection of utilitarian morality' freed from the 'selfish' immoral doctrines of reward and punishment that were part of the teachings of the corrupted Pauline Church.[44]

This accounts too for the strenuous Manichean demands made on individual character by Mill's altruistic religion of humanity.[45] The full extent of Mill's unorthodoxy was not disclosed until he published *Auguste Comte on Positivism* (1865) and his step-daughter released the *Three Essays on Religion* (1874) after his death. Readers of the former would have noticed that Mill commended Comte's idea that 'a religion may exist without belief in a God, and that a religion without a God may be, even to Christians, an instructive and profitable object of contemplation'. The concept of a Grand Etre was capable of supporting reverence for past and future generations, and even, in contrast to Comte's opinions on useless plants, of endorsing a duty of care for those 'animal races which enter into real society with man'. Mill's Benthamite training would have extended this category to include all animals capable of suffering pain, whether or not they had a connection with man.[46] But Mill conceded that '[t]he

[43] Fawcett's interest in this question is documented fully in Leslie Stephen's *Life of Henry Fawcett* (London, 1885), ch. 7.

[44] CW, X, p. 218.

[45] Stefan Collini gives the best account of the 'culture of altruism' and Mill's role as public moralist in his *Public Moralists; Political Thought and Intellectual Life in Britain, 1850–1930* (Oxford, 1991).

[46] For Bentham's defence of animal rights see his *Introduction to the Principles of Morals and Legislation*, ed. J. H. Burns and H. L. A. Hart (London, 1970), ch. XVII, pp. 282–3n.

strong sense [Comte] always shows of the worth of the inferior animals, and of the duties of mankind towards them, is one of the very finest traits of his character'.[47]

The reception given to *Three Essays on Religion* by Christians and secular admirers alike proves how wise Mill was not to court publicity for his views during his lifetime.[48] Admirers bitterly regretted the unnecessary, even damaging, concessions to Christianity in the last-written of the essays, that on theism. Christians condemned the entire set, though there was little that was truly novel in any of the essays. Mill does not go quite as far as David Hume in undermining the argument from design, even though the final essay was written with the benefit of having read Darwin's *Origin of the Species*, a work that Mill was prepared to accept as a powerful hypothesis. Nevertheless, the idea that following Nature has any moral as opposed to prudential force receives some severe handling from the perspective of inductive science; and there could be a sideswipe at Ruskinians in Mill's remark that '[t]hose in whom awe produces admiration may be aesthetically developed, but they are morally uncultivated'.[49] Mill matches other claims for a divinely sanctioned morality when he rejects the idea that non-religious views of morality must result in short-sighted forms of Epicureanism.

[T]he supposition, that human beings in general are not capable of feeling deep and even the deepest interest in things which they will never live to see, is a view of human nature as false as it is abject. Let it be remembered that if individual life is short, the life of the human species is not short; its indefinite duration is practically equivalent to endlessness; and being combined with indefinite capability of improvement, it offers to the imagination and sympathies a large enough object to satisfy any reasonable demand for grandeur of aspiration. If such an object appears small to a mind accustomed to dream of infinite and eternal beatitudes, it will expand into far other dimensions when those baseless fancies shall have receded into the past.[50]

## Ruskin's environmentalism

Ruskin's environmentalist credentials owe a good deal to Wordsworth for reasons that are not dissimilar to Mill's debt to the same source. The equivalent to Mill's Pyrenean walks was Ruskin's infant memory of being

[47] See CW, X, pp. 332–4.
[48] See K. W. Britton, 'John Stuart Mill on Christianity', in J. M. Robson and M. Laine, eds, *James and John Stuart Mill: Papers of the Centenary Conference* (Toronto, 1976), pp. 20–34; and J. Hamburger, 'Religion and *On Liberty*', in M. Laine, ed., *A Cultivated Mind: Essays on J. S. Mill presented to John M. Robson* (Toronto, 1991), pp. 139–81.
[49] CW, X, p. 384.      [50] Ibid., p. 420.

shown Friar's Crag on Derwentwater in the Lake District, the district to which he retired during the final period of his increasingly troubled life. One could even trace parallels between Mill's botanical interests and those of Ruskin in mineralogy and geology, with the hammering of the geologists playing its part in chipping away at the Evangelical foundations of Ruskin's religion while providing the time-scale essential for Darwin's theory of natural selection to show its paces. But if attention is confined to rhetoric alone Ruskin owes nothing to political economy apart from deep antagonism, a desire to invert the entire logic of the enterprise as he chose to interpret it.

Beneath the rhetoric, however, there are good grounds for thinking that Ruskin borrowed more from Mill than he was prepared to acknowledge once he had resolved, in the 1860s, 'to make it the central work of my life to write an exhaustive treatise on Political Economy'.[51] Although this resolution was unfulfilled, the final decades of his writing life were certainly devoted to the elaboration of the implications of his motto: 'There is no Wealth but Life'.[52] Ruskin's marginal notes on his copy of Mill's *Principles* made in 1849 or thereabouts were mostly commendatory, and it would not be difficult to cull from the *Principles* a number of opinions that in substance if not style he shared with Mill. The most obvious have been cited above: Mill's dislike of the prospect of a world permanently devoted to competitive striving; the belief that improvements in machinery had so far increased the gap between rich and poor without relieving the burden of physical labour; and the endorsement of a zero-growth society in which the quality of life would take precedence over the cruder, though as yet still essential, quantitative measures of improvement. When he returned to the *Principles* for ammunition to attack the 'commercial' science in *Unto This Last*, Ruskin grudgingly acknowledged that Mill differed 'from the common writing of political economists in admitting some value in the aspect of nature, and expressing regret at the probability of the destruction of natural scenery'. For polemical purposes, however, on this occasion at least, Ruskin treated such regrets flippantly as 'sentimental' anxieties. 'England may, if it so chooses, become one manufacturing town', but the need for food would ensure that in the world at large there would always be places devoted to peaceful and joyous agrarian pursuits.[53] On other occasions he supported *petite* as opposed to *grande culture*, peasant proprietorship, and the payment of compensation for tenants' improvements – the less controversial aspects of Mill's land tenure reform programme. Mill's concern for the preservation of commons was another shared interest, though it earned him no praise from Ruskin, possibly because

[51] *Munera Pulveris* in *Works*, XVII, p. 143.    [52] Ibid., p. 110.    [53] *Works*, XVII, p. 143.

Mill and Fawcett gave it the kind of 'liberal' or radical turn he came to dislike. It may also be significant that unlike his 'romantic' predecessors Ruskin did not attack Malthus. While he found nothing so 'melancholy as the speculations of political economists on the population question', he accepted the Malthusian conclusion and statement of the problem of establishing 'how many human beings ought to be maintained on a given space of habitable land'.[54] No mention of anything so coarse as birth control soils Ruskin's pages, and there is no sign of any grasp of the law of diminishing returns. Ruskin's rhetoric moves between arcadia and apocalypse: the idea of asymptotes is absent.

Markets, for Ruskin, could never generate anything more than a set of exchange values that reflected the degraded tastes of existing consumers and the corrupt habits of producers who sought to cultivate and profit from those tastes. As in the case of his practice as an art critic, pronouncing on the intrinsic worth of paintings and architectural styles, Ruskin's *forte* lay not in analysing exchange values but in making pronouncements on 'vital' values, where the judgement was a matter of absolute rightness or wrongness in the Platonic sense. Any morally acceptable outcome of economic decisions would require a complete transformation in the mentalities of economic agents, supplemented by an idealized paternal state performing extensive duties in the field of what became known as social welfare. The state would partly deal with the casualties of the existing system as well as those incurred during the process of transition away from a market economy.

But what was the destination of the process? Proleptic readings of this aspect of Ruskin's political economy speak of the modern cradle-to-grave welfare state and suggest parallels with 'ethical investment' policies and consumer boycotts of goods produced under unfriendly environmental or social conditions.[55] A more historical interpretation would treat it as one of the lessons Ruskin derived from his reading of Xenophon's *Oeconomicus*, where the fortunes of master, mistress and servant are linked together within a self-sufficient household or estate that exists outside any market framework, and where the economic problems of deciding what to produce and how it should be consumed are fused by being determined by a single authority, the *pater* or *mater familias*. Although Ruskin was articulating this position at the same time that the marginal revolution was in

---

[54] *Unto This Last* in *Works*, XVII, p. 105.

[55] For a critical examination of Ruskin's credentials as inspiration for the welfare state see J. Harris, 'Ruskin and Social Reform', in D. Birch, ed., *Ruskin and the Dawn of the Modern* (Oxford, 1999), pp. 7–55. Modern environmentalists are divided between those who espouse green consumerism and those who believe that reduced levels of consumption should be the chief goal. See J. Elkinton and J. Hailes, *The Green Consumer Guide* (London, 1988) and S. Irvine, *Beyond Green Consumerism* (London, 1989).

train, he showed no interest in the writings of neo-classical economists, with their heightened awareness of the psychology of consumption. In any event, the neo-classical economists' problem stood at the opposite pole from the one occupied by Ruskin. It was concerned with the collective consequences of myriads of households making decisions on the basis of the opportunities offered in the markets for goods and labour – a world subject to continual changes in tastes and technology, but with no master intelligence to guide its fortunes.

One could describe Ruskin's vision as utopian or *post*-economic, though that risks confusion with Mill's equally idealistic vision of a zero-growth society that might be encouraged to evolve, through improved education and reformed institutions, beyond the present 'phase of industrial society'. Mill's stationary state was one in which both the population and its stock of accumulated capital were in a continuous state of dynamic equilibrium, with both elements being subject to improvement. While there would be no net additions to the capital stock, renewal of the existing stock would embody higher forms of technology designed to increase leisure and improve the quality of life. Ruskin's Xenophonic household, like other arcadian visions, presumes the capacity to achieve permanent stasis. The human agents may develop, but their way of life, their technology in the broadest sense, remains unchanged and hence incapable of provoking disturbance. As evidence of this it is possible to cite one of the policies that Ruskin shared with orthodox economists: he claimed to be 'an utterly fearless and unscrupulous free-trader' on the grounds that free trade would put an end to competition between nations.[56] The only way in which this could occur would be if the competition to establish superior advantage coalesced into a situation in which any acquired or natural comparative advantages remained unchanged. It makes the ideal Ruskinian economy one in which full employment and abundance for all are attained according to the existing state of technology and via a definitive redistribution of tasks, tastes and, to a lesser extent, incomes.[57]

Another major difference over socialism exists. Ruskin differentiated his proposals for social reform from all contemporary forms of redistributive socialism, believing equality to be an impossible goal. Mill was not enamoured of forms of state socialism, but he attached high priority to equality, hoping to see an end to the existing relationship between capital and labour and the abolition of dependent forms of wage-earning. As he said in his *Autobiography*, '[t]he social problem of the future' would

---

[56] *Works*, XVII, p. 72.
[57] For an extended interpretation of Ruskin as a theorist of stasis see J. C. Sherburne, *John Ruskin or the Ambiguities of Abundance* (Cambridge, MA, 1972).

be 'how to unite the greatest individual liberty of action, with a common ownership in the raw material of the globe, and an equal participation of all in the benefits of combined labour'.[58]

## Economic man, market failure and welfare economics

Ruskin's misunderstandings of Mill are legion, though often based on verbal quibbles.[59] One of these, however, his attack on Mill's 'economic man' assumption, provides a useful way of underlining something that remained essential to the economists' – classical and neo-classical – perspective on the deficiencies or limits of market rules and criteria. It also gives access to one of the ways in which Marshall sought to deal with this line of criticism in his welfare economics, that new branch of neo-classical economics that was codified by his pupil and successor in the Cambridge Chair, Arthur Cecil Pigou.[60]

'There is no Wealth but Life' is based on a version of the ethic of the Sermon on the Mount concerning our duties of love. Mill, as we have seen, had already appropriated this as a perfect statement of the utilitarian ethic. Ruskin, on the other hand, believed that it contrasted with the self-interest assumptions of orthodox political economy in being purged of covetousness. Within the Evangelical tradition in which he had been raised there were many examples of providentialist accounts of the social order that treated self-interest in the normal enlarged sense as essential to the Divine plan.[61] By taking self-interestedness to mean only a narrow and inherently dishonest form of selfishness that often involved the naked use of superior bargaining power, Ruskin was exploiting a rhetorical opportunity rather than engaging with this tradition.

But what lent operational (i.e. non-rhetorical) significance to Ruskin's covetous interpretation – in principle at least – are his observations on the ways in which wealth could be purchased at the expense of 'illth', goods being counterbalanced by bads, those forms of production and consumption that were at the expense of life. Although his normal practice is absolutist, on such matters Ruskin resorts to an implicit language of quantity and degree when speaking of additions and subtractions, the pluses and minuses in the calculation. Followed further, this track leads from his

---

[58] CW, I, p. 239.

[59] For a blow-by-blow analysis of this see J. T. Fain, *Ruskin and the Economists* (Nashville, 1956).

[60] See Pigou's *The Economics of Welfare* (London, 1920), originally published as *Wealth and Welfare* (London, 1912).

[61] The most extensive examination of Evangelical thinking can be found in B. Hilton's *The Age of Atonement; The Influence of Evangelicalism on Social and Economic Thought, 1785–1865* (Oxford, 1988), though Ruskin does not feature in this account.

usual either/or treatment of moral absolutes into one that economists find more congenial, the world of more or less, a world in which optimal solutions that minimize sacrifice or maximize welfare subject to constraints are sought. Ruskin's attitude to such balancing acts would appear to have been hostile: in jurisprudential terms, he treated them as part of the inferior realm of equity rather than justice. Nevertheless, any counter-positioning of wealth against illth in this world, as opposed to a planned utopia in which no conflict between priorities is permitted to occur, implies the ability on somebody's part to perform such balancing acts. The marginal revolution is relevant here because it provided a means of making the concept of maxima and minima behind the idea of an optimal solution more explicit and precise than it had been earlier. It also enabled distinctions to be made between marginal social costs and benefits and their private equivalents, thereby giving the concept of positive and negative externalities more precise meaning than it had in classical treatments of social costs, including environmental damage and the effects of monopoly power.

Ruskin showed no interest in these developments, but since we know that he had read Adam Smith it is tempting to believe that his views on what became known as 'alienated labour' derived from a buried memory of Smith's account of the grave human costs associated with the division of labour in the *Wealth of Nations*.[62] It could not have been borrowed from Ruskin's favourite sources at this time, from Plato, Xenophon, Horace and Cicero, and the views of Marx on the subject were not known to him. Mill too, as we have seen, was particularly keen to draw attention to the human and environmental costs of economic growth – costs that were not registered or regulated by market mechanisms. Exposing the social and economic costs of monopoly was one of the original motives behind cultivating political economy. It is the leitmotif of central parts of the *Wealth of Nations*, and one of Mill's didactic roles when speaking about co-operative experiments was to point out to socialists that the opposite of competition was not co-operation but monopoly.[63] Orthodox economics, from Smith to Marshall, has always stressed the view that the interests of unorganized consumers should take precedence over the organized interests of producers, especially those that profess to be trading in the public interest. Where lack of consumer power or consumer ignorance

[62] The classic statement of the problem can be found in A. Smith, *An Inquiry into the Nature and Causes of the Wealth of Nations*, bk V, ch. 1; see the Glasgow edition of *The Works and Correspondence of Adam Smith*, ed. E. C. Mossner and I. S. Ross, 2nd edn (Oxford, Clarendon Press, 1987), V.i.f. 50–61.

[63] *Principles* in CW, III, pp. 794–6.

prevails, alternative forms of public regulation or provision have to be explored.

Marshall's welfare economics was designed to provide a way of exploring such questions. An important feature of his self-appointed mission was to overcome the conflict between ethics and economics, or rather, perhaps, construct a via media between them.[64] He repudiated the 'hedonic' utilitarian emphasis imparted by the Jevonian version of the science, partly by the simple expedient of replacing Mill's economic man with 'man in the ordinary business of life'. The shift was intended as another way of blurring the distinction between selfish and self-interested behaviour, where the latter could be applied to what Marshall usually called 'noble' ends. It is a sign of Marshall's sensitivity to all currents of opinion during the third quarter of the century that he denied that in the process of getting and spending there was any point in distinguishing between what was selfish and what was altruistic. As in all such matters, he argued, whether we think of the continuous functions of calculus or the continuities of Darwinian evolution, there was an unbroken spectrum between self-regarding and social concerns.

In saying this, however, Marshall was not hiding behind a neutral professional stance: he could be as disdainful as Ruskin in his condemnation of consumption habits that did not conform with social function.[65] Nor was Marshall afraid to employ a term that was earlier more closely associated with the 'feudal' position, as becomes obvious from the title he gave to an important lecture in 1907, 'Social Possibilities of Economic Chivalry'. Indeed, this represented Marshall's version of Ruskin's programme for a moral revitalization of the behaviour of the 'captains of industry', a phrase taken from Carlyle. They were enjoined to take 'a delight in doing noble and difficult things because they are noble and difficult'.[66] It also has to be pointed out, however, that for a post-Darwinian thinker such as Marshall, hopes were fortified by the idea that the path towards this goal had already been smoothed by those evolutionary processes associated with competitive modern forms of technological innovation.

Marshall had met Ruskin in Oxford during the latter's tenure of the Slade Chair, and it may be significant that, like Mill before him, he made

---

[64] Much of what follows is covered in greater detail in the essay on Marshall written by Stefan Collini and myself in S. Collini, D. Winch and J. Burrow, *That Noble Science of Politics* (Cambridge, 1983), pp. 311–37.

[65] A. Marshall, *Principles of Economics*, 9th variorum edition with annotations by C. W. Guillebaud (London, 1961), 2 vols, vol. I, pp. 134–7, 720.

[66] See A. Marshall, *Collected Essays, 1872–1917*, ed. P. Groenewegen (Bristol, 1997), 2 vols, vol. II, p. 595.

no attempt to answer Ruskin's critique of the science he was in the process of turning into a serious professional pursuit. Ruskin is cited only twice in the *Principles of Economics* (1890), and on both occasions in tandem with Carlyle, with William Morris added on another occasion. If the older economists had been clearer in stating that material wealth was not the main aim of human effort, Marshall claimed,

they would have escaped many grievous misrepresentations; and the splendid teachings of Carlyle and Ruskin as to the right aims of human endeavour and the right uses of wealth, would not then have been marred by bitter attacks on economics, based on the mistaken belief that the science had no concern with any motives except the selfish desire for wealth, or even that it inculcated a policy of sordid selfishness.[67]

He later coupled Carlyle and Ruskin when making a double distinction: first, between the views of earlier economists and those 'harsh employers and politicians, defending exclusive class privileges early in the last century'; and secondly, between Carlyle and Ruskin and their followers. While the leaders were credited with 'brilliant and ennobling poetical visions' the followers were guilty of holding 'the great economists responsible for sayings and deeds to which they were really averse'. 'As the imitators of Michael Angelo copied only his faults, so Carlyle, Ruskin and Morris find today ready imitators, who lack their fine inspirations and intuitions.'[68]

One has to be careful when reading this kind of thing in Marshall: 'poetical' takes away some of the emphasis on 'splendid' or 'brilliant and ennobling'. 'Fine inspirations and intuitions' is also double-edged when one remembers Marshall's commitment to science, to what he called 'hard thinking'. It was Marshall, after all, who praised Morris's *News from Nowhere* as a stimulus to 'aspiration', as being 'a joy for ever': it embodied 'unmixed good' precisely because it did not 'profess to be practical'.[69]

Marshall's response to the Carlyle-Ruskin-Morris critique of capitalism was to seek ways of highlighting and measuring the gap between private and social costs and benefits, those cases in which following market signals led to a preponderance of illth over wealth. He persisted in his attempts to measure the total satisfaction that consumers derived from their expenditure on goods via his concept of consumers' surplus, the collective version of something that is more easily grasped in its individual possessive form. For the most part he applied this apparatus to tax and subsidy issues arising from monopolies and the existence of industries

---

[67] A. Marshall, *Principles*, vol. I, p. 22.    [68] Ibid., p. 47; see too vol. I, p. 789n.
[69] A. Marshall, 'Social Possibilities of Economic Chivalry', in *Collected Essays*, vol. II, p. 593.

characterized by his own distinction between increasing or decreasing returns.[70] This enabled him to make an effective point in any debate with
continental economists (and their domestic adherents within the liberal
optimist school associated with Cobden) who argued that 'maximum social satisfaction' would be achieved in all cases where demand and supply
were in competitive equilibrium. But Marshall was too cautious, too im-
pressed by the advantages of free enterprise over bureaucratic control,
to employ the tools of consumers' and producers' surplus to advocate
bold new forms of state regulation or management of such industries.
Nevertheless, he offered the apparatus as a means of arriving at an im-
partial assessment of all the costs and benefits that needed to be taken into
account by 'the rapid growth of collective interests, and the increasing
tendency towards collective action in economic affairs'.

Marshall's strategy of combining a cool head with a warm heart succeeded, however temporarily, in retaking the high moral ground that had
been annexed by late Victorian critics of capitalism. For a time he even
convinced those Fabian heirs to Mill's legacy, Sidney and Beatrice Webb.
He certainly shared many of the late Victorian environmental concerns
with better housing, access to fresh air and public parks that were part
of the response to the problems of the built environment in the world's
most highly urbanized country. If, as Marshall believed, Malthusian pressures were dormant in Britain at that time, the accumulated results of
rapid urban growth on the quality of life could now be tackled more
squarely. By contrast with Mill, however, this lack of immediate concern
with the sustainability of economic growth on Malthusian grounds means
that Marshall's economics is more concentrated on 'amenity' and urban
renewal than the larger environmental issues tackled by both Mill and
Ruskin.

Welfare economics opens up a new lineage because, alongside neo-
Malthusian extrapolations, it provides a foundation for what has become
the economists' chief contribution to the problems of choice posed by
environmental problems: cost-benefit analysis, with consumers' surplus
supplying the rationale for 'willingness to pay' criteria when assessing
the impact of environmental damage.[71] Much of this would have appeared strange to Mill, and there are many latter-day Wordsworthians and
Ruskinians who would prefer an environmental ethic that is more holistic,
with the economists' 'scientific' choice procedures being replaced with
something more akin to religious reverence. They are not convinced that

[70] Marshall, *Principles*, bk V, ch. XIII.
[71] For the modern economist's approach see D. Pearce, *Economic Values and the Natural
World* (London, 1993).

the economic leopard has changed its individualistic spots, despite the inclusion of 'passive', 'existence', and 'inheritance' values within the calculus, with 'sustainability' built in as a side condition.[72] Indeed, neither of the main positions considered here would probably satisfy those who seek a more wholehearted ecocentric ethic: both Christianity and the religion of humanity are decidedly anthropocentric.

Although genealogies, like chronicles, have their uses, they are rightly judged to be of limited value as history; they often tell us more about the needs of those who construct them than they do about their historical subjects. Constructing supportive genealogies survives as part of the search for a defensible modern environmental ethic of the kind that Ruskin found in Christianity and classical mythology, that Mill discerned in a new religion of humanity, and Marshall hoped for in a society becoming rich enough to make ethical sacrifices while continuing to enjoy the benefits of economic and moral progress. But affirming one's own values by the indirect means provided by a preferred lineage has some parasitic qualities that are best avoided by historians.

---

[72] See, for example, D. Wiggins, 'Nature, Respect for Nature, and the Human Scale of Values', *The Aristotelian Society*, C (2000), pp. 1–32.

# 7 Tönnies on 'community' and 'civil society': clarifying some cross-currents in post-Marxian political thought

*Jose Harris*

## I

Among the many attempts to retrieve something of value out of the supposed wreckage of Marxian social and political thought, two of the most prominent have been the advocacy of various forms of 'communitarianism', and the widespread revival of interest in notions of 'civil society'. Both of these concepts are notoriously protean in character; both have captured the imagination of present-day theorists and political actors across the right, left and centre of politics; and each of them has been used in recent debate to encompass a very broad range of moral and theoretical positions, some of which appear to be not merely diverse but mutually contradictory.

Thus writers on 'civil society' differ sharply on whether the term includes or explicitly *excludes* the institutions of the state – and, if the latter, on whether it refers to all forms of associational life or only to those which have a place in the 'public sphere'.[1] Bodies currently advocating 'civil society' as a practical programme range from the Institute for the Study of Civil Society (initially linked to the Institute for Economic Affairs), whose prime concern is with the revival of small-scale voluntary action, through to the Institute for Global Civil Society (based at the London School of Economics), whose aims include the promotion and enforcement of

---

[1] Classic civil society theories were divided between a British tradition, stemming from Cicero, Hobbes, Locke and Ferguson, which located state institutions within civil society, and a later German tradition, represented by Hegel, Marx and Riehl, which saw state and civil society as separate. The modern revival of civil society thought, even in Britain, has largely followed the German conception. For a critique of this separation see M. Walzer, 'The Civil Society Argument', in R. Beiner, ed., *Theorizing Citizenship* (Albany, NY, 1995), pp. 167–70; and J. Harris, 'From Richard Hooker to Harold Laski: changing perceptions of civil society in British political thought', in *Civil Society in British History: Ideas, Identities, Institutions* (Oxford, forthcoming, 2003). For further references, see the Introduction, n. 14 above.

'universal' human rights.[2] Writers on communitarian themes likewise profoundly disagree as to whether 'community' means merely the collective enhancement of individual goals, or the existence of a social and moral order that is ontologically and historically prior to the individual.[3] Rather less remarked upon is the fact that the overarching terms 'community' and 'civil society' have themselves come to be used by some current theorists as though they were complementary and even interchangeable. A 'civil and decent society', Amitai Etzioni tells us, theoretically and practically requires the existence of 'community'; while Roger Scruton's *Dictionary of Political Thought* identifies communitarianism with 'the ideal . . . of a civil society, neither led nor controlled by the state, but existing as something over and above the sum of the individuals who compose it'.[4] And at a more prosaic and practical level conflation of the two terms is writ large in much of the polemical literature of both post-Thatcherite liberal conservatism and Blairite New Labour. David Willetts's *Civic Conservatism* (1994) insisted that the restoration of community was inseparable from a revival of 'civil institutions', 'civic responsibility' and 'the checks and balances of civil society'; while Tony Blair's Beveridge memorial lecture on the abolition of child poverty (1999) specifically promised the 're-building of moral community' via a restoration of the 'institutions of civil society'.[5] In each of these contexts, and in many other academic and political settings, 'community' and 'civil society' have been invoked as partners in reviving civic identity and in humanizing and moralizing the impersonal operation of market-driven economic change.

To historians of political thought, however, this extreme elasticity of language may well seem somewhat puzzling. Whilst acknowledging the many diverse ways in which the two terms have been used within past traditions and contexts, they may well protest that to reduce the overall categories of 'community' and 'civil society' to virtual synonyms is to empty them of all effective meaning. It may be pointed out that the two concepts have had totally different pedigrees over many centuries in the

[2] D. Green, *Reinventing Civil Society: The Rediscovery of Welfare Without Politics* (London, 1993); R. Whelan, *Helping the Poor* (London, 2001); H. Anheier, M. Glasius and M. Kaldor, eds, *Global Civil Society 2001* (Oxford, 2001).
[3] C. Taylor, *Philosophical Arguments* (Cambridge, MA, 1995), ch. 10; M. Sandel, *Liberalism and the Limits of Justice* (Cambridge, 1982; 2nd edn 1998).
[4] A. Etzioni, *The Spirit of Community: Rights, Responsibilities and the Communitarian Agenda* (London, 1995), pp. 37–44; R. Scruton, *A Dictionary of Political Thought* (London, 1996), p. 92.
[5] D. Willetts, *Civic Conservatism* (London, 1994), pp. 5, 11–13, 21; R. Walker, ed., *Ending Child Poverty: Popular Welfare for the 21st Century* (Bristol, 1999); T. Blair, 'Beveridge Revisited: A Welfare State for the 21st Century', in Lord Butler of Brockwell, ed., *Builders of the Millennium* (Oxford, 2000).

history of political theory and practice, and that they have typically implied two very different conceptions of law, property rights, moral order, political relationships, and human self-awareness and subjectivity. 'Civil society' in its many various guises has nearly always had implications of individualism, rational choice, contractual relationships and formal legal structures; whereas 'community' in all but its most transcendent religious forms has had connotations of historical particularity, locality, solidarity, and civic-cum-social ties based on 'face-to-face' human relationships and intimately shared traditions. Historically, many proponents of civil society have viewed 'public' virtues as categorically distinct from virtues of the private kind, whereas theorists of community have more often seen them as closely interdependent. We live in a culture where the relation of words to things is fluid and deeply contested; but even so it is difficult to avoid the suspicion that what is on offer in this conflation of two such contrasting themes is, not the forging of powerful new insights and meanings, but a lapse into confusion, linguistic carelessness, moral exhortation and blandness.

In trying to prise apart this confusion I shall look more closely at the analysis offered by one of the few major socio-political theorists to have attempted to address both these concepts simultaneously, and at the same time to distinguish them radically from each other. Ferdinand Tönnies's *Gemeinschaft und Gesellschaft*, first published in Leipzig in 1887, has long been acknowledged in Europe and North America as a classic work on the theory of *Gemeinschaft* or 'community'; but the second leg of Tönnies's argument, on the nature and characteristics of *Gesellschaft* or 'society', has received much less critical and contextual attention. In particular, the fact that Tönnies's '*Gesellschaft*' specifically referred not just to 'society' in a sociological sense, but to 'civil society' in the wider-ranging political, legal and economic senses variously deployed by Hobbes, Adam Ferguson, Kant, Hegel and Marx, has been largely ignored.[6] Likewise, the underlying theoretical framework of Tönnies's work has been not so much forgotten as never adequately acknowledged. When first published in 1887 it was generally believed to be a Marxian propagandist tract; when reissued in the 1920s it was reinterpreted by some as a plea for extreme ethnic and Teutonic nationalism; and after 1945 it was widely portrayed in German historiography as part of the

---

[6] F. Tönnies, *Gemeinschaft und Gesellschaft* (1887), translated as *Community and Civil Society*, ed. J. Harris (Cambridge, 2001). On Tönnies's debt to the Anglo-Scottish conception of 'civil society', as opposed to the newer and still hazy concept of mere 'society', see Harris, pp. xxi–xxii, xxiv–xxvii, 64; and E. G. Jacoby, *On Social Ideas and Ideologies* (New York, 1974), pp. 121–82. All references to *Gemeinschaft und Gesellschaft* in this chapter are to the 2001 Cambridge University Press edition.

politics of anti-modernism and cultural despair that had fostered fascism and national socialism.[7]

Tönnies himself, however, conceived of his work in none of these lights: he believed that he was devising a timeless and morally neutral analytical matrix, suitable for application to all social and political structures and all historical settings, in the manner attempted in Aristotle's *Politics* or Hobbes's *Leviathan*. Just how far this overall enterprise was successful is something that cannot be reviewed in detail here (though the very fact that the core theme of *Gemeinschaft und Gesellschaft* was so persistently misinterpreted suggests that, initially at least, it was a signal failure!). In this chapter I want simply to exhume the hidden foundations of Tönnies's portrayal of 'community' and 'civil society', and to look at the ways in which he related them to broader philosophical, psychological, legal, linguistic and economic themes and settings. I shall suggest that, although one may well find fault with his difficult, idiosyncratic, and often tortuous method of exposition, Tönnies is nevertheless highly persuasive on the need for two quite distinct analytical models: and that although elements of 'community' and 'civil society' can and nearly always do exist alongside one another in any real historical setting, Tönnies's depiction of them makes it difficult to go along with recent expressions of the view that they logically 'require' one another, that they point towards similar kinds of mutualist and co-operative arrangements, or that they even mean one and the same thing. I shall suggest also that (as he himself predicted would be the case[8]) there are certain aspects of Tönnies's bi-polar analysis that are more instantly recognizable in the global polity of the early twenty-first century than they were when he first forged them in 1887.

## II

So, let us look more closely at Tönnies's *Gemeinschaft und Gesellschaft*, and the difficulties of interpretation that it often poses. One point that should be mentioned in advance is that, despite his acknowledgement of a debt to many earlier theorists, Tönnies's terminology and his understanding of community and civil society did not precisely coincide with those of any of his mentors. Like Kant he identified civil society with the advance of legal rationality and abstract rights, but he was very far from sharing Kant's

---

[7] See Tönnies, *Community and Civil Society*, pp. xxiv, xxix–xxx; A. Mitzman, *Sociology and Estrangement: Three Sociologists of Imperial Germany* (New Brunswick, 1973), pt two; R. Dahrendorf, *Society and Democracy in Germany* (1965; English edn: London, 1968), pp. 127–30.

[8] Letter to F. Paulsen, 12 January 1888, in *Ferdinand Tönnies und Friedrich Paulsen: Briefwechsel 1876–1908*, ed. O. Klose, E. G. Jacoby and I. Fischer (Kiel, 1961), pp. 243–4.

view that these were closely linked with 'universal justice' and enhanced personal freedom.[9] On the contrary, like Hegel and Marx, he portrayed the processes of civil society as often predatory and a battlefield of private interests; but unlike them (and much more in tune with theorists of the English and Scottish schools) he envisaged civil society as specifically embracing the institutions of state and commonwealth as well as the economic sphere.[10] His account of the setting-up of a civil commonwealth closely resembled that of Thomas Hobbes, but he nevertheless sharply dissented from Hobbes's wholly negative portrayal of pre-civil social relations in family-based and tribal communities.[11] He dissented also from other nineteenth-century German theorists like Wilhelm Riehl, whose conception of civil society included guilds and self-governing corporations – bodies which Tönnies thought more properly belonged within the tradition of *Gemeinschaft*.[12] Among the authorities cited in his text Tönnies's understanding of his two master concepts perhaps most closely followed that of the Scottish Enlightenment theorist, Adam Ferguson, who had portrayed 'civil society' as the necessary condition of wealth-creation, science and civic peace – but also as fraught with possibilities of faction, decadence, cultural corruption and institutional decline.[13]

Another reason why Tönnies's arguments are so easy to misinterpret is that he set himself the task of trying to fuse analytical political and social science into a seamless web with narrative and descriptive history. His original subtitle (omitted from later editions) promised a comparison of the 'pure forms' of communism and socialism, as embodied in concrete historical epochs and cultures.[14] His text frequently cited the accounts of the historic shift from status to contract advanced by Gierke and Sir Henry Maine; his analysis of industrial, entrepreneurial and financial change was largely derived from the historical sections of the *Wealth of Nations*, *Das Kapital* and the *Critique of Political Economy*; and there was also frequent reference to a cyclical pattern of world history, involving a continuous transition from rustic virtue, through small-scale civic republics to large-scale metropolitan empires, eventually climaxing in irresolvable

---

[9] H. Reiss, ed., *Kant's Political Writings* (Cambridge, 1970), pp. 45–6.
[10] T. M. Knox, ed., *Hegel's Philosophy of Right* (Oxford, 1942), pp. 123, 156, 189, 353–6; Tönnies, *Community and Civil Society*, pp. 67–8, 89–91.
[11] Tönnies, *Community and Civil Society*, pp. xxvi–xxvii; cf. Thomas Hobbes, *Leviathan*, ed. M.Oakeshott (Oxford, 1957), pp. 109, 155.
[12] W. H. Riehl, *Naturgeschichte des Volkes*, II: *Die Bürgerliche Gesellschaft* (Stuttgart, 1856).
[13] Tönnies's account was much less optimistic than Ferguson's; but see A. Ferguson, *An Essay on the History of Civil Society* (Cambridge, 1995), pp. 194–264.
[14] Tönnies, *Community and Civil Society*, pp. xv, xl. The 1887 subtitle, 'An Essay on Communism and Socialism as Historical Social Systems' was toned down in later editions to 'Fundamental Concepts in Pure Sociology'.

conflict, revolutionary breakdown, and moral and social collapse.[15] In addition, as a citizen of the second (and later third) German Reich Tönnies found numerous parallels to the later stages of this cycle in the history of his own times, a point that could be illustrated with much textual and biographical detail.

Yet to place too much emphasis on the historical dimension to *Gemeinschaft und Gesellschaft* can be more than a little misleading. It fosters the false impression, gained perhaps by a majority of Tönnies's readers and critics, that the central thrust of his work was to endorse and recommend the close-knit kinship-based structures of the archaic world, and to condemn the contractually based competitive individualism of modern market societies. This was not, however, Tönnies's main intention. On the contrary, like his mentor Thomas Hobbes, he believed that the study of historical facts and narratives was pointless, except in so far as those facts and narratives demonstrated some analytical model or theorem about human relations and power structures within human society in general.[16] And in the introduction to his first edition of 1887 he tells us that his underlying aim is not the mere retailing of history but the methodological one of merging and reconciling the historical empiricism of David Hume with the formal rationalism and apriorism of Kant.[17] Thus, despite the many references to specific historical examples – and despite also the flavour of regret for the past that often suffused his narrative – Tönnies viewed the concepts of *Gemeinschaft* and *Gesellschaft*, and the clusters of secondary concepts that were attached to them, as analytical tools designed to explicate the general characteristics of all human social organization. They were not normative judgements about different types of social behaviour, nor were they meant to be precise factual descriptions of particular social systems or specific historical events.

Nor should Tönnies's enterprise be confused with a straightforward comparison between socialism and competitive capitalism, or between collectivism and individualism. He held little brief for the incessant debates on these subjects that dominated much popular political and economic discussion of the later nineteenth century in Germany, Britain, America and elsewhere – which he believed went no further than trivial commentary on rival party programmes.[18] And far from equating late nineteenth-century socialism with communitarianism, one of the most distinctive features of Tönnies's account was that he identified 'democratic' and 'state' socialism with the eventual culmination and apogee of many trends and processes within contemporary market-based civil

---

[15] Ibid., pp. 64–91, 216–21, 258–61, and *passim*.    [16] Ibid., pp. xxv, 9–10.
[17] Ibid., pp. 3–14.    [18] Ibid., p. 10.

society. In other words socialism was not, as many imagined, a more peaceful, prosaic and constitutionalist version of 'communism', but – even more so than liberalism or corporate capitalism – it was communism's polar opposite (i.e., socialism was the end version of the capitalistic process whereas communism was a reversion to its earliest beginnings).[19] Again, however, such commentary on contemporary political movements was not Tönnies's primary exegetical concern. His portrayal of the dichotomy between *Gemeinschaft* and *Gesellschaft* was designed to penetrate to much deeper levels – to an excavation of the underlying cognitive, psychological, productive, reproductive and religious determinants of all organized social life, and of the ways in which these forces found expression in economic, legal and political institutions. Despite his claims about reconciling Hume and Kant, his analysis was rooted in an epistemology that was fundamentally Kantian: it entailed the identification of a series of a priori interpretative 'forms' whose existence made intelligible the great mass of psychological, biological, cultural and institutional detail embedded in all human action and in social and productive arrangements.[20]

Tönnies applied this methodology to all different levels of human experience. At the most basic level, he portrayed all social actions and arrangements as being traceable back to two different forms of human consciousness – which were in turn linked to different forms of perception, understanding, rationality, and styles of human freedom. On the one hand there was what Tönnies termed '*Wesenwille*', variously translatable as 'natural', 'essential', or 'intuitive' will (and the 'will' component of the German word also corresponded to such English terms as determination, design, mental outlook, or conscious purpose). This 'natural will' was a kind of conscious but spontaneous spill-over from the biological sphere. It coincided with the unreflecting common sense or natural reason of everyday life, and it was characterized by a very weak sense of differentiation between individual and group, between mental and material processes, and between subject and object.[21] Contrasted with natural will there was what Tönnies (again following the terminology of Kant) initially called '*Willkür*' but was in later editions to replace with the invented word '*Kürwille*' (a term variously translatable as rational, arbitrary, or artificial will, or even as the autonomous 'free will' [*liberum arbitrium*] of Augustinian Christian theology).[22] This 'rational' will was characterized by a very high degree of abstraction from the external physical world, by a very heightened sense of individual identity and of separation between subject and object, and by reason in the form not of intuitive common sense, but

[19] Ibid., pp. xx, xl, 260–1.   [20] Ibid., pp. xl, 3–5, 95–99.
[21] Ibid., pp. 95–113, 133–7.   [22] Ibid., pp. xvii, 6.

of fine-tuned goal-directed rational calculation. In their most extreme forms the two types of will expressed and generated two very distinct types of human psyche – the relatively un-self-conscious natural 'Self' or 'Soul'; and the hyper-self-conscious abstract 'Person' (the latter a psychological entity artificially manufactured by continuous engagement in the abstract mental processes of ratiocination and rational choice). Whereas the spontaneous and unreflecting 'Self' was the archetypal participant in Tönnies's 'community', the hyper-conscious self-regarding 'Person' was the archetypal rational actor in his conception of 'civil society'.[23] These two different kinds of wills were latent in all individuals, in both sexes, and in all age-groups; but Tönnies believed that the creative and intuitive faculties of women, children, and people without formal education flourished best in a well-ordered community; whereas civil society universalized 'the lord and master going out into the street and market-place', forcing women (and by analogy all other subordinate groups) eventually to adapt and recreate themselves in the images and roles of adult men.[24]

This dualistic portrayal of the human will was of course by no means new in European thought; it had deep roots and affinities in the long history of Aristotelian versus Augustinian constructions of human nature. What was distinctive about Tönnies's approach was his systematic and detailed projection of it into different kinds of concrete practices, beliefs, social structures, creative arts, and private and public institutions. Thus in the world of *Wesenwille* or natural will, knowledge of all kinds – from basic survival techniques through to the highest forms of intellect and wisdom – was communicated by practice, example, repetition and social habit; whereas in the world of *Kürwille* or rational will, knowledge was transmitted by formal theorems, systematized data, and by hiring the services of 'experts' (it was purchased like any other commodity from priests, doctors, counsellors, financial advisers or university professors).[25] In the exercise of *Wesenwille* language itself was rooted, almost literally like a 'vegetable', in biological, material, and everyday human activities and functions; whereas in the exercise of *Kürwille* exact rational calculation both required and was further advanced by the forging of signs that were abstract, standardized, unambiguous and artificial. (The invention of artificial language, clinically detached from conventional usage, was in Tönnies's view one of the most indispensable tools and trademarks of advanced scientific knowledge.)[26] The practice of *Wesenwille* generated, and

---

[23] Ibid., pp. 118–27, 138–9, 172, 179–83.
[24] Ibid., pp. 152–75.    [25] Ibid., pp. 145–6.
[26] Ibid., pp. 33–5, 169. On Tönnies's enthusiasm for 'artificial' language as a prerequisite for the advancement of knowledge, see his articles on 'Philosophical Terminology', *Mind*, new ser., 8 (1899), pp. 289–332, 467–91, and 9 (1900), pp. 46–60.

was in turn generated by, clusters of day-to-day habits and practical rules that built up like coral reefs into localized customary morality; whereas in the sphere of *Kürwille* or rational will individuals were either free to make their own rules, or were bound merely by the formal logic of abstract universals. *Wesenwille* treated art, religion and human creativity as part of the immanent stuff of everyday life, as things that everyone could do or share in, like breathing, walking and sexuality; whereas *Kürwille* treated them as areas of scientific knowledge, abstract doctrine, media stardom and special inspiration.[27]

These dualistic modes of perception, self-consciousness, language, morals and belief Tönnies portrayed as the fundamental clue to deciphering the contrasting characters and institutional structures of 'community' and 'civil society'. The awareness of 'Self', as deeply enmeshed in and only weakly differentiated from both natural functions and the wider social group, complemented a vision of the material world as a finite and conditional resource closely intertwined with the activities of everyday life, and available for communal and cross-generational use and occupation: a way of thinking about 'possessions' and 'public goods' that was peculiar to *Gemeinschaft*. By contrast the highly abstracted rational 'Person' viewed the world as full of alien objects, all requiring instant appropriation, and capable of being objectively measured and continuously exchanged: a vision of absolute 'property' that was intrinsic to *Gesellschaft*.[28] Communal ownership, particularly of land, fostered (so Tönnies believed) a conception of 'common law' derived from shared experience, custom, memory and precedent; whereas private ownership of property required formal legal rules, contracts, certified documents, and notions of abstract rights.[29] The un-self-conscious will of the inhabitants of community took it for granted that kinship structures, family life, neighbourhood ties, functional roles, and the sharing of common tasks of work were all necessary, morally mandatory, immutable and 'given'; whereas the rational will of the denizens of civil society saw all such things as arbitrary, malleable and contingent – whom you associated with, where you lived, and what you did for a living all being matters of open-ended and reversible choice and negotiation. Moral attitudes in community were transmitted and policed by feelings of stigma and shame, purity and danger, operating through the organ of individual 'conscience'; while moral

[27] Tönnies, *Community and Civil Society*, pp. 104–5, 113, 127–8, 145–51, 164–5, 239–41.
[28] Ibid., pp. 36–9, 182–4, 188–9, 193–4.
[29] Ibid., pp. 211–21. Tönnies cited England as a place where such market-driven developments had overridden the common law, but it would have been more accurate to say that the English common law had itself developed many aspects of economic and legal 'rationality'.

attitudes in civil society were transmitted and policed by politeness, good manners, rational self-interest and, above all, by the continuous pressure of encircling 'public opinion'.[30]

## III

Such dichotomies, in Tönnies's view, similarly determined the different forms of association and structures of authority within the political sphere, which he termed the *Gemeinwesen* or Commonwealth. The antinomy of natural and rational will could be starkly discerned in the contrast between the close-knit kin-based ties and institutions of tribal societies, and modern rational-bureaucratic structures whose primary purpose was the supervision and legal enforcement of contract. But here as in other spheres it is a mistake to suppose that Tönnies automatically identified community with primitive or archaic cultures, and civil society with 'modern' pluralistic and cosmopolitan ones. On the contrary, he depicted the political functions and institutions of a developed *Gemeinschaft* system as being outwardly very similar to those found in a market-oriented *Gesellschaft*. In both systems, Tönnies portrayed 'sovereignty' as ultimately stemming from the assent of the mass of the people, women as well as men. In both there were likely to be representative assemblies, and public administrative arrangements for defence, distribution of resources, and enforcement of law. And in both systems an analytical and practical distinction needed to be made between loose, limited and transient 'associations', and more permanent collectivities or 'corporations' that acquired a common legal or political personality.[31]

Nevertheless these outward points of comparability disguised certain inner structures and underlying principles that in Tönnies's view made 'communities' and 'civil societies' fundamentally quite distinct from each other. In a community, collective political 'personality' would have evolved incrementally over time in a manner largely invisible to the casual observer; whereas in civil society its origin would be clearly marked by some specific legal enactment, written constitution, or sequence of constitutive events. Likewise, shared political identity in a community was an product of time – of past experience, of common historical memory and pre-memory; whereas in civil society it was largely a product of

---

30  Ibid., pp. 108–46, 161–4, 241–3, 248. On Tönnies's continuing interest in 'public opinion' as the source of moral authority in civil society, see his *Kritik der Öffentlichen Meinung* (Berlin, 1922).

31  Tönnies, *Community and Civil Society*, pp. 17–19, 201–8, 233–6, 254. This was no mere academic distinction, as may be seen in the struggles over the precise legal status of trade unions that went on in many parts of Europe, but particularly in Great Britain, for much of the twentieth century.

space – of the random contiguity of disparate human beings of many different identities and origins who happened to be living side-by-side in the same geographical area. In both cases the framework of law was a man-made, 'positive' thing; but in a community, law would have grown cumulatively through earlier decisions and precedents, whereas in civil society it was the product of juristic and administrative rationality, formal statutory legislation, and the assertion of abstract rights. (The latter process Tönnies viewed as particularly embodied in the modernist revival and 'codifying' agenda of Roman civil law, increasingly dominant in the legal systems of continental Europe.)[32] In terms of government, Tönnies's *Gemeinschaft* closely resembled an Oakeshottian 'enterprise association', where even in peacetime the vast bulk of material resources was managed and allocated on the lines of a military commissariat (rather similar to the model of a 'civic economy' prescribed by John Ruskin in *Unto This Last* and *The Political Economy of Art*, and favoured by many theorists of the British labour movement earlier in the twentieth century).[33]

By contrast government in *Gesellschaft*, at least in its initial stages, was primarily concerned merely with regulating the legal framework of competition and contract, and with maintaining public order and relations with other states. Under both regimes, governmental structures and practices actively reinforced the psychological outlooks upon which they drew: as in the much later analysis of Michel Foucault, Tönnies's account posited a tight reciprocal relationship between modes and methods of public administration and the inner constituents of human subjectivity.[34]

Similar dichotomies underpinned ideas about representation, and about how popular 'sovereignty' was to be practically expressed. Thus within a classic community, access to a share in the exercise of political power was basically rooted in 'function'. In very early communities such power was concentrated in the procreative, hunting, dispute-settling and patriarchal functions of male heads of households. In more developed communities it was more widely dispersed through the roles of military leaders, priests and judges, and membership of skilled occupational groups: and in modern communities it sought expression (though usually with dwindling success) through such movements as workers' co-operatives, guild socialism, professional corporations, and other

---

[32] Ibid., pp. 211–21.

[33] M. Oakeshott, *On Human Conduct* (Oxford, 1975), pp. 114–19; E. T. Cook and A. Wedderburn, eds, *The Library Edition of the Works of John Ruskin* (London, 1903–12), vol. XVI, pp. 9–10 and vol. XVII, pp. 17–23, 43–56.

[34] M. Foucault, *Histoire de la Folie* (Paris, 1961); M. Foucault, *Surveiller et Punir: Naissance de la Prison* (Paris, 1975); G. Burchell, 'Peculiar Interests: Civil Society and Governing "The System of Natural Liberty" ', in G. Burchell, C. Gordon and P. Miller, eds, *The Foucault Effect: Studies in Governmentality* (Chicago, 1991), pp. 119–51.

self-governing vocational groups.[35] Within a civil society, however, participation in the exercise of political authority – despite certain outward institutional similarities – took a quite different form. The fragmented, freely choosing, goal-oriented rational actors of *Gesellschaft* could never in themselves hope to comprise a cohesive collective unit or political personality; but the practical imperatives of commerce and exchange required that each of them needed some higher power of this kind to enforce the rules of contract against his fellow-citizens. The result was their coming-together to create a Hobbesian-style 'artificial person' – either a prince or an assembly or a mixture of the two – which, like the board of a joint-stock company, was invested with the autochthonous powers of the individual members or 'mandators' and represented their rights and interests, both in disputes with each other and against external enemies. This company-law model of the structure of the state embodied in Tönnies's view the essence of national political constitutions and of organized power relationships in advanced, market-based, 'civil society'.[36] Paradoxically, however, the very minimalism of this system – initially designed simply to facilitate private commercial transactions – contained the seeds of its opposite: a system that Tönnies portrayed as a gradually emerging civic, cultural, legal and administrative totalitarianism. This came about because, by eliminating all lesser customary, corporate and communitarian sources of authority, the state came increasingly to be coterminous with society at large and with 'the idea of Society as a single all-embracing rational subject'.[37] By using coercion to secure the enforcement of contract, the state implicitly created precedents for other kinds of overriding sovereign intervention in the balance of market forces and the distribution of economic power. And by destroying *Gemeinschaft* and universalizing the ethic of 'rational choice', the modern state was inadvertently opening up a Pandora's box of boundless and ungovernable popular desires (that element of 'insatiability' noted by many recent writers on the implications of global markets). Far from providing an autonomous counterweight to state power, in Tönnies's account the citizens or stakeholders of civil society were therefore both implicitly responsible for authorizing the growth of the 'absolute' state, and complicit in the conditions of their own ultimate destruction.[38]

## IV

Detailed examples of Tönnies's account of the practical working out of his community/civil society dichotomy could be cited ad nauseam in relation

[35] Tönnies, *Community and Civil Society*, pp. 30–2, 152–4, 194–5, 209–10, 228–33.
[36] Ibid., pp. 183–6, 233–9.    [37] Ibid., p. 237.
[38] Ibid., pp. 164–5, 217–21, 236–9, 248–9, 260–1.

to all different levels of private and public experience. He perceived both models as latent in all political contexts, and one or other of them as in the ascendant in all historical epochs. *Gemeinschaft* had reached its apogee in the early Roman republic and in the 'free cities' of late medieval and early modern Europe. *Gesellschaft* was exemplified in the history of the Roman Empire, and in Tönnies's own day by the explosion of global capitalism that had followed the American Civil War and German unification (an expansion which he expected to continue for a prolonged, though not indefinite, historical future). Yet, as suggested above, to interpret Tönnies's narrative simply as lamenting the transition from one kind of social system to another is misleading. On the contrary, when defending himself against charges of utopianism and anti-modernism, Tönnies throughout his life was to maintain that the dichotomies he had identified were not purely time-specific, but were universal and dialectical. Both concepts were 'ideal types', or 'typical exemplars' (explanatory models invented by Tönnies more than a decade before their use by Max Weber): and the attitudes and arrangements which they exemplified would always coexist and compete with each other in any historical or institutional setting.[39] Thus a political assembly in a modern state might be the artificial creation of a specific and formal constitutive act, but it would at the same time be composed of people who were at least residually linked together by ties of kinship, neighbourhood, culture, language and history. Similarly, any actual human being would simultaneously be subject both to *Wesenwille* (spontaneity, kinship loyalties, habit, and private conscience) and to *Kürwille* (calculation, market forces, fashion, and the pressures of public opinion) – even though in global market society the latter set of pressures would usually tend to prevail.

Moreover, despite his often lyrical account of the highest forms of community, it is a mistake to see Tönnies as an unambiguous moral advocate for one particular kind of social order rather than another. In his own personal life he experienced, as did many of his contemporaries, a constant uneasy tension between two deeply contrasting ways of life and thought. As a Schleswigian small-townsman, a German patriot, a personal friend of romantic poets such as Storm and Fontane, and a critic of the cultural anarchy wrought by markets, he was drawn to the deep structures of *Gemeinschaft*: but as a republican and a rationalist, a disciple of Hobbes and Kant, and the friend and mentor of many Jewish and non-German intellectuals, he was drawn to the universalism, cosmopolitanism and legalistic egalitarianism that he perceived in *Gesellschaft*. Moreover, Tönnies constantly maintained (against Gierke and other contemporary communitarians) that modernity could not 'jump over its own shadow';

[39] Ibid., pp. xvi, xxv, 140–3, 156, 179n.

i.e., that whether one liked it or not, the advance of civil society, legal rationality, and market institutions – and the accompanying transformation of the individual human psyche – was largely irresistible.[40] It might be contained and modified by certain limited countervailing arrangements (such as guilds, co-operatives, humanistic education, social welfare policies, government 'regulation', and measures to protect family life), but unless or until current civilization eventually collapsed it could not be wholly reversed or rejected.

Tönnies's personal interest in communitarian social experiments and civic reform movements in his own day might seem to indicate that, despite the points made above, he was a kindred spirit with recent commentators who believe that community and civil society are, if not exactly synonymous, nevertheless close partners, and that communitarianism can somehow be painlessly grafted onto the fragmented structures of societies dominated by global markets. In fact the whole thrust of *Gemeinschaft und Gesellschaft* was to argue just the opposite. It was to suggest that the two systems of thought and practice coexisted in a state of profound tension and antagonism, that each had quite different human benefits and costs, and that the advance of the one form of social life necessarily negated and subverted the core principles of the other. Thus in Tönnies's view community fostered emotions and relationships that were deeply satisfying but limited in range, whereas civil society fostered emotions and sympathies that were wide-ranging and 'universalist' but often transient and shallow. The very intimacy and depth of community meant that it was necessarily 'exclusive', whereas the very impersonality and 'thinness' of civil society meant that it could be open, 'inclusive' and tolerant of individual difference.[41] The advance of *Gesellschaft* inevitably undermined established communities and settled cultures; while defence of *Gemeinschaft* necessarily disadvantaged strangers, migrants and minorities. Habits and attitudes which in a community constituted the highest forms of virtue – such as powerful group loyalties, piety, and giving priority to the interests of family and friends – were subtly reclassified by the ethic of civil society as outlooks that were at best private and a-social, and at worst the triggers of favouritism, fanaticism, corruption and terror. Whenever civil society appeared to mobilize principles of altruism, civic solidarity and individual 'public spirit', what was really being observed was either a calculated cosmetic exercise, or a rearguard action by the proponents of community trying to soften the impact of unlimited free competition. And, similarly,

---

[40] F. Tönnies, *Die Sitte* (1909), tr. A. Farrell Borenstein as *Custom: An Essay on Social Codes* (New York, 1961), pp. 135–6.
[41] Tönnies, *Community and Civil Society*, pp. 17–19, 32–6.

whenever a community became more pluralistic or libertarian or relaxed its policies towards newcomers, what was really happening was that it was transforming itself into a civil society. Long-standing debates about 'domestic' versus 'equal-rights' feminism, when viewed through the lens of *Gemeinschaft und Gesellschaft*, likewise appeared not simply as alternative routes towards women's emancipation, but as deeply antagonistic rival constructions of human psychology, sexuality, culture and social structure. And one of Tönnies's most arresting, even shocking, conclusions was that the very rationalism, egalitarianism, and would-be universalism of *Gesellschaft* might in the long run lead to a far more intolerable aggregation of state power than could ever emerge from the relatively limited, localized, and disparate structures favoured by *Gemeinschaft*.

All of this seems to indicate that, despite many current aspirations to the contrary, there can be no easy and pain-free partnership between the theory and practice of enhanced 'community' on the one hand and the theory and practice of civil society on the other. What, if any, are the implications of this dichotomy for current debates among theorists, politicians, and ordinary citizens who are looking for new forms of human co-operation and collaboration, other than those simply dictated by markets? It would clearly be absurd to suggest that a text written in the 1880s should be seen as a tract for the early twenty-first century; but the analysis set out in *Gemeinschaft und Gesellschaft* nevertheless offers some important clues to current social trends, and throws a powerful searchlight on many areas of misconception. It suggests, for example, that policies for 'inclusion', 'anti-discrimination' and 'stakeholder democracy' – all proclaimed in recent times as strategies for the strengthening of 'community' – are much better understood as sophisticated and predictable developments of *Gesellschaft*. Conversely, attempts to revive voluntarism, self-help, mutualism, and neighbourhood support groups – all frequently identified as the very essence of civil society – should more properly be seen as reassertions of the spirit of *Gemeinschaft*. Similarly, it implies that policies of 'multi-culturalism', which draw eclectically upon the competing rhetorics of both community and civil society, require much more rigorous analysis – and much more awareness of the costs involved in both directions – than they have received so far. It indicates that the 'bowling alone' phenomenon, widely identified over the past decade as corrosive of civil society in both Britain and North America, is in fact one of its underlying psychological predicates.[42] Tönnies's analysis also casts doubt

---

[42] D. Selbourne, *The Principle of Duty: An Essay on the Foundations of the Civic Order* (London, 1994); R. D. Putnam, *Bowling Alone: The Collapse and Revival of American Community* (New York, 2000).

upon how far either of his master-constructs can be relied upon to tame or restrain the globalization of markets – community being simply too weak and impoverished, and civil society too complicit in market processes, to supply the moral, regulatory, and 'civilizing' counterweights to markets that their respective advocates often claim. And his characterization of 'socialism' as the eventual site, not of community but of the most developed form of global civil society, helps to explain the amazing speed with which democratic socialist parties were able to transfer their loyalties to markets, once they had disencumbered themselves of their lingering ideological affinities with now-vanished 'communist' regimes.[43]

All these points may perhaps be read as suggesting that Tönnies's stance on contemporary market society is wholly critical and negative. Yet, as suggested above, his concerns were analysis and explanation rather than prescription; and his central thesis – that there are two sharply differentiated analytical models of perception, rationality, selfhood, property and law, which are latent to a greater or lesser degree in all economic, cultural and political structures – remains powerful and persuasive. These models represent major clashes of interest and principle in many areas of public life, often not adequately captured by the now largely exhausted dichotomies of socialism versus capitalism, states versus markets; and their costs and benefits need to be weighed accordingly. As with parallel debates over the merits of 'liberty' versus 'equality', the real interest of the argument between *Gemeinschaft* and *Gesellschaft* lies, not in which model emerges the outright winner, but in how far it proves possible to negotiate a (doubtless painful and difficult) accommodation between the two. Tönnies's stark characterization of his two models as 'community' and 'civil society' may seem to fly in the face of much casual everyday language, just as it did when his book was first published in 1887:[44] but his approach seems more useful for the advance of historical understanding than the shallow conflation and confusion of these terms in much current political rhetoric.

[43] Tönnies, *Community and Civil Society*, pp. 260–1.
[44] Ibid., pp. xli, 17–19.

# 8 German historicism, progressive social thought, and the interventionist state in the United States since the 1880s

*Axel R. Schäfer*

In the spring of 1887, during the heyday of the Gilded Age, the *Contemporary Review* printed an article by the chief editorial writer of a Midwestern newspaper which voiced the heretical opinion that 'the *laissez-faire* doctrine of government is as foreign to the true genius of social and political life in the Western States as is the ultra-socialistic doctrine'. The author listed public land policies, railroad land grants, inspection laws, agricultural loans, public health legislation, schooling, and licensing laws as examples of widely accepted domains of government intervention. 'Legislation intended to enforce certain standards of morality', he added, 'is perhaps more prolific and vigorous in the United States . . . than anywhere else in the world.'[1]

What appeared to be the outburst of a minor prairie radical was in fact the considered view of Albert Shaw, a genteel reformer who became a leading light in progressive journalism, was a friend of Woodrow Wilson's, and later advised Theodore Roosevelt. More importantly, Shaw's article reflected not only homegrown scepticism about free market capitalism, but also the growing significance of European social thought in American reform. Shaw was a prominent member of the newly established American Economic Association (AEA), which at the time was not only a professional organization of dissenting economists, but also a clearinghouse for European ideas critical of *laissez faire*.[2] The AEA included social

---

[1] A. Shaw, 'The American State and the American Man', *Contemporary Review* 51 (1887), pp. 711, 707. For useful discussions of the interventionist role of nineteenth-century American government see S. Fine, *Laissez Faire and the General-Welfare State: A Study of Conflict in American Thought, 1865–1901* (Ann Arbor, 1956), pp. 18–25; and O. A. Pease, 'Urban Reformers in the Progressive Era', *Pacific Northwest Quarterly* 62 (1971), p. 52.

[2] Shaw wrote the article in the *Contemporary Review* a few years after he had completed his Ph.D. under Ely at Johns Hopkins University. His mentor later generously supplied him with references and suggestions for his year-long study tour of Europe. See R. T. Ely to Albert Shaw, 24 August 1888 and 8 October 1888, Albert Shaw Papers, Manuscripts and Archives Section, New York Public Library, New York. On A. Shaw see L. J. Graybar, *Albert Shaw and the Review of Reviews: An Intellectual Biography* (Lexington, 1974).

scientists, politicians, reformers and journalists, and provided a microcosm of the growing transnational network of reformers and academics in US reform politics. Its leading founders, the economists Edmund J. James, Richard T. Ely and Simon N. Patten, were trained in Germany and had absorbed the German historical school of economics' critique of *laissez-faire* liberalism. They maintained that the state was 'an agency whose positive assistance is one of the indispensable conditions of human progress'.[3]

The transfer of ideas through this transatlantic network underpinned the American reformers' critique of liberal market capitalism and formed a powerful, if disjointed, element in pre-World War I progressivism in the US. Young, educated, mostly middle-class Americans became the crucial mediators of German social thought and reform. In addition to Shaw, Ely, James and Patten they included, among others, the economists Henry Carter Adams and Thorstein Veblen, the sociologists George Herbert Mead, Albion W. Small, Edward A. Ross and Charles Henderson, the philosopher John Dewey, the social workers Florence Kelley and Edward T. Devine, the urban reformers Frederic C. Howe and John Graham Brooks, the city planners Benjamin C. Marsh and Frederick Law Olmsted, Jr., the scholar and civil rights campaigner W. E. B. Du Bois, the insurance reformer Isaac M. Rubinow, and the political scientists Frank J. Goodnow and Ernst Freund. The reformers paid close attention to numerous German developments in areas such as municipal reform, city planning, conservation, schooling, cartelization, social insurance and labour laws. Although the shared experience of living and studying in Germany did not result in a singular intellectual outlook on the part of the fledgling progressives, the perception, adaptation and transformation of foreign reforms helped shape the intellectual world of progressivism, and subsequently influenced the features of the American welfare state.[4]

---

[3] American Economic Association, 'Statement of Principles', quoted in J. Dorfman, 'The Role of the German Historical School in American Economic Thought', *American Economic Review* 45 (1955), p. 27. For a useful discussion of Ely see B. G. Rader, *The Academic Mind and Reform: The Influence of Richard T. Ely in American Life* (Lexington, 1966); on S. Patten see D. M. Fox, *The Discovery of Abundance: Simon N. Patten and the Transformation of Social Theory* (Ithaca, 1967). Useful general studies of the relationship between the German historical school and American reform include J. Herbst, *The German Historical School in American Scholarship: A Study in the Transfer of Culture* (Ithaca, 1965); J. C. Myles, 'German Historicism and American Economics: A Study of the Influence of the German Historical School on American Economic Thought', PhD diss., Princeton University, 1956; and Dorfman, 'Role of the German Historical School, pp. 17–28.

[4] For a recent discussion of the transatlantic reform network and the impact of progressivism on American social policy see D. T. Rodgers, *Atlantic Crossings: Social Politics in a Progressive Age* (Cambridge, 1998), pp. 409–46.

Shaw's article indicates that American progressives initially used references to German precedents to underpin the rehabilitation of the state in American genteel reform and to give credence to renewed calls for moral control and regulatory intervention in the age of the robber baron. However, as progressive social thinkers explored further the philosophical implications of German historicism, they increasingly sought to formulate a theory of reform that went beyond moral control or regulating the market in reaction to the excesses of industrial capitalism. Rather than searching for pragmatic policies designed to create order and a modicum of social justice within the given framework of capitalist market society, they based their reform proposals on a critique of the philosophical underpinnings of *laissez faire*. They stripped market ideology of its spurious claims to universal validity, naturalness and metahistorical essence, and suggested a new social conception of democracy. They historicized capitalism, advanced a relativistic understanding of morality, and parted with the rights orientation of liberal reform. Moreover, instead of revolting against the moral pitfalls of industrial society, they maintained that the normative transformations and social interdependencies characteristic of industrial capitalism could be used to create new avenues of public participation and control in order to overcome market society.

Hence, one of the most intriguing aspect of the transatlantic reform connection is that the progressives disentangled the imported social ideas from their paternalist German roots and used them to develop a radical theory of social reform. Nonetheless, a closer look at the development of US social and economic policies also reveals the ambiguities of progressive thought. It suggests that progressive ideas both transformed and buttressed the corporate capitalist order. The consumer-focused analysis of progressive social thought became a mainstay of twentieth-century economic policy; its emphasis on political participation and industrial democracy, however, became marginalized.[5]

## The German historical school and American genteel reform

The time period when Ely, Patten, Du Bois and other future progressives were students at American and German universities has long been recognized as an era of intense intellectual ferment. German scholars provided

---

[5] For an excellent intellectual history of transatlantic reform thought see J. T. Kloppenberg, *Uncertain Victory: Social Democracy and Progressivism in European and American Thought, 1870–1920* (New York, 1986). I have also explored these ideas in more detail in A. R. Schäfer, *American Progressives and German Social Reform, 1875–1920: Social Ethics, Moral Control, and the Regulatory State in a Transatlantic Context* (Stuttgart, 2000).

much of the vocabulary used by progressive social thinkers to question *laissez-faire* theory and the philosophical underpinnings of liberalism. They replaced the Enlightenment language of the rational autonomous individual, natural rights, economic man and the social contract with the language of interdependence, organic social growth, historical customs and social ethics. Prominent advocates of the German historical school of economics, such as Gustav Schmoller, Adolf Wagner, Johannes Conrad and Karl Knies explained that the hallowed tenets of *laissez faire*, ranging from the law of supply and demand to the iron law of wages, were not scientific truths, but simply ways of ideologically legitimating economic self-interest. Declaring justice the goal of economics, they taught their American students to think of the economic organization of society as reflecting culturally specific 'ethical and customary views [*sittlichen Anschauungen*]', not universal economic laws. Instead of positing market relations as a universal feature of human relations, they argued that the concept of the market and of self-interested rational individuals was the result of traditions and practices that had developed historically and expressed time-bound norms and values.[6]

The German historical school of economics offered an attractive assortment of ideas to the progressives. Its advocates were critical of both utilitarian and metaphysical ethics, yet not entirely given to moral subjectivism. They advanced a theory of historical relativism, but their view of history was distinctly teleological. They embraced state intervention, but encouraged civic engagement and public participation. They provided a philosophical rationale for the reformers to transcend *laissez faire* without challenging its middle-class foundations. They also appealed to the revivalist temper, moral sentiments and civic energy of progressivism. Moreover, they outlined a theory of ethics which rescued moral feelings from their confinement to the realm of sentimentality and attributed cognitive power and epistemological insight to them. They also linked social progress, civilizational advancement and ethical self-realization to the objectification of these moral feelings in public institutions.[7]

---

[6] G. Schmoller, 'Die sociale Frage und der preußische Staat', in *Zur Social- und Gewerbepolitik der Gegenwart. Reden und Aufsätze* (Leipzig, 1890), pp. 55–6. The sociologists Max Weber and Werner Sombart, for example, regarded the allegedly natural laws of the market simply as expressions of a culture-specific spirit of entrepreneurial individualism that enshrined the accumulation of wealth as the goal of economic endeavour. In the same vein, Weber regards the 'spirit of capitalism' as a set of historically developed attitudes, not as a natural or inevitable result of all economic activity. See F. K. Ringer, *The Decline of the German Mandarins: The German Academic Community, 1890–1933* (Cambridge,1969), pp. 144–5; F. Meinecke, *Die Entstehung des Historismus* (Munich, 1946), p. 339; M. Weber, *The Protestant Ethic and the Spirit of Capitalism*, tr. T. Parsons (New York, 1958).

[7] For the ideas of the historical school of economics, see especially T. Veblen, 'Gustav Schmoller's Economics', in *The Place of Science in Modern Civilization and Other Essays*

In the 1880s and early 1890s the main intellectual impact of the reformers' European sojourn was still largely confined to rehabilitating the state as a major factor in the development of American society. Shaw's above-mentioned article indicates that genteel reformers demanded moral control and regulatory intervention. They combined Protestant revulsion against the moral pitfalls of corporate capitalism and Republican concerns about the power of corporations and urban party machines with Hamiltonian beliefs in the beneficent influence of government promotionalism. In the words of Simon Patten, they had 'a high regard for such institutions as the Republican Party and the Presbyterian Church as agents of social change'.[8]

The German-trained economist Henry Carter Adams's influential theory of the state typified this genteel approach. Adams called for state 'conditioning' of economic relations and for restrictions on the accumulation of profits, although they should be 'high enough not to destroy the force of self-interest'. Income, he argued, should be sufficient 'for the satisfaction of the necessities of life, and enjoyments of life', but not serve a 'morbid ambition to be rich'.[9] Adams, who had studied under Wagner and Knies in the late 1870s, argued that the principle of free competition was not the same as *laissez faire*. In his view, the principle did not absolve the state from its duty both to secure to society the benefits of competition and to safeguard against its evils.[10] In historicist terms he reasoned that no society ever existed without a code of ethics.[11] Adams exemplified a strong undercurrent in progressivism that sought to put restrictions on economic behaviour in an attempt to revive an older tradition of moral limitations on economic conduct, without eliminating competition and market economics. In the words of the social worker Edward T. Devine, the state was obligated to 'fix the levels below which the exploitation of

(New York, 1932), pp. 252–78; and Herbst, *German Historical School*. The impact of Schmoller's ethical emphasis on American social scientists is illustrated by the fact that his 1881 essay 'Gerechtigkeit in der Volkswirtschaftslehre' was translated into English. See G. Schmoller, 'The Idea of Justice in Political Economy', *Annals of the Academy of Political and Social Science* 4 (1894), pp. 697–737. Other classic works of the historical school of economics include K. Knies, *Die politische Ökonomie vom geschichtlichen Standpuncte* (Braunschweig, 1853); W. Roscher, *Ansichten der Volkswirtschaft aus dem geschichtlichen Standpunkte* (Leipzig, 1861); and B. Hildebrand, *Die Nationalökonomie der Gegenwart und Zukunft und andere gesammelte Schriften* (Jena, 1922).

[8] Fox, *Discovery of Abundance*, p. 14.

[9] Henry C. Adams to James B. Angell, 25 March 1886, p. 2; Henry C. Adams, 'Berlin Diary', 20 December 1878, p. 17, and 4 January 1879, p. 31, Henry C. Adams Papers, Bentley Historical Library, University of Michigan, Ann Arbor.

[10] Henry C. Adams to James B. Angell, 25 March 1886, p. 4, Henry C. Adams Papers. See also Henry C. Adams, 'The Relation of the State to Industrial Action', *Publications of the American Economic Association* 1 (1887), pp. 465–549.

[11] Henry C. Adams, 'Opening Address for School of Applied Ethics', 1891, p. 6, Henry C. Adams Papers.

workers and consumers would not be tolerated', and above which 'the principles of free competition might safely and advantageously be left free to operate'.[12]

In the same vein, the sociologist Albion Woodbury Small personified the combination of moral reform and corporatist longing of German-inspired progressive thought. Small left for Germany in 1879 to study in Berlin under Wagner and Schmoller. In 1905, he founded the American Sociological Society and launched the *American Journal of Sociology*. Small advocated state intervention to ensure that business remained aware of its social responsibility toward the social organism. He also devised plans for the co-operative control of industries by labour and management, for employee stock-ownership, and for workingmen's housing, schooling and insurance. Nonetheless, he wanted to preserve a hierarchical system in the economic and social realm. Although he advocated worker co-operation, he did not want employees to be entitled to the same decision-making power as the employers.[13]

Throughout his writings, Small emphasized the organic unity of society, the necessity for social planning, and the development of a scientific system of ethics. He stressed the need for co-operation between the classes, and regarded workers and employers as two components in an organic system of production. He hailed the German cameralist tradition as 'the most effective economizer of national energy', because 'the incapable masses of the German people were divided into squads and disciplined for civic duties'. He also spoke highly of Bismarck's social legislation, while warning against the dangers of the German bureaucracy.[14]

Adams's and Small's historicist rehabilitation of the state was designed to present intervention as part and parcel of the established trajectory of American society. They embraced both moral reform and regulatory intervention. The potential conflict between these approaches, however, appears to have been of little concern to the genteel reformers. While moral reform considers the moral community to be the necessary normative basis of a society, regulatory intervention is based on the notion of a community of rational interest. Moral reform aims to enforce fixed rules of moral conduct by imposing, for example, blue laws, prohibition and anti-prostitution legislation; regulatory agencies aim to ensure the functioning of the market and to make the pursuit of self-interest in a competitive environment socially beneficial.

[12] E. T. Devine, *When Social Work Was Young* (New York, 1939), p. 4.
[13] G. Christakes, *Albion W. Small* (Boston, 1978), pp. 17, 94–5. See also C. Bernert, 'From Cameralism to Sociology with Albion Small', *Journal of the History of Sociology* 4 (1982), pp. 32–63.
[14] A. W. Small, *The Cameralists: The Pioneers of German Social Polity* (Chicago, 1909), pp. xv, 17.

## The critique of *laissez faire*

As progressive social thinkers began to explore further the ideas imported from Europe and to reflect upon social relations in the age of corporate capitalism, a new progressive theory of reform was born that bore little resemblance to the moralism and regulationism of Shaw, Adams and Small. This was a crucial moment in the intellectual history of progressivism which warrants closer analysis. Inspired by late nineteenth-century thought, ranging from pragmatism to the teachings of the German historical school, a new generation of progressive thinkers ushered in a thoroughgoing revision of the hallowed teachings of utilitarianism, empiricism and rationalism. They renounced the epistemological and ethical grounding of nineteenth-century liberalism which had provided the intellectual impetus for moral reform and regulatory intervention along the lines of Small and Adams. Their new theory of reform combined a radical re-evaluation of *laissez-faire* economics with a critique of liberal reform, a new interpretation of industrial capitalism, and a theory of democracy based on social ethics.[15]

### Historicizing capitalism

At the centre of the progressive critique of liberal economic thought stood the reinterpretation of Adam Smith. In offering a new look at the god-father of classical economic liberalism, the German-trained progressives and the historical school hoped to beat their orthodox liberal antagonists with their own weapons. The reformers charged that liberal economic theory had reduced Smith's ideas to a set of unchangeable economic laws, effectively suppressing the fact that Smith was, first and foremost, a moral philosopher who was aware of the close link between economic conduct and ethical codes. They maintained that Smith neither absolutized man as autonomous, acquisitive and self-interested, nor regarded freedom as grounded purely in private property. By historicizing Smith they hoped both to recover the moral content of his economic theories and to expose the fallacies of *laissez faire*.

---

[15] For the intellectual cross-currents of the age see Kloppenberg, *Uncertain Victory*; D. Ross, *Modernist Impulses in the Human Sciences* (Baltimore, 1994); H. S. Hughes, *Consciousness and Society: The Reorientation of European Social Thought, 1890–1930* (New York, 1958); M. White, *Social Thought in America: The Revolt against Formalism* (New York, 1949): and Fine, *Laissez Faire and General-Welfare State*. The notion that truth is a social product, that meanings are contingent and provisional, and that there are no universal categories or totalizing theories are important elements of both post-structuralist and progressive thought. For a discussion of the similarities between progressive social thought and post-structuralism see M. Stokes, 'Progressivism, Poststructuralism, and the Writing of American History', in D. K. Adams and C. A. van Minnen, eds, *Religious and Secular Reform in America: Ideas, Beliefs, and Social Change* (Edinburgh, 1999), pp. 205–29.

Gustav Schmoller maintained that Smith's self-seeking motive in economic pursuits was restricted and shaped by ethics, social customs and cultural traditions. He argued that Smith did not conceive of the 'dangers of a perverted spirit of usury, of a shameless, boundless, and avaricious spirit of acquisition [*Die Gefahren eines entarteten Wuchergeistes, eines scham- und schrankenlosen, habsüchtigen Erwerbsgeistes*]' of *laissez-faire* capitalism. According to Schmoller, Smith's faith in competition relied on the presence of internalized moral restrictions embedded in society, mainly the sense of 'justice and propriety [*Gerechtigkeit und Schicklichkeit*]' of the 'strict spirit of Calvinism'.[16] His attempt to rescue the moral content of the Scotsman's theories from the tight grip of orthodox liberals was eagerly taken up by American students of historicism. Albion Small, for example, maintained that Smith's ethical convictions had been suppressed and that the social sciences needed to return 'to a basis of moral philosophy . . . like that upon which Adam Smith rested his economic reasoning'.[17]

Above and beyond arguing that Smith's theories expressed moral preconceptions, rather than scientific truths, the progressive economists also maintained that producer capitalism as an economic system expressed the moral codes and intellectual horizon of its specific historical and cultural setting, and not absolute and universal laws. In the words of Thorstein Veblen, self-interest was merely 'a phase of the modern cultural situation'. The character of business organization, he explained, conformed 'to the circumstances of the time, not to any logical scheme of development from small to great or from simple to complex'.[18] Likewise, Schmoller substituted historical relativism for the liberal belief in the universal operation of Malthus's law of population growth, the iron law of wages, and the law of supply and demand. The historical analysis of capitalism thus helped reformers undermine liberalism's claim that the market was scientific and natural and that self-interest and acquisition were the sole motivations of human action.[19]

---

[16] G. Schmoller, 'Adam Smith', in *Charakterbilder* (Munich, 1913), p. 132. The essay originally appeared in 1901. For an incisive analysis of Smith and other economic thinkers see also T. Veblen, 'Preconceptions of Economics', in Wesley C. Mitchell, ed., *What Veblen Taught: Selected Writings of Thorstein Veblen* (New York, 1936), pp. 39–150. See also M. Weber, *Protestant Ethic*.

[17] A. W. Small, *Adam Smith and Modern Sociology* (Chicago, 1907), p. 11, quoted in J. Herbst, 'From Moral Philosophy to Sociology: Albion Woodbury Small', *Harvard Educational Review* 29 (1959), p. 235.

[18] Veblen, 'Gustav Schmoller's Economics', pp. 277–8.

[19] D. T. Rodgers provides a good discussion of the progressives' understanding of the market in political rather than scientific terms in *Atlantic Crossings*, pp. 78, 79–80.

### Relativizing morality

In addition to a historicizing capitalism, a relativistic understanding of morality was crucial for the emergence of a progressive theory of reform. The historicist concept of ethics and economics as linked in a process of mutual construction and as mirroring each other had wide-ranging implications for progressive social thought. If economic realities were reflections of culturally specific moral codes, then changes in moral norms would transform *laissez-faire* capitalism. By the same token, if social ethics mirrored economic realities, changes in the structures of capitalism would result in the transformation of moral norms.

In support of the first proposition – that changes in moral codes would engender changes in economic realities – the historical school offered an evolutionary and teleological conception of ethics. Derived from romanticism and Hegelian idealism, historicists regarded ethical development as part of a cultural and civilizational process which did not simply end with the self-interested rationality of autonomous and acquisitive individuals. Schmoller contended that man's moral energies, his '*sittliche Kräfte*', were, in the course of history, transformed into customs and objectified in institutions. 'Custom and law lend permanence and stability to ideas of morality, and effect the agreement of men about that which ought to be.' He maintained that both informed rational decisions in matters of economic justice and the 'psychological processes whose final result is the judgement which finds the distribution just or unjust' would determine social ethics and the extent of public control in a society. Thus, Schmoller insisted that vague feelings of justice would gradually grow into conscious judgements. 'And the more they rise to judgments and standards of valuation, the more the mental temperaments are condensed through the medium of public discussion, to decisions which possess distinct characteristics and criteria, the more we have before us mass-judgments . . . which are clear, firm and generally admitted.'[20]

In keeping with this theory of ethics, Schmoller regarded history as the gradual realization of a consciousness of social justice from an unreflected feeling of equity, social balance and just distribution of income. The specific content of justice could not be defined, since its realization was tied to a historical process that could not be predicted. The ethical theories of the historical school thus combined the belief in conscious action with a profound concern with subconscious motivations and subjective feelings. In the words of the economist Joseph Schumpeter, historicists saw 'people act according to rules which have not been reasoned out and

---

[20] Schmoller, 'Idea of Justice', pp. 28, 19, 12–13.

often appear to them as imperatives which cannot be discussed'.[21] This concern also anticipated the pragmatist focus on psychology and volition as determinants of reality, social systems and economic institutions. According to William James, for example, economic and social action could not be understood as the result of objective problems, but rather of inner psychological and philosophical desires.[22]

This evolutionary approach also indicates that social ethicism, unlike genteel moralism, regarded the ethical community as no longer based on fixed moral norms. Progressive social thinkers regarded values neither as grounded in metaphysical rights and the moral autonomy of rational subjects, as Kantian liberals maintained, nor as strategies of adaptation, as Darwinists suggested. Instead, the progressives saw ethics as socially and culturally constructed, and the ethical community as founded on institutions which allowed for ever widening political participation and social interaction. These institutions, they argued, would engender the development of a new ethic of interdependence commensurate with the social realities of urban and industrial life.[23]

### The rejection of liberal reform

The progressives' relativistic and evolutionary conception of ethics culminated in another crucial departure from the matrix of liberalism, namely the critique of the liberal rights-oriented reform tradition. The reformers challenged not only *laissez-faire* economics and liberalism's extrinsic and utilitarian ethics, but also its natural rights philosophy and deontological grounding. Justice, in their view, was not the same as equality, or even equal opportunity, and thus pointed beyond the liberal tradition of equal rights.[24] As disturbing as it may sound, the fact remains that the first significant twentieth-century social reform movement in the US had little use for the extension of civil and political rights as an avenue of social change.

---

[21] J. Schumpeter, *Economic Doctrine and Method: An Historical Sketch* (New York, 1954), p. 177.

[22] See W. James, *The Varieties of Religious Experience: A Study in Human Nature* (New York, 1902).

[23] Good examples that reflect this view in progressive thought and reform include F. C. Howe, *The City: The Hope of Democracy* (New York, 1905); L. S. Rowe, *Problems of City Government* (New York, 1908); A. W. Small, *Between Eras from Capitalism to Democracy* (Kansas City, 1913); and C. R. Henderson, *Social Elements, Institutions, Characters, Progress* (New York, 1911).

[24] Schmoller, like many progressives, argued for social reform on the basis of social equity, *suum cuique*, the distribution of reward and punishment according to the individual's needs and contributions to the social organism. See 'Idea of Justice', pp. 708–9, 715.

For many progressives influenced by historicism the traditional liberal concept of individual rights had lost its meaning in the context of an interdependent urban and industrial society. Suffrage and constitutionalism did not seem to offer solutions to the problems of industrial exploitation, urban congestion, business monopolies and cut-throat competition. The right to vote had not helped workers fight industrial exploitation. Legal recourse had not been a remedy for the devastating effects of industrial accidents. By the late nineteenth century the rights debate which had gripped reform circles in the United States around the time of the Civil War had dissipated. An 'inverse relationship between welfare and civil rights policies . . . in which support for one combined with opposition to the other' characterized the Progressive Era.[25]

Although numerous progressive thinkers, such as Louis Brandeis and W. E. B. Du Bois, supported expanded civil and social rights, the rights discourse was not dominant in progressivism. The reformers tended to argue their case on the basis of social efficiency and ethical demands, not on the basis of extending individual or collective rights. Even the socialist Florence Kelley found it more expedient to use the rhetoric of social ethics and women's needs for special protection than to argue for workers' rights. Likewise, recent scholarship contends that maternalist welfare activism was based on attending to specific social needs, not on the demand for social rights.[26] Many reformers were hesitant to extend suffrage, tended to ignore the problems of race inequality, and even embraced manifestations of rights violations in the foreign countries they sought to emulate.[27] The glowing reports about German urban reform, including those by Shaw and Ely, often favoured the country's discriminatory three-class voting system.[28]

---

[25] E. L. McDonagh, 'The "Welfare Rights State" and the "Civil Rights State": Policy Paradox and State Building in the Progressive Era', *Studies in American Political Development* 7 (1993), p. 252. See also Rodgers, *Atlantic Crossings*, pp. 41–2, 53–4, 143.

[26] On maternalism and the rights discourse see K. K. Sklar, *Florence Kelley and the Nation's Work: The Rise of Women's Political Culture, 1830–1900* (New Haven, 1995), and L. Gordon, *Pitied But Not Entitled: Single Mothers and the History of Welfare* (Cambridge, 1994); see also F. Kelley, *Modern Industry in Relation to the Family, Health, Education, Morality* (New York, 1914).

[27] A concise history of the relationship between progressivism and race is still missing. For an excellent account of the race issue in the settlement house movement see E. Lasch-Quinn, *Black Neighbors: Race and the Limits of Reform in the American Settlement House Movement, 1890–1945* (Chapel Hill, 1993); for a typical progressive view on race see R. S. Baker, *Following the Color Line: American Negro Citizenship in the Progressive Era* (New York, 1908). I have explored this issue in A. R. Schäfer, 'W. E. B. Du Bois, German Social Thought, and the Racial Divide in American Progressivism, 1892–1909', *Journal of American History* 87 (2001), pp. 925–49.

[28] For examples of progressive support for the Prussian three-class voting system see R. T. Ely, 'Administration of the City of Berlin', *Nation* 34 (23 March 1882), pp. 245–6;

While this repudiation of liberal reform can easily be seen as reactionary, the disdain for rights in favour of social ethics was not simply a reflection of middle-class morality and deep-seated conservatism. On the contrary, the rejection of the rights discourse marked the intellectual departure of many progressives from their liberal heritage and portended the emergence of genuinely radical ideas. Granting further civil or procedural rights was no longer a solution in the progressives' view, since the idea of individual rights had originated in the specific historical context of the eighteenth century and could not be regarded as a universal moral imperative. Neither was extending civil rights of any use as a means of transcending the utilitarian ethics, self-interested rationality and empiricist epistemology of liberalism. Many progressive social thinkers made the criticism that civil, political and social rights ultimately served to tie people to the norms and practices of liberal capitalist society by encouraging competitive behaviour and individual ambition. Since rights-oriented reform uses state regulatory power to protect private property, contractual rights and the autonomy of the individual, it does not aim to overcome market society, but to enable the individual to function in it.

By the same token, liberal reform, indebted to eighteenth-century thinkers, sought to restrain the concentration of political power through constitutional limits on government and expanded suffrage, rather than to control the processes of commodification. In contrast, progressives contended that the concentration of economic power and the problem of social fragmentation needed to be addressed. Industrial society, Thorstein Veblen and others argued, had not only changed the conditions of production, it had also transformed social relations and undermined the rights-based conception of the individual. According to John Dewey, 'a right, individual in residence, is social in origin and intent'. He insisted that political rights could only be meaningful as a basis for the participation of individuals in the democratic construction of social ethics.[29]

One of the key translators of these undercurrents of the historical school into progressive social thought was Simon Patten. He set sail for Germany in 1876 to study in Halle under Johannes Conrad. An original, though

A. Shaw, 'Government of German Cities', *Century* 48 (1894), pp. 296–305; and R. C. Brooks, 'City Government by Taxpayers: The Three-Class Election System in Prussian Cities', *Municipal Affairs* 3 (1899), pp. 396–423.

[29] J. Dewey and J. Tufts, *Ethics* (New York, 1908), p. 440. For Veblen's concept of the disjuncture between social realities and natural rights philosophy see Mitchell, ed., *What Veblen Taught*. The debate about the social construction of rights, and whether justice is a matter of guaranteeing natural rights of the autonomous subject or of pursuing culturally conditioned ideas of the social good, continues in modern liberal thought. See, for example, John Rawls, *A Theory of Justice* (Oxford, 1972), M. J. Sandel, *Liberalism and the Limits of Justice* (Cambridge, 1982), and J. Rawls, *Political Liberalism* (New York, 1993).

often obfuscating, thinker, Patten understood the radical implications of historicism and formulated a distinctive critique of American liberal democracy on this basis. Under the influence of Conrad, he began to look at society as an organism, and at man as defined by social networks. In tune with many German-trained progressives, Patten considered a democracy which was based on the representation of competing social interests less than adequate, because it subordinated conscience to expediency, and reduced the role of consciousness to that of rational adjustment to the social and economic status quo. Patten charged that the American view of freedom was 'a political concept that has no content but freedom from control'. Constitutional limitations 'put the freedom of person above group welfare'. While the Germans had not yet risen to the level of democracy of the English-speaking countries, Americans had not emancipated themselves from an individualistic conception of liberty which the Germans had long abandoned for a superior concept of liberty based on interdependence.[30]

For Patten and others, liberty was not defined negatively as protection from intrusion, but positively as developing meaning in the context of humans interacting in the making of their own laws. On this basis progressive thinkers rejected the primacy of the right over the good and questioned the civil rights agenda of liberal reform. They constructed democracy no longer in terms of protecting individual rights and market relations, but in terms of social ethics.[31]

### The ethical potential of industrial capitalism

As mentioned earlier, the second proposition which emerged from the progressives' close reading of historicism was that changes in capitalism would bring about changes in social ethics. Building upon Hegelian, Marxist and historicist ideas, many progressives maintained that the new avenues for social interaction and participation opened up by industrial capitalism could become the basis for challenging market society, liberalism, and the concept of the autonomous, acquisitive individual. Schmoller himself regarded the growing complexity and interdependence of social relations in industrial societies as a moral process. 'The further the division of labor progresses, the more inextricably will the thread of intercourse involve the individual in an insoluble social community,' he concluded, arguing that these new relations based on economic interaction attained a moral character, since they united people for a common

---

[30] S. N. Patten, 'The German Way of Thinking', *Forum* 54 (1915), pp. 22–3.
[31] On Patten see Fox, *Discovery of Abundance*; see also J. Dorfman, *The Economic Mind in American Civilization* (New York, 1959), 3 vols, vol. III, pp. 182–8.

purpose.[32] In the same vein, many American reformers maintained that the formation of new social ethics and the attachment to norms and values needed to be understood as part and parcel of the dynamics of industrial capitalism.

In embracing this view, progressive social thinkers parted with the genteel yearning for an idealized past of moral rectitude and producer capitalism which had grown in the soil of Protestant morality, Republican social thought and Hamiltonian federalism. They not only asserted that the social realities of industrial capitalism themselves pointed toward the overcoming of the ideological and economic underpinnings of *laissez-faire* capitalism, but also replaced the historical school's search for ethics embedded in history with the search for ethics embedded in industrial society. Progressive thinkers, such as John Dewey and George Herbert Mead, rarely engaged in a misty-eyed idealization of organic social relations and traditional folkways challenged by the processes of commodification. Expressing a generally favourable view of industrial society, they regarded the alleged destruction of communal ties and traditional moral codes in modern society as less of a problem than the persistence of quasi-feudal structures in the economy, buttressed by a subservient political and legal system.[33]

In a manner reminiscent of Karl Marx, the progressives linked the development of democratic social ethics to the development of industrial capitalism which contained within itself an unfulfilled social potential. Industrial society, they argued, revealed that man's existence was relational and interdependent, and showed that social development relied upon co-operative efforts and co-ordinated productive output. John Dewey, for example, insisted that the breakdown of customary morals and social ties in industrial modernity actually increased opportunities for initiative and endeavour, providing multiple stimuli for the application of the creative human will. 'The history of setting free individual power in desire, thought, and initiative,' he reasoned, 'is, upon the whole, the history of the formation of more complex and extensive social organization.' Increasing social and economic interconnectedness worked toward the creation

---

[32] Schmoller, 'Idea of Justice', p. 23.

[33] Although Dewey himself was intensely critical of German thought and politics, his ideas are the best expression of specific epistemological and ethical ideas in progressivism that German-trained reformers arrived at on the basis of their adaptation of historicism. See J. Dewey, *German Philosophy and Politics* (New York, 1915). George Herbert Mead, who was also trained in Germany, postulated that meaning was not intrinsic, but derived from human interaction in specific contexts. His concepts, which were later called 'symbolic interactionism', can be seen as the sociological foundation for this conception of ethics. See R. M. Crunden, *Ministers of Reform: The Progressives' Achievement in American Civilization, 1889–1920* (New York, 1982), pp. 25–38.

of a progressive and moral society, Dewey contended. The stranglehold of small groups and exclusive loyalties was broken and 'some institution grows up to represent the interests and activities of the whole as against the narrow and centrifugal tendencies of the constituent factors'. This worked to the benefit of individual moral development, since modern society 'with its multiple occupations, its easy intercourse, its free mobility, its rich resources of art and science, will have only too many opportunities for reflective judgment and personal valuation and preference'.[34]

The organic community of progressivism was thus not marked by recovering historical ties and loyalties, but by the rational development of social ethics and sensitivities as a result of social experience in industrial society. Dewey regarded communication not simply as a functional instrument to co-ordinate social action, but as an event that enabled individuals to open themselves up to others and allowed for experiences which resulted in the attachment to norms and values. He insisted that the processes of communication and participation would enable individuals to develop an inner sense that their freedom and happiness were tied to their social being.[35]

### Progressive democracy and the state

By defining reform less as intervention to control the excesses of *laissez faire* than as building upon the social potentialities of industrial capitalism, progressives faced a dilemma. While industrial society afforded new opportunities for political participation, it also threatened to undermine democracy. In Dewey's view the concentration of economic power and the emergence of industrial culture had led to an ambivalent situation. On the one hand, industrial civilization created a new awareness that 'all modern life . . . is completely bound up with and dependent upon facilities of communication, intercourse, and distribution'. On the other hand, it posed a serious threat to social progress by depriving masses of people of the opportunity to develop their talents and become active participants in the democratic discourse.[36]

Hence, Dewey and others did not see social progress simply as the automatic outcome of the increasing interconnectedness of society. Rather, they considered progress to be the result of society actively enabling the individual to pursue moral growth through social integration and participation. 'Practical conditions should be afforded which will enable

---

[34] Dewey and Tufts, *Ethics*, pp. 438, 435, 434.
[35] See H. Joas, *Die Entstehung der Werte* (Frankfurt, 1997), p. 184.
[36] Dewey and Tufts, *Ethics*, p. 477.

[the individual] effectively to take advantage of the opportunities formally open,' Dewey asserted, because only humans who 'are exempt from external obstruction . . . become aware of possibilities, and are awakened to demand and strive to obtain more positive freedom'. He argued that industrial relations needed to be reconstructed in ways which allowed for the participation and interaction of individuals in order to encourage social responsibility, meaningful labour, the formulation of ethical goals, and the scrutiny of political and economic decisions. He demanded the creation of 'new civic and political agencies' to afford these opportunities and allow for the development of 'a *generalized* individualism which takes into account the real good and effective – not merely formal – freedom of *every* member of society'.[37] Like Schmoller, Dewey maintained that the improvement of institutions was both the result and the origin of the refinement of man's ethical nature. In his eyes, the social sciences were the key to solving social problems and to suggesting new civic institutions for the moral end of developing 'the welfare of society as an organized community of attainment and endeavor' in such fields as sanitation, social legislation, recreation, factory inspection and city planning. In the words of Albion Small, sociology was 'a moral philosophy conscious of its task, and systematically pursuing knowledge of cause and effect within this process of moral evolution'.[38]

This progressive conception of reform differed not only from homegrown moralism and the liberal insistence on protecting individual rights; it also differed from paternalist statism. Progressives are often criticized for paving the way for the bureaucratic welfare state. Their enchantment with German public policy, their critique of market economics, their repudiation of the liberal rights discourse, and their moralism has caused many scholars to maintain that the reformers justified and promoted the emergence of large-scale bureaucratic intervention.[39] Yet a closer look at the evidence reveals that neither the adaptation of German thought nor that of German reform models caused progressives to promote a

---

[37] Ibid., pp. 439, 472.

[38] Ibid., p. 473; A. W. Small, 'Technique as Approach to Science: A Methodological Note', *American Journal of Sociology* 27 (1922), p. 650. W. Eucken termed Schmoller's approach '*ethisch-biologische Fortschrittsidee*'. See Eucken, 'Wissenschaft im Stile Schmollers', *Weltwirtschaftliches Archiv* 52 (1940), pp. 468–506.

[39] See, for example, S. B. Hays, *Conservation and the Gospel of Efficiency: The Progressive Conservation Movement, 1890–1920* (Cambridge, 1959); R. H. Wiebe, *The Search for Order, 1877–1920* (New York, 1967); G. Kolko, *The Triumph of Conservatism: A Reinterpretation of American History, 1900–1916* (New York, 1963). On the development of state administrative capacities see B. C. Campbell, *The Growth of American Government: Governance from the Cleveland Era to the Present* (Bloomington, 1995), and S. Skowronek, *Building a New American State: The Expansion of National Administrative Capacities, 1877–1920* (New York, 1982).

paternalist state. On the contrary, in historicist thought the state's role was not codified and prescribed.

German-trained progressives agreed with Schmoller that the issue was not one of state intervention versus market rule. 'I was never taught in Germany that the greater the activity of the state the better,' Ely noted, 'I was taught to examine into the grounds for state action as well as for private action.' As Dewey put it, 'The question really involved is not one of magnifying the power of the State against individuals, but is one of making individual liberty a more extensive and equitable matter.'[40] Moreover, the advocates of the social ethics model of reform abandoned the genteel attempt to find a trajectory of statism in the American past. They distrusted and reviled the often corrupt and inefficient institutions of American government. Their glance across the Atlantic was part of the progressive attempt to fight genuinely American manifestations of social welfare policies, such as the abused pension system. They also resented the urban political machines, which offered jobs and a measure of social security to a working-class clientele in exchange for votes and loyalty.[41]

Progressivism was thus not primarily an attempt to strengthen the state and bureaucratic control over the free market. Instead, the progressives' call for a broader public sphere, ranging from urban parks to municipal ownership of utilities, needs to be understood in the context of their belief in the ethical effects of new public institutions. The campaigns for urban reform, city planning and compulsory health insurance, for example, neither demonized the state nor embraced large-scale bureaucratic solutions. They were based on a philosophy of reform which sought to understand the social dynamics of industrial capitalism in order to overcome market society and its attendant moral codes, and to promote an expanded sphere of public control and democratic decision-making.[42]

[40] K. H. Kaufhold, 'Gustav von Schmoller (1838–1917) als Historiker, Wirtschafts- und Sozialpolitiker und Nationalökonom', *Vierteljahrschrift für Sozial- und Wirtschaftsgeschichte* 75 (1988), p. 235; Richard T. Ely to Henry W. Farnam, 16 November 1906, Henry Farnam Papers, Manuscripts and Archives Section, New York Public Library, New York; Dewey and Tufts, *Ethics*, p. 481.

[41] For a good discussion of the political meaning of the reformers' fight against patronage democracy see T. Skocpol, *Protecting Soldiers and Mothers. The Political Origins of Social Policy in the United States* (Cambridge, 1992), pp. 261ff. On the relationship between reformers and urban machines see ibid., pp. 96–101. By the same token the reformers objected to the paternalistic social policies advocated by big business. In fact, they often found private business more centralized and bureaucratic than the state. For a good discussion see E. Berkowitz and K. McQuaid, *Creating the Welfare State. The Political Economy of Twentieth Century Reform* (Lawrence, KA, 1992), pp. 112ff.

[42] For details on the campaigns for health insurance and city planning see Schäfer, *American Progressives*, pp. 79–188.

## Two conceptions of progressive democracy

Historicizing the market, relativizing morality, rejecting rights-oriented reform, reinterpreting the social and ethical implications of industrial capitalism, and rejecting statism were the main components of the emerging progressive theory of democracy and its interventionist agenda. The goal of progressives was to uncover the social foundations of industrial capitalism and to use them to construct a concept of democracy beyond *laissez faire*, moral regulation and limited government. In his incisive critique of progressivism, however, Christopher Lasch maintains that progressive social thought was torn between what he calls conceptions of participatory democracy and distributive democracy.[43] This conflict reveals both the radicalism of progressivism and the way in which progressive social ethics provided a new rationale for market relations under the conditions of consumer capitalism.

Lasch sees John Dewey, Herbert Croly, Thorstein Veblen, Louis Mumford and Van Wyck Books as the main advocates of the participatory view of democracy. Displaying strong affinities with French syndicalism and British guild socialism, they regarded the revival of craftsmanship, meaningful labour, and control over the workplace as prerequisites for a democratic culture. Fearing that large-scale production would undercut the sense of responsibility necessary for a democratic order, they were primarily concerned with instilling democratic mental habits and republican virtues in individual producers through participatory structures in the workplace.[44] In the words of John Dewey, democracy was 'the effective embodiment of the moral ideal of a good which consists in the development of all the social capacities of every individual member'. The primary goals of government intervention were to democratize the workplace, broaden the sphere of public control, and ensure equal opportunity of participation for all as a prerequisite for social progress, political tranquillity and moral growth. The real justification for democratic government lay in its potential for promoting social ethics, not in its protection of individual rights. Structured participation and communication, Dewey asserted, made people aware of their interdependence and gave them an opportunity to rationally connect with each other, solve specific problems of an interdependent industrial society, and open up new avenues for ethical self-realization.[45] In the words of W. E. B. Du

---

[43] C. Lasch, *The True and Only Heaven: Progress and Its Critics* (New York, 1991), pp. 345–6.
[44] Ibid., pp. 340–2, 345–8.
[45] Dewey and Tufts, *Ethics*, pp. 474ff. Hans Joas argues that Dewey ends up 'sacralizing' democracy, which contradicts his reasoned ethical relativism. Joas, *Entstehung*, pp. 187, 194.

Bois, it was the duty of the state to interfere in order to link industrial pursuits to the ethical development of the social organism and ensure the welfare of the whole. Democracy was not a functional arrangement or a mechanical problem, but a system that gave meaning and significance to human strivings.[46]

Dewey's concept of democratic reform pursued two goals. First, his scheme of social and moral development was designed to safeguard against 'explosive change and intermittent blind action and reaction', allowing instead for the 'graduated and steady reconstruction' of society. In this regard, Dewey expressed the fear of radical change which marked both historicism and progressivism. Second, Dewey sought to make sure that society heeded the lessons of evolutionism. In pragmatist fashion he held out the promise that democratic society, in order to preserve its progressive dynamics and further the development of social complexity, 'will not subordinate individual variations, but will encourage individual experimentation in new ideas and new projects'.[47] To quote Du Bois again, a true democratic government needed to recognize 'not only the worth of the individual to himself, but the worth of his feelings and experiences to all' in order to realize 'the broadest justice for all citizens'. Shutting out a people on the basis of race was actually diminishing the progress of humanity as such, since 'there is lost from the world an experience of untold value'.[48]

In regard to the distributive view of democracy, Lasch singles out Simon Patten and the journalist Walter Weyl as two crucial advocates. According to Lasch, the distributive approach associates democracy with prosperity and universal abundance. It pursues the democratization of leisure and consumption, rather than of industrial relations. Access to consumer goods, rather than political participation, is the overriding concern. Distributive democracy adopts the concept of a surplus economy and links progress to the democratization of consumption, seeing the broadening of consuming powers as the impetus for social improvement. It also acknowledges that the age of abundance demands a new morality outside the old mantra of hard work, self-sacrifice, discipline and loyalty. Defining progressivism as a consumers' movement, its advocates are primarily concerned with techniques of distributing the fruits of labour in a large-scale industrial capitalist setting through taxation, welfare-state building, and growth-oriented economic planning.[49]

Patten and others drew very different lessons than Dewey from studying the interdependencies of industrial society. They focused on the immense

---

[46] W. E. B. Du Bois, *Darkwater: Voices from Within the Veil* (New York, 1920), pp. 158–9.
[47] Dewey and Tufts, *Ethics*, pp. 446, 485.    [48] Du Bois, *Darkwater*, p. 144.
[49] Lasch, *True and Only Heaven*, pp. 68–71, 342–4.

increase in productive output through technology and organizational efficiency. They linked human self-realization to the ability to consume and enjoy abundance, rather than to exerting control over the workplace, meaningful labour, and democratic participation. Patten, who frequently corresponded with leading German scholars, including Schmoller and Max Weber, was fascinated with the subjectivist implications of historicism and developed a 'potentially explosive theory of social surplus'.[50] Like Schmoller, he insisted that the law of supply and demand was only partially the result of natural processes. Schmoller had concluded that '[d]emand and supply are summary terms for the magnitudes of opposing groups of human wills. The causes and conditions of these magnitudes are partly natural, mostly, however, human relations and powers, human deliberations and actions.'[51] In the same vein, Patten declared that 'laws, customs, habits, democratic feelings, ethical ideals constitute the subjective environment' that tended to 'eradicate those mental and physical peculiarities due to local, objective conditions'. He maintained that 'color, for example, adheres not in the object, but is placed there by the observer. The same faculty is utilized by the individual to objectify his habitual choices. He thinks of them as adhering in the object although created by himself.'[52] Expanding on this dynamic and evolutionary interplay of objective and subjective forces, Patten challenged the wisdom of the iron law of wages and free market economics. He used Conrad's argument that abundance, rather than scarcity, was the long-term trend in the economy and lambasted free trade, because it encouraged single-crop agriculture which resulted in a lack of variety in agricultural goods and weakened health conditions.[53] According to Patten the supply of goods under the conditions of liberal capitalism was not a response to objective demand, but the result of political interests which limited both the amount and quality of economic production. All of this left a mark on Patten's student Rexford Tugwell and his ideas on agriculture during the New Deal.

## Progressive thought and US social policy

The dual agenda of this volume – to recover intellectual traditions critical of the free market and to show that the functioning of markets was prescribed by distinct cultural and institutional contexts – raises the question to what extent the two trajectories of progressive thought shaped

[50] Dorfman, *Economic Mind*, p. 188.    [51] Schmoller, 'Idea of Justice', p. 19.
[52] S. N. Patten, 'The Organic Concept of Society', *Annals of the Academy of Political and Social Science* 5 (1894), pp. 89, 91–2.
[53] Dorfman, *Economic Mind*, p. 183.

American social and economic policy. Of course, linking social thought to actual policies is fraught with danger. Economic interests and political path-dependency are usually considered to be more convincing as explanations for policy development. Moreover, the American system of social provision is a complex mesh of public, non-profit and private programmes, and of state, local, and federal government involvement, which defies easy categorization. However, as recent studies have shown, progressive social thought provided the basic parameters for twentieth-century social science thinking on poverty and the welfare state.[54]

Within the confines of this essay, a closer look at two characteristics of the American system of social provision will have to suffice to highlight the interplay of progressive social thought and social policy. The first is that American social policy in the twentieth century was primarily designed as a politics of economic growth and was marked by a shift in focus from production to consumption. In this context the progressive-era reinterpretation of the market, at least the distributive model with its theories of the consumer economy, appears to have made some inroads in shaping policies. World War I, Christopher Lasch maintains, was the single most important factor in the shift towards the dominance of an 'assimilationist, consumerist, distributive version of the democratic dogma', primarily because of the focus on productive output, the lessons of centralization, the marginalization of both socialist and syndicalist views, and the disillusionment with democratic politics and public opinion in the aftermath of war.[55] The Great Depression and World War II further contributed to this dominance. During and after the war, government retreated from control and regulation of business and embraced federal fiscal policies as the main social policy tool, paving the way for post-war 'military Keynesianism'. The fear of another depression, the lessons of the wartime boom, and the atmosphere of the Cold War channelled liberal thought in the direction of growth-inducing policies without economic restructuring. Social policies were designed to boost consumer spending through subsidies, tax breaks, full employment policies and deficit spending.[56]

Moreover, it can be argued that the concepts of the self advanced by Dewey, Patten and others formed the basis of a personality structure required by consumer capitalism. The reformers' focus on social relations as constituting the individual's identity, on subconscious desires

[54] See, for example, A. O'Connor, *Poverty Knowledge: Social Science, Social Policy, and the Poor in Twentieth-Century U.S. History* (Princeton, 2001).
[55] Lasch, *True and Only Heaven*, p. 360.
[56] For useful discussions of the use of fiscal policies as a social policy tool during and after World War II see M. Sherry, *In the Shadow of War: The United States Since the 1930s* (New Haven, 1995); A. Wolfe, *America's Impasse: The Rise and Fall of the Politics of Growth* (New York, 1980); A. Brinkley, *Liberalism and Its Discontents* (Cambridge, 1998).

as defining social reality, and on the need for new moral codes commensurate with an economy of abundance, were key intellectual shifts in the transition from producer to consumer capitalism. Though rejecting the nineteenth-century view of self-interested individuals competing in the marketplace, advocates of both the participatory and the distributive model embraced the concept of the flexible, adaptable individual whose social and moral make-up was derived from the experience of social interaction. The progressives' assumption that industrial society had swept away historical ties and traditions and produced individuals freed from history in fact replicates the 'blank slate' concept and the state of nature of Lockean liberalism and recasts the foundation myth of the American republic.[57]

If the politics of growth indicate the partial adoption of one strand of progressive reinterpretations of the market, the second feature of the American system of social provision – that character issues and moral norms have retained a prominent role in debates on social policy – reveals a more ambivalent picture. Character issues, morals testing, gender discrimination, and racialized welfare provision are part and parcel of the American system of social provision, and have made a sustained comeback in recent years.[58] 'Moral tales', as the economist Robert Reich calls them, define social problems and frame the welfare debate. Recent research has shown that even during Lyndon B. Johnson's Great Society programmes in the 1960s, when the most fervent effort was made to part with the tradition of morally charged categorizing, the aim remained to convert the poor, who were still seen as intrinsically hedonistic, improvident, unable to defer gratification, and trapped in cycles of dependency.

On this count progressive social thought seems to have failed to leave its mark. Modern social policies institutionalize traditional moral reform, rather than its progressive critique. They focus on adjusting individual

---

[57] For an excellent analysis of the intellectual shift from nineteenth-century notions of economic man to twentieth-century concepts of 'social selfhood' see J. Sklansky, *The Soul's Economy: Market Society and Selfhood in American Thought, 1820–1920* (Chapel Hill, NC, 2002). For insights on the tension between traditional moral codes and consumer capitalism see D. Bell, *The Cultural Contradictions of Capitalism* (New York, 1976). For the link between progressive and pragmatist social thought and consumer society, as well as its defence, see R. Rorty, *Philosophy and Social Hope* (London, 1999).

[58] For useful discussions of the meaning of morality in social policy see, e.g., J. Handler and Y. Hasenfeld, *The Moral Construction of Poverty. Welfare Reform in America* (Newbury Park, London, 1991); R. B. Reich, *Tales of a New America* (New York, 1987). Reich, a Harvard economist, was Secretary of Labor in the first Clinton administration. On the Great Society see A. O'Connor, 'Neither Charity Nor Relief: The War on Poverty and the Efforts to Redefine the Basis of Social Provision', in D. T. Critchlow and C. H. Parker, eds, *With Us Always: A History of Private Charity and Public Welfare* (Lanham, MD, 1998).

behaviour, rather than on extending democracy in the workplace. However, we can hardly let the progressives off the hook. Moralism is not just part of the rhetorical arsenal of conservatives. The terminology of welfare dependency, dysfunctional families, culture of poverty, deficiencies of poor communities, or, to use the term frequently heard in Britain these days, 'social exclusion', is fundamental to progressive social thinking and its focus on social interaction as the basis for value formation. The interactionist ethic of progressivism formulated a normative code, which, by tying values to social interaction, became the basis of declaring the poor deficient in the development of their social ethics. Poverty was thus defined as a problem of insufficient socialization, rather than as a problem of economic exploitation and inequality. As Alice O'Connor has shown, this analysis helped channel progressive energies either into addressing the alleged deficiencies of poor families and communities through social work intervention, rehabilitative measures, and workfare policies, or into macro-economic planning to remove barriers to labour force participation and encourage economic growth.[59]

It can thus be argued that while progressive thought helped shape the consumer economy, welfare policies remained tied to the normative code of nineteenth-century producer capitalism. One of the remarkable phenomena in US social policy is that the welfare state is rhetorically largely separated from consumer society. While consumer society relies upon the willingness of consumers to spend and indulge, welfare politicians talk about the need for a work ethic, self-discipline, responsibility and moral self-control. Consumer culture has destigmatized behavioural norms associated with infantile behaviour among the middle classes, particularly in the wake of the adaptation of middle-class norms to the requirements of consumer capitalism in the 1960s. At the same time, welfare policies have sought to stigmatize the same norms among the poor. Thus, while the poor are chided for becoming 'dependent' on welfare, equivalent behaviour patterns among the middle classes are defined as conducive to the workings of the consumer economy.

Part of the reason why progressive thought was more successful in promoting consumer culture than in shaping social and economic policy was that the reformers failed to pursue more forcefully a syndicalist and participatory vision of self-governed decentralized economic units without embracing the large-scale state. This participatory vision had found expression, for example, in the early social insurance campaigns and the city planning movement in the late nineteenth and early twentieth centuries as part of the transatlantic exchange discussed in this essay. In contrast, the

[59] O'Connor, *Poverty Knowledge*, pp. 14–19.

distributive view encouraged the development of habits of consumption, but did little to promote civic consciousness, public control, meaningful labour and workplace codetermination. As progressivism came to be identified with distributive democracy, the emphasis on values and ethics was increasingly hijacked by conservatives and used to remoralize the debate on poverty.

## Conclusion

The analysis of the transatlantic dimension of progressive social thought provides new insights into the intellectual foundations of progressivism and challenges assumptions about the nature of American reform. It suggests that progressive reform thought was a significant intellectual tradition in its own right, rather than just an expedient instrument applied to improve the efficiency of large-scale industrial production, to adapt nineteenth-century society to the requirements of twentieth-century capitalism, or to build a welfare state that focused on social order and bureaucratic control.

The transatlantic vantage point reveals that in the course of integrating the historicist concepts of their German mentors the reformers abandoned the philosophical parameters of nineteenth-century liberalism and suggested a radical theory of social reform. Progressive social thought after the historicist turn questioned the belief in fixed moral norms that underpinned the earlier genteel reformers' calls for controlling the excesses of capitalism. It parted with the liberal rights-oriented reform tradition, criticized regulatory intervention designed to uphold the competitive market, and remained sceptical of paternalistic state control.

In its stead, the reformers historicized market society, advanced a relativistic conception of morality, detached democratic development from the assertion of individual rights, and linked social progress to democratizing the industrial order. Historicizing the market enabled them to understand capitalism as a historical construct, rather than an expression of the natural order of human relations; maintaining that moral codes were dependent on contingent institutions and cultural practices allowed the reformers to argue that human moral development resulted from social interaction; the critique of the rights discourse helped them understand that the concept of individual rights was not based on metaphysical truths, but perpetuated the norms and values of capitalist market society; the rejection of bureaucratic control allowed them to rescue their democratic feelings from the temptations of 'reform from above' and to understand the democratizing potential of European social reform.

However, while many progressives envisaged an organic society based on social ethics, they did not seek to recover an idealized past in order to reconstruct social cohesion. Instead, they suggested that the interaction and participation of human beings in new democratically governed public institutions would replace the motivation of self-interest and calculating reason with a new ethical community born of experiences and sentiments that developed from an awareness of interdependence. Moreover, many progressives applied historicist interpretations to the study of industrial society. Since historicizing the market had removed the naturalist trappings from capitalism, and relativizing morality had stripped reform of its foundationalist heritage, industrial capitalism and reform could only be understood in relationship to each other. They maintained that the interdependencies and social interaction in industrial capitalism would yield new social ethics, which would engender calls for a broader sphere of public control and new, non-commercial, public institutions.

This interactionist translation of historicism yielded two distinct strands of progressive thinking. On the one hand, advocates of the participatory view of democracy focused on industrial democracy and self-governing institutions. On the other hand, proponents of the distributive view of democracy made access to consumer goods and wealth distribution their overriding concern. In the context of the emerging American welfare state the distributive view amounted less to a radical critique of liberal economics than to an intellectual justification of consumer capitalism. Its advocates embraced a personality structure that stressed flexibility and adaptation, rejected traditional moral codes, and saw consumer demands and subconscious desires as engines of social and economic progress. While the distributive conception became institutionalized in social and economic policies, the participatory approach was increasingly marginalized. This failure of progressive social thought to bridge the gap between consumer society and social ethicism had significant consequences, since it allowed both the capitalist politics of growth and conservative moralistic rhetoric to dominate American social and economic policy in the long term.

# 9 Civilizing markets: traditions of consumer politics in twentieth-century Britain, Japan and the United States

*Patricia Maclachlan and Frank Trentmann*

At the turn of the twenty-first century, consumers and politics stand in a paradoxical relationship. Never before have consumers in advanced economies had it so good. According to the proponents of more open and competitive global markets, consumers have been the principal beneficiaries of deregulation and trade liberalization in the 1980s and 1990s. At the same time, there has been a wave of consumer protests at international summits and in local politics against the democratic, economic and ethical costs of globalization. How should we explain this paradox?

One school of thought views the recent consumer protests as a reaction to the global processes of capitalist branding and production[1] – processes that created the very communicative and cultural openings for the development of a critical global consumer movement. This account is a good social movement story, popular with the critics of trade liberalization, but it is marred by a number of conceptual and empirical problems. First, by treating the recent wave of consumer activism in isolation from the network of national and international consumer movements and their ideological evolution in the twentieth century, the globalization narrative ignores the persistence of different traditions of consumer politics. Just as deregulatory processes have diverged across countries, so, too, have the ideological definitions and political uses of 'the consumer'. Second, the narrative helps explain how consumer movements arise in response to changes in the political economy, yet fails to explore how the movements themselves have contributed to the structure and dynamics of political economies. Finally, the globalization perspective pays too much attention to the institutional foundations of consumer-related policies and neglects the myriad ways in which ideology shapes the nature of 'consumption'

The authors would like to thank Mark Bevir for comments, and Frank Trentmann also the ESRC and AHRB for award L 34341003.
[1] See, for example, N. Klein, *No Logo* (New York, 1999).

in different societies and locates and legitimizes the position of the 'consumer' in relation to the state, civil society and the market.

In contrast to political scientists who have turned to institutional or legal structures to explain cross-national differences in consumer politics and policy,[2] our discussion seeks a more historically informed understanding of the different ideological traditions that shaped the formation of organized consumer groups and definitions of consumers' interests. This chapter will explore the evolution of these traditions in twentieth-century Great Britain, the United States, and Japan, where consumers have banded together to civilize capitalism in very different ways. Our aim is to reinsert the role of traditions and beliefs into studies of consumer politics as a way of understanding the ideas and norms informing policy making and its institutional practices. What states and other institutions do for consumers is partly determined by what organized consumers define as their needs, rights and responsibilities and by what they see as the legitimate agencies of reform. Institutions are not idea-free containers. How consumers define themselves over time and are defined by others matters. Far from being new or surprising reactions to globalization, the current wave of international consumer protests, we argue, needs to be reconnected to the historical evolution of nationally specific forms of consumer movements and ideas about the rightful place of the consumer in relation to the state, civil society and the market.

## The ideological foundations of consumer politics at the turn of the twentieth century

Consumers emerged as more vocal and demanding actors in many parts of the globe at the turn of the twentieth century, as the terrain of politics broadened into new mass and street politics. Consumption became politicized as mass parties competed for electoral support and new expectations of rights – ranging from political to economic to maternal rights – energized 'subjects' to think of themselves as 'citizen-consumers'. The range of consumer activism is impressive, from the American meat boycotts of the early 1900s to the protests of German voters against high prices in Wilhelmine Germany.[3] The conditions of scarcity during the

---

[2] See S. K. Vogel, 'When Interests Are Not Preferences: The Cautionary Tale of Japanese Consumers', *Comparative Politics* (January 1999), pp. 187–207; P. L. Maclachlan, *Consumer Politics in Postwar Japan: The Institutional Boundaries of Citizen Activism* (New York, 2002).

[3] C. Nonn, *Verbraucherprotest und Parteiensystem im wilhelminischen Deutschland* (Düsseldorf, 1996); T. Lindenberger, 'Die Fleischrevolte am Wedding. Lebensmittelversorgung und Politik in Berlin am Vorabend des Ersten Weltkriegs', in M. Gailus and H. Volkmann,

second half of World War I generated even higher levels of agitation and violence, from the street struggles of Barcelona and Berlin in 1918 to the mass demonstrations against profiteering and the increasing cost of living in cities from Melbourne to London.[4] These protests were by no means simple variations on the older food riot; on the contrary, they symbolized the new politicization of consumption that had begun by the turn of the twentieth century. The political meanings of consumption, as well as the political ambitions of consumers, however, diverged significantly according to the distinctive ideas and beliefs in different societies.

While elsewhere protesters sought to move consumption from the margins to the centre of political discourse by resorting to boycotts, demonstrations or electoral pressure, in Edwardian Britain consumption was at the centre of popular politics and the Liberal governments' policy of unilateral free trade. The successful defence of free trade in the elections of 1906 and 1910 rested in part on the co-operative movement and the Women's Co-operative Guild, the largest social movement and the largest independent women's organization at the time.[5] The politicization of consumption was aided by radical, liberal and conservative free trade bodies that turned to new techniques of political communication, extending the political world of leaflets and speeches, to demonstrations in seaside resorts, nocturnal slide-shows, travelling exhibitions and shop-window displays that contrasted the cheap prices of commodities under free trade with the higher prices of protectionist Germany. Free trade culture marginalized other traditions of consumer politics, such as the socialist consumerism of the suffragette Teresa Billington-Greig, who attacked non-working consumers for exploiting and corrupting the true

---

eds, *Der Kampf um das tägliche Brot: Nahrungsmangel, Versorgungspolitik und Protest 1770– 1990* (Opladen, 1994), pp. 282–304; M. Friedman, *Consumer Boycotts: Effecting Change Through the Marketplace and the Media* (London, 1999), pp. 68ff.

[4] B. J. Davies, *Home Fires Burning: Food, Politics and Everyday Life in World War I Berlin* (Chapel Hill, NC, 2000); T. Kaplan, 'Female Consciousness and Collective Action: the Case of Barcelona, 1910–1918', *Signs: Journal of Women in Culture and Society* 7 (1982), pp. 545–66; J. Smart, 'Feminists, Food and the Fair Price: the Cost of Living Demonstrations in Melbourne, August–September 1917', *Labour History* 50 (1986), pp. 113–31; B. Waites, 'The Government of the Home Front and the "Moral Economy" of the Working Class', in P. H. Liddle, ed., *Home Fires and Foreign Fields: British social and military experience in the first world war* (London, 1985), pp. 175–93; M. Geyer, 'Teurungsprotest, Konsumentenpolitik und soziale Gerechtigkeit während der Inflation', *Archiv für Sozialgeschichte* 30 (1990), pp. 181–215; F. Trentmann, 'Bread, Milk, and Democracy: Consumption and Citizenship in Twentieth-Century Britain', in M. Daunton and M. Hilton, eds, *The Politics of Consumption* (Oxford, 2001), pp. 129–63.

[5] For the co-operative movement, see P. Gurney, *Co-operative Culture and the Politics of Consumption in England, 1870–1930* (Manchester, 1996); G. D. H. Cole, *A Century of Co-operation* (Manchester, 1945).

interests of consumers.[6] Where consumption became connected to citizenship, as in the writings of the progressive J. A. Hobson, this mainly occurred within the framework of free trade – a connection that would come under stress during World War I.

The strong affinity between consumer politics and free trade at the level of ideas and social movements privileged a view of 'consumption' and consumer interests that turned to civil society rather than the state for protection, redress and representation. At the same time that consumers' interests were identified with cheap prices, those interests derived a moral and political legitimacy by being imagined as organic and unitary. Consumer interests were not represented as diverse, pluralistic, or even opposed to those of businesses, as is common amongst many contemporary consumer advocates. Rather, free traders appealed to the public interest of consumers, a collective interest shared by housewives (cheap food) and industrial consumers (cheap raw materials).[7] Free Trade consumer politics here developed and amplified the emerging association between a consumer interest and the public interest that can already be found among water and gas users who organized municipal consumer protests in the late Victorian period.[8] By 1903, in its defence of free trade, the Treasury asserted unequivocally that 'the consumer . . . is the whole nation'.[9]

If the close identification between free trade and the national interest provided one pillar of support for this organic consumer politics, the other pillar was the prevailing vision of civil society.[10] For just as free trade fed the collective interests of consumers in a material sense, so, too, was it believed to nurture the civic sensibilities of consumer-citizens. Co-operators pictured the repeal of the protectionist Corn Laws (1846) as the starting point of the history of self-governing associations. Radical women's groups and progressive politicians saw in free trade a favourable setting for training citizens, making people more aware of the ethical and social motivations and consequences of purchasing decisions, and preparing them for full citizenship in democratic associations like the Women's

---

[6] T. Billington-Greig, *The Consumer in Revolt* (London, 1912). For more on middle-class women gaining access to the public spaces of consumer society, see now E. D. Rappaport, *Shopping for Pleasure: Women and the Making of London's West End* (Princeton, 2000).

[7] H. Cox, ed., *British Industries and Free Trade* (London, 1903).

[8] For a visual representation, see the East London Water Consumers' Defence Association, 'The Eastern Question Must be Settled' (1898), a poster which portrays 'public opinion', in Public Record Office, London, COPY 1, 143 folio 165.

[9] Public Record Office, London, T 168/54, 'The Conditions and Effects of "Dumping"' (7 July 1903).

[10] F. Trentmann, 'National Identity and Consumer Politics', in P. O'Brien and D. Winch, eds, *The Political Economy of British Historical Experience, 1688–1914* (Oxford, 2002), pp. 215–42.

Co-operative Guild (WCG).[11] In the context of the rapidly advancing commercialization of public and private life, the importance of this civic vision cannot be overestimated, for it allowed Liberals and Radicals to distance themselves from the charge of promoting materialist individualism. In free trade politics, consumption as the right to cheap food was discursively divorced from consumption more generally, and thus also from the pathologies associated with its hedonistic, selfish, addictive or conspicuous forms found abroad. As Lloyd George, the Chancellor of the Exchequer, kept telling Edwardian audiences, it was protectionism (not free trade) that promoted a materialistic culture utterly alien to civic, God-fearing Britons: 'I am confident that Tariff Reform means Socialism . . . Not the Christian Socialism of a few enthusiastic Englishmen, but the godless Socialism of Continental materialism.'[12]

Consumer politics, in short, relied on market forces that would in turn be civilized by a self-regulating civil society. In contrast to many European societies at the time, the political space for anti-Semitic, corporate attacks and state policies directed at institutions of consumer society like the department store was circumscribed.[13] But while British consumers may have benefited from marginally lower food prices than consumers burdened by protectionist duties elsewhere, free trade culture also bracketed a wide range of other consumer issues and reform instruments. The emphasis on cheapness as a benchmark of consumer satisfaction hampered discussions of product quality, consumer-related information, and the consequences of unregulated trade for employment, labour conditions and public health. As the international food and commodity chain became longer, it was unclear how the ethical sensibilities of the British consumer would exercise their positive influence on ever more distant and fragmented processes of production and trade and weave the promised

---

[11] See further F. Trentmann, 'Commerce, Civil Society and the "Citizen-Consumer" ', in *Paradoxes of Civil Society: New Perspectives on the Evolution of Civil Society in Modern Britain and Germany* (Oxford and New York, 2000/2003), pp. 306–31.

[12] British Library of Political and Economic Science, London, Coll. Misc 246, ff. 97, interview with Harold Begbie of the *Daily Chronicle*.

[13] Several German states, for instance, had introduced special taxes on department stores, a practice followed after the war by France as well as some states in the United States. For the critique and politicization of modern consumer society, see U. Spiekermann, *Warenhaussteuer in Deutschland: Mittelstandsbewegung, Kapitalismus und Rechtsstaat im späten Kaiserreich* (Frankfurt/Main, 1994); Hans-Peter Ullmann, 'Der Kaiser bei Wertheim: Warenhäuser im wilhelminischen Deutschland', in C. Dipper, ed., *Europäische Sozialgeschichte: Festschrift für Wolfgang Schieder* (Berlin, 2000), pp. 223–36; D. Briesen, *Warenhaus, Massenkonsum und Sozialmoral: zur Geschichte der Konsumkritik im 20. Jahrhundert* (Frankfurt/Main, 2001). By contrast, see the connections in late Victorian Britain between imperial patriotism and the Ladies' Guide Association's mapping of public consumer spaces, discussed in Rappaport, *Shopping*, p. 133.

web of peace and harmony around the globe.[14] The adherence to unilateral free trade went hand in hand with a deep-seated respect for national sovereignty that made it impossible to use the unique power of
the British market to press for improved social conditions for workers
abroad. At home, the fantasy of a self-regulating competitive market left
consumers without safeguards against monopolistic competition such as
price-fixing. Free traders portrayed trusts and cartels as alien creatures of
foreign protectionism, a simplifying equation that retarded competition
policy in Britain.[15]

The triumphant vision of consumers civilizing capitalism from within
an expanding – but distinctly national – civil society masked a larger distrust of an active state. Free trade was seen to strengthen the institutions
of liberal democracy precisely by sheltering the political system from the
power of special interests. In this view, although the House of Commons,
which voted on taxation, could be seen as offering a virtual representation to all consumers – those with and without the vote – there was no
space here for a special representation of consumer interests. For many
co-operators, the very act of granting the state regulatory powers over
the food trade ran the unacceptable risk of concentrating power in the
hands of elected officials who might become the enemies of consumers.
Municipal controls over milk or coal, argued Honora Enfield of the WCG
in 1920, were a bad idea not only because they might hurt the co-operative
business, but also because there was no way to ensure that municipal governments would keep an eye on prices, product quality and distribution
processes or prevent controls from falling into the hands of selfish capitalists during labour disputes.[16]

The emphasis on cheapness and self-regulation in the free trade culture hindered the introduction of protective regulatory measures for consumers at a time when new forms of mass production and retailing were
putting consumers increasingly at risk. As a result, consumers lacked
adequate representation both within the state and on the street, while
health, safety and other regulatory measures were comparatively backward. On the eve of World War I, for example, many American cities had
already introduced milk safety standards and pasteurization, but it was
still legal to sell tubercular milk in Britain. The Sale of Food and Drugs

---

[14] One of the few free traders who noted this was J. A. Hobson who observed that a growing
product chain might create a '[d]ecentralisation of ends and motives', thus unravelling a
shared 'social meaning' between participants in trade, *Industrial System* (London, 1909),
p. 310.

[15] D. J. Gerber, *Law and Competition in Twentieth Century Europe: Protecting Prometheus*
(Oxford, 2001).

[16] A. H. Enfield, *The Place of Co-operation in the New Social Order* (London, 1920), p. 6.

Act (1875) – the basis of British food law until after World War II –
focused on weeding out fraud rather than solving pollution problems or
improving general standards of public health. The mutually reinforcing
image of an organic consumer interest as the public interest and of a neutral state disadvantaged the development of administrative thinking about
specific consumer problems. Food reform, an area of increasing significance to consumer groups concerned about public-health risks, lacked
ideological and administrative support within the state.[17] British consumers might have gained access to cheap food, but their distrust of
the state and narrow definition of cost meant that the 'cheap loaf' dis-
tracted them from a host of more direct forms of consumer protection and
regulation.

British consumer politics in late nineteenth- and early twentieth-
century Britain, then, presents us with an interesting paradox: nowhere
was consumption more central to political culture and social mobilization,
and yet there were few legal, institutional or policy-oriented measures to
protect consumers. The intense significance of consumer politics corre-
lated with the very narrow definition of what counted as consumption
in mass politics, namely, access to essential foodstuffs or 'necessaries'.
The way in which the political meaning of consumption was thus defined was far from natural. The standard of living in Edwardian Britain
exceeded that of other European societies, which failed to produce the
same consumer politics. Many Edwardian Liberals and Radicals participated in an expanding world of consumption, ranging from tourism and
pension policies to cultural entertainment and new technologies. The free
trade tradition blended out this diverse set of consumer issues and interests. Put differently, in Britain free trade consumer politics privileged a
generic image of the consumer as someone primarily interested in cheap
foodstuffs, masking politically explosive questions about the competing
interests and identities of consumers with competing value systems and
lifestyles, among as well as between classes.[18] The ideological framing of
consumption in free trade culture, then, points to a remarkable contra-
diction in Britain at the turn of the twentieth century: at the very time

---

[17] The targets of British legislation were retailers, rather than producers who had been
left to their own devices in the pursuit (or abuse) of quality. For this, and the weak
record of the Local Government Board, see J. Phillips and M. French, 'Adulteration and
Food Law, 1899–1939', *Twentieth Century British History* 9/3 (1998), pp. 350–69. This
contrasts with the more bureaucratic and punitive powers of states like Germany, where
the law of 1879 empowered the police to search for unsafe foods, and the United States,
where new agencies, such as the Bureau of Chemistry, were created within the federal
system to address the increasingly complex field of food policy.

[18] For different value systems and interests within working-class culture, see P.
Johnson, 'Conspicuous Consumption and Working-Class Culture in Late-Victorian and
Edwardian Britain', *Transactions of the Royal Historical Society* 38 (1988), pp. 27–43.

that consumer culture was expanding and diversifying its goods, services, spaces and aesthetics, consumer politics was contracting around the essentials of life.

In the United States, consumption also emerged as an increasingly sensitive issue in popular politics at the turn of twentieth century. However, consumer activism failed to produce a coherent discursive and sociopolitical alliance that could rival that of hegemonic free trade in Britain. There was certainly plenty of evidence of consumer activism during this period. Consumers organized boycotts against the high price of meat in 1902, protested against rent levels in 1904 and 1907–8, pressed for accurate weights and measures, and took to the streets against the rising cost of living in 1917. They established a number of advocacy groups, including the National Consumers' League (NCL, 1899), the National Anti-Food Trust League (1909), and the Housewives League (1911) of New York. Their efforts to politicize consumption, however, were often stymied by an alliance of business groups and Southern Democrats that came to dominate the legislative process in Congress. Though not supporters of free trade as such, this alliance was also wary of any form of regulatory controls over the affairs of free enterprise. Consequently, while Congress and the White House were willing to pass legislation like the 1906 Meat Inspection and Pure Food and Drug Acts to correct the more egregious affronts to consumer interests, consumer protection was primarily achieved *indirectly* through competition policy – policy that benefited business as much as, if not more than, consumers.

US consumer groups in the early twentieth century had a number of distinctive beliefs, the most significant of which was a close affinity with the ideas and objectives of the labour movement. Consumer interests were rarely separated from producer interests. As wage labour expanded, 'the living wage' became increasingly important to the workers' sense of citizenship.[19] Indeed, the dominant consumer organizations focused far more on improving wage levels and working conditions than on lowering prices, expanding choice, or improving the conditions of purchase. The National Consumers' League led by Florence Kelley saw purchasing power as leverage in the battle for improved labour conditions, especially of women and children. To promote 'ethical consumption,' the NCL distributed 'white lists' of shops and producers that adhered to proper labour and production standards. The burden of improving the conditions of work, meanwhile, lay with the nation's housewives. In many cases, consumer activism was influenced by socialist ideology. Activists like Kelley,

---

[19] L. B. Glickman, *A Living Wage: American Workers and the Making of Consumer Society* (Ithaca, NY, 1997).

who joined Eugene Debs' Socialist Party, were inspired by the tradition of evolutionary socialism that sought to gradually strengthen trade unions and reduce the capitalists' appropriation of surplus value from workers.[20]

Whereas the free trade tradition in Britain privileged 'cheapness' and in general accepted that the poor working conditions surrounding the production of sweated goods were problems best solved by producing nations, the NCL directly confronted the relationship between cheapness and labour standards and prioritized the latter in its activism.[21] Consumers were not only partly responsible for solving some of the problems shouldered by the nation's workers: they were also the source of those problems. As Josephine Shaw Lowell proclaimed in 1925, '[t]he responsibility for some of the worst evils from which producers suffer rests with the consumers, who seek the cheapest markets regardless of how cheapness is brought about'.[22] In contrast to Britain, then, the centre of the American tradition of ethical consumption lay ultimately in the world of production, rather than consumption.

The tradition of individual rights was a second, distinct source of American consumer activism, a legal-political orientation that was reinforced by the role of the legal system as a significant point of political access for social movements in the United States. The NCL worked closely with Louis Brandeis during the pre-war years in a progressive alliance for protective labour legislation. The historic affinity between the language of rights and questions of consumption – a connection that can be traced back to the War of Independence[23] – also provided a bridgehead for new battles over civil rights. In the late 1920s and 1930s, the NCL linked the campaign for ethical consumption and labour legislation to that against racial discrimination and political authoritarianism in the South: the racial division of the South constituted both a denial of black rights and, by exercising a downward pressure on wages, a threat to the social rights of whites to a decent wage.[24]

The social and civic discourse informing consumer politics in the United States in the early twentieth century thus encouraged images of the consumer that moved beyond those of free trade Britain. While

---

[20] L. R. Y. Storrs, *Civilizing Capitalism: The National Consumer's League, Women's Activism, and Labor Standards in the New Deal Era* (Chapel Hill, NC, 2000), pp. 16f.

[21] Similar arguments about the dangerous halo of cheapness at any cost were made on the British left but were marginalized by the free trade revival; see F. Trentmann, 'Wealth versus Welfare: the British Left between Free Trade and National Political Economy before the First World War', *Historical Research* 70/171 (1997), pp. 70–98.

[22] Cit. in Storrs, *Civilizing Capitalism*, p. 19.

[23] T. H. Breen,' "Baubles in Britain": The American and Consumer Revolutions of the Eighteenth Century', *Past and Present* 119 (1988), pp. 73–104.

[24] Storrs, *Civilizing Capitalism*, chs 5, 6.

women played an equally decisive role in both movements at both the leadership and grassroots levels, the Consumers' League in America quickly developed a view of the 'consumer' that was much more than the British image of the purchaser of the 'cheap loaf' and other necessaries. Initially, the NCL's image of consumers was that of women as disinterested agents of the public interest, a trope that can be traced to eighteenth-century ideas of sympathetic femininity in which women, thanks to their supposed distance from the corrupting world of commerce, claimed to speak on behalf of humanity in consumer boycotts of slave products.[25] By the inter-war years, the campaign for racial justice and labour legislation complicated this gendered tradition and legitimized the right to consume of Southern black men. Given the NCL's attention to the conditions of labour and production, it is not surprising that its focus on goods extended beyond the free trade fixation on basic foodstuffs. Much of the early NCL activism targeted middle-class women and understood itself as an experiment in applied economics that would reveal the centrality of the consumer to the economy at large, a generic approach that also found its way into the writings of economists, including Simon Patten's *New Basis of Civilization* (1907).[26] For the NCL, the consumer was the purchaser of a potentially infinite range of commodities: ' "Every person who buys anything, from a bun to a yacht, is a consumer." '[27] Here was a socially open and flexible framing of consumption as a dynamic relationship between users and producers connected through a potentially infinite world of goods. And this view would facilitate the consumer movements' embrace of social Keynesianism during the 1930s and 1940s, which aimed to raise the purchasing power and comfort of the American people.

In contrast to the United States and Britain, consumption in pre-war Japan failed to develop into a legitimate sphere of human activity. From the late 1860s until the end of World War II, as the Japanese poured their collective energies into rapid economic modernization and imperial expansionism, consumers were encouraged not to consume but to save – to contribute to the resource base of an expanding economic and military infrastructure. Purchasing and consuming goods and services,

[25] K. Davies, 'A Moral Purchase: Femininity, Commerce and Abolition, 1788–1792', in C. Grant and E. Eger, eds, *Women, Writing and the Public Sphere: 1700–1830* (Cambridge: 2000), pp. 133–59.
[26] K. Kish Sklar, 'The Consumers' White Label Campaign of the National Consumers' League, 1898–1918', in M. Judt, S. Strasser and C. McGovern, eds, *Getting and Spending: European and American Consumer Societies in the Twentieth Century* (Cambridge, 1998), pp. 25ff.
[27] As the League's official history, *The First Quarter Century*, put it in 1925; cit. in Storrs, *Civilizing Capitalism*, p. 22.

meanwhile, were portrayed as highly self-centred acts that did virtually nothing to advance the interests of the nation. This was nowhere more apparent than in one of the more oft-quoted slogans of the era: 'Luxury is the enemy!'[28]

Against this backdrop, popular mobilization in support of consumer-related objectives was viewed as nothing less than radical. During the 1910s and 1920s, a period of significant – albeit limited – democratic experimentation, a small consumer co-operative movement arose in close affiliation with the Christian socialist, communist and labour movements. This motley association of political fringe groups opposed the growth of large corporations and their close ties to government, the widening gap between rich and poor, and a host of other problems attributed to tightening state control over the population. The co-ops, for their own part, emphasized labour rights, gender equality, and the Rochdale pioneers' principles of open membership and democratic control. Partly as a result of these cultural and political constraints, the co-ops failed to contribute to an enduring 'mass politics' that would energize and empower consumers; nor, for that matter, did they contribute to meaningful public discussions of the relationship between democratic principles and consumption.

The negative connotations surrounding 'consumption' had deep cultural origins. Although consumption in the West had also been imbued with negative overtones in the past,[29] the concept suffered from a particularly negative image in Japan. Part of the problem was the very make-up of the term 'consumption' (*shôhi*): *shô* means 'to extinguish' and *hi* connotes 'waste'. At a time of rapid industrialization, the socially accepted role of consumers was to contribute to the national resource base for future economic expansion by saving, rather than spending. Thus, it should come as no surprise that the co-op leaders often encountered resistance from ordinary Japanese when trying to recruit them into 'consumer co-operatives' (*shôhisha kumiai*).[30] Who, after all, would want to be openly associated with the self-seeking and non-productive activities of 'consumers' (*shôhisha*, lit., one who extinguishes and wastes), particularly during the 1930s when self-sacrifice in support of the 'national polity' (*kokutai*) had become a carefully cultivated public virtue?

[28] See further S. Garon, 'Luxury Is the Enemy: Mobilizing Savings and Popularizing Thrift', *Journal of Japanese Studies* 26/1 (2000), pp. 41–78.
[29] See R. Porter, 'Consumption: Disease of the Consumer Society?', in J. Brewer and R. Porter, eds, *Consumption and the World of Goods* (London, 1993), pp. 58–81; L. B. Glickman, 'Born to Shop? Consumer History and American History', in L. B. Glickman, ed., *Consumer Society in American History: A Reader* (Ithaca, NY, 1999), p. 1.
[30] A. Yamamoto, *Nihon seikatsu kyôdô kumiai undôshi* [The history of Japan's lifestyle co-operative movement] (Tokyo, 1982), p. 674; Maclachlan, *Consumer Politics*, p. 79.

As Japan mobilized for total war, the increasingly authoritarian state forcibly disbanded the consumer co-operative movement along with all other social movements and interest groups that represented whatever semblance of a civil society Japan may have had at the time. Consumers had become captured subjects of a pro-producer nation state.

## Consumer politics in transformation

Our discussion has distinguished among three dominant national traditions of consumer politics at the turn of the twentieth century: the radical-liberal tradition of free trade and civil society in Britain, the American tradition based on individual rights and progressive labourism, and the pro-labour but underdeveloped tradition of pre-democratic Japan. These national traditions were by no means fixed or self-perpetuating. As the next section will show, the inter-war years gave rise to new ideas about consumption – many of them the product of economic scarcity – that were to shape consumer politics through the post-war periods of economic development and affluence.

If 'cheapness' had been the dominant watchword of British consumer politics under free trade, it became increasingly marginalized in response to a number of inter-related developments during and after World War I: increasing demand for stable supplies and improved public health, and the emergence of new ideas about consumer regulation in the public interest. Inflation and the scarcity of foodstuffs during 1916–19, followed by economic depression and mass unemployment, raised new questions about how to protect consumers against insecure supplies and business cycles, and how to balance the interests of consumers and producers. As critics of liberal markets emphasized, consumers did not necessarily gain in the long run from extreme cheapness. Price fluctuations, by harming investment, destabilizing industrial relations and creating incentives for profiteering and special interest politics, hurt the interests of consumers, citizens and producers alike.[31] For many in the co-operative movement and the WCG the war highlighted the chaotic nature of markets and the need for state regulation of basic foodstuffs and raw materials. An advisory Consumers' Council (1918–21) investigated high prices, distribution, and costs of production of essential foods, such as milk, and in the process sharpened a sense of the consumer interest and its claim on protection from the state against profiteers and cartels.[32] The consumer interest, in this view, now lay with secure access to regular supplies of

---

[31] E. M. H. Lloyd in *Nation and Athenaeum* (9 December 1922), pp. 384f.
[32] Trentmann, 'Bread, Milk and Democracy', pp. 146ff.

food at stable prices, rather than unregulated imports. In Britain, as on the continent, this concern with food security prompted Labour and social democrats to embrace state regulation as a way of reconciling the interests of consumers and producers.[33] The plethora of proposals for import boards, long-term imperial contracts, purchasing controls, and 'Buy British' campaigns during the inter-war years reflected this repositioning of the consumer within society and polity as someone whose interests and identities as a shopper and a housewife should be balanced against a concern for the conditions of producers – both domestic and imperial.[34] If these proposals largely failed to transform policy in the Conservative-dominated inter-war years, they nonetheless left their mark on the earlier type of radical-liberal consumer politics: organized consumers increasingly looked to political institutions – rather than the market – to provide the instruments of economic governance.

The rediscovery of political institutions added an important new international dimension to consumer politics. For the attention to market imperfections and cycles in international trade suggested not only the potential strengths of the state, but also its limitations as an agent of regulation. If freedom of trade had failed to safeguard consumers against trusts, monopolists and price-fixing, it was not clear that unilateral state action would fare any better against combinations of international capital, such as the American-dominated meat trust. Here again, the free trade assumption that markets reconciled the interests of consumers and producers was discredited by the war. New internationalists campaigned (in vain) for a world economic council.[35] The question of consumption acquired more generally a new salience in international politics in the 1930s, when ideas of coordinating consumption by regulating prices and imports became tied at the League of Nations to what was called 'economic appeasement': raising the level of consumption to overcome the depression and international economic friction.[36] Consumption here is not to be confused with the Keynesian interest in the propensity to consume. While Keynesians developed the macro-economic potential of consumption, they also rendered the substance of purchasing

---

[33] C. Nonn, 'Vom Konsumentenprotest zum Konsens: Lebensmittelverbraucher und Agrarpolitik in Deutschland 1900–1955', in H. Berghoff, ed., *Konsumpolitik: Die Regulierung des privaten Verbrauchs im 20. Jahrhundert* (Göttingen, 1999), pp. 32ff.

[34] See, for instance, C. Addison, 'The Nation and Its Food', (1929), in P. Redfern, ed., *Self and Society: Second Twelve Essays, Social and Economic Problems from the Hitherto Neglected Point of View of the Consumer* (London, 1930).

[35] F. Trentmann, 'The Erosion of Free Trade: Political Culture and Political Economy in Great Britain, c. 1897–1932' (PhD thesis, Harvard University 1999), chs 5 and 6.

[36] S. Turnell, 'F. L. McDougall: eminence grise of Australian economic diplomacy', in *Australian Economic History Review*, 40/1 (March, 2000), pp. 51–70.

irrelevant by reducing consumption to little more than a demand function. The internationalism underlying 'economic appeasement', by contrast, was informed by a tight connection between public health and consumption.

Together, the twin demands of public health and stable, coordinated supplies broadened both the political targets and the self-understanding of the popular consumer movement. Co-operators' demands for food rich in vitamins or milk unpolluted by tuberculosis helped shift the definition of the consumer interest from cheapness to access to nutritious food at reasonable prices. 'Cost of living' campaigns by Labour Party women in the 1930s and 1950s broadened the criteria of cost for consumers to include public health considerations as well as market prices. 'Under-consumption' thus acquired nutritional overtones that gave food and health policies the legitimacy to address broader social and macroeconomic problems. Turning consumers into healthy citizens held out the additional prospect of saving farming communities from destitution during the 1930s. The public-health connection between domestic and international concerns inserted a new sense of global obligation into British consumer activism that would articulate itself in ambitious demands for a world food council in the 1940s and 1950s. The universal language of nutrition could place the interests and duties of British consumers in the same political and analytic framework as those of non-European consumers. Even though British consumers might be better off than, say, their Nigerian or Greek counterparts, there was a shared human interest in overcoming vitamin deficiencies. Hunger became understood as a systemic global problem requiring the reform of global political economy, rather than national reforms or charitable responses to natural disasters. The Co-operative Party was very self-conscious about the global change in perspective this entailed for ethical consumers in more privileged parts of the world:

Fifty years ago would anyone have _thought_ about a WORLD food problem? When famine struck India, or the potato blight struck Ireland, other people heard of _India's_ or _Ireland's_ food problem. They were sympathetic and sent what help they could. But they didn't think about a _world_ food problem that the WORLD should do something about solving. The first step toward solving it has been taken when we _talk_ about a _world_ problem.[37]

New concerns about public health, stable prices, and secure access transformed the general understanding of 'consumers', their nature, their interests, and the agencies best equipped to deal with them. One reason

---

[37] Hull Archives, Co-operative Party discussion paper (1955), FAO 55/3/1806, topic 1 (1), emphases in orig.

for the success of radical-liberal free trade, we have argued, had been its ability to place an unproblematic organic image of the consumer at the centre of Edwardian politics – an image that precluded discussions about the socio-cultural consequences of consumerism. Consumers were left to pursue their interests through the market: civil society, meanwhile, acted as a self-regulating agency that would foster civic virtues and behaviour. The debate about scarcities and nutrition, profiteering and trusts shattered underlying assumptions about the market, and, by doing so, opened a Pandora's box of questions about the nature of consumer demand and when and where it might be in the public interest to protect or regulate it.

As calls for consumer regulation intensified, so, too, did arguments about the extent of consumer rationality and the need for consumer education. First, there was a growing concern about ignorant, passive consumers eroding the spirit of democracy. 'The consumer', Harold Laski charged in 1928, 'has done little or nothing to control his environment . . . He does not announce his wants; he waits for the profit-maker to discovery such of his wants as it is worth his while to supply. But since the quality of his citizenship largely depends upon what there is for him to consume, ignorance of his wants means . . . the absence of a civic context to this aspect of his life.'[38] The future of citizenship depended increasingly on the state's ability to satisfy demand, and that ability required the state to take a more active role in making demand more 'articulate' and 'informed'. Second, questions of how to improve consumer rationality and information came to the fore in applied psychology. Rather than viewing consumers simply as instinctive automatons that responded passively to the signals of the advertising world, psychologists in inter-war Britain, like Frank Watts, began to develop a more complex view of consumers' changing subjectivity in which advertisers carried the civilizing mission of elevating consumer desires and interests.[39] Third, public health discourse imposed new educational requirements on consumers. If one source of inadequate nutrition was poverty, a second, according to John Boyd Orr and the League of Nations Mixed Committee, was widespread 'ignorance

[38] H. J. Laski, 'The Recovery of Citizenship' (1928), in P. Redfern, ed., *Self and Society: First Twelve Essays, Social and Economic Problems from the Hitherto Neglected Point of View of the Consumer* (London, 1930), p. 7.

[39] In contrast to the popular image of a hegemony of psychological theories of total human manipulation in the 1950s and 1960s, as pronounced by the Frankfurt School, more complex views of consumption and subjectification continued to be developed in British psychology after World War II; see Peter Miller and Nikolas Rose, 'Mobilizing the Consumer: Assembling the Subject of Consumption', *Theory, Culture and Society*, 14/1 (1997), pp. 1–36.

of food values or carelessness and indifference'.[40] Consumers needed to be taught more intelligent habits. Finally, at the policy level, the model of consumption based on free trade and free markets was replaced with a technocratic model of consumer protection based on expanded information flows, education, and product-testing. Consumers, the progressive think-tank Political and Economic Planning (PEP) argued in the 1930s, did not automatically benefit from markets because they stood in an asymmetrical power relationship with big firms and lacked the knowledge to navigate the marketplace effectively. Overcoming this asymmetry of information would reorder consumer culture and make it more rational and scientific for the overall benefit of society. The rationale for consumer protection that would inspire the establishment of the Consumers' Association in 1957 was born.[41]

In the United States during the inter-war years, the political meanings of consumption and the status of the consumer-as-citizen were extended and radicalized no less than in Great Britain. Both countries experienced a critique of free markets as the consumer's best friend and the establishment of private product-testing organizations. What distinguished America was the duality of consumer politics. On the one hand, the private vision of consumer activism was concerned, perhaps even obsessed, with creating powerful independent consumers – Davids who could battle the Goliaths of the corporate world of producers and advertisers. On the other hand, there emerged a collective vision of a consumers' republic, in which consumers-as-citizens were connected through the state in a campaign to raise the purchasing power of the people. This was the consumer politics of the New Deal. These extremes clearly fed off each other, not least in their shared picture of the enemy – the evil, unaccountable, price-fixing firm. Whereas in Britain the erosion of free trade deprived consumer politics of its centre and led to a proliferation of competing visions and ideas, in America there crystallized a new democratic politics of consumption in the New Deal in the 1930s. And whereas a good deal of progressive consumer activism in Britain focused on extending basic rights to health and nutrition to consumers, in America the ambition was

[40] *Final Report of the Mixed Committee of the League of Nations on the Relation of Nutrition to Health, Agriculture, and Economic Policy* (League of Nations Document No. A. 13. 1937. II. A.), p. 33.

[41] C. Beauchamp, 'Getting *Your Money's Worth*: American Models for the Remaking of the Consumer Interest in Britain, 1930s–1960s', in M. Bevir and F. Trentmann, eds, *Critiques of Capital in Modern Britain and America: Transatlantic Exchanges 1800 to the Present Day* (Basingstoke and New York, 2002), pp. 127–50; M. Hilton, 'The Fable of the Sheep', *Past and Present* 174 (2002), esp. pp. 229ff.

to create nothing less than a self-sustaining mass consumer society in which all citizens could share in the comforts of the American way of life.

It was the positive embrace of mass consumption as the citizen's passport to democracy that distinguished American trends in the inter-war years. Consumption was not only connected to civic qualities but now appeared to be a prerequisite of democratic life. 'The consumer' and 'the citizen' were increasingly paired in the same breath. Although organized consumer activism suffered setbacks as a result of the producer-oriented policies of the 1920s, several undercurrents prepared for a coalescence of the language of consumption (living cost, purchasing power, prices) and the language of democratic citizenship (rights, participation, representation) that would flow into the New Deal policies of the second half of the 1930s and early 40s. First, consumption became politicized from within business itself. Advertisers, for example, began to fuse political and commercial metaphors, equating individuals' acts of purchase with civic acts of voting. Political democracy, in this view, was built on a consumer democracy in which all citizens had access to goods. Admittedly, such ideas rested on highly elitist representations of the consumer that all but ignored the labouring masses.[42] A more inclusive approach came from progressive businessmen like Edward Filene, the department store owner, and associated think-tanks like the Twentieth-Century Fund. Their campaigns in the 1920s for rationalizing distribution and lowering prices looked forward to a market of mass-produced goods for all. For the working classes to become full citizens, they needed a 'cultural wage' enabling them to participate in consumer society.[43] Such arguments were indicative of a broadening of the social groups invoked as 'consumers' that would facilitate collaboration between labour and consumer activists and democratic appeals to a 'consuming public'. Thus, while the League for Independent Republican Action, a third party established in 1929, still looked to small merchants and white-collar workers as ' "represent[ing] most adequately the interests of the consumer," '[44] New Dealers like Leon Henderson, the consumer adviser to the National Recovery Administration (NRA), imagined ' "farmers and laborers, that

---

[42] C. McGovern, 'Consumption and Citizenship in the United States, 1900–1940', in Strasser, *Getting and Spending*, pp. 37 ff.; see also R. Marchand, *Advertising the American Dream: Making Way for Modernity, 1920–40* (Berkeley, 1985); and now L. Cohen, *A Consumers' Republic: The Politics of Mass Consumption in Postwar America* (New York, 2003).

[43] M. Jacobs, 'The Politics of Purchasing Power: Political Economy, Consumption Politics, and State-building in the United States, 1909–1959' (PhD thesis, University of Virginia, 1998).

[44] Dewey (1931), cit. in L. Cohen, 'The New Deal State' in Strasser, ed., *Getting and Spending*, p. 117.

is consumers"' when arguing for increased purchasing power as the lever of economic growth.[45]

The democratic broadening of the consumer constituency went hand in hand with a growing emphasis on the substantive contributions consumers needed to make to preserve democracy. Private consumer testing-organizations, like Consumers' Research (1927) and its progressive break-away Consumers Union (1936), favoured remedies different from the redistributive policies and institutional reforms of the New Deal, but they all turned to the consumer as the potential saviour of democracy from the clutches of big business. For Chase and Schlink, the founders of Consumers' Research, and popular sociologists like Robert and Helen Lynd, the authors of *Middletown* (1929), the helpless consumer was a symptom of the citizen's loss of sovereignty. As the Lynds noted, consumers were kept 'economically illiterate' by business and advertisers. They were bombarded with product choices, novelties and styles that made them helpless slaves of profiteering producers. *Your Money's Worth*, the title and motto of Chase and Schlink's bestseller in 1927, was not only meant to give consumers the goods and prices to which they were entitled but also to cultivate their sense of pride and independence as good republican citizens and, in the process, to redress the balance of power between citizens and oligopoly. Consumers' Research fused a technocratic vision of expert-provided information, scientific product-testing, and planning with a republican vision of independent citizens.[46]

---

[45] A. Brinkley, *End of Reform: New Deal Liberalism in Recession and War* (New York, 1995), p. 71. While the broad-based identity of all citizens as consumers would dominate amongst New Dealers, some groups, like the NRA Women's Division, retained a more limited, sectional view of the consuming class as that of middle-class housewives, distinct from the working class; see M. Jacobs, ' "Democracy's Third Estate": New Deal Politics and the Construction of a "Consuming Public" ', *International Labor and Working-Class History* 55, Spring 1999, pp. 27–51.

[46] For Consumers' Research, the consumer was essentially a private person – Schlink was suspicious of consumerism as a social movement or political programme and sought to keep consumption separate from labour issues, whereas Consumers Union carried on the earlier progressive identification of the consumer as worker. The vision of Consumers' Research, in short, was not to reform capitalism but to restore markets. The discussion here and below draws on L. Glickman,'The Strike in the Temple of Consumption: Consumer Activism and Twentieth-Century American Political Culture', *The Journal of American History* 88 (June 2001), pp. 99–128; Hayagreeva Rao,'Caveat Emptor: The Construction of Nonprofit Consumer Watchdog Organizations', *American Journal of Sociology* 103/4 (1998), pp. 103, 4, 912–961; Beauchamp, 'Getting *Your Money's Worth*'. For the following discussion, see also Meg Jacobs,' "How About Some Meat": The Office of Price Administration, Consumption Politics, and State Building from the Bottom Up, 1941–1946', *The Journal of American History* 84/3 (1997), pp. 84, 3, 910–41; and now Cohen, *Consumers' Republic*.

The New Deal developed a complementary institutional strategy of empowering citizen-consumers by resorting to state agencies to redress the power asymmetry in the marketplace. The idea of raising the consuming capacity of Americans to pull the economy out of the depression placed the twin political goals of fighting oligopoly and preserving democracy at the centre of the American state. Theories of under-consumption compelled reformers to look beyond the older programme of anti-trust policies as the primary mechanism for consumer protection. As the economist Leon Keyserling and Senator Robert Wagner argued, the state had to play an active role in tackling the disparity between wages and prices in order to correct the 'failures' of consumer demand. Although producers came to dominate the National Recovery Administration, it is clear that even they supported the New Deal as means of redistributing income.

New Deal policies mobilized consumers and sharpened their sense of political and economic entitlement. The Federal Housing Administration, the Home Loan Corporation, and a number of other New Deal agencies expanded the consumer voice in national politics by advocating stronger consumer-protection measures, while others, like the Tennessee Valley Authority, became bastions of grassroots consumer activism.[47] Partly to overcome the institutional power of producers, New Deal consumer advocates encouraged grassroots activism by asking consumers to report and protest against the high prices of such commodities as bread and meat. After America's entry into the war, rationing and price controls were linked to state-sponsored popular campaigns in which consumers kept an eye on profiteering – a veritable 'kitchen gestapo' in the view of Republican and business critics. Consumers' rights to redress were recognized and their exercise encouraged; consumers could now sue for being overcharged. By 1945, over two million women shoppers had reported price violations. The extent to which these actions increased purchasing power is debatable, but there is little doubt that New Deal policies broadened the public meaning of consumption and the sense of entitlement that came with it. The NRA's Consumer Advisory Board (CAB) explicitly looked beyond the immediate act of purchase: ' "The consumers' interest is not to be regarded as limited to the retail market for consumers' goods . . . An adequate safeguarding of the consumers' interest . . . calls for a complete check upon industrial processes from the raw material to the finished good and its distribution to the ultimate consumer." '[48] The principle of consumer protection offered a new leverage for groups fighting against discrimination in a variety of markets.

[47] L. Cohen, 'The New Deal State', in Strasser, ed., *Getting and Spending*, pp. 120f.
[48] Cit. in Jacobs, ' "Democracy's Third Estate" ', p. 37.

African-American groups stressed that ' "Negroes, too, are Consumers" ' and extended the logic of price controls in shops to the housing market where black renters faced discriminatory high prices.[49] President Franklin D. Roosevelt, in his 1944 state of the union address, testified to this expanded sense of consumer entitlement when he called for an economic bill of rights. For the first time in American history, the consumer interest had been upheld by the state as a legitimate manifestation of the public interest.

## Consumerism after world war II

The decades of the post-war period were ones of both change and continuity for consumer politics in Britain, the United States and Japan. In each country, consumers redefined themselves and their relationships with state and market actors as new political opportunities for activism arose and economic affluence and new technologies produced a host of new consumer grievances. The post-war era did not, however, constitute a clean break with the past; to the contrary, consumerism in each context was conditioned by many of the principles and values that had arisen before World War II.

In contrast to American and British consumerism, the formative years for Japanese consumerism were those of the immediate post-war era – an era of extreme economic scarcity and unprecedented opportunities for consumer activism. Occupation authorities encouraged ordinary Japanese to mobilize in support of political objectives, viewing even radical forms of citizen activism as effective vehicles for grassroots democratization in a country that was accustomed to being governed from above. As the Japanese people were granted the rights and privileges of citizenship, many flocked to the labour unions, the political parties, professional interest groups, and also to the consumer co-operatives and women's organizations that eventually assumed a leading role in the post-war consumer movement. In the process, they began to discard their identities as subjects of a pro-producer state and to redefine their roles in the political economy. They did not, however, shed their sense of responsibility toward the overall well-being of the nation; now, as before, consumers were imbued with a sense of economic nationalism that contributed to a distinctive approach to consumption.

Japan's early post-war consumer activists embraced a simple but pressing goal: the elevation of the national standard of living from below the subsistence line. To that end, they linked arms with workers, farmers

---

[49] Jacobs, ' "How About Some Meat" ', p. 927.

and small businessmen – the victims of economic scarcity – against big business, black marketeers, and the now defunct rationing system. As this eclectic alliance of consumers and small producers struggled to restore the flow of basic goods and services into the marketplace, consumer advocates began to fashion a distinctive conceptualization of the 'consumer'. At the most fundamental level, a consumer was a survivor – an individual struggling to feed, clothe and house both herself and her family. Second, a consumer was a citizen, both of civil society (*shimin*) and the national polity (*kokumin*). The *kokumin* dimension of the consumer identity reflected the activists' concern for the state of the national economy and their willingness to ally with producer groups in order to strengthen that economy. Housewives, who played a leading role in the movement, rarely forgot they were married to producers. Consumers thus became standard bearers of the 'public interest' – defined in national, economic terms – and in ways that reflected the intellectual underpinnings of the pre-war *kokutai* (national polity). Third, and in keeping with the intellectual overlap between consumerism and trade-unionism before the war, a consumer was also a worker or small producer, or the spouse or dependent of a worker or small producer. Finally, the consumer was the purchaser and user of goods and services in the marketplace. Even more than in the United States and Great Britain, here was a multifaceted, holistic tradition that viewed consumption primarily as a mechanism for improving the overall health of the *nation*.

Since the term 'consumer' was still imbued with negative overtones during the post-war period, some activists adopted the term *seikatsusha*, or 'lifestyle person'. Thus, many 'consumer co-operatives' (*shōhisha kumiai*) became known as 'lifestyle co-operative unions' (*seikatsu kyōdō kumiai*, or *seikyō*). A politically innocuous but ingenious concept embraced by other citizen groups as well, *seikatsusha* and its derivatives enabled consumer activists to gloss over the conceptual conflicts inherent in the loose alliance between consumers and producer groups. It also reinforced the movement's reluctance to take a more adversarial approach toward producers, a tendency that left unchallenged the political supremacy of producers during the first decade or so of the post-war era.

Japan's distinctive consumer identity and the political alliances that underscore it explain some of the idiosyncratic priorities of the movement. Advocates have, until very recently, been staunch opponents of any form of governmental privatization or deregulatory schemes.[50] This is in

---

[50] As the Japanese government supports legislation designed to protect consumers in a freer market setting, many advocates have softened their opposition to deregulation; see Maclachlan, *Consumer Politics*.

marked contrast to British and American advocates, many of whom have supported elements of the 'neo-liberal' reform movements of their respective countries for the sake of lower prices and greater choice. Japanese advocates willingly sacrificed cheapness to the stability of supply, which, they believed, could only be guaranteed through state ownership of basic national services and close bureaucratic supervision of the activities of private firms. The movement's position reflected far more than a traditional obedience to authority; it also symbolized advocates' unwillingness to subject their allies in the vulnerable small-business sector to the vicissitudes of freer markets. Similar calculations have defined the movement's position on the liberalization of the domestic rice market. Most advocates would gladly pay high prices for domestic rice in return for the survival of Japanese farmers – another long-standing movement ally – and the economic security of the nation.

The nationalist sentiments underpinning the movement's refusal to promote agricultural liberalization also reflect health and safety considerations. As in Britain and the United States, Japanese consumers since the 1950s have paid increasing attention to product safety as medical advances enhanced the population's awareness of public-health hazards and market expansion and mass production led to the increased use of synthetic additives in food products. In Japan, however, the prioritization of safety and purity reached new heights as a result of traditional beliefs and values. Shintô, Japan's closest approximation to a native religion, puts great store in ritual purity, a value that has become manifest in everything from household cleanliness to personal hygiene and food safety. Religious concerns have been corroborated by traditional views of disease as the product of contamination.[51] It should come as no surprise, then, that Japanese consumers try to avoid imported food products containing post-harvest chemicals and synthetic additives – particularly those that are not used by domestic producers. Indeed, many consumers have asserted that cultural, safety and nationalist considerations warrant the placement of food products outside the mainstream commodity market.[52] A failure to do so, Takeuchi Naokazu of the Consumers Union once proclaimed, would allow foreign producers (and Americans in particular) to 'occupy the stomachs' of the Japanese people.[53] These anti-globalization sentiments are a major source of trade

---

[51] See E. Ohnuki-Tierney, *Illness and Culture in Contemporary Japan: an Anthropological View* (Cambridge, 1984), pp. 21–50; Maclachlan, *Consumer Politics*, pp. 178–80.
[52] M. Shoshichi, 'Food Should Not Be Compared with Industrial Products', *Japan Economic Journal* (22 May, 1984), pp. 20–1.
[53] T. Naokazu, *Nihon no shôhisha wa naze okoranai no ka* [Why Don't Japanese Consumers Get Mad?] (Tokyo, 1990), p. 104.

frictions with US producers, many of whom operate on the assumption that consumers everywhere should be ultimately motivated by cheapness and choice.

Another defining feature of Japanese consumerism has been a highly ambivalent attitude toward the state. On the one hand, consumers have been unusually dependent on government for services that in many Western countries are normally provided by private organizations. One reason for this has been a long-standing tendency among consumers and political authorities alike to view consumer protection as a state respon-sibility, rather than a right of individual consumers. The lack of strong civil-law protections for consumers simply strengthened the state's posi-tion as the only logical guarantor of consumer interests. But as might be expected in a country where producer interests are extolled, the state has not always lived up to its responsibilities toward consumers. The bureau-cracy has plenty of regulatory measures on the books, but only a handful of those measures address the interests of consumers directly. Many of the 'consumer' bureaux and sections of the national ministries, meanwhile, have done little to address the non-material grievances of consumers, preferring instead to promote higher levels of 'consumption' as part of the post-war state's broader goal of economic development.

By the early 1960s, as the country moved beyond economic recon-struction and into an era of rapid growth, and particularly after 1968, when the passage of the Consumer Protection Basic Law opened the consumer decision-making process to at least nominal consumer rep-resentation, consumer activists grew increasingly critical of the state, its partnership with business, and its failure to address consumer interests as either a discrete policy objective or as part of a broader social-democratic project. The state, according to this line of reasoning, had come to neglect the democratic rights of consumers in its preoccupation with material-istic objectives, and, in the process, was obstructing the development of a vibrant civil society. Inspired by the elevation of basic consumer rights in American politics and Ralph Nader's adversarial approach to consumerism, Japanese advocates became more vocal proponents of the 'citizen' (*shimin*) dimension of the consumer (or *seikatsusha*) identity, en-couraging ordinary Japanese to assert their rights as consumer-citizens.[54] This marriage between the consumer and citizen identities is by no means an exclusively Japanese phenomenon; as we have seen, it has also char-acterized British and American consumerism since the inter-war period.

[54] P. Maclachlan, 'The Struggle for an Independent Consumer Society: Consumer Ac-tivism and the State's Response in Postwar Japan', in F. Schwartz and S. J. Pharr, eds, *The State of Civil Society in Japan* (New York and Cambridge, forthcoming).

What distinguishes the Japanese case was the state's almost complete lack of involvement in the cultivation of citizen-consumers. To varying degrees, both the British and American states endorsed consumer citizenship as an integral component of the political economy and took significant steps to achieve some semblance of balance between producer and consumer interests. In Japan, by contrast, the post-war materialist state has viewed consumer and producer interests as part of a zero-sum relationship – a relationship that, for the sake of the overall health of the 'national economy' (*kokumin keizei*, lit. the people's economy), should be balanced in favour of producers.

Today, it is clear that Japanese consumerism is changing. Most significantly, there is mounting evidence that consumption has become a more acceptable part of society and the political economy. A decade of economic recession has bred a passion for cheapness among consumers, illustrated by the proliferation of discount and second-hand shops, while also weakening the political power of business. After the pro-business Liberal Democratic Party's (LDP) temporary fall from power in 1993, politicians of virtually all political persuasions have grown somewhat more attentive to the interests of consumer-citizens and, in the process, have presided over a small but significant increase in consumer-friendly policies and legislation. Deregulation in particular has increased pressure on politicians and bureaucrats to do more to provide consumers with the information they need to function successfully in freer markets. Finally, and in keeping with the public's deepening consciousness of civil and consumer rights, the number of professed representatives of consumer interests has proliferated. Once dominated by large consumer advocacy groups and, to a lesser extent, their allies in the legal and scholarly communities and opposition parties, the public discourse on what is in the consumer's best interest is now shaped by a diverse cross-section of society, from politicians to bureaucrats, and professional consumer advocates to small, grassroots citizen groups and social movements.

This is not to suggest, however, that the Japanese have embraced a Jeffersonian view of the consumer as an independent and self-interested member of the political economy. For although Japanese consumers have downplayed their small-producer identities and have made considerable progress in terms of asserting their interests as consumers and citizens, the consumer identity is still imbued with a deep-seated concern for the nation as a whole. At the local level, for instance, consumer activists since the early 1990s have allied with producer groups in support of common objectives like community development, the promotion of recycling programmes, and a host of other quality-of-life issues that are of concern to all citizens. Meanwhile, advocates and their close allies in the farming community continue to support agricultural protectionism, even though it means higher prices for consumers. Finally, consumers more generally still tend to prefer domestic – as opposed to foreign – manufactured goods, and for reasons that have more to do with economic nationalism than product quality. In sum, Japanese consumer-citizens still live in a producer-oriented society and remain committed to resolving consumer/producer conflicts in ways that benefit the political-economic community as a whole.

American consumerism after World War II both built on and departed from pre-war trends. The sociological identity of the 'consumer' continued to expand and articulated increasingly pronounced gender and racial hierarchies in post-war society. After decades of equating consumption with the affairs of housewives, for example, more attention was focused on the charge card toting 'Mr. Consumer' who accompanied his wife to the shopping mall. And for all its unfulfilled economic and social promises, the vision of a democracy of consumers continued to inform the strategies for civic inclusion embraced by many groups suffering from discrimination.[55] African-Americans, for instance, campaigned for fair treatment by retailers and an end to credit discrimination. In the course of the 1960s the balance between equal opportunities and the right or entitlement to consumer goods tipped in favour of the latter, as welfare recipients campaigned for greater benefits in the belief that full citizenship implied the right to be part of a commercial consumer culture.[56]

Two trends would transform the overall shape of consumer politics in the 1960s: the elevation of consumer interests on both the Congressional and White House agendas and the rise of adversarial grassroot consumerism (Naderism). President Kennedy's speech to Congress in 1962 articulating a 'Consumer Bill of Rights' symbolized the rise of consumption and consumer welfare up the government agenda. Kennedy stressed the rights to product safety, to choice, to information, and to be heard in the corridors of political power; the right to redress was added a few years later. The speech was made at a time of rising 'public expectations about the capacity of government to improve the quality of

---

[55] See Cohen, *Consumers' Republic*. The earlier, female identification of the consumer was never complete; before World War I, for example, US free traders invoked a male consumer, Modern Archives Centre, Churchill College (Cambridge), Char 2/44 f. 108, *Tariff Reform Matter*, no. 15 (1910), by the Tariff Reform Committee of the Reform Club, New York.

[56] F. Kornbluh, 'To Fulfill Their "Rightly Needs": Consumerism and the National Welfare Rights Movement', *Radical History Review* 69 (1997), pp. 76–113.

life in American society'.[57] At the same time, it built on pre-war republican trends in consumer politics that stressed the individual consumer's independence in the marketplace. But while pre-war consumer republicanism emphasized the provision of unbiased information to consumers, the post-war variation stressed the empowerment of consumers through formal recognition of consumer rights. Kennedy's speech helped sparked an upsurge in consumer activism. By the mid-1960s, consumer advocates had allied with pro-consumer political entrepreneurs in Congress in support of consumer-friendly legislative initiatives and had taken advantage of the expansion of the consumer's new rights to sue in order to politicize the problems of unsafe products, fraud, and lack of choice.[58] By the end of the decade, the US had passed more consumer legislation than any other country.

As during the New Deal years, consumption in the 1960s was closely tied to citizenship, but the social and political meanings of this connection had fundamentally changed. Whereas the New Deal vision had focused on consumption as a way to enhance national wealth and welfare and had sought to incorporate citizens into the state, in the 1960s consumerism was linked to citizenship as a way to empower the consumer vis-à-vis the state and big business. If one side of the Naderite coin was the *Taming of the Giant Corporation* (1976), the other was the taming of the federal government by reforming campaign finance and increasing governmental transparency – processes that would make the government more accountable and accessible to citizens. Arguably, this third wave of consumerism built on the republican tradition of the private citizen that had inspired Consumers' Research in the 1920s.

Consumer activists' adversarial approach to consumer–producer relations reflected and reinforced this repositioning of consumer interests in American politics.[59] As Nader's band of 'Raiders' and other advocacy organizations rushed to expose the consumer-related transgressions of both industry and state, many portrayed consumer and producer interests as diametrically opposed to one another. The adversarial nature of consumer politics eventually backfired. By the early 1970s, big business had regrouped and was putting pressure on government to tone

---

[57] D. Vogel, *Fluctuating Fortunes: The Political Power of Business in America* (New York, 1989), p. 40.

[58] See R. N. Mayer, *The Consumer Movement: Guardians of the Marketplace* (Boston, 1988); Vogel, *Fluctuating Fortunes*; and J. M. Berry, *Lobbying for the People: The Political Behavior of Public Interest Groups* (Princeton, 1977).

[59] For the confrontational nature of the French grassroots consumerism, see G. Trumbull, 'Strategies of Consumer-Group Mobilization: France and Germany in the 1970s', in Daunton and Hilton, eds, *Politics of Consumption*, pp. 261–82.

down the alleged excesses of public interest politics.[60] In keeping with the movement's historically based distrust of the state, many consumer organizations supported the notion of state disengagement from the affairs of private business and the reform of state agencies. But Ronald Reagan's ascension to power, his pro-producer stance and the introduction of supply-side economics were more than the movement could withstand. By the early 1980s, consumer advocates once again found themselves on the margins of national politics. The heyday of post-war consumer activism was over.

The relationship between consumption and citizenship evolved differently in post-war Britain. While a broad consensus emerged in the United States during the 1960s behind the notion of a consumer democracy, early post-war Britain witnessed the continued erosion of the dominant organic radical-liberal representation of a consuming public and its replacement by a plurality of competing consumer interests and traditions. The co-operative strand declined and faced new organizational and intellectual rivals, from more technocratic consumer protection and advisory groups, like the Consumers' Association, to new grassroots movements and particular interest groups concerned with everything from food hygiene to ecology. But whereas consumerism slipped to the margins of American political discourse in response to deregulatory trends in the 1980s, in Britain in the 1980s and 90s it returned to the centre of political culture, contributing to the debate about the future of social welfare and active citizenship.

The contestation between rival conceptions of the consumer interest accelerated after the war. Debates about austerity and, later, affluence produced a cacophony of consumer voices advocating everything from price controls and fairness to freer markets and more consumer choice.[61] By the late 1950s, it had become customary to 'make an amusing speech' on consumer issues, in the words of one MP, but rare to link citizenship and consumption explicitly.[62] The report of the 1959 Molony Committee on Consumer Protection defined consumer interests narrowly in terms of consumer education and protection against unsafe products and corrupt

---

[60] See Vogel, *Fluctuating Fortunes*.

[61] For the growing popularity of Conservative proposals to restore consumer choice, see I. Zweininger-Bargielowska, *Austerity in Britain: Rationing, Controls and Consumption 1939–1955* (Oxford, 2000). Cf. J. Hinton, 'Militant Housewives: The British Housewives' League and the Attlee Government', *History Workshop Journal* 38 (1994), pp. 128–56.

[62] F. Willey, 20 March 1959, cit. in M. Hilton, 'Consumer Politics in Post-War Britain', in M. Daunton and M. Hilton, eds, *Politics of Consumption*, p. 243, with further discussion of the Molony Committee, which led to the government-funded Consumer Council in 1963.

sales practices. Consumer interests were expanded with the passage of the 1973 Fair Trading Act to include a wide range of services, but consumer politics remained largely focused on protection. One reason for this narrowing was the development of a semi-corporatist political system centred in the national bureaucracy that encouraged the accommodation of diverse societal interests.[63] In response, advocacy organizations like Consumers' Association and the government-funded National Consumer Council (1975) focused on influencing government legislation in co-operation with business interests, rather than building a movement of consumer-citizens within civil society or confronting businesses head-on in a Naderite fashion.

The renewed interest in consumers as citizens during the 1980s and 1990s was paradoxically linked to the triumph of neo-liberal reforms. As commercial imperatives, quasi-markets, consumer choice and other market principles infused the welfare state and denationalized industries, the 'consumer' returned to the centre of political discourse. What was particularly interesting about this process was the fact that it was initially propelled from within the political system, not civil society. This British process was part of a more general broadening of the political terrain and image of the consumer at a multilateral level. The European Union, which at its inception had viewed consumers as little more than passive beneficiaries of market integration, embraced a growing number of consumer principles in the resolution of 1975 and the Maastricht Treaty of 1992. And in 1985, the United Nations began advocating a health principle and the distribution of essential goods and services.[64] Efforts to make governmental services more responsive to consumers were an essential part of neo-liberalism on both sides of the Atlantic. What has been distinctive in Britain is the fervour and comprehensiveness with which consumerism has entered and redefined public services all round, an ambition symbolized by the *Citizen's Charter*, which applied the principles of choice,

---

[63] Maclachlan, *Consumer Politics*, p. 47; see also G. Smith, *The Consumer Interest* (London, 1982).

[64] S. Locke, 'Modelling the Consumer Interest', in B. Doern and S. Wilks, eds, *Changing Regulatory Institutions in Britain and North America* (Toronto, 1998), pp. 162–86. In the course of the 1980s, the European Council emphasis moved away from consumer rights towards consumer choice. The 1992 Maastricht Treaty can be read as a shift in direction towards consumers' right to regulation. For this see H.-W. Micklitz and S. Weatherill, 'Consumer Policy in the European Community: Before and After Maastricht', *Journal of Consumer Policy* 16 (1993), pp. 16, 285–321. For the importance of the EU in facilitating consumer co-operation, see A. Young, 'European Consumer Groups: multiple levels of governance and multiple logics of collective action', in J. Greenwood and M. Aspinwall, eds, *Collective Action in the European Union: interests and the new politics of associability* (London, 1998), pp. 149–75.

value-for-money, openness, courtesy and redress to 'wherever there is no effective competition or choice for the individual consumer'.[65]

In recent British governments the relationship between consumers and citizens has remained ambiguous – an ambiguity that reflects how porous and problematic these two categories and identities have become. At times, the cultivation of 'confident consumers' has been viewed as a way of rescuing people from political apathy and economic powerlessness. In other contexts, the consumer has been portrayed as a utility-maximizing individual.[66] Although many consumer activists have challenged this stark distinction between the economistic individual and the public citizen, what is important here is that the debate about the relationship between consumers and citizens has been revitalized. Once political language moved from that of rights to welfare and public utilities to that of freer markets with its emphasis on consumption and choice, it inevitably raised questions of consumer representation. Citizenship and consumption began to shade into each other again. Consumers, for their own part, have responded and contributed to this debate by mobilizing at greater rates, while the Consumers' Association and the National Consumer Council have looked beyond the framework of liberal parliamentary democracy for new opportunities for consumer representation and involvement in all public bodies as well as government, demanding greater recognition of the diversity of consumers' interests and the needs of disadvantaged consumers.[67] The debate about consumer involvement has been a significant step in the transition from government to governance.

Although many consumer advocates supported the deregulation of public services even prior to Margaret Thatcher's reforms, they

---

[65] *The Citizen's Charter – Five Years on*, Cm 3370 (1996), p. 2. For different perspectives on public sector reform, see J. Potter, 'Consumerism and the Public Sector: How Well Does the Coat Fit?' *Public Administration* 66 (1988), 149–64; J. Harris, 'State Social Work and Social Citizenship in Britain: From Clientelism to Consumerism', *British Journal of Social Work* 29 (1999), pp. 915–37; J. Gabe and M. Calnan, 'Health Care and Consumption', in S. J. Williams, J. Gabe and M. Calnan, eds, *Health, Medicine and Society: Key Theories, Future Agendas* (London, 2000), pp. 255–73; Y. Gabriel and T. Lang, *The Unmanageable Consumer: Contemporary Consumption and Its Fragmentations* (London, 1995), ch. 10; J. Clarke, 'Consumerism', in G. Hughes, ed., *Imagining Welfare Futures* (London, 1998), pp. 13–54.

[66] As the British prime minister, Tony Blair, has remarked recently, 'the public know . . . that they are more than consumers of public servants [sic]. A patient in A & E [accident and emergency] demanding his hand is stitched up acts as a consumer fuming at the delay. But when he sees a car crash victim rush past him on a trolley he acts as a citizen, understanding that a more urgent case comes first.' A. Blair, *The Courage of Our Convictions: Why Reform of the Public Services is the Route to Social Justice* (London, 2002), p. 26. See also Labour's Citizen's Charter (1991).

[67] Recent examples are NCC, *Involving Consumers: Everyone Benefits* (2002); Consumers' Association, *Setting Aside the CAP* (2002).

subsequently began to highlight tensions between consumer interests and market-oriented reforms of public services. How, for example, should competing claims between different groups of consumers be adjudicated? What would happen in the event of a conflict between the rights to safety and fair prices, or other basic consumer rights? These and other questions compelled advocates to pay more attention to the collective nature of the consuming public as more than the sum total of utilitarian individuals. As the NCC has noted, for instance, low-income consumers are not only interested in low prices, they also have social and environmental concerns.[68] And like their Japanese counterparts after World War II, consumers have become concerned about the employment prospects of small producers and the stability of local communities.

As in the United States and Japan, the expansion of consumer interests to include environmentalism, social justice and sustainable development has been facilitated by heightened international communication among national consumer movements through such organizations as Consumers International. Enhanced communication has in turn encouraged British consumers to pay more attention to the international consequences of production, consumption and free trade. Pressure by British consumer groups for the EU to reform the Common Agricultural Policy, for example, is driven not only by a desire for cheaper food products at home, but also by a concern for the effects of European farming subsidies on the environment and on farmers in less developed countries.[69]

When consumers are left to their own devices in deregulated, privatized economies, some might expect them to focus on the maximization of their individual economic interests. This is precisely what happened in the United States, where a 'winner-take-all' approach to consumer–producer relations combined with the elevation of the social and economic status of producers marginalized collective consumer voices during the 1980s and encouraged a utilitarian approach to consumption. Early critics of the neo-liberal reform movement feared much the same for Britain, as they bemoaned the potential loss of a collective language of politics following the transformation of public services into marketable commodities. But in the final analysis, privatization and deregulation have arguably had the opposite effect on British consumer politics: once politicians and civil servants turned to more active consumers as agents of civic and economic renewal, it became difficult to control a cycle of growing expectations and assertiveness. As British people learn how to navigate public services and freer markets as conscious consumers, they have become increasingly

[68] National Consumer Council, *Feeding in to Food Policy* (London, 2001).
[69] Consumers' Association, *Setting Aside the CAP* (2002).

aware of the social, political and economic consequences of the act of purchasing goods and services. There is also evidence of an upsurge in activism around consumer issues – particularly at the local level. Significantly, people in Britain use their consumer voices to express collective interests and grievances as well as personal ones.[70] After a period of focusing on the material interests of shoppers, consumerism has re-emerged as an umbrella movement for issues ranging from consumption, to economic justice, social inclusion, and civil rights.

## Conclusion

Against a narrative of global convergence, this discussion has highlighted the importance of different traditions for the changing identity and political place of consumption in twentieth-century Britain, the United States and Japan. More specifically, we have shown that the relationship among consumers, states and markets has varied both cross-nationally and over time. In Britain, the free trade citizen-consumer of the late nineteenth and early twentieth centuries was succeeded by a plurality of consumer identities and groups. This pluralization assisted the relative marginalization of consumer interests in the mid-twentieth century by more producer- and statist-oriented traditions of economic planning and welfare. In recent years, however, consumers have moved back to the centre of national political discourse as the country revisits questions of civil society in the wake of economic reform. In the United States, the ethical consumerism which focused on conditions of labour at the turn of the twentieth century transmuted in the 1930s into a democratic vision of a more affluent society with access to goods for all. That vision was partly achieved during the post-war period, but at a distinct price: it sharpened social and racial hierarchies and, after a brief period of political supremacy that put producers on the defensive, sparked the fragmentation of the collective consumer identity as business regained the upper hand. Finally, in post-war Japan, the strength of consumerism as a social movement depended heavily on its ability to incorporate the materialist dimensions of consumption into a nationalist political agenda that emphasized the economic health of the nation and, consequently, enhanced the power of producers in the political economy.

---

[70] A recent Mori survey for the National Consumer Council in Britain found an almost even balance of motivations behind consumer activism. 24% of responses were 'to support the community', 23% 'to help other people', 22% 'got very angry about service provided', and 20% 'to help support myself/my family'; NCC, *Consumer Activism Omnibus Survey* (London, 2002).

The evolution of these distinct forms of consumerism did not correlate with cycles of material deprivation or affluence. Rather, the strength and sustainability of consumer politics depended on the ability of movements to connect with and contribute to national definitions of citizenship and the public good. Thus, consumer movements flourished when they worked within traditions that enabled them to translate questions of material needs into promises of social and political inclusion; when the prevailing political winds disadvantaged such synergy, as they did in Japan in the first half of the twentieth century, early post-war Britain, and in the United States during the 1980s and 1990s, consumer movements found themselves relegated to the sidelines of political discourse.

These observations have implications for social movements more generally. Contrary to the so-called 'resource mobilization' approach to social movements,[71] they suggest that the political 'success' of a social movement depends on far more than access to resources such as allies within the political system; it also rests on the ability of movements to frame their objectives in ways that complement or contribute to broader cultural norms and prevailing ideas about democracy and political economy. This chapter stresses the importance of looking beyond the action-reaction model of relations between organized consumers and political economies favoured by critics of globalization. At crucial times – in late Victorian and Edwardian Britain and in 1940s–60s America – organized consumer politics was an important pillar of the liberal politico-economic settlement that shaped global as well as local politics.

The experiences of consumerism in Britain, the United States and Japan should give proponents of a 'global consumerism' pause. For although a significant amount of convergence has taken place among the principles and aspirations of different national consumer movements, consumerism continues to have local roots. Through each of the three periods examined in this discussion, consumers defined themselves primarily in relation to *national* political economies and in accordance with *national* political cultures and traditions. Contemporary consumers may be in the business of civilizing global markets, but they do so in ways that both reflect and contribute to the longevity of domestic political cultures and local markets.

[71] See J. D. McCarthy and M. N. Zald, 'Resource Mobilization and Social Movements: A Partial Theory', *American Journal of Sociology* 82/6 (1977), pp. 1212–41; A. Oberschall, *Social Conflict and Social Movements* (Englewood Cliffs, NJ, 1973); J. Q. Wilson, *Political Organizations* (New York, 1973).

# 10 The ideologically embedded market: political legitimation and economic reform in India

## Rob Jenkins

### Introduction

India's shift to a market-oriented development strategy during the 1990s was made possible by the political skill of elites operating within established, yet flexible, state and non-state institutions. This often showcased the less democratic elements of the liberal parliamentary tradition – what has been called 'reform by stealth'.[1] Underhanded tactics, aided by propitious international circumstances during most of the 1990s, may well have sufficed to promote the initial stages of India's process of marketization. But by the end of the decade, the continued deployment of unsavoury dissent-management tactics had revealed themselves as insufficient to the task of consolidating, politically, India's *second-generation* reform agenda. The new phase represented an attempt to move beyond macro-economic stability and deregulation to the creation of durable structures to mediate state–market interaction – a much more demanding brief.

This chapter argues that second-generation reforms will require not just institutional adaptability, but also for ideas about the market to embed themselves within India's unique ideological context, where a range of political traditions – backed by powerful organizational expressions – appear within the public arena. When politics is examined as more than a machine for processing actor preferences, it becomes visible as a site where fluctuating yet stable relations among competing ideological traditions are also established. This is because the form and legitimacy of markets depend ultimately on the political cultures in which they are embedded.

Not only does the market share the ideological stage with three other powerful political formations – lower-caste assertiveness, Hindu nationalism, and issue-based social activism – but all three of these competitors share a partial claim to the most potent anti-market ideological tradition in India over the past century: *swadeshi*, a multifaceted Indian variety of

---

[1] R. Jenkins, *Democratic Politics and Economic Reform in India* (Cambridge, 1999).

economic nationalism. The fate of the market as an idea in Indian politics will depend on its interaction with *swadeshi*'s competing incarnations.

The remainder of this chapter proceeds as follows. The next section introduces changes in the understanding of markets in the development discourse; outlines the political dimensions of India's shift towards a market-oriented development strategy during the 1980s and 1990s; and situates the market amidst three other ideological tendencies that were maturing at the same time. The third section surveys the renewed political interest by all three groups in the idea of *swadeshi*. The fourth section examines the efforts of the coalition government led by the Bharatiya Janata Party (BJP) to redefine the Hindu nationalist variety of *swadeshi*. The final section concludes by reviewing the main arguments and advancing a few further points on the relationship between *swadeshi* and (1) institutional analysis, and (2) the regionalization of Indian politics.

### Embedded markets, Indian policy reform and the ideological context

The 1980s and 1990s witnessed the ascendancy of the idea that markets are a powerful – perhaps the *most* powerful – mechanism for allocating resources efficiently and fuelling increased productivity, growth and wealth-creation. Many governments around the world adopted market-oriented economic philosophies, and devised national development strategies in conformity with the principles underlying them. And yet, in light of the east Asian economic crisis of the late 1990s and other signs of vulnerability in the global economy, there has been widespread scepticism about the broader 'projects' with which the idea of 'competitive markets' has often been associated. The de-coupling of belief in the power of markets from the more extreme positions of market fundamentalism has been found not only on the receiving end of economic evangelism, but in the high church itself. The World Bank has, for all its faults as an institution, shown itself capable of rethinking the nature and role of markets. Its institutional position on these questions evolved substantially during the 1990s.

Bank researchers and operational personnel working in rural development, corporate governance and industrial policy acknowledged the importance of embeddedness. This culminated in the public rebukes to the Washington Consensus model of the market economy delivered by the former World Bank chief economist Joseph Stiglitz after he left the Bank in 2000.[2] But this was part of a larger, gradual process. By the

---

[2] J. Stiglitz, *Globalization and Its Discontents* (London, 2002).

mid-1990s, many components of the Bank had already shed the more simplistic models of market activity. In short, despite continued protestations to the contrary from familiar critics, the work of neo-liberal economists, and in particular development economists applying the new institutional economics within professional settings like the World Bank, has succeeded in forging a far more nuanced understanding of the ways in which markets rely upon existing patterns of social interaction. The charge that neo-liberal economics ignores power relations is no longer true, if indeed it ever was. That it underestimates the significance of beliefs, culture and traditions is substantially more correct.[3]

Polanyi conceived of markets not only as rooted in a larger social totality, but also as the product of conscious political construction. For markets to be sustainable, they must be capable of at least staking a claim to furthering the ethical basis of social life. This is simultaneously an argument about equity and efficiency. That market competition should not be permitted to destroy the social fabric into which markets are woven – that human compassion and civility must be preserved – is not only a plea that the market's role as means rather than ends should be recalled; it is also a warning not to kill the goose that laid the golden egg. Which is why prominent men of wealth, such as investment guru George Soros, have taken pains to quote Polanyi.[4] Markets are sustained and fleshed out as practices only within the context of ideological traditions.[5] And it is through the politics of ideas – not simply the political economy of interest representation, or the impersonal mechanisms of government institutions – that such traditions are formed. The overlapping social and cultural settings in which economic life is embedded help to stabilize and regulate market functioning. But they also perform a third service: they help to *legitimize* particular market outcomes, and therefore particular types of markets.[6] What is legitimate emerges largely through repeated practice. But it also emerges, at least in part, from the struggle between competing traditions.

If it is now widely understood that markets are inherently socially embedded, there is still a great deal of diversity in the way in which this embeddedness operates and is conceptualized. The Indian case demonstrates that analysis of the political sustainability of market-oriented reform must look beyond merely the institutional dimension of politics, and

---

[3] See P. Hall, ed., *The Political Power of Economic Ideas* (Princeton, 1989).
[4] G. Soros, *Crisis of Global Capitalism: Open Society Endangered* (London, 1998).
[5] See ch. 1 above.
[6] These points have been made eloquently, in a slightly different context, by the Indian social activist and writer Rajni Bakshi. See her 'Beyond Market Fundamentalism', *The Hindu* (Chennai, 24 September 2000).

inquire into the constitutive role of beliefs and traditions. The domain of political ideologies – and questions relating to their plasticity, the movements and traditions from which they emerge, and the skill with which they are deployed – are as important as the institutional environment with which they interact.

The unveiling of a new economic liberalization programme by the Government of India in 1991 was driven at least partly by the demands of one of its larger creditors, the World Bank. This was not the first time that multilateral agencies were implicated in forcing market policies onto India's economic agenda. India's 1965–6 devaluation crisis, a dress rehearsal for 1991 in many ways, resulted in some piecemeal relaxation of market controls, and more importantly has stood as an icon of national embarrassment in political debate ever since.

What made 1991 different, however, was that the political leadership of India's national government, largely out of financial compulsion, decided not only to plunge towards greater reliance on market mechanisms, but also, simultaneously, to integrate the Indian economy (or selected portions thereof) to the international economic system – through exposure to capital and goods markets, participation in international organizations and regimes, and through the harmonization of Indian institutions of economic governance with those prevailing internationally.

These issues did not suddenly appear on the agenda in 1991, of course. Ideas about all aspects of markets – the configuration of property rights, the arrangements for ensuring fair competition, and even the means by which economic actors and activities are to be taxed – have fuelled fierce political debate in India for most of its existence as an independent state. Market advocates were on the ascendant throughout most of the 1980s, reflected in the somewhat hesitant but symbolically important reform programme undertaken by Rajiv Gandhi's government in the second half of the decade. When Rajiv turned back to statism in the latter part of his five-year term, India's neo-liberals were seen to have been thwarted in their aim of longer-term hegemony by a consortium of powerful domestic constituencies whose political clout could forestall pro-market change.[7]

So when markets made an ideological comeback in 1991, no one was predicting a long political shelf life for them. The entrenched interest groups arrayed against greater market orientation in policy were formidable and battle-tested in their ability to exercise veto power. Moreover, both formal and informal political institutions had been compromised such that they allowed disproportionate influence for groups like

[7] P. Bardhan, *The Political Economy of Development in India* (Oxford, 1984).

public-sector workers. And yet the reform programmes introduced, and sustained, in the 1990s proved to have greater staying power than those of the 1980s, despite the more precarious parliamentary majority for the ruling party the second time around.

The general scholarly consensus has been that a combination of social division, institutional adaptation and interest-group reconfiguration helped to keep market-reorientation politically feasible during the first generation of reforms, though at great cost to the institutional inheritance of Indian politics.[8] Serious doubts have been expressed as to whether more complex reform challenges might be handicapped by this politics of de-institutionalization. In managing the first generation of reforms, political leaders sought 'the relegation of reforms to a secondary political status',[9] and did not seek to promote, at the levels of rhetoric and conviction, the democratic possibilities of various market principles – for instance, the market's ability to threaten status hierarchies. Not surprisingly, then, the neo-liberal market as a political idea failed to acquire legitimacy within the ideological environment of 1990s India.[10] Through a decade of reforms, neo-liberalism's reluctant vanguard had relied on institutional loopholes, faux-populist gimmicks and a good deal of 'political skill'.[11] They had not found an idiom through which to 'normalize', through political discourse, market-orientated policies.

The lack of legitimacy of the neo-liberal (global) market in India appears in two dimensions: general political attitudes about the market and the specific configuration of ideological forces arrayed against it. The study of India is striking for the sheer range of physical and conceptual locations in which ideas about markets crop up. Burton Stein noted the market-like qualities of financial contributions to South Indian temples.[12] Robert Wade has revealed the workings of a 'market for public office' in India that regulates appointments to government jobs.[13] Given these associations, it is not surprising that suspicion of the market has been

[8] Jenkins, *Democratic Politics*, ch. 7; J. Sachs, A. Varshney and N. Bajpai, eds, *India in the Era of Economic Reforms* (New Delhi, 1999).

[9] A. Varshney, 'Mass Politics or Elite Politics? India's Economic Reforms in Comparative Perspective', *Policy Reform* 2 (1998), pp. 301–35.

[10] Arguably, of course, the ideology of the market was spread through the channels of production and consumerism – including mass advertising, entertainment and media; but I take this to be a non-political ideology, or political only to the extent it fosters de-politicization.

[11] Jenkins, *Democratic Politics*, ch. 6.

[12] B. Stein, 'The Economic Function of a Medieval South Indian Temple', and 'The State, the Temple and Agricultural Development: A Study in Medieval South India', in *All the Kings' Mana: Papers on Medieval South Indian History* (Madras, 1984).

[13] R. Wade, 'The Market for Public Office: Why the Indian State Is Not Better at Development', *World Development* 13/4 (1985), pp. 467–97.

widespread. The leading Indian corporate executive Gurchuran Das reflected on why it might exist:

Often I ask myself, why is it that so many Indians, especially intellectuals, hate the market. There are two reasons I can think of. One, *no one is in charge* in the market economy and this causes enormous anxiety. And two, we tend to equate the market with businessmen. Since we think that businessmen are crooked we tend to transfer this negative image to the market . . . This suspicion of markets is magnified when it comes to the global marketplace, for there *truly no one is in charge*.[14]

This is not a very convincing explanation for the market-aversion of India's intelligentsia, which as Das implies is just the tip of a public-opinion iceberg. Far from believing that there is no agency controlling the direction and pace of the global economy, the market's critics in India are most spectacularly of the view that certain governments and concentrations of private capital determine the global economy's very shape. America's government and firms – as well as US-dominated international organizations (like the World Bank and IMF) – are common embodiments of the market in this discourse. Ironically, the one thing that binds together the three other tendencies in Indian politics (represented by the politics of Mandal, Mandir, and Movement, to be discussed later) is that *none* of them is driven by a belief that 'no one is in charge' of the market. The idea of the self-regulating market has found India difficult soil to penetrate.

Kaushik Basu has written that India's economic life, past and present, 'cannot be understood if one ignores the variables that conventional analysis has taught us to ignore – the social norms, culture, beliefs, and the fabric of social interaction'.[15] Several underwear advertisements from 1984 – all from the Delhi edition of the *Indian Express*, an English-language daily – struck him as especially revealing. Taken together they document a price war among retailers. But they also 'represent a common effort by firms to counter the widespread Indian mistrust of business'. The first advertisement contained, alongside the thirty-three-rupees-per-item pitch, a statement of the proprietor's personal business credo: his last mortal act would be to 'pray to god to send me again to the great land of India, so that I can give more hosiery service to my countrymen'. Rather than simply identifying the business-owner's generic commitment to the consumer's welfare, Basu argues, the advertisement 'appeals to morals

[14] G. Das, 'Why Indians Hate Capitalism', *Times of India* (17 March 1993).
[15] K. Basu, 'India and the Global Economy: Role of Culture, Norms and Beliefs', *Economic and Political Weekly* (Mumbai, 6 October 2001). See also his *Prelude to Political Economy: A Study of the Social and Political Foundations of Economics* (Oxford, 2000).

beyond the marketplace . . . it appeals to the seller's patriotism'. The second advertisement (placed by a competing shop) contained another personal mission statement – the proprietor this time promising 'to sell hosiery item worth up to Rs 200 for only Rs 25 because I am the son of that respectable mother who did not desire bungalows from me, but desired the service of my nation'. This kind of nationalist bravado can be found in many other countries, but Basu argues that '[i]n India there is a disproportionate effort to couch business in morality, to show that the low price of the big sale is not a business strategem but an act of honour'.

While there may be no definitive evidence of the existence of the phenomenon Basu emphasizes – the excessive taint associated with commercial activity, and the corresponding tendency to clothe ambition in the language of national service – many people *believe* that this belief exists. There is, in other words, a strong intellectual and popular tradition in India, as there is in many other formerly colonized countries, associating private-sector economic activity with foreign commercial interests and, thence, to the humiliation of alien rule. The *manipulation* of markets by political interests during the era of colonial rule – and the extent to which a commercial society was introduced by force, at much expense to the lives and livelihoods of local people – has given the market a tarnished image throughout Asia, Africa and Latin America.

The habit of associating the market with foreign domination, though widespread as a political phenomenon, has varied from country to country. At least three factors account for the intensity of this syndrome in India. First, as Basu points out, India's first interaction was with the East India Company rather than with the crown. This promoted a 'fear of multinationals and a mistrust of business and trade [that] would get etched in the collective memory of India'. The country, as a result, 'would design its economic policy in the shadow of this memory'. Second, Indian politics could draw on the popular belief that Hindu tradition – the weight of *dharma*, or sacred law and duty – required not only regulation of commercial activity, but also an active sequestering of the market itself, lest the taint of commerce infect less-soiled realms of society, or worse, disrupt the divinely sanctioned division of labour through which the trading, ruling, priestly and labouring limbs of the body politic were each quarantined in their own respective *varna* categories. Third, Indian resistance to foreign rule – and especially commercial domination – had given birth to its own idiom, that of *swadeshi*, an idea that has been the subject of constant reinvention throughout the twentieth century, and beyond. Ostensibly an idea about the relationship between community and outsider, the idea has, in practice, been central to virtually all debates about economic behaviour, and hence markets, in India.

The market's moral standing is just one facet of its complex character, however. At least as important is the array of ideological forces – expressed in each case by substantial political organizations – that are arrayed against it. In theoretical discussions, the market is normally situated dichotomously, opposite the state, or else situated at one point of a triangle, with the state and civil society perched upon the other two. It is these kinds of relationships that have guided the institutional analyses highlighted above. But it is also possible to locate the market ideologically, within a quartet of forces seeking to mould the shape of Indian politics during the 1990s: Market, Mandir, Mandal, and Movement.[16]

*Mandir* (temple) refers collectively to the politically organized manifestations of Hindu nationalism. The movement, which dates itself to the first quarter of the twentieth century – making it co-terminous with much Eastern and Southern European nationalism – promotes a particularly muscular vision of India's (Hindu) national identity. The base of the Mandir political hierarchy is the Rashtriya Swayamsevak Sangh (RSS), a mass, membership-based organization that promotes the deepening of Hindutva (or 'Hindu-ness') in all spheres of life – through educational programmes, social welfare provision, and the staging of religious festivals that also serve as a form of political mobilization. The RSS and its associated organizations are ostensibly interested in reviving the glory of the ancient Hindu kingdoms. Critics see RSS politics as a thinly disguised political vehicle for upper-caste reaction against lower-caste political assertiveness (see Mandal below). That too is a simplistic view. The fact is that pragmatic and extreme versions of Mandir politics have long co-existed, even (as Jaffrelot has pointed out) oscillating according to a strategic logic.[17] This oscillation can be found on economic issues as well.

The BJP is the parliamentary face of the RSS – not that BJP officials always follow the RSS line at all times. Prime Minister Atal Behari Vajpayee (who heads the National Democratic Alliance coalition government in New Delhi) is the 'leader' of the BJP. The protracted RSS-led campaign to (re)construct the Ram temple (the origin of the Mandir

---

[16] Numerous articles in the Mumbai-based *Economic and Political Weekly* have used variations of the Mandal-Market-Mandir analytical framework, as have Stuart Corbridge and J. Harriss in *Reinventing India: Liberalization, Hindu Nationalism and Popular Democracy* (Cambridge, 2000). The way in which the terms are employed in this paper builds on ideas found in an earlier paper, which added the fourth category (the increasingly important sphere of Movement politics). See R. Jenkins, 'La Réforme économique liberale et les diverses conceptions de la démocratie en Inde', in S. Mappa, ed., *Le Lien social du Nord au Sud* (Paris, 1999), pp. 328–54.

[17] C. Jaffrelot, *The Hindu Nationalist Movement and Indian Politics, 1925 to the 1990s* (London, 1996).

label) in the northern state of Uttar Pradesh drove the BJP's electoral rise in the late 1980s and early 1990s. By 1998 the party was no longer politically untouchable, and it headed a diverse coalition government, with good representation among regional parties. Fresh elections in 1999 only strengthened the BJP's position.

*Mandal* is a common term for the politics of assertive subaltern identity, particularly its electoral aspect, which took on vastly increased significance following the decision of a centre-left government in 1990 to implement (after a ten-year delay) the recommendations on affirmative action in government service set forth in the report of the Mandal Commission (which is named after its chairman, Mr B. P. Mandal). This shifted the fault line of Indian politics from rural/urban issues, which had been successfully pushed onto the national agenda during the 1970s and 1980s by various farmers' movements, to one based on an upper/lower caste cleavage. The politics of Mandal has become increasingly complex of late, with regional variations emerging on an almost constant basis, and a heightened awareness of how the benefits from reservation policy are being spread among the various Other Backward Classes (OBCs), the administrative term for localized kinship/ethnic/occupational groups officially designated as having been historically discriminated-against, and therefore eligible for quotas in public employment and state scholarships.

*Movements* are those purposive collectivities that nevertheless adopt a loose, inclusive, network form rather than the organizational model embodied by functionally differentiated, systemically integrated corporate entities (like business associations or service/entitlement-oriented NGOs), or the more formal of the Rudolphs' 'demand groups'[18] (like students). At first glance, it might appear that each of the other three political forces could claim to be a movement in its own right, making this category superfluous. But Movement politics deserves its own category if we refer specifically to the Indian case where the reference is to campaigning organizations that are (a) not based primarily on identity politics, (b) critical of the Indian state's developmentalist ideology, and (c) not specifically linked to any political party. During the 1990s, groups like the Narmada Bachao Andolan, which fought against exorbitant infrastructure projects that displaced large numbers of people, created a broad-based platform from which to act as chief critics of market-based policies. The National Alliance of People's Movements, as well as countless single-issue campaigning networks, emerged partly as a result of the displacement of socialist ideological politics by caste-based (Mandal)

---

[18] This term was coined in L. I. Rudolph and S. H. Rudolph, *In Pursuit of Lakshmi: The Political Economy of the Indian State* (Chicago, 1987).

politics, which shifted the burden of progressive opposition to these newly emergent 'non-party political formations'.[19]

These four ideological traditions (if we include the market) have over-lapping constituencies. One key point of differentiation among them concerns how best to establish lasting social cohesion, the basis for economic activity. The Market itself seeks to do this through voluntary exchange relationships centred on individual enterprise and risk-taking behaviour; it thus considers itself non-exclusivist, and is relatively open to the world beyond India. The politics of Mandir, which has many different strands, represents a move towards a form of majoritarianism that, to the extent it highlights Muslims as 'enemies within' (that is, by definition, originating without), is both exclusivist and isolationist. Hindu nationalists have thus developed a policy favouring '*internal* economic liberalization' but not 'globalization'. '*M*andalization', on the other hand, refers to a process whereby certain, previously marginalized, groups not only play the game of party politics (that is, they legitimize the organized political sphere of procedural democracy), but (significantly) do so as representatives of independent parties, not as factions of larger 'broad-based', upper-caste-dominated parties. Cohesion, in this vision, is to be structured around the social realities of caste and community, and effected through adherence to *non*-market principles of affirmative action. Finally, *M*ovement politics considers inequality and the lack of meaningful participation in democratic life the main sources of social fragmentation. The strategies for rectifying these flaws are as numerous as the movements that make up this category, but one point of common ground is the Gandhian belief in the unifying capacity of ongoing struggle.

Of course, the ideological environment could be represented in numerous alternative ways. Situating the market amidst these three other traditions has the virtue of helping to show what it is up against – in the marketplace of ideas, as it were. Moreover, an important reason why it has been so difficult for the market to take root politically in this environment is that each of the other three tendencies – Mandal, Mandir and Movement – shares a partial claim to one of the most evocative mobilizing ideas in modern Indian political discourse: *swadeshi*.

## Contested conceptions of *swadeshi*

The 'coming together' of Mandal, Mandir and Movement around the idea of *swadeshi* has usually taken place more figuratively than in concrete

---

[19] For an excellent definition and analysis of this phenomenon – which he calls Movement Groups – see D. L. Sheth, 'Globalizing Democracy versus Deepening of Democracy: The Post-Cold War Discourse', paper for the Lokayan Seminar on 'Globalization and South Asia', Centre for the Study of Developing Societies, Delhi, October 2001.

form. *Swadeshi* ('of one's own country') is the kind of political idea that because of its abstract nature tends to accumulate a multitude of competing definitions.[20] Forever linked with the boycott of goods, and the use of this tactic against British imports and Western-*style* products during the freedom struggle, *swadeshi* acquires meaning largely in relation to a cluster of cognate terms associated with the anti-colonial nationalist movement – such as national 'self-reliance' and 'self-rule' (or *swaraj*), which can be realized at the level of individual consciousness, the village community or the national polity. *Swadeshi*, at heart, describes a variety of political assertion that insists upon the value of the local or indigenous over the remote.

Following the 'articulate and sustained opposition to British imports' in the late nineteenth century, *swadeshi*'s 'first peak' as a campaigning slogan was in the Bengal movement against imported cloth, and indeed cloth woven through foreign means involving advanced mechanization. Interestingly, the movement was sparked off by a political act (Lord Curzon's partitioning of Bengal), rather than any change in economic policy.[21] This is a pattern that continues today: the contemporary *swadeshi* upsurge is as much a reaction against India's political engagement with (and exposure to) the outside world – manifested most notably in the closer alliance between the governments of India and the United States – as it is a revolt against the specific economic policies themselves. Differences, of course, remain. In the early twentieth century the Bengali Nobel Laureate Rabindranath Tagore became the poet of *swadeshi*, while also publishing essays on practical matters such as an indigenous form of governance for India ('*Swadeshi Samaj*'). No such figure exists today, and the artistic and literary dimension to *swadeshi* is missing from its avatar in contemporary Indian politics.

Despite the figurative rather than literal quality of their meeting of minds on *swadeshi*, the forces of Mandir, Movement and Mandal have at least been mutually aware. The leaders of the RSS-linked economic front organization, the Swadeshi Jagran Manch (SJM), the main manifestation of swadeshi in *Mandir* politics, have repeatedly stated that they have been able to propel *swadeshi* back into mainstream political discourse (that is, as an active mobilizing principle, rather than an organizational shibboleth) only with the 'assistance' of Gandhian organizations like the Azadi Bachao Andolan (Save Our Independence Movement) and the Karnataka Rajya Raitha Sangha (a farmers' organization) – groups more

---

[20] These are illuminatingly analysed in S. Sarkar, *The Swadeshi Movement in Bengal* (New Delhi, 1973).
[21] C. A. Bayly, *Origins of Nationality in South Asia: Patriotism and Ethical Government in the Making of Modern India* (Delhi, 1998), p. 198.

closely associated with Movement politics and leftist intellectuals than with the Mandir constituency embodied by the SJM. We shall return to the Mandir category in the discussion of the BJP's government/party conflict over *swadeshi* and its approach to market integration.[22]

The category of *Movement* politics is, in places, highly influenced by the idea of *swadeshi*. It should be, since this is the natural home of contemporary 'Gandhians', who come in a bewildering number of varieties that outsiders seek to classify at their own peril. Nevertheless, Gandhi and *swadeshi* are inextricably linked: his 'second' *swadeshi* movement (the Bengal movement of 1903–8 being the first) was part of the process by which he turned the elite-oriented Indian National Congress of the early twentieth century into the mass-based organization it became by the 1930s and 1940s. Particularly after Gandhi's 'ascension to the leadership of Congress in 1920, [*swadeshi*] became a vehicle for mobilising India's vast rural populace'.[23] The Gandhian ideal of homespun cloth was a potent symbol of the need for people to participate actively (and constructively) in public life. Through spinning Gandhi could enact *swadeshi*'s moral message of self-reliance. The spinning wheel became part of the Congress flag, and later the flag of the new Republic. The loose poetic licence Gandhi took with the original idea of *swadeshi* was typical of his political style. Bhikhu Parekh reminds us that it was Gandhi's 'practice to take over terms familiar to his audience and to define them in the way he thought proper without much worrying about their conventional meanings; for example, his definitions of satya, swaraj, swadeshi, and brahmacharya'.[24] This tradition continues today in Indian politics.

In an essay called 'Gandhi and the Market', L. C. Jain, one of India's leading economic planners in the post-independence period, reveals something of what Gandhi instilled through the use of *swadeshi*. Gandhi stressed the cultivation of, on the one hand, self-respect and self-reliance, and on the other, an ethic of concern for the effect of one's economic actions on those to whom one is in proximity. Jain recounts a study tour he undertook in the 1950s to review ways of improving production in the handicraft and hand-woven products sector. He quotes the craftspeople he met as having said: 'If we are here today, even if half alive, it is because

[22] Some SJM leaders claim closer support from left-leaning issue-oriented movement activists like Gene Campaign and the Narmada Bachao Andolan, *Sunday* (7–13 June 1998), p. 23. Certainly the position statements of *swadeshi*'s left and right wings sound similar themes on flagship global market issues like the WTO. See 'RSS Meet Cautions Centre about WTO Provisions', *The Hindu* (14 March 1999).

[23] S. R. B. Leadbeater, *The Politics of Textiles: The Indian Cotton Mill Industry and the Legacy of Swadeshi* (New Delhi, 1993), p. 16.

[24] B. Parekh, *Colonialism, Tradition and Reform: An Analysis of Gandhi's Political Discourse* (New Delhi, 1989), p. 130.

of Gandhiji.' When Jain asked them why, '[t]hey all gave the same answer: swadeshi'. Some said 'not only did Gandhiji teach us swadeshi but, along with it, the ousting of the foreign. It was as rewarding and life-giving as the swadeshi.'[25] This implies, among other things, that *swadeshi* was not solely, or even primarily, about opposition to alien rule. It was about the negative impact of markets on society generally, and the personal moral commitment required to overturn the powerful forces of the status quo. Self-knowledge and self-actualization, two further concepts that Gandhi ingeniously fused with *swadeshi*,[26] were the primary purpose, the 'ousting of the foreign' merely an added bonus.

Gandhi did at certain points call for the lifting of government controls on market activities (especially during food crises). The irony is that when political groups began to rediscover this facet of Gandhi's thought in the 1980s and 1990s, it was used to promote precisely the opposite values to those espoused by Gandhi. Gandhi, Jain argues, 'rejected governmental control so that the strings of the economy could be in the hands of the people . . . The structure of the new economic policy has no relationship with Gandhi's ideas and is its very opposite. The new economic policy is going so far as to separate the market from the villages and global-ising them.'[27] The more conventional view, of course, is that Gandhi contributed to the marginalization of the market principle in Indian policy making. This was grounded in clear analysis: 'Gandhi considered that the mills starved villages of rural employment; in consequence the swadeshi movement encouraged a set of values in relation to industrial development which questioned the legitimacy of the very existence of an organised mill sector. As a political legacy after independence these values were translated into government textile policy.'[28]

Either way, Gandhi's *swadeshi* orientation furnished the votaries of Mandir politics with a point of entry into secular constituencies. The RSS has used *swadeshi* as a critical means of appropriating Gandhi, as if to neu-tralize the association of the RSS with Gandhi's assassin. This strategy has not gone unanswered. Disgust with the BJP's 'rank opportunism' – making political mileage out of indirect association with the Mahatma – reached a peak in late 1997 in reaction to the RSS's scheduling of its 'Mass Contact Programme on Swadeshi' to coincide with Gandhi-related festivities for the fiftieth anniversary of India's independence. Stung by

---

[25] L. C. Jain, 'Gandhi and the Market', *Lokayan Bulletin* 12/3 (1995), p. 6.

[26] Pinto, for instance, says that '[o]ne of the contemporary ways by which Gandhi's vision of swadeshi takes effect is through self-reliance'. V. Pinto, *Gandhi's Vision and Values: The Moral Quest for Change in Indian Agriculture* (New Delhi, 1998), p. 111.

[27] Jain, 'Gandhi and the Market', p. 10.

[28] Leadbeater, *The Politics of Textiles*, p. 16.

this criticism, a BJP general secretary retorted angrily that 'Mahatma Gandhi is not the monopoly of the Congress party'. This referred to the Congress Party president's remark that the forces of Mandir were attempting to 'hijack' Gandhi. Noorani argues that 'the issue is not one of anyone "monopolizing" a national hero but of a [Hindu nationalist] political movement opposing him ferociously while he lived, rejecting his ideology for decades and suddenly hailing him . . . all the while continuing to espouse a credo fundamentally antithetical to his'.[29]

This is a widely held view among Movement Gandhians and others inspired by some aspect of Gandhi's life. Ashok Chousalkar argues that the RSS's adoption of the Mahatma took place much earlier, during the agitations against Indira Gandhi's declaration of a state of internal Emergency in the mid-1970s. The precursor party to the BJP, the Jan Sangh, ended up sharing power with centre-left parties in the Janata Party-led coalition government in the late 1970s. When the Jan Sangh was reincarnated in 1980 as the BJP, with the moderate A. B. Vajpayee as its leader, it 'wanted to claim the political legacy of the Janata Party. Therefore, it did not change Janata Party's philosophy of Gandhian socialism.'[30]

But arguably the appropriation of Gandhi by the forces of Mandir politics took place a long time earlier. During the 1950s, modified versions of *swadeshi* thought were emerging through the 'Integral Humanism' of Deendayal Upadhyaya, a former president of the Jan Sangh.[31] Upadhyaya's philosophy is a Hindu chauvinist form of Gandhian socialism. Upadhyaya's thought is, remarkably, still being elaborated by contemporary Hindutva ideologues, the attempt to increase proximity to Gandhi never far from the surface.

The forces of *Mandal* politics reflect greater ambivalence about *swadeshi*. On the one hand there is a natural affinity: *swadeshi* has often been promoted as a way of resisting the attempt of foreign business interests to immiserate the rural poor – overwhelmingly from the lower castes – who are routinely portrayed as embodying all that is authentic about traditional village life. Programmatically, moreover, Mandal is in conflict with the market: affirmative action relies on a large state to distribute jobs to lower-caste people, whereas advocates of the market press for a more streamlined state, staffed by fewer (better-trained)

---

[29] A. G. Noorani, *The RSS and the BJP: A Division of Labour*, 2nd edn (Delhi, 2001), p. 49.

[30] A. Chousalkar, 'BJP and the Ethnic Constitution of the Nation', *Economic and Political Weekly* (Bombay, 12 February 2000), p. 535.

[31] Some of these ideas also emerged in an interview with M. C. Sharma, the BJP's chief whip in the upper chamber of the Indian parliament and an economic theorist with the Swadeshi Jagran Manch who has published a book on the *Economic Philosophy of Deendayal Upadhyaya*, New Delhi, 5 March 2002.

employees. Thus is Mandal nudged further into *swadeshi*'s anti-market embrace.

On the other hand, there is a palpable sense of mistrust of the idea at a fundamental level in some quarters of the Mandal constituency. That the attempted appropriation of Gandhi by the forces of Mandir has taken place through the medium of *swadeshi* is part of this aversion. But things Gandhian have always been suspect among the practitioners and supporters of Mandal politics. The strong condemnation of Gandhi's views on untouchability, voiced by the Dalit leader and fellow freedom fighter D. R. Ambedkar, both before and after independence, had long ago depressed Gandhi's stock in the Mandal camp. Thus, given the inescapable Gandhi–*swadeshi* connection, *swadeshi* has been less in evidence in the programmes of caste-based parties than one might otherwise have expected. An informal discussion on *swadeshi* among a contemporary group of social activists, as reported by Bakshi, reveals the continued mistrust: 'Swadeshi was not an unquestioned gospel for all the participants. The Dalit activists resisted the term "Swadeshi" because of its contemporary associations with the [RSS]. Besides, for them the concept of Swadeshi was meaningless unless it included land reforms and a firm stand on the hierarchical and exploitative caste structure.'[32]

Mandal politics has also shied away from *swadeshi* because of the less heroic uses to which the notion was put in earlier nationalist campaigns. Guha examines 'some of the disciplinary aspects of the Swadeshi Movement of 1903–1908', finding that '[c]oercion had already established itself as a means of mobilization for Swadeshi quite early in the campaign'. That is, popular support for the boycotts of foreign goods was not always as unanimous as subsequent generations have been led to believe. Many of the boycotts were certainly less voluntary than their organizers suggested publicly. Guha reproduces extracts from colonial reports stating that 'there was massive indulgence in physical coercion' of people who refused to support the boycott, or threatened to do so.

More importantly, from the perspective of Mandal politics, there was also 'social coercion' which 'came in the form of caste sanctions which meant, in effect, withdrawal of ritual services, refusal of inter-dining, boycott of wedding receptions and funeral ceremonies, and other pressures amounting to partial or total ostracism of those considered guilty of deviation from *swadeshi* norms'.[33] The denial of ritual services – the cleansing of pollution – to those who refuse to abide by the boycott

---

[32] R. Bakshi, *Bapu Kuti: Journeys in Rediscovery of Gandhi* (New Delhi, 1998), p. 310.
[33] R. Guha, *Dominance without Hegemony: History and Power in Colonial India* (New Delhi, 1998), p. 110.

was to trap a Hindu irretrievably in a state of impurity. And since status within the caste hierarchy related critically to the degree of one's freedom from ritual uncleanliness, the imposition of this discipline could condemn its victim to total excommunication. No wonder that those who wanted Swadeshi to win out in a short and swift campaign settled on this device as their most favoured weapon.[34]

Guha argued not only 'that mobilization for the Swadeshi Movement relied on caste sanction to no mean extent',[35] but also that by using the idiom of caste to enforce the voluntary boycotts, the *swadeshi* campaign became part of a larger pattern of Hindu revivalism, through whose 'ideology . . . the image of the Brahman was promoted as that of the mentor and warden of Hindu society'. The result – not likely to appeal to the forces of Mandal – was 'a political ethos soaked so thoroughly in Hinduism' that it made 'the discrimination between purity and pollution', the barriers between dominant and oppressed castes, 'a defining principle of nationalist conduct'.[36]

## Governance, Mandir politics and the redefinition of *swadeshi*

*Swadeshi*, then, engages with virtually all of the key ideas associated with the market – competition, exchange, inequity, impersonality, economies of scale and scope. It is also suffused through all three of the ideological traditions highlighted above as competing for influence with the market in the arena of contemporary Indian politics. Thus the nature and extent of the legitimacy a market-orientation attains in policy making – how it becomes ideologically embedded – will depend in part on the battle between competing conceptions of *swadeshi*. The most prominent site for that battle is between the government and organizational wings of Mandir politics.

During the mid-to-late 1990s, the BJP's highlighting of *swadeshi* raised great expectations among SJM activists, who at the time had misapprehended the ruling party's intentions: the BJP government had employed *swadeshi* as, above all, a way of burnishing its Gandhian credentials. Once the BJP-led government came to power, and showed its true pragmatic orientation, the *swadeshi* activists in Mandir politics were to be bitterly disappointed. Because of the organizational strength of these critics from within the Hindu nationalist fold, who could draw on the resources of the RSS network, the BJP has been forced to address *swadeshi* critics of the market. This, as we shall see, has led the BJP to seek a redefinition of the Mandir conception of *swadeshi*.

[34] Ibid., p. 117.     [35] Ibid., p. 111.     [36] Ibid., p. 119.

*Swadeshi*-oriented critics of the market focus on what they see as its two basic negative attributes: first, its tendency to compromise sovereignty (because of the market's ability to act as a channel of 'foreign economic dominance'); and second, its documented tendency to erode the foundations of the social order (by promoting various forms of mobility). Part of the BJP-led coalition government's response to this two-pronged attack has been to adopt its own idiosyncratic 'national interest' version of *swadeshi*, through which the government permits itself to engage with external economic actors, and even to bind India's economy to international markets, in those instances when it deems such actions necessary for the strengthening of the nation. This form of *swadeshi* may help to neutralize charges that continued movement in the direction of market-led policy is contributing to further economic subjugation from abroad, but it does nothing to counter the second kind of charge – that markets lead to social breakdown. And it is this that is becoming the rallying cry among an influential element within the Swadeshi Jagran Manch.

As Baldev Raj Nayar has argued, the version of *swadeshi* that has been put forward by the pragmatists within the political leadership of the Hindu right is closely aligned with the idea of 'national interest'. Nayar argues that the Jan Sangh's nationalism has always contained a pragmatic streak. The party's first election manifesto, in 1951, advocated the 'revival of Bharatiya culture and revitalization of true Bharatiya nationalism on its basis, with such adjustments as may be necessary to make our country truly modern, progressive and strong'. This is the larger doctrinal framework within which the 'national interest' school of *swadeshi* rose to prominence.[37]

This broader framework was applied in the chapter of the BJP's 1998 manifesto entitled 'Our Swadeshi Approach: Making India and Global Economic Power'. As the manifesto put it: 'India, too, must follow its own national agenda . . . [and] the broad agenda of the BJP will be guided by Swadeshi or economic nationalism . . . Swadeshi simply means "India First". This is the governing principle of all nations.' Nayar makes the important observation that *swadeshi* 'is not to be understood simply in the narrow sense of protectionism', clarifying this point by quoting from the 1998 manifesto: 'By Swadeshi one means that the local resources and talents have the full scope for development in national interest.'[38]

[37] *BJP Election Manifesto* 1951, pp. 10–11, cited in Baldev Raj Nayar, 'The Limits of Economic Nationalism: Economic Policy Reforms Under the BJP-Led Government', paper prepared for the conference on 'India and the Politics of Developing Countries: Essays in Honour of Myron Weiner', 24–6 September 1999, Kellogg Institute of International Studies, University of Notre Dame, Indiana.

[38] *BJP Election Manifesto* 1998.

This view was elaborated by the BJP's Yashwant Sinha (who has been both finance and external affairs minister).[39] Sinha echoed the idea of *swadeshi* as a way of pursuing national interest in an almost market-like setting: 'Swadeshi actually means competition, going out to the world and winning.'[40] Sinha is seeking to connect the idea of *swadeshi* with an understanding of the multidimensionality of national power, stating: 'I understand swadeshi basically as a concept which will make India great.' Through this means he makes the link between *swadeshi* and economic power by drawing on the role of military power as a signifier of national greatness:

Nuclear tests [undertaken by the BJP government soon after taking office in early 1998] were Swadeshi, because they made India powerful. Now India must be a powerful economic nation to match its military might, and the only way you can become an economic power is by being able to test your strengths against others. Which means going out into the world and competing – or letting the world come in and compete.

The government's flash of *nuclear swadeshi*, according to one reading of Sinha, means that it need not be defensive about its abandonment of *economic swadeshi*. Sinha argued that it was nonsense to think that '[a]fter the nuclear tests . . . we will go the East India Co. way, or that transnationals will come in and take over, or that they will exercise undue influence'. The association of *swadeshi* with the struggle against foreign domination, or with the need to promote security through inward-looking policies, 'are all concepts which are not valid any more. And therefore, swadeshi, globalizer, and liberalizer are not contradictions in terms. I personally think that globalization is the best way of being Swadeshi.'[41]

One news analysis argued that 'Mr Sinha's remarks must be galling for the swadeshi lobby as he was seen as their nominee for the finance minister's post.' Others were irked as well. Elaborating on the earlier charge that the BJP had 'stolen the word from the Congress', one Congress MP claimed that it had done so clumsily. Sinha was incapable, he wrote, of composing a '500-word essay on swadeshi'.[42]

But the nuclear tests had shaken not just the confidence of America's CIA analysts, who reportedly learned of the detonations from CNN, but also some of the key alignments in domestic politics as well. This worked to Sinha's advantage. The outside world has difficulty grasping

[39] *Business Today* (22 January 1998), pp. 98–101.
[40] 'Swadeshi is competition, not return to dark ages: Sinha', *Economic Times* (11 September 1998).
[41] *Business Today* (22 January 1998), pp. 98–101.
[42] M. S. Aiyar, 'Saffron Swadeshi: Does the BJP's Economics Derive from Gandhi or Golwalkar?', *India Today* (20 April 1998), p. 29.

how important the nuclear tests were in strengthening the BJP's rhetoric of national interest *swadeshi*, neutralizing other forms in the process. As one editorial put, 'one of the first casualties' of the nuclear tests 'has been swadeshi'.[43]

The realpolitik vision of national interest *swadeshi*, however, also served to undermine *swadeshi*'s moral appeal. National interest *swadeshi* becomes a classic reaffirmation of the position taken by the realist school of international relations, which emphasizes a belief in the essential amorality of the inter-state system, where might makes right. The amorality stems from the fact that there is no universally legitimate and effective higher enforcement authority above the state to regulate conflict and that, as a result, every state must provide for its own security. And yet this bleak message is emerging at a time – the early twenty-first century – when the moral dimension of *swadeshi* is more evident than at any time since Gandhi's death. According to one statement of BJP policy: 'It is . . . necessary to revive the spirit of Swadeshi. This will save us from reckless imitation, from unnecessary and excessive dependence on foreign capital and create in us a tendency of restraint and avoidance of conspicuous consumption.'[44] Another example of concern with the moral fabric of the nation can be found in attempts to reconsider what 'the founding fathers of the Indian Renaissance and the leaders of the anti-colonial resistance' thought of *swadeshi*. New theoretical interpretations contend that the great nationalist leaders were 'opposed not to Videshi (that is, [things/ideas] originating in foreign countries) but to Aupaniveshi (that is, [anything] having its source in Aupaniveshik Manasikta or colonial mentality)'.[45]

Given this fluid political and ideational landscape it is not surprising that, ideologically speaking (or at least at the level of party manifestos), the Congress and BJP views on *swadeshi* and the market began to bleed into one another a bit around the time of the 1999 election. As one commentary put it:

The consensus appears to have evolved gradually, with the Congress talking of 'self-reliance', which in a way is a tacit acceptance of the fact that BJP's 'swadeshi' agenda does have its appeal. At the same time, since BJP is only a part of the NDA [National Democratic Alliance], it has been forced to tone down its swadeshi rhetoric. Hence both manifestos seem to have found a common meeting ground.[46]

---

[43] *Times of India* (19 May 1998).    [44] *BJP Election Manifesto* 1998.
[45] P. C. Joshi, 'Countering Aupaniveshik Manasikta: Swaraj and Swadeshi in Indian Social Science', *Mainstream* (24 May 1997), pp. 13–24.
[46] *Outlook* (New Delhi, August 1999).

And yet this indicates little more than an indeterminate degree of 'passive parliamentary consensus'. This is different from a shared political programme, the absence of which is likely to prevent the emergence of any substantive joint activity or outcome. Still, it is a step in *some* direction – forward or back we do not yet know, but tending to bring to the fore divisions between the BJP and the RSS.

## Conclusion

The Indian experience of introducing market reforms demonstrates the importance of analysing the ideological field left uncaptured in interest-based institutional analysis. In India, a market-orientation in policy making has been confronted by various forms of *swadeshi*, a notion invoked by actors from across the political spectrum. Further research will be required to determine the factors most influencing whether conflicts among these visions remain contained mainly within the ruling party's organizational structures – that is, between the RSS's 'hardline activists' and the 'party pragmatists' in the BJP-led government – or whether they spread further into other domains, pitting the pragmatists against a combination of SJM functionaries and organizations representing the politics of Mandal and Movement. Some of the answer, however, may lie in the relationship between *swadeshi* and (1) the nature of institutional analysis, and (2) the regionalization of Indian politics. Each is examined briefly below.

First, *swadeshi* has long been used as a vehicle for building institutions and coalitions based on perceptions of overlapping interests. For instance, Gandhi's closeness to several industrialists is often remarked upon as a source of contemporary industry's willingness to build a coalition around the *swadeshi* idiom. But this tradition goes much further back than Gandhi's period of influence over the Congress. As Dharma Kumar reminds us, Bombay in the first decade of the twentieth century was 'in the midst of a great boom. At the same time, India generally was engulfed by an enthusiastic swadeshi agitation to which the Tatas [a large Indian business conglomerate] appealed in their prospectus. The Tatas... were an ideal group to take advantage of this fortunate conjuncture of conditions.'[47]

Many of contemporary India's leading industrialists now claim to have overcome their initial aversion to market competition, and to have

---

[47] D. Kumar, *The Cambridge Economic History of India – Volume II, c. 1757–c. 1970* (Cambridge, 1982), p. 590.

embraced liberalization. Those of this ilk prefer to save their protectionist special-pleading for private negotiations with government officials. Other business leaders have flirted with *swadeshi* on occasion, emphasizing the need for the government to create a 'level playing field' for indigenous capital in the face of multinational competition. This took its most concrete form in the early 1990s with the rather ad hoc Bombay Club, a group of business leaders who questioned the pace and sequencing of market liberalization, not whether reform was needed at all. This lent further legitimacy to *swadeshi* ideas that had been marginalized due to their association with the (at the time) politically untouchable RSS.

Second, the regionalization of Indian politics has, through a variety of mechanisms, put additional decision-making power in the hands of state governments. States have had to use the very limited resources available to them to compete among themselves (and with destinations outside India) for inward investment. In doing so, they were among the only group of political leaders in India that *did* deploy their rhetorical skills to make the political case for market orientation. Regional level political elites with something like a political vision for markets can be found in a handful of India's states. Chandrababu Naidu in Andhra Pradesh is an unabashed modernizer.[48] He has, in contrast to his counterparts in the neighbouring state of Tamil Nadu, publicly associated himself with the reformist agenda, subsuming it within a larger vision of a more responsive form of government. Why conditions in Andhra Pradesh should have made him so inclined is a matter of some controversy.[49]

At least some others are found elsewhere, most notably in Karnataka, where chief minister S. M. Krishna has earned praise. But even mafia-tainted Sharad Pawar, chief minister of Maharashtra during the late 1980s and early 1990s, was able to ground market reforms in something approaching a legitimating ideology, one that considered politics a fair transaction, in which the voter could expect service or go elsewhere (which helps to explain why Pawar was ousted in 1995). The Communist Party of India-Marxist (CPI-M) during Jyoti Basu's reign as chief minister (1977–2000) is another example of political regionalism helping the market to embed itself ideologically. This had much to do with Basu's skill at portraying *parts* of liberalization as a liberation for West Bengal from 'central planning' – not because the CPI-M was opposed to planning, but because

---

[48] C. Naidu (with Sevanti Ninan), *Plain Speaking* (New Delhi, 2000).

[49] For a comparison of the political strategies underlying economic reform in these two states, see L. Kennedy, 'Contrasting Responses to Economic Reform in Andhra Pradesh and Tamil Nadu', in Rob Jenkins, ed., *Regional Reflections: Comparing Politics Across India's States* (Oxford University Press, forthcoming).

the 'central' part had deprived the region of what it saw as its fair share of national resources. State-level politicians are key linkage elites with huge potential to draw on regional political idioms to legitimate 'market-orientation'.[50] Their actions and rhetoric will be a huge influence on the ability of the market to become ideologically embedded in India.

[50] P. R. Brass, *The New Cambridge History of India, IV-1: The Politics of India Since Independence*, 2nd edn (Cambridge, 1994).

# 11 The locational and institutional embeddedness of electronic markets: the case of the global capital markets

*Saskia Sassen*

We might expect today's global financial market to be generally unlike other current and past markets and to approximate, and even enact, key principles of neo-classical market theory. The prevalent representation of this market as electronic, transjurisdictional, and globally interconnected indicates that more than any other type of market it is well captured by neo-classical theory. According to this account, demand and supply forces are less hindered in the case of financial markets by the frictions of time and distance and the imperfections of knowledge. Market supply and demand can thus carry more weight in the coordination and regulation of the financial sector than they are likely to in other markets and sectors. Therewith market forces can be seen to strengthen the weight of liberal dynamics in the political order.

Today's global capital market is indeed a complex formation markedly different from earlier global financial markets and from other types of markets in the past and today. Largely electronic and consisting of the movement of dematerialized instruments, this market can be expected to be largely disembedded from the social worlds characterizing the functioning of most markets. Hence this market would represent old notions and their current reincarnations of the market as a depersonalized force that can further the development of contemporary capitalism. It is in fact a powerful market with vast shadow effects over just about all economic sectors, with often significant transformative force.

This chapter interrogates the neo-classical representation of these two characteristics of the global capital market – its distinctiveness as a market and its transformative effect. It examines the possibility that this market evinces distinctive modalities of embeddedness such that these can escape the categories used to capture the embeddedness of other types of market. This would have implications for prevalent notions about the kind of agency – depersonalized and modernizing – associated with this electronic, global and transjurisdictional market. One feature in these notions is the presumed neutrality ascribed to advanced technology, such

224

that high inputs of the latter can be expected to reduce and perhaps even eliminate the weight of 'traditional' forces.

The first section is a brief discussion of how the key features in mainstream economic representations of the global electronic market for capital would seem to be one of the closest approximations to the basic economic model of the market, itself presented as an approximation to the actual functioning of markets, albeit the one with the greatest explanatory power. To examine the validity of this point it is actually important to show that the current market for capital is different from earlier phases in this market, in good part due to the specific capacities associated with the new computer-centred interactive technologies. The second section then examines in what ways this market is different. In the third section I argue that even as it is different, it remains deeply embedded and conditioned by non-market and non-digital dynamics, agendas, contents, powers. One consequence is that its representation as a depersonalized mode of coordination and as a modernizing force that strengthens liberalism may well be unwarranted.

## Has the ultimate market arrived?

Among the key assumptions in economic models aimed at approximating the actual operation of markets is the assumption that markets are open, which in turn ensures the operation of demand and supply forces, therewith in turn ensuring their openness. Among the key propositions in these types of models is the crucial role of competition and its pressure on innovation, which functions as a stimulus for technological development and thereby brings about more competition, and so on. In this type of analysis, governments, courts and even firms are encumbrances which *can* weigh down market operation. They are factors constituting social structures and thereby can potentially detract from market dynamics. Insofar as markets are the best mechanisms for allocating scarce resources, governments, courts, firms, and whatever is an obstacle to their functioning, are represented as undesirable. Finally, when markets function as they are meant to, they can be seen as representations of a general theory of how people interact.

Applied to what is a common representation or understanding of the global market for capital, this bundle of assumptions and propositions would seem to be as close an approximation to the actual market as has been possible yet. Because it is increasingly an electronic market, with pervasive use of cutting-edge computer applications, it is open to millions of simultaneous investors and conceivably able to maximize the chances that market participants have basically instantaneous access to the same information no matter where they are. This should then ensure that supply and demand forces are in full operation, guided by information universally available to participants. Since it is a market centred in an industry that produces dematerialized outputs these can respond 'freely' to demand-supply forces in that they experience little if any distance friction or other obstacles to circulation which can distort the operation of demand-supply forces. Crucial to this possibility is the fact that growing numbers of governments have been persuaded or led to deregulate the industry and its markets, thereby enhancing the operation of supply and demand forces, rather than being encumbrances to the operation of these forces. Further, as a global, deregulated, and electronic market it has particular capabilities for overriding existing jurisdictions.

In brief, one might posit that this is as close an approximation to the model of supply and demand as one might hope for: a market that is not encumbered by geography, weight, unequal access to information, government regulation, or particularistic agendas given its highly technical character and the participation of millions of investors. Has the ultimate market arrived?

Insofar as an economic analysis of markets excludes firms, states and courts from its explanatory variables, the global market for capital would seem to be a good case through which to explore these assumptions and propositions. In saying this, one of my assumptions is that today's global market for capital is actually distinct and needs to be differentiated from earlier cases of worldwide financial markets. There is by no means agreement on this assumption. The next section briefly seeks to explain the main reasons for my asserting that it is different. Some of these differences with past financial markets and with other types of markets today are in turn the features that conceivably would seem to make this market one of the closest approximations to the economists' model of the market.

## The market for capital today

There has long been a market for capital and it has long consisted of multiple, variously specialized, financial markets.[1] It has also long had global components.[2] Indeed, a strong line of interpretation in the literature is that today's market for capital is nothing new and represents a return to an earlier global era at the turn of the twentieth century and,

---

[1] See B. Eichengreen and A. Fishlow, *Contending with Capital Flows* (New York, 1996).
[2] See G. Arrighi, *The Long Twentieth Century: Money, Power and the Origins of Our Times* (London, 1994).

then again, in the inter-war period.[3] And yet, I will argue that all of this holds at a high level of generality, but that when we factor in the specifics of today's capital market some significant differences emerge with those past phases. There are, in my reading, two major sets of differences. One has to do with the level of formalization and institutionalization of the global market for capital today, partly an outcome of the interaction with national regulatory systems that themselves gradually became far more elaborate over the last hundred years.[4] I will not focus on this aspect here.[5] The second set of differences concerns the transformative impact of the new information and communication technologies, particularly computer-based technologies (henceforth referred to for short as digitization). In combination with the various dynamics and policies we usually refer to as globalization they have constituted the capital market as a distinct institutional order, one different from other major markets and circulation systems such as global trade.

One of the key and most significant outcomes of digitization on finance has been the jump in orders of magnitude and the extent of worldwide interconnectedness. Elsewhere I have posited that there are basically three ways in which digitization has contributed to this outcome.[6] One is the use of sophisticated software, a key feature of the global financial markets today and a condition which in turn has made possible an enormous amount of innovation. It has raised the level of liquidity as well as increased the possibilities of liquefying forms of wealth hitherto considered non-liquid. This can require enormously complex instruments; the possibility of using computers not only facilitated the development of these instruments, but also enabled their widespread use insofar as much of the complexity could be contained in the software. It allows users who might not fully grasp either the mathematics or the software design issues to be effective in their deployment of the instruments.

Second, the distinctive features of digital networks can maximize the implications of global market integration by producing the possibility of simultaneous interconnected flows and transactions, and decentralized

---

[3] See P. Hirst and G. Thompson, *Globalization in Question: The International Economy and the Possibilities of Governance* (Cambridge, 1996).

[4] See Rodney Bruce Hall and Thomas J. Biersteker, eds, *The Emergence of Private Authority in Global Governance* (Cambridge, 2002); and P. C. Cerny, 'Structuring the Political Arena: Public Goods, States and Governance in a Globalized World', in R. Palan, ed., *Global Political Economy: Contemporary Theories* (London, 2000), pp. 21–35.

[5] For a discussion of this feature see S. Sassen, *The Global City: New York, London, Tokyo*, new edn (Princeton, 2001), chs 4 and 5, and S. Sassen, *Losing Control? Sovereignty in an Age of Globalization* (New York, 1996), ch. 2.

[6] See Sassen, *Global City*, chs 5 and 7, and S. Sassen, ed., *Global Networks/Linked Cities* (London, 2002).

access for investors. Since the late 1980s, a growing number of financial centres have become globally integrated as countries deregulated their economies. This non-digital condition raised the impact of the digitization of markets and instruments.

Third, because finance is particularly about transactions rather than simply flows of money, the technical properties of digital networks assume added meaning. Interconnectivity, simultaneity, decentralized access, all contribute to multiply the number of transactions, the length of transaction chains (i.e., distance between instrument and underlying asset), and thereby the number of participants. The overall outcome is a complex architecture of transactions. The combination of these conditions has contributed to the distinctive position of the global capital market in relation to other components of economic globalization. We can specify two major features, one concerning orders of magnitude and the second the spatial organization of finance. In terms of the first, indicators are the actual monetary values involved and, though more difficult to measure, the growing weight of financial criteria in economic transactions, sometimes referred to as the financialization of the economy. Since 1980, the total stock of financial assets has increased three times faster than the aggregate GDP of the twenty-three highly developed countries that formed the OECD for much of this period; and the volume of trading in currencies, bonds and equities has increased about five times faster and now surpasses it by far. This aggregate GDP stood at US$30 trillion in 2000 while the worldwide value of internationally traded derivatives reached over US$65 trillion in the late 1990s, a figure that rose to over US$80 trillion by 2000 and stood at US$168 trillion by late 2001. To put this in perspective we can make a comparison with the value of other major high-growth components of the global economy, such as the value of cross-border trade (c. US$8 trillion in 2000), and global foreign direct investment stock (US$6 trillion in 2000).[7] Foreign exchange transactions were ten times as large as world trade in 1983, but seventy times larger in 1999, even though world trade also grew sharply over this period.[8]

As for the second major feature, the spatial organization of finance, it has been deeply shaped by regulation. In theory, regulation has operated as one of the key locational constraints keeping the industry, its firms

---

[7] See IMF 2001; BIS 2002.

[8] The foreign exchange market was the first one to globalize, in the mid-1970s. Today it is the biggest and in many ways the only truly global market. It has gone from a daily turnover rate of about US$15 billion in the 1970s, to US$60 billion in the early 1980s, and an estimated US$1.3 trillion today. In contrast, the total foreign currency reserves of the rich industrial countries amounted to about US$1 trillion in 2000.

and markets, from spreading to every corner of the world.[9] The wave of deregulations that began in the mid-1980s has lifted this set of major constraints to geographic spread. Further, since today it is a highly digitized industry, its dematerialized outputs can circulate instantaneously worldwide, financial transactions can be executed digitally, and both, circulation and transactions, can cut across conventional borders. This raises a host of locational issues that are quite specific and different from those of most other economic sectors.[10] The large-scale deregulation of the industry in a growing number of countries since the mid-1980s has brought with it a sharp increase in access to what were still largely national financial centres and it enabled innovations which, in turn, facilitated its expansion both geographically and institutionally. This possibility of locational and institutional spread also brings with it a heightened level of risk, clearly a marking feature of the current phase of the market for capital.

Though there is little agreement on the subject, in my reading these current conditions make for important differences between today's global capital market and the period of the gold standard before World War I.[11] In many ways the international financial market from the late 1800s to the inter-war period was as massive as today's. This appears to be the case if we measure its volume as a share of national economies and in terms of the relative size of international flows. The international capital market in that earlier period was large and dynamic, highly internationalized and backed by a healthy dose of Pax Britannica to keep order. The extent of its internationalization can be seen in the fact that in 1920, for example, Moody's rated bonds issued by about fifty governments to raise money in the American capital markets.[12] The depression brought on a radical decline in the extent of this internationalization, and it was not till very recently that Moody's was once again rating the bonds of about fifty governments. Indeed, as late as 1985, only fifteen foreign governments

---

[9] Wholesale finance has historically had strong tendencies towards cross-border circulation, whatever the nature of the borders might have been. Venice-based Jewish bankers had multiple connections with those in Frankfurt, and those in Paris with those in London; the Hawala system in the Arab world was akin to the Lombard system in Western Europe. For a detailed discussion see Arrighi, *Twentieth Century*.

[10] See, e.g., L. Budd, 'Globalization, Territory and Strategic Alliances in Different Financial Centers', *Urban Studies* 32/2 (1995), pp. 345–60.

[11] See also R. B. Hall and T. J. Biersteker, eds, *The Emergence of Private Authority in Global Governance* (Cambridge, 2002) and S. Maxfield, *Gatekeepers of Growth* (Princeton, 1997).

[12] See T. Sinclair, 'Passing Judgment: Credit Rating Processes as Regulatory Mechanisms of Governance in the Emerging World Order', *Review of International Political Economy* 1/1 (Spring 1994), pp. 133–59.

Table 1 *Financial Assets of Institutional Investors, 1990 to 1997, selected countries, (bn USD)*

| Country | 1990 | 1993 | 1996 | 1997 |
|---|---|---|---|---|
| Canada | 332.6 | 420.4 | 560.5 | 619.8 |
| France | 655.7 | 906.4 | 1278.1 | 1263.2 |
| Germany | 599.0 | 729.7 | 1167.9 | 1201.9 |
| Japan | 2427.9 | 3475.5 | 3563.6 | 3154.7 |
| Netherlands | 378.3 | 465.0 | 671.2 | 667.8 |
| United Kingdom | 1116.8 | 1547.3 | 2226.9 | n/a |
| United States | 6875.7 | 9612.8 | 13382.1 | 15867.5 |
| Total OECD | 13768.2 | 19013.9 | 26001.2 | n/a |

*Source:* Based on OECD, International Direct Investment Statistical Yearbook 1999, Table 8.1.

were borrowing in the US capital markets. Not until after 1985 did the international financial markets re-emerge as a major factor.[13]

One type of difference concerns the growing concentration of market power in institutions such as pension funds and insurance companies. Institutional investors are not new. What is different beginning in the 1980s is the diversity of types of funds and the rapid escalation of the value of their assets. There are two phases in this short history, one going into the early 1990s and the second one taking off in the later 1990s. Just focusing briefly on the first phase, and considering pension funds, for instance, their assets more than doubled in the US from $1.5 trillion in 1985 to $3.3 trillion in 1992. Pension funds grew threefold in the UK and fourfold in Japan over that same period, and they more than doubled in Germany and in Switzerland. In the US, institutional investors as a group came to manage two-fifths of US households' financial assets by the early 1990s, up from one fifth in 1980. Further, today the global capital market is increasingly a necessary component of a growing range of types of transactions, such as the diversity of government debts that now get financed through the global market: increasingly kinds of debt that were thought to be basically local, such as municipal debt, are now entering this market. The overall growth in the value of financial instruments and assets also is evident with US institutional investors whose assets rose from 59 per cent of GDP in 1980 to 126 per cent in 1993.

---

[13] Switzerland's international banking was, of course, the exception. But this was a very specific type of banking and does not represent a global capital market, particularly given the fact of basically closed national financial systems at the time.

Besides the growth of older types of institutional investors, the late 1990s also saw a proliferation of institutional investors with extremely speculative investment strategies. Hedge funds are among the most speculative of these institutions; they sidestep certain disclosure and leverage regulations by having a small private clientele and, frequently, by operating offshore. While they are not new, the growth in their size and their capacity to affect the functioning of markets certainly grew enormously in the 1990s and they emerged as a major force by the late 1990s. According to some estimates they numbered 1,200 with assets of over $150 billion by mid-1998,[14] which was more than the $122 billion in assets of the total of almost 1,500 equity funds as of October 1997.[15] Both of these types of funds need to be distinguished from asset management funds, of which the top ten are estimated to have $10 trillion under management.[16] A second set of differences has to do with the properties that the new information technologies bring to the financial markets, already briefly addressed earlier. Two sets of properties need to be emphasized here: one, instantaneous transmission, interconnectivity and speed; and the other, increased digitization of transactions and the associated increase in capacities to liquefy assets. Gross volumes have increased enormously. And the speed of transactions has brought its own consequences. Trading in currencies and securities is instant thanks to vast computer networks. Further, the high degree of interconnectivity in combination with instantaneous transmission signals the potential for exponential growth.

A third major difference is the explosion in financial innovations, also partly discussed above. Innovations have raised the supply of financial instruments that are tradable – sold on the open market. There are significant differences by country. Securitization is well advanced in the US, but just beginning in most of Europe. The proliferation of derivatives has furthered the linking of national markets by making it easier to exploit price differences between different financial instruments, i.e., to arbitrage.[17] By 1994 the total stock of derivatives sold over the counter or traded in exchanges had risen to over US$30 trillion, a historical high; this had doubled to US$65 trillion only a few years later, in 1999.

[14] See, e.g., BIS 1999.    [15] See, e.g., UNCTAD 1998.

[16] The level of concentration is enormous among these funds, partly as a consequence of M&As driven by the need for firms to reach what are de facto the competitive thresholds in the global market today. For more details see Sassen, *Global City*, ch. 7.

[17] While currency and interest-rate derivatives did not exist until the early 1980s and represent two of the major innovations of the current period, derivatives on commodities, so-called futures, have existed in some version in earlier periods. Famously, Amsterdam's stock exchange in the seventeenth century – when it was the financial capital of the world – was based almost entirely on trading in commodity futures.

Table 2 *Cross-border Transactions in Bonds and Equities\**, *1975 to 1998, selected years (percentage of GDP)*

|               | 1975 | 1980 | 1985 | 1990 | 1995 | 1998 |
|---------------|------|------|------|------|------|------|
| United States | 4    | 9    | 35   | 89   | 135  | 230  |
| Japan         | 2    | 8    | 62   | 119  | 65   | 91   |
| Germany       | 5    | 7    | 33   | 57   | 172  | 334  |
| France        | n/a  | 5    | 21   | 54   | 187  | 415  |
| Italy         | 1    | 1    | 4    | 27   | 253  | 640  |
| Canada        | 3    | 9    | 27   | 65   | 187  | 331  |

*Source:* Bank for International Settlements, *Annual Report 1999*, April 1998 – June 1999, p. 10.
\* denotes gross purchases and sales of securities between residents and non-residents.

One indicator of this growing importance of cross-border transactions is the value of cross-border transactions in bonds and equities as a percentage of GDP in the leading developed economies. Table 2 presents this information for a handful of these countries and shows the recency of this accelerated increase. For instance, the value of such transactions represented 4 per cent of GDP in 1975 in the US, 35 per cent in 1985 when the new financial era was in full swing, but had quadrupled by 1995 and risen to 230 per cent in 1998. Other countries show even sharper increases. In Germany this share grew from 5 per cent in 1975 to 334 per cent in 1998; in France it went from 5 per cent in 1980 to 415 per cent in 1998. In part, this entails escalating levels of risk and innovation driving the industry. It is only over the last decade and a half that we see this acceleration.

The drive to produce innovations is one of the marking features of the financial era that begins in the 1980s. The history of finance is in many ways a long history of innovations. But what is perhaps different today is the intensity of the current phase and the multiplication of instruments that lengthen the distance between the financial instrument and actual underlying asset. This is reflected, for instance, in the fact that stock market capitalization and securitized debt, before the financial crisis of 1997–8, in North America, the EU, and Japan amounted to $46.6 trillion in 1997, while their aggregate GDP was $21.4 and global GDP was $29 trillion. Further, the value of outstanding derivatives in these same sets of countries stood at $68 trillion, which was about 146 per cent of the size of the underlying capital markets.[18]

[18] For a full description of assumptions and measures see IMF 1999: 47.

## In the digital era: more concentration than dispersal?

Today, after considerable deregulation in the industry, the incorporation of a growing number of national financial centres into a global market, and the widespread use of electronic trading, the actual spatial organization of the industry can be seen as a closer indicator of its market-driven locational dynamics than was the case in the earlier regulatory phase. This would hold especially for the international level given the earlier prevalence of highly regulated and closed national markets; but also in some cases for domestic markets, given barriers to inter-state banking, e.g. in the US.

There has, indeed, been geographic decentralization of certain types of financial activities, aimed at securing business in the growing number of countries becoming integrated into the global economy. Many of the leading investment banks have operations in more countries than they had twenty years ago. The same can be said for the leading accounting, legal, and other specialized corporate services whose networks of overseas affiliates have seen explosive growth.[19] And it can be said for some markets: for example, in the 1980s all basic wholesale foreign exchange operations were in London. Today these are distributed among London and several other centres (even though their number is far smaller than the number of countries whose currency is being traded).

But empirically what stands out in the evidence about the global financial markets after a decade and a half of deregulation, worldwide integration, and major advances in electronic trading is the extent of locational concentration and the premium firms are willing to pay to be in major centres. Large shares of many financial markets are disproportionately concentrated in a few financial centres. This trend towards consolidation in a few centres is also evident within countries. Further, this pattern towards the consolidation of one leading financial centre per country is a function of rapid growth in the sector, not of decay in the losing cities. The sharp concentration in leading financial markets can be illustrated with a few facts.[20] London, New York, Tokyo (notwithstanding a national economic recession), Paris, Frankfurt and a few other cities regularly

[19] See R. J. Johnston, P. J. Taylor and M. J. Watts, eds, *Geographies of Global Change: Remapping the World* (Malden, MA, 2002) and see generally GAWC.

[20] Among the main sources of data for the figures cited in this section are the International Bank for Settlements (Basel); IMF national accounts data; specialized trade publications such as *Wall Street Journal's WorldScope*, *MorganStanley Capital International*, *The Banker*, data listings in the *Financial Times* and in *The Economist* and, especially for a focus on cities, the data produced by Technimetrics, Inc. (now part of Thomson Financial, 1999). Additional names of standard, continuously updated sources are listed in Sassen, *Global City*.

Table 3 *The 10 Biggest Stock Markets in the World (USD Billions) by Market Capitalization*

| Stock Market | Market Capitalization 2001 | 2001 Percentage of Members Capitalization | Market Capitalization 2000 | 2000 Percentage of Members Capitalization |
|---|---|---|---|---|
| NYSE | 11,026.6 | 41.4% | 11534.6 | 37.1% |
| Nasdaq | 2,739.7 | 10.3% | 3597.1 | 8.8% |
| Tokyo | 2,264.5 | 8.5% | 3157.2 | 7.3% |
| London | 2,164.7 | 8.1% | 2612.2 | 7.0% |
| Euronext | 1,843.5 | 6.9% | 2271.7 | 5.9% |
| Deutsche Borse | 1,071.7 | 4.0% | 1270.2 | 3.4% |
| Toronto | 611.5 | 2.3% | 766.2 | 2.0% |
| Italy | 527.5 | 2.0% | 768.3 | 1.7% |
| Swiss Exchange | 527.3 | 2.0% | 792.3 | 1.7% |
| Hong Kong | 506.1 | 1.9% | 506.1 | 1.6% |
| Total for Federation Members | 26,610.0 | 87.5% | 31,125.0 | 76.4% |

Compiled from the 2001 Annual Report p. 92 with calculations of percentages added. Euronext includes Brussels, Amsterdam and Paris. 2001 figures are year end figures.

appear at the top *and* represent a large share of global transactions. This holds even after the September 11 attacks that destroyed the World Trade Center (albeit that this was not largely a financial complex) in New York and were seen by many as a wake-up call about the vulnerabilities of strong concentration in a limited number of sites. Table 3 below shows the extent to which the pre-September 11 levels of concentration in stock market capitalization in a limited number of global financial centres held after the attacks. Table 4 shows the foreign listings in the major markets, further indicating that location in a set of financial markets is one of the features of the global capital market, rather than a reduced need for being present in multiple markets. London, Tokyo, New York, Paris (now consolidated with Amsterdam and Brussels as Euronext), Hong Kong and Frankfurt account for a major share of worldwide stock market capitalization. London, Frankfurt and New York account for an enormous world share in the export of financial services. London, New York and Tokyo account for over one third of global institutional equity holdings, this as of the end of 1997 after a 32 per cent decline in Tokyo's value over 1996. London, New York and Tokyo account for 58 per cent of the foreign exchange market, one of the few truly global markets; together with Singapore, Hong Kong, Zurich, Geneva, Frankfurt and Paris, they account for 85 per cent in this, the most global of markets.

Table 4 *Foreign Listings in Major Stock Exchanges*

| Exchange | 2000 Number of Foreign Listings | 2000 Percentage of Foreign Listings | 2001 Number of Foreign Listings | 2001 Percentage of Foreign Listings |
|---|---|---|---|---|
| Nasdaq | 445 | 11.0% | 488 | 10.3% |
| NYSE | 461 | 19.2% | 433 | 17.5% |
| London | 409 | 17.5% | 448 | 18.9% |
| Deutsche Borse | 235 | 23.9% | 241 | 24.5% |
| Euronext | – | | – | |
| Swiss Exchange | 149 | 36.2% | 164 | 39.4% |
| Tokyo | 38 | 1.8% | 41 | 2.0% |

Compiled from the 2001 Annual Report p. 86 with calculations of percentages added. Euronext includes Brussels, Amsterdam and Paris. 2001 figures are year end figures.

This trend towards consolidation in a few centres, even as the network of integrated financial centres expands globally, is also evident within countries. In the US, for instance, New York concentrates the leading investment banks with only one other major international financial centre in this enormous country, Chicago. Sydney and Toronto have equally gained power in continental-sized countries and have taken over functions and market share from what were once the major commercial centres, respectively Melbourne and Montreal. So have São Paulo and Bombay, which have gained share and functions from respectively Rio de Janeiro in Brazil and New Delhi and Calcutta in India. These are all enormous countries and one might have thought that they could sustain multiple major financial centres. This pattern is evident in many countries.[21] Consolidation of one leading financial centre in each country is an integral part of the growth dynamics in the sector rather than the result of losses in the losing cities. There is both consolidation in fewer major centres across and within countries *and* a sharp growth in the numbers of centres that become part of the global network as countries deregulate their economies. Bombay, for instance, became incorporated in the global financial network in the early 1990s after India (partly) deregulated its financial system. This mode of incorporation into the global network is often at the cost of losing functions that these cities may have had when

---

[21] In France, Paris today concentrates larger shares of most financial sectors than it did 10 years ago and once-important stock markets like Lyon have become 'provincial', even though Lyon is today the hub of a thriving economic region. Milan privatized its exchange in September 1997 and electronically merged Italy's 10 regional markets. Frankfurt now concentrates a larger share of the financial market in Germany than it did in the early 1980s, and so does Zurich, which once had Basel and Geneva as significant competitors.

they were largely national centres. Today the leading, typically foreign, financial, accounting and legal services firms enter their markets to handle many of the new cross-border operations. Incorporation in the global market typically happens without a gain in their global share of the particular segments of the market they are in even as capitalization may increase, often sharply, and even though they add to the total volume in the global market. Why is it that at a time of rapid growth in the network of financial centres, in overall volumes, and in electronic networks, we have such high concentration of market shares in the leading global and national centres? Both globalization and electronic trading are about expansion and dispersal beyond what had been the confined realm of national economies and floor trading. Indeed, one might well ask why financial centres matter at all.

## The continuing utility of spatial agglomeration

The continuing weight of major centres is, in a way, countersensical, as is, for that matter, the existence of an expanding network of financial centres. The rapid development of electronic exchanges, the growing digitization of much financial activity, the fact that finance has become one of the leading sectors in a growing number of countries, and that it is a sector that produces a dematerialized, hypermobile product, all suggest that location should not matter. In fact geographic dispersal would seem to be a good option given the high cost of operating in major financial centres. Further, the last ten years have seen an increased geographic mobility of financial experts and financial services firms.

There are, in my view, at least three reasons that explain the trend towards consolidation in a few centres rather than massive dispersal.

(a) *The importance of social connectivity and central functions*. First, while the new communications technologies do indeed facilitate geographic dispersal of economic activities without losing system integration, they have also had the effect of strengthening the importance of central coordination and control functions for firms and, even, markets.[22] Indeed for firms in any sector, operating a widely dispersed network of branches and affiliates and operating in multiple markets has made central functions far more complicated. Their execution requires access to top talent, not only inside headquarters but also, more generally, access to innovative milieux – in technology, accounting, legal services, economic forecasting, and all

---

[22] This is one of the seven organizing hypotheses through which I specified my global city model. For a full explanation see Sassen, *Global City*, especially the preface to the new edition.

sorts of other, many new, specialized corporate services. Major centres have massive concentrations of state of the art resources that allow them to maximize the benefits of the new communication technologies and to govern the new conditions for operating globally. Even electronic markets such as NASDAQ and E*Trade rely on traders and banks which are located somewhere, with at least some in a major financial centre. The question of risk and how it is handled and perceived is yet another factor which has an impact on how the industry organizes itself, where it locates operations, what markets become integrated into the global capital market, and so on.

One fact that has become increasingly evident is that to maximize the benefits of the new information technologies firms need not only the infrastructure but a complex mix of other resources. In my analysis organizational complexity is a key variable allowing firms to maximize the utility/benefits they can derive from using digital technology.[23] In the case of financial markets we could make a parallel argument. Most of the value added that these technologies can produce for advanced service firms lies in so-called externalities. And this means the material and human resources – state-of-the-art office buildings, top talent, and the social networking infrastructure that maximizes connectivity. Any town can have fibre optic cables, but this is not sufficient.[24]

A second fact that is emerging with greater clarity concerns the meaning of 'information.' There are two types of information.[25] One is the datum, which may be complex yet is standard knowledge: the level at which a stock market closes, a privatization of a public utility, the bankruptcy of a bank. But there is a far more difficult type of 'information', akin to an interpretation/evaluation/judgement. It entails negotiating a series of data and a series of interpretations of a mix of data in the hope of producing a higher order datum. Access to the first kind of information is now global and immediate from just about any place in the highly developed world thanks to the digital revolution. But it is the second type of information that requires a complicated mixture of elements – the social infrastructure for global connectivity – which gives major financial centres a leading edge.

It is possible, in principle, to reproduce the technical infrastructure anywhere. Singapore, for example, has technical connectivity matching Hong Kong's. But does it have Hong Kong's social connectivity? At a higher level of global social connectivity we could probably say the same

[23] See ibid., pp. 115–16.
[24] See L. Garcia, 'The Architecture of Global Networking Technologies', in Sassen, ed., *Global Networks/Linked Cities*.
[25] See Sassen, *Global City*, ch. 5.

for Frankfurt and London. When the more complex forms of information needed to execute major international deals cannot be got from existing data bases, no matter what one can pay, then one needs the social information loop and the associated de facto interpretations and inferences that come with bouncing off information among talented, informed people. It is the weight of this input that has given a whole new importance to credit rating agencies, for instance. Part of the rating has to do with interpreting and inferring. When this interpreting becomes 'authoritative' it becomes 'information' available to all. The process of making inferences/interpretations into 'information' takes quite a mix of talents and resources as well as a professional subculture. In brief, financial centres provide the social connectivity which allows a firm or market to maximize the benefits of its technical connectivity.

b) *Cross-border mergers and alliances.* Global firms and markets in the financial industry need enormous resources, a trend which is leading to rapid mergers and acquisitions of firms and strategic alliances among markets in different countries. These are happening on a scale and in combinations few would have foreseen as recently as the early 1990s. There are growing numbers of mergers among respectively financial services firms, accounting firms, law firms, insurance brokers, in brief, firms that need to provide a global service. A similar evolution is also possible for the global telecommunications industry which will have to consolidate in order to offer a state-of-the-art, globe-spanning service to its global clients, among which are the financial firms.

I would argue that yet another kind of 'merger' is the consolidation of electronic networks that connect a very select number of markets. There are a number of networks that have been set up in the last few years to connect exchanges. In 1999 NASDAQ, the second largest US stock market after the New York Stock Exchange, set up Nasdaq Japan and in 2000 Nasdaq Canada. This gives investors in Japan and Canada direct access to the market in the US. Europe's more than thirty stock exchanges have been seeking to shape various alliances. Euronext (NEXT) is Europe's largest stock exchange merger, an alliance among the Paris, Amsterdam and Brussels bourses. The Toronto Stock Exchange has joined an alliance with the New York Stock Exchange (NYSE) to create a separate global trading platform. The NYSE is a founding member of a global trading alliance, Global Equity Market (GEM) which includes ten exchanges, among them Tokyo and NEXT. Also small exchanges are merging: in March 2001 the Tallinn Stock Exchange in Estonia and its Helsinki counterpart created an alliance. A novel pattern is hostile takeovers, not of firms, but of exchanges, such as the attempt by the owners of the

Stockholm Stock Exchange to buy the London Stock Exchange (for a price of US$3.7 billion).

These developments may well ensure the consolidation of a stratum of select financial centres at the top of the worldwide network of thirty or forty cities through which the global financial industry operates.[26] Taking an indicator such as equities under management shows a similar pattern of spread and simultaneous concentration at the top of the hierarchy. The worldwide distribution of equities under institutional management is spread among a large number of cities which have become integrated in the global equity market along with deregulation of their economies and the whole notion of 'emerging markets' as an attractive investment destination. In 1999, institutional money managers around the world controlled approximately US$14 trillion. Thomson Financials (1999), for instance, has estimated that at the end of 1999, twenty-five cities accounted for about 80 per cent of the world's valuation. These twenty-five cities also accounted for roughly 48 per cent of the total market capitalization of the world which stood at US$24 trillion at the end of 1999. On the other hand, this global market is characterized by a disproportionate concentration in the top six or seven cities. London, New York and Tokyo together accounted for a third of the world's total equities under institutional management in 1999.

These developments make clear a second important trend that in many ways specifies the current global era. These various centres don't just compete with each other: there is collaboration and division of labour. In the international system of the post-war decades, each country's financial centre, in principle, covered the universe of necessary functions to service its national companies and markets. The world of finance was, of course, much simpler than it is today. In the initial stages of deregulation in the 1980s there was a strong tendency to see the relation among the major centres as one of straight competition when it came to international transactions. New York, London and Tokyo, then the major centres in the system, were seen as competing. But in my research in the late 1980s on these three top centres I found clear evidence of a division of labour already then. They remain the major centres in the system today with the addition of Frankfurt and Paris in the 1990s. What we are seeing now

---

[26] We now also know that a major financial centre needs to have a significant share of global operations to be such. If Tokyo does not succeed in getting more of such operations, it is going to lose standing in the global hierarchy notwithstanding its importance as a capital exporter. It is this same capacity for global operations that will keep New York at the top levels of the hierarchy even though it is largely fed by the resources and the demand of domestic (though state-of-the-art) investors.

is an additional pattern whereby the cooperation or division of functions is somewhat institutionalized: strategic alliances not only between firms across borders but also between markets. There is competition, strategic collaboration and hierarchy.

In brief, the need for enormous resources to handle increasingly global operations, in combination with the growth of central functions described earlier, produces strong tendencies towards concentration and hence hierarchy even as the network of financial centres has expanded.

(c) *De-nationalized elites and agendas.* National attachments and identities are becoming weaker for global firms and their customers. This is particularly strong in the West, but may develop in Asia as well. Deregulation and privatization have weakened the need for national financial centres. The nationality question simply plays differently in these sectors than it did even a decade ago. Global financial products are accessible in national markets and national investors can operate in global markets. For instance, some of the major Brazilian firms now list on the New York Stock Exchange, and by-pass the São Paulo exchange, a new practice which has caused somewhat of an uproar in specialized circles in Brazil. While it is as yet inconceivable in the Asian case, this may well change given the growing number of foreign acquisitions of major firms in several Asian countries. Another indicator of this trend is the fact that the major US and European investment banks have set up specialized offices in London to handle various aspects of their global business. Even French banks have set up some of their global specialized operations in London, inconceivable a decade ago and still not avowed in national rhetoric.

One way of describing this process is as what I call an incipient and highly specialized denationalization of particular institutional arenas.[27] It can be argued that such denationalization is a necessary condition for economic globalization as we know it today. The sophistication of this system lies in the fact that it only needs to involve strategic institutional areas – most national systems can be left basically unaltered. China is a good example. It adopted international accounting rules in 1993, necessary to engage in international transactions. To do so it did not have to change much of its domestic economy. Japanese firms operating overseas adopted such standards long before Japan's government considered requiring them. In this regard the 'wholesale' side of globalization is quite different from the global consumer markets, in which success necessitates altering national tastes at a mass level. This process of denationalization

---

[27] See Sassen, *Losing Control*, ch. 1, and S. Sassen, *Denationalization: Territory, Authority and Rights in a Global Digital Age* (Princeton, forthcoming 2004).

has been strengthened by state policy enabling privatization and foreign acquisition. In some ways one might say that the Asian financial crisis has functioned as a mechanism to denationalize, at least partly, control over key sectors of economies which, while allowing the massive entry of foreign investment, never relinquished that control.[28] Major international business centres produce what we could think of as a new subculture, a move from the 'national' version of international activities to the 'global' version. The long-standing resistance in Europe to M&As, especially hostile takeovers, or to foreign ownership and control in East Asia, signal national business cultures that are somewhat incompatible with the new global economic culture. I would posit that major cities, and the variety of so-called global business meetings (such as those of the World Economic Forum in Davos and other similar occasions), contribute to denationalize corporate elites. Whether this is good or bad is a separate issue; but it is, I would argue, one of the conditions for setting in place the systems and subcultures necessary for a global economic system.

## The global capital market and the state

The explosive growth in financial markets, in combination with the tight organizational structure of the industry described in the preceding section, suggest that the global capital market today contributes to a distinct political economy. The increase in volumes per se may be secondary in many regards. But when these volumes can be deployed, for instance, to overwhelm national central banks, as happened in the 1994 Mexico and the 1997 Thai crises, then the fact itself of the volume becomes a significant variable.[29] Further, when globally integrated electronic markets

---

[28] For instance, Lehman Brothers bought Thai residential mortgages worth half a billion dollars for a 53% discount. This was the first auction conducted by the Thai government's Financial Restructuring Authority which is conducting the sale of $21 billion of financial companies' assets. It also acquired the Thai operations of Peregrine, the HK investment bank that failed. The fall in prices and in the value of the yen has made Japanese firms and real estate attractive targets for foreign investors. Merril Lynch's has bought 30 branches of Yamaichi Securities, Société Générale Group is buying 80% of Yamaichi International Capital Management, Travelers Group is now the biggest shareholder of Nikko, the third largest brokerage, and Toho Mutual Insurance Co. announced a joint venture with GE Capital. These are but some of the best-known examples. Much valuable property in the Ginza – Tokyo's high priced shopping and business district – is now being considered for acquisition by foreign investors, in a twist on Mitsubishi's acquisition of Rockefeller Center a decade earlier.

[29] The new financial landscape maximizes these impacts: the potential deregulation of commercial banks and ascendance of securities industry (with limited regulation and significant leverage), the greater technical capabilities built into the industry, and aggressive hedging activities by asset management funds. Rather than counteracting the excesses of the securities industries, banks added to this landscape by accepting the forecast of

can enable investors rapidly to withdraw well over US$100 billion from a few countries in South East Asia in the 1997–8 crisis, and the foreign currency markets had the orders of magnitude to alter exchange rates radically for some of these currencies, then the fact of digitization emerges as a significant variable that goes beyond its technical features.[30]

These conditions raise a number of questions concerning the impact of this concentration of capital in markets that allow for high degrees of circulation in and out of countries. Does the global capital market now have the power to 'discipline' national governments, that is to say, to subject at least some monetary and fiscal policies to financial criteria where before this was not quite the case? How does this affect national economies and government policies more generally? Does it alter the functioning of democratic governments? Does this kind of concentration of capital reshape the accountability relation that has operated through electoral politics between governments and their people? Does it affect national sovereignty? And, finally, do these changes reposition states and the inter-state system in the broader world of cross-border relations? These are some of the questions raised by the particular ways in which digitization interacts with other variables to produce the distinctive features of the global capital market today. The responses in the scholarly literature vary, ranging from those who find that in the end the national state still

long-term growth in these economies, thus also adding to the capital inflow and to the fairly generalized disregard for risk and quality of investments, and then joining the outflow. Furthermore, at the centre of these financial crises were institutions whose liabilities were perceived as having an implicit government guarantee, even though as institutions they were essentially unregulated, and thus subject to so-called 'moral hazard' problems, that is, the absence of market discipline. Anticipated protection from losses based on the IMF's willingness to assist in bailing out international banks and failed domestic banks in Mexico encouraged excessive risk-taking. It is not the first time that financial intermediaries with substantial access to government liability guarantees pose a serious problem of moral hazard, as became evident in the US savings and loan crisis.

[30] Global capital market integration which had been praised in much of the 1990s for enhancing economic growth became the problem in the East Asian financial crisis. Although the institutional structure for regulating the economy is weak in many of these countries, as has been widely documented, the fact of global capital market integration played the crucial role in the East Asian crisis as it contributed to enormous overleveraging and to a boom-bust attitude by investors, who rushed in at the beginning of the decade and rushed out when the crisis began even though the soundness of some of the economies involved did not warrant that fast a retreat. The magnitude of debt accumulation, only made possible by the availability of foreign capital, was a crucial factor: in 1996 the total bank debt of East Asia was $2.8 trillion, or 130% of GDP, nearly double that from a decade earlier. By 1996 leveraged debt for the median firm had reached 620% in South Korea, 340% in Thailand and averaged 150% to 200% across other East Asian countries. This was financed with foreign capital inflows which became massive outflows in 1997.

exercises the ultimate authority in these matters[31] to those who see an emergent power gaining at least partial ascendance over national states.[32]

For me these questions signal the existence of a second type of embeddedness: the largely digitized global market for capital is embedded in a thick world of national policy and state agencies. It is so in a double sense. First, as has been widely recognized, in order to function these markets require specific types of guarantees of contract and protections, and specific types of deregulation of existing frameworks.[33] An enormous amount of government work has gone into the development of standards and regimes to handle the new conditions entailed by economic globalization. Much work has been done on competition policy and on the development of financial regulations, and there has been considerable willingness to innovate and to accept whole new policy concepts by governments around the world. The content and specifications of much of this work are clearly shaped by the frameworks and traditions evident in the North Atlantic region. This is not to deny the significant differences among the US and the EU, for instance, or among various individual countries, but rather to emphasize, first, that there is a clear Western style that is dominant in the handling of these issues and, secondly, that we cannot simply speak of 'Americanization' since in some cases Western European standards emerge as the ruling ones.

Secondly, in my reading, today the global financial markets are not only capable of deploying the raw power of their orders of magnitude but also of producing 'standards' that become integrated into national public policy and shape the criteria for what has come to be considered 'proper' economic policy.[34] The operational logic of the capital market contains

---

[31] See, e.g., E. Gilbert and E. Helleiner, eds, *Nation-States and Money: The Past, Present and Future of National Currencies* (London, 1999); S. D. Krasner, *Sovereignty: Organized Hypocrisy* (Princeton, 1999); L. Pauly, 'Global Markets, National Authority and the Problem of Legitimation: the case of finance', in Hall and Biersteker, eds, *Emergence of Private Authority*.

[32] See, e.g., L. Panitch, 'Rethinking the Role of the State in an Era of Globalization', in J. Mittelmann, ed., *Globalization: Critical Reflections*, International Political Yearbook, vol. IX (Boulder, CO, 1996), p. xx, and Sassen, *Losing Control*.

[33] See S. Picciotto and R. Mayne, *Regulating International Business: Beyond Liberalization* (London, 1999); P. G. Cerny, *The Changing Architecture of Politics* (London, 1990); Cerny, 'Structuring the Political Arena'; G. Garrett, 'Global Markets and National Politics: Collision Course or Virtuous Circle', *International Organization* 52/4 (1998), pp. 787–824; E. O. Graham and J. D. Richardson, *Global Competition Policy* (Washington, DC, 1997).

[34] I try to capture this normative transformation in the notion of a privatizing of certain capacities for making norms which in the recent history of states under the rule of law were in the public domain. (I am not concerned here with cases such as, e.g., the Catholic Church, an institution that has long had what could be described as private norm-making capacities, but is of course a private institution, or is meant to be that.) Today what are

criteria for what leading financial interests today consider not only sound financial, but also economic policy. These criteria have been constructed as norms for important aspects of national economic policy making going far beyond the financial sector as such.[35]

These dynamics have become evident in a growing number of countries as these became integrated into the global financial markets. For many of these countries, these norms have been imposed from the outside. As has often been said, some states are more sovereign than others in these matters.[36] One of the more familiar elements that has become a norm of 'sound economic policy' is the new importance attached to the autonomy of central banks, anti-inflation policies, exchange rate parity and the variety of items usually referred to as 'IMF conditionality'.[37] The IMF has been an important vehicle for instituting standards that work to the advantage of global financial firms and markets, very often to the detriment of other types of economic actors.[38]

Digitization of financial markets and instruments played a crucial role in raising the orders of magnitude, the extent of cross-border integration, and hence the raw power of the global capital market. Yet this process

actually elements of a private logic emerge as public norms even though they represent particular rather than public interests. This is not a new occurrence in itself for national states under the rule of law; what is perhaps different is the extent to which the interests involved are global. For a fuller discussion see Sassen, *Losing Control*, ch. 2 and Sassen, *Denationalization*.

[35] This is not to deny that other economic sectors, particularly when characterized by the presence of a limited number of very large firms, have exercised specific types of influence over government policy making. See, e.g., J. Dunning, *Alliance Capitalism and Global Business* (London, 1997); Graham and Richardson, *Global Competition Policy*.

[36] A particular feature that matters for my current research on denationalization is the fact that many states, more precisely, specific agencies and departments within states, have participated in the formation and implementation of these conditions and rules.

[37] Since the South East Asian financial crisis there has been a revision of some of the specifics of these standards. For instance, exchange rate parity is now posited in less strict terms. The crisis in Argentina that broke in December 2001 has further raised questions about aspects of IMF conditionality. But neither crisis has eliminated the latter.

[38] See, e.g., L. Ferleger and J. R. Mandle, eds, *Dimensions of Globalization*, special millennial issue of *The Annals*, vol. 570 (July 2000). One instance here is the IMF's policy which makes it cheaper for investors to provide short-term loans protected by the IMF at the expense of other types of investments. The notion behind this capital standard is that short-term loans are generally thought to have less credit risk, and as a result the Basel capital rules weight cross-border claims on banks outside the OECD system at 20% for short-term loans under one year, and at 100% if over a year. This encouraged short-term lending by banks in developing countries. Borrowers, given lower rates, took short-term loans. The result was the accumulation of a large volume of repayment coming due in any given year. Thus Basel risk weights and market risk do not interact properly as a signal. According to the Basel risk weights it was safer to lend to a Korean bank than to a Korean conglomerate as the latter would incur a 100% weight capital charge, compared to 20% for a bank. The official position was thus to extend more loans to the banks than to the conglomerates.

was shaped by interests and logics that typically had little to do with digitization per se, even though the latter was crucial. This makes clear the extent to which these digitized markets are embedded in complex institutional settings. Secondly, while the raw power achieved by the capital markets through digitization also facilitated the institutionalizing of certain finance-dominated economic criteria in national policy, digitization per se could not have achieved this policy outcome.

## Conclusion

The vast new economic topography implemented through the emergence and growth of electronic markets is but one element in an even vaster economic chain that is in good part embedded in non-electronic spaces. There is today no fully virtualized market, firm or economic sector. Even finance, the most digitized, dematerialized and globalized of all sectors, has a topography that weaves back and forth between actual and digital space. This essay sought to show that these features produce a type of double embeddedness in the case of today's global and largely digitized market for capital.

On the one hand the globalization itself of the market has raised the level of complexity of this market and its dependence on multiple types of non-digital resources and conditions. Information technologies have not eliminated the importance of massive concentrations of material resources but have, rather, reconfigured the interaction of capital fixity and hypermobility. The complex management of this interaction is dependent in part on the mix of resources and talents concentrated in a network of financial centres. This has given a particular set of places, global cities, a new competitive advantage in the functioning of the global capital market at a time when the properties of the new ICTs could have been expected to eliminate the advantages of agglomeration, particularly for leading and globalized economic sectors, and at a time when national governments have lost some authority over these markets. In theory, the intensification of deregulation, and the instituting of policies in various countries aimed at creating a supportive cross-border environment for financial market transactions, could have dramatically changed the locational logic of the industry. This is especially the case because it is a digitized and globalized industry that produces dematerialized outputs. It could be argued that the one feature that could keep this industry from having a very broad range of locational options would be regulation. With deregulation that constraint should be disappearing. Other factors, such as the premium paid for location in major cities, should be a deterrent to locate there, and the new developments of telecommunications should reduce the need for such central locations.

On the other hand, these new technologies have raised the orders of magnitude and capabilities of finance to thresholds which make it a sector distinct from other major sectors in the economy. The effect has been a financializing of economies and the growing weight of the operational logic of financial markets in shaping economic norms for policy making. This is significant in two ways. No matter how globalized and electronic, finance requires specific regulatory conditions and hence depends partly on the participation of national states to produce these conditions. The other is that this participation has taken the form of introducing into public policy a set of criteria that reflect the current operational logic of the global market for capital. The formation of a global capital market has come to represent a concentration of power that is capable of influencing national government economic policy, and by extension other policies.

The organizing effort in this essay was to map the locational and institutional embeddedness of the global capital market. In so doing, it also sought to signal that there might be more potential for governmental participation in the governance of the global economy than much current commentary on globalization allows for given its emphasis on hyper-mobility, telecommunications and electronic markets. But the manner of this participation may well be quite different from long-established forms. Indeed, we may be seeing instances where the gap between these older established conceptions and actual global dynamics – particularly in the financial markets – is making possible the emergence of a distinct zone for transactions and governance mechanisms, which, although electronic and cross-border in some of its key features, is nonetheless structured and partly located in a specific geography. By emphasizing the embeddedness of the most digitized and global of all markets, the market for capital, the analysis presented here points to a broader conceptual landscape within which to understand global electronic markets today, both in theoretical and in policy terms.

# Index

Adams, Henry Carter, 146, 149, 150–151
Adanson, Michel
  *Familles des Plantes*, 41
advertising and consumer politics, 184
agency, 2–3, 5, 14, 23
agricultural history, 11
  ploughs, 37–39
  in Scotland, 25–26
agricultural societies, 11, 34–35, 44
  in France, 31–32, 36–37, 42
  in Ireland, 29–31, 32–34, 42
  promotion of new technology, 37–39
  and rationality, 39–40
  in Scotland, 32
  *see also* networks
agriculture
  and High Toryism, 87
  and Malthus, T. R., 80
  and physiocracy, 58
Alder, Ken, 37
Alison, Archibald, 84–86
alliances, *see* mergers and alliances
Ambedkar, D. R., 216
American Economic Association (AEA),
  145
American progressivism, *see* progressivism,
  American
American Sociological Society, 150
anglophobia, 60–61, 64, 67–69
Arbuthnot of Norfolk, 38
Aristotle, 49
  *Politics*, 132
Ashley, Lord, 87, 89
associations, 16, 96–99, 100, 138–139
  *see also* civil society; guilds
autonomy, 23
Azadi Bachao Andolan, 212

Badeau, Nicolas, 62, 63
Baker, John Wynn, 33–34
Bank Charter Act, 1844, 82–83
Basu, Jyoti, 222–223

Basu, Kaushik, 207–208
beliefs, 5, 19–24
  *see also* traditions
Bentham, Jeremy, 68, 69, 106
Bertin, Louis-François, 31
Beuvin, Claude, 36
Bharatiya Janata Party (BJP), 209,
  214–215, 217–221
  *see also* Hindu nationalism
Billington-Greig, Teresa, 172
bimetallism, 14, 84
Bismarck, Otto von, 150
BJP, *see* Bharatiya Janata Party (BJP)
*Blackwood's Edinburgh Magazine*, 76, 82,
  84, 87, 89
Blair, Tony, 130
Blanquet, 42
Blanqui, Adolphe, 93–94
Boissier de la Croix de Sauvages,
  François, 42
Bombay Club, 222
bonds and equities, 232, 239
Books, Van Wyck, 162
botany, 39–43
Bourgeois, Léon, 103
Brandeis, Louis, 155, 178
Brenner, R., 27–29
Brentano, Lujo, 96
Brissot de Warville, Jacques-Pierre, 63, 65
Brooks, John Graham, 146
Buffon, Georges Louis Leclerc, 40–41
  *Natural History*, 40
Burke, Edmund, 87
Byron, George Gordon, Lord, 114

capitalism, 3–5
  and American progressivism, 146,
    151–152, 157–159
  and consumer politics, 175
  and ethics, 157–159
  and German historicism, 151–152,
    157–159

capitalism (*cont.*)
and High Toryism, 75
*see also* markets
capital market, global, *see* global capital
market
Carlyle, Thomas, 105, 107, 125–126
*Chartism*, 76
'Signs of the Times', 76, 77
caste, 210
*see also* Mandal
Castel de Saint-Pierre, Charles-Irénée, 53
Catholicism, 69
*see also* religion
centres, financial, *see* financial centres
Chadwick, Edwin, 80
Chase, Stuart and Frederick J. Schlink
*Your Money's Worth*, 187
China, financial market in, 240
Chousalkar, Ashok, 215
Christianity, 57–61
*see also* religion
Citizen's Charter, 197
citizenship
and consumption, 14, 171–173, 184,
185–190, 192–193, 194, 195,
196–200
*see also* democracy
civil rights, *see* rights
civil society, 2, 7–8, 15, 19
and community, 16, 17–18, 139–144
and consumer politics, 173–175, 200
definitions of, 129–131
and ethics, 137–138
and guilds, 95–96, 100–104
and state, 138–140
Tönnies, F. on, 131–144
*see also* Gesellschaft
Clavière, Etienne, 64–65
Clément, Ambroise, 93
Cobden, Richard, 89
Coleridge, Samuel Taylor, 73, 76, 77, 78,
87, 105, 106, 114
*Lay Sermons*, 74
colonization, 86, 208
commerce, *see* markets
Common Agricultural Policy, 199
Commons Preservation Society, 116,
118
Communist Party of India-Marxist
(CPI-M), 222–223
communitarianism, *see* community
and civil society, 16, 17–18, 139–144
definitions of, 129–131
and ethics, 137–138
and state, 138–140

Tönnies, F. on, 131–144
*see also Gemeinschaft*
community, 99
computer technology, *see* digitization and
the global capital market
Comte, Auguste, 113, 118–119
Condorcet, Antoine Nicolas, Marquis de,
63, 65
connectivity, social, *see* social connectivity
Conrad, Johannes, 148, 156
Conservative Party
and free trade, 71–72, 74
and liberalism, 73
and markets, 71–73
origins of, 70–71
and political economy, 71–73
and protectionism, 71–72
*see also* Toryism, High
Constant, Benjamin, 12–13, 19, 49–51,
68–69
on political economy, 47–48
on religion, 69
consumer politics, 5, 14–15
activism in, 170–172, 177, 188–190,
194–196
and advertising, 184
in Britain, 172–177, 181–185,
196–201
and capitalism, 175
Citizen's Charter, 197
and citizenship, *see* citizenship and
consumption
and civil society, 173–175, 200
consumer education, 184–185
and democracy, 175, 185–189
and ethics, 177–179, 183–184, 200
food prices, 174–177, 181–183
food safety, 175–176, 183, 184–185
and free trade, 172–177, 181–183,
200
and globalization, 170–171
and governance, 198
and international politics, 182–183
in Japan, 179–181, 189–194, 200–201
and the labour movement, 177–178
and lifestyle culture, 176–177
and neo-liberalism, 197
and New Deal, 185–189
protection and regulation, 124,
175–176, 177, 181–185, 188–189,
190–192, 194–196
and radicalism, 173–174
and religion, 191
and rights, 178–179, 188, 194
and traditions, 170–181, 200–201

and the United Nations, 197
in the United States, 177–179, 185–189,
  194–196, 200–201
and women, 179
*see also* consumption
Consumer Protection Basic Law, 192
Consumers' Association, 185, 196, 197,
  198
Consumers' Council, 181
Consumers International, 199
Consumers' Research, 187, 195
Consumers Union, 187, 191
consumption
  and American progressivism, 163–164,
    165–166, 167–168, 169
  and citizenship, 14, 171–173, 184,
    185–190, 192–193, 194, 195,
    196–200
  and production, 177–178, 181–183,
    190, 193
  *see also* consumer politics
contextualism, 8–9
convertibility, abandonment of, 81–84
co-operative movement, 172
  in Japan, 180
  *see also* consumer politics
co-ordination, social, *see* social
  co-ordination
Cork
  Cuverian Society of Cork, 42
corporations, *see* guilds
*Courier de Provence*, 65
Creuzé-Latouche, J.-A., 63
Croly, Herbert, 162
culturalism, 9–10
culture, lifestyle, *see* lifestyle culture
culture and markets, 16
culture-and-society tradition, 106
currency policy, 81–84, 85–86
Curzon, Lord, 212

Darwin, Charles
  *Origin of the Species*, 119
Das, Gurchuran, 207
decentred theory, 7
democracy
  and American progressivism, 156–157,
    159–161, 162–163
  and consumer politics, 175, 185–189
  distributive, 162, 163, 168, 169
  and German historicism, 159–161,
    162–163
  and guilds, 103
  participatory, 162–163, 167, 169
  *see also* citizenship

democratic republicanism, *see*
  republicanism, democratic
denationalization of global capital market,
  240–241
derivatives in global capital market,
  231–232
Devine, Edward T., 146, 149
Dewey, John, 146, 156, 158–160, 161,
  162–163, 165
Diderot, Denis, 40
digitization and the global capital market,
  11–12, 225, 227–228, 231, 236–238,
  244–245
disembedding, 29, 38
  *see also* embeddedness
Disraeli, Benjamin, 87
D'Ivernois, François, 51–52
Drumont, Edouard, 102
Du Bois, W. E. B., 146, 147, 155, 162, 163
Duguit, Léon, 103
Dumont, Etienne, 65
Dupan, Jacques Mallet, 54
Dupont de Nemours, Pierre-Samuel, 50,
  62–63, 65
  *Physiocratie*, 52
Durkheim, Emile, 17, 91, 96–97, 100–104
  *La division sociale du travail*, 100
  'Le Socialisme', 103
Du Roveray, Jacques-Antoine, 65

East India Company, 208
Eastwood, David, 12, 13–14
economic man, 123–128
economy, political, *see* political economy
*Edinburgh Review*, 88
education, consumer, *see* consumer
  politics, consumer education
Ely, Richard T., 146, 147, 155, 161
embeddedness
  of global capital market, 11–12,
    224–225, 243–246
  of markets, 2, 10–19, 44, 202–205
  *see also* disembedding
Emerson, Ralph Waldo, 106
emigration, 108
empire, 86, 208
enclosure, 35
Enfield, Honora, 175
Engels, Friedrich, 84
Enlightenment, rural, 34
entrepreneurs, 3
environmentalism, 16–17
  and ethics, 115–119
  and Marshall, A., 127
  of Mill, J. S., 105, 106–119

environmentalism (*cont.*)
  and religion, 115–119
  of Ruskin, J., 105–106, 107, 119–123
equities and bonds, 232, 239
ethics, 15, 16
  and American progressivism, 148–150,
    153–159, 169
  and civil society, 137–138
  and community, 137–138
  and consumer politics, 177–179,
    183–184, 200
  and environmentalism, 115–119
  and German historicism, 148–150,
    153–159
  and industrial capitalism, 157–159
  and markets, 2–5, 57–61, 66–68,
    153–154, 204, 206–208
  and political economy, 125
  and poverty, 166–168
  and *swadeshi*, 220
E*Trade, 237
Etzioni, Amitai, 130
Euronext (NEXT), 238

farmers, *see* peasants
fascism and guilds, 104
Fawcett, Henry, 116, 117, 120–121
Federal Housing Association, 188
feminism, 108, 143
  *see also* women
Ferguson, Adam, 131, 133
Filene, Edward, 186
finance, international, *see* global capital
  market
financial centres, 11–12, 228–229,
    233–241, 245–246
Fontane, Theodor, 141
food prices, 174–177, 181–183
food safety, 175–176, 183, 184–185,
    191–192
Foucault, Michel, 8, 28, 139–141
France
  agricultural societies in, 31–32, 36–37,
    42
  anglophobia in, 60–61, 64, 67–69
  guilds in, 17, 92–94, 100–104
  Institut National, 63, 64
  liberalism in, 47, 91–92, 93–94
  physiocracy in, 46, 57–61
  political economy in, 12–13, 46, 64–69
  relationship with Britain in 1700s, 53–54
  republicanism in, 12–13, 49, 61–69,
    103
  revolution, *see* French Revolution
free trade, 13, 15, 49, 86–89, 93–95

and the Conservative Party, 71–72, 74
and consumer politics, 172–177,
    181–183, 200
and Ruskin, J., 122
free will, *see* will
French Revolution, 49
  and guilds, 91–92
  and physiocracy, 62–63
  and political economy, 12–13, 61–64
  and Rousseau, J.-J., 54–55
Freund, Ernst, 146

Gall, Lothar, 94
Gambles, Anna, 87
Gandhi, Indira, 215
Gandhi, Mahatma, 15, 221
  and markets, 213–214
  and *swadeshi*, 213–216
Gandhi, Rajiv, 205
Gellner, Ernest, 28, 29
*Gemeinschaft*, 16, 104, 131–144
  *versus Gesellschaft*, 139–144
  and self, 136, 137
  and will, 135–137
  *see also* community
*Gemeinschaft und Gessellschaft*, 17–18,
    131–144
German historicism, *see* historicism,
  German
Germany
  associations in, 96–100
  guilds in, 17, 94–97, 133
  liberalism in, 94–95
  self-government in, 99–100
*Gesellschaft*, 16, 104, 131–144
  *versus Gemeinschaft*, 139–144
  and person, 136, 137
  and will, 135–137
  *see also* civil society
Giddens, A., 29
Gierke, Otto von, 17, 91, 96–100, 133, 141
  *Deutsches Genossenschaftsrecht*, 97
Gladstone, William, 86
global capital market, 11–12, 19
  bonds and equities in, 232
  denationalization of, 240–241
  derivatives in, 231–232
  and digitization, 11–12, 225, 227–228,
    231, 236–238, 244–245
  embeddedness of, 224–225, 243–246
  financial centres in, 228–229, 233–241,
    245–246
  financial innovations and, 231–232
  interconnectivity of, 227–228, 231
  and mergers and alliances, 238–240

regulation of, 227, 228–229
and social connectivity, 5, 236–238,
    245–246
standards in, 243–244
and the state, 241–245
transactions in, 227–228, 232
as ultimate market, 225–226
see also hedge funds; pension funds
Global Equity Market, 238
globalization, 11, 22, 24
and consumer politics, 170–171
in India, 205–206
of markets, 144
Goodnow, Frank J., 146
governance, 5–10, 19–24
and consumer politics, 198
and markets, 12, 18–19
and post-structuralism, 8
and social history, 9–10
Great Transformation, 27–28
green politics, see environmentalism
Grief, Avner, 44
Guha, R., 216–217
guilds, 17
and civil society, 95–96, 100–104
and democracy, 103
and fascism, 104
in France, 92–94, 100–104
and the French Revolution, 91–92
in Germany, 94–97, 133
and Hegel, G. W. F., 95–96
and liberalism, 91–92, 93–104
and markets, 104
nature of, 90–91
see also associations

Hacking, Ian, 29
Haller, Albrecht von, 57
Harris, Jose, 16, 17–18
Haupt, Heinz-Gerhard, 16, 17
health, public, see public health
hedge funds, 231
Hegel, G. W. F., 95–96, 131, 133
    Elements of the Philosophy of Right, 95
Helvétius, 69
Henderson, Charles, 146
Henderson, Leon, 186
High Toryism, see Toryism, High
Hill, Octavia, 106
Hindu nationalism, 209–210, 217–221
    see also Bharatiya Janata Party (BJP)
historicism, German, 14, 145–150
and capitalism, 151–152, 157–159
and democracy, 159–161
and ethics, 148–150, 153–159

and laissez faire, 148, 151–161
and liberalism, 154–157
and markets, 148
Hobbes, Thomas, 131, 133, 134, 141
    Leviathan, 132
Hobson, J. A., 173
Hodgskin, Thomas
    Popular Political Economy, 76
hollowing out, see governance
Home Loan Corporation, 188
Housewives League, 177
Howe, Anthony, 86
Howe, Frederic C., 146
human consciousness, see self
Hume, David, 47, 56, 119, 134, 135
Huskisson, William, 85, 86

ideas and markets, 2–3, 11
India
    economic reform, 5, 15–16, 202–203,
        205–206, 221–223
    globalization, 205–206
    Hindu nationalism, 209–210, 217–221
    institutions, 221–222
    neo-liberalism, 15–16, 205–206,
        221–223
    nuclear tests, 219–220
    regionalization of, 222–223
    statism, 205
    suspicion of markets, 206–208
    see also Mandal; Mandir; Movement
        politics; swadeshi
Indian National Congress, 213
individualism, 76–78, 98–99, 160
information technology, see digitization
    and the global capital market
innovations, financial, 231–232
Institute for Global Civil Society, 129
Institute for the Study of Civil Society, 129
institutional investors, 230–231
institutions, 7, 19, 153–154
    and American progressivism, 160
    in India, 221–222
    and Tönnies, F., 138–139
Institut National, 63, 64
interconnectivity
    and the global capital market, 227–228,
        231
    see also social connectivity
international finance, see global capital
    market
International Monetary Fund (IMF), 244
international politics and consumer
    politics, 182–183
interpretive theory, 19–24

intervention, state, *see* state intervention
investors, institutional, 230–231
Ireland, agricultural societies in, 29–31, 42

Jäger, Hans, 96
Jain, L. C.
    'Gandhi and the Market', 213–214
James, Edmund J., 146
James, William, 154
Janata Party, 215
Jan Sangh, 215, 218
Japan, consumer politics in, 179–181,
    189–194, 200–201
Jenkins, Robert, 15–16
Johnson, Lyndon B., 166
justice, *see* ethics

Kant, Immanuel, 131, 132, 134, 135,
    141
Karnataka Rajya Raitha Sangha, 212
Kelley, Florence, 146, 155, 177
Kennedy, J. F., 195
Keyserling, Leon, 188
Knies, Karl, 148, 149
Koerner, Lisbet, 40
Koyré, Alexandre
    *From the Closed World to the Infinite
    Universe*, 28
Krishna, S. M., 222
Kumar, Dharma, 221
*Kürwille*, *see* will

labour movement and consumer politics,
    177–178
*laissez faire*, 13, 47, 145–146
    and American progressivism, 151–161
    critique of, 148
    and German historicism, 151–161
    *see also* liberalism; state intervention
Lake District, preservation of, 112
Lasch, Christopher, 162–163, 165
Laski, Harold, 184
Latour, Bruno, 37
la Tour du Pin La Charce, René de, 102
League for Independent Republican
    Action, 186
League of Nations, 182, 184
Leavis, F. R., 106
Legret, 93
Liberal Democratic Party, Japan, 193
liberalism, 9, 18–19
    and the Conservative Party, 73
    in France, 47, 91–92, 93–94
    and German historicism, 154–157
    in Germany, 94–95

and guilds, 91–92, 93–104
and Say, J.-B., 66
*see also* free trade; *laissez faire*;
    neo-liberalism; progressivism,
    American
Liberal Party, 70–71
life sciences, 39–43
lifestyle culture, 15
    and consumer politics, 176–177
Lille, guilds in, 92
Linnaeus, Carolus, 39, 40–42
Liverpool, Lord, 71
Livesey, James, 11
Lloyd George, David, 174
London Stock Exchange, 239
Lowell, Josephine Shaw, 178
Lynd, Robert and Helen
    *Middletown*, 187
Lyon, agricultural society in, 31

Maastricht Treaty, 197
Macaulay, Thomas Babington, 110, 112
Machiavelli, Niccolò di Bernardo dei, 49
Maclachlan, Patricia, 14–15
Madden, S., 34–35
Maine, Sir Henry, 133
Malthus, Thomas Robert, 78–81, 85
    *Essay on the Principle of Population*, 76–78
    and Ruskin, J., 121
    and Southey, R., 77, 78–79
    and Wordsworth, W., 115–116
    *see also* neo-Malthusianism
Mandal, 15, 210, 211
    and markets, 215
    and *swadeshi*, 215–217
Mandir, 15, 209–210, 211
    and *swadeshi*, 212–213, 214–215,
    217–221
market, global capital, *see* global capital
    market
market failure, *see* markets, failures of
markets
    and American progressivism, 168
    and Christianity, 57–61
    and colonization, 208
    and the Conservative Party, 71–73
    and culture, 16
    embeddedness of, 2, 10–19, 44,
    202–205
    and ethics, 2–5, 57–61, 66–68, 153–154,
    204, 206–208
    failures of, 14, 75–76, 85–86, 123–128
    and German historicism, 148
    globalization of, 144
    and governance, 12, 18–19

and guilds, 17, 104
and High Toryism, 13–14, 74–78
and ideas, 2–3, 11
Indian suspicion of, 206–208
and Ruskin, J., 121–122
and Gandhi, M., 213–214
and Mandal, 215
and peasants, 27–28, 44
and physiocracy, 57–61
and practices, 2–3, 11, 148, 204
and regulation, 2, *see also* state
 intervention
and state, 1–2, 6–8, 14
and *swadeshi*, 217–223
and Tönnies, F., 143–144
and traditions, 2–5, 18–19, 148,
 202–205, 211
ultimate market, 225–226
and the World Bank, 203–204
*see also* capitalism; free trade; global
 capital market; *laissez faire*;
 protectionism; supply and demand
Marsh, Benjamin C., 146
Marshall, Alfred, 16, 107, 123, 125–127
and environmentalism, 127
*Principles of Economics*, 126
'Social Possibilities of Economic
 Chivalry', 125
Marx, Karl, 131, 133
*Critique of Political Economy*, 133
*Das Kapital*, 133
Maurice, F. D., 114
Maxwell, John, 25–26
Mead, George Herbert, 146, 158
meanings, *see* beliefs
mergers and alliances, 238–240
Mill, John Stuart, 2, 16–17
*Auguste Comte on Positivism*, 118–119
*Autobiography*, 113, 114
and emigration, 108
environmentalism of, 105, 106–119
and feminism, 108
influence of Wordsworth, W., on,
 112–117
influence on Ruskin, J., 120–123
and neo-Malthusianism, 107–111
*On Liberty*, 108
and political economy, 123–128
*Principles of Political Economy*, 106, 109,
 113, 116, 120
and production, 109
and religion, 115–119
and socialism, 122–123
and Southey, R., 117
*Subjection of Women*, 108

*Three Essays on Religion*, 118, 119
*Utilitarianism*, 118
Mirabeau, Gabriel Honoré Riquetti de, 65
Mirabeau, Victor Riquetti, Marquis de,
 57–58
*L'Ami des hommes*, 57
modernity
and peasants, 3–4, 27–29
and traditions, 3–5, 11
*see also* rationality
modern republicanism, *see* republicanism,
 modern
Molesworth, R. M., 30–31
Molony Committee on Consumer
 Protection, 196
monarchy and physiocracy, 60
monetary policy, 14, 81–84, 85–86
Montchrétien, Antoyne de
*Traicté de l'œconomie politique*, 53
Montesquieu, Charles Louis, 62
Montpellier, Société royale des sciences,
 31, 36, 42
Moody's rated bonds, 229
Moore, James, 33
morality, *see* ethics
Morris, William, 105, 126
*News from Nowhere*, 126
Mounier, Jean-Joseph, 54
Mouret of Saint-Jean de Bruel, 37
Movement politics, 210–211, 213
Muir, John, 106
Mumford, Louis, 162
Murray, Denis, 43

Nader, Ralph, 192, 195
*Taming of the Giant Corporation*, 195
Naidu, Chandrababu, 222
Naismith, J., 39
Naokazu, Takeuchi, 191
Napoleon Bonaparte, 47, 64
Narbonne, Archbishop of, 31
Narmada Bachao Andolan, 210
NASDAQ, 237, 238
National Alliance of People's Movements,
 210
National Anti-Food Trust League, 177
National Consumer Council (NCC), 197,
 198, 199
National Consumers' League (NCL),
 177–179
National Democratic Alliance, 209–210
nationalism, Hindu, *see* Hindu nationalism
National Recovery Administration (NRA),
 186, 188
 Consumer Advisory Board, 188

National Trust, 106, 112
natural history, 39–43
Navarre, Antoine, 36
Nayar, Raj, 218
neo-liberalism
  and consumer politics, 197
  in India, 15–16, 205–206, 221–223
  see also liberalism
neo-Malthusianism, 107–111
  see also Malthus, Thomas Robert
networks, 6–7, 11, 21
  see also agricultural societies; social
    connectivity; social co-ordination
New Deal, 185–189
new political economy, 1, 2
  see also political economy
New York Stock Exchange (NYSE), 238
Nisbet, Robert, 102
Noorani, A. G., 215
North, Douglas, 45
nuclear tests in India, 219–220

Oastler, Richard, 87
O'Connor, Alice, 167
Olmsted, Frederick Law, Jr, 146
Orr, John Boyd, 184

Pagès, Jacques, 37
Paine, Thomas, 63, 65
Paley, William, 76
Parekh, Bhikku, 213
Paris, Société Royale d'Agriculture, 36
Parmentier, 34
Patten, Simon N., 146, 147, 149,
    156–157, 163–164, 165
  New Basis of Civilization, 179
Pawar, Sharad, 222
peasants
  and markets, 27–28, 44
  and modernity, 3–4, 27–29
  rationality of, 26–28, 35–37, 44–45
  and religion, 31
Peel, Sir Robert, 14, 81, 82, 85, 86, 88–89
pension funds, 230
person, 136, 137
  see also self
physiocracy
  and agriculture, 58
  and Christianity, 57–61
  in France, 46
  and the French Revolution, 62–63
  and markets, 57–61
  and monarchy, 60
  and political economy, 52, 57–61
  and religion, 52

and Rousseau, J.-J., 57–58, 61
and Say, J.-B., 50
Pigou, Arthur Cecil, 123
Pitt, William, 70–71, 81, 86
ploughs, 37–39
poets
  and political economy, 73–74, 78–79,
    115–116
  see also individual poets
Polanyi, Karl, 3–4, 27, 43, 204
Political and Economic Planning (PEP),
    185
political economy, 15
  and the Conservative Party, 71–73
  and ethics, 125
  in France, 12–13, 46, 64–69
  and the French Revolution, 61–64
  and High Toryism, 73–89
  and Mill, J. S., 123–128
  monetary policy, 81–84, 85–86
  and physiocracy, 52, 57–61
  and poets, 73–74, 78–79, 115–116
  and Rousseau, J.-J., 46, 52, 54–57, 69
  and Ruskin, J., 123–128
  and Say, J.-B., 46–47
  and Southey, R., 73–74
  see also new political economy
poor laws, 79
population control, see Malthus, Thomas
    Robert
positivism, 20–24
post-structuralism, 8, 22
poverty and ethics, 166–168
practices, 5, 19–24
  and markets, 2–3, 11, 148, 204
Preuss, Hugo, 100
production
  and consumption, 177–178, 181–183,
    190, 193
  Mill, J. S. and, 109
progressivism, American, 14, 145–150
  and capitalism, 151–152, 157–159
  and consumption, 163–164, 165–166,
    167–168, 169
  and democracy, 156–157, 159–161,
    162–163
  and ethics, 148–150, 153–159, 169
  and individualism, 160
  and institutions, 160
  and laissez faire, 151–161
  and liberalism, 154–157
  and markets, 168
  and social policy, 165–168
  and welfare, 165–168
protection, social, see social protection

protectionism, 86–89, 93–95
  and the Conservative Party, 71–72
public health, 175–176, 183, 184–185,
  191–192
Pultenay, William, 25

Quesnay, François, 46, 57, 58, 59
  *Despotisme de la Chine*, 61

radicalism, 18
  and consumer politics, 173–174
Ram temple, 209
Ranulf, Svend, 104
Rashtriya Swayamsevak Sangh (RSS), 209,
  214–215, 217, 221
rationality, 11, 28–31
  and agricultural societies, 39–40
  of peasants, 26–28, 35–37, 44–45
  *see also* modernity
Rawnsley, Canon, 106
Reagan, Ronald, 196
reason, *see* rationality
reform, *see* progressivism, American
reform, economic, *see* India, economic
  reform
regulation, 2, 227, 228–229
  *see also* consumer politics, protection and
    regulation; state intervention
Reich, Robert, 166
religion
  and Constant, B., 69
  and consumer politics, 191
  and environmentalism, 115–119
  and Mill, J. S., 115–119
  and peasants, 31
  and physiocracy, 52
  and Ruskin, J., 115
  and Say, J.-B., 66, 69
  *see also* Christianity; Hindu nationalism
republicanism, 9–10
  democratic, 12, 49–51, 64–69
  in France, 12–13, 49, 61–69, 103
  modern, 12, 49–50, 51, 54–57, 64–65,
    69
  and Say, J.-B., 64–69
Reybaz, Pierre-Saloman, 65
Ricardo, David, 77, 79, 80, 81–82, 89
  *Principles of Political Economy*, 75
Rickman, John, 77
Riehl, Wilhelm, 133
rights, 15, 154–157, 178–179, 188, 194
Rivière, P.-P.-F.-J.-H. Le Mercier de la
  *De l'Ordre naturel et essentiel des sociétés
    politiques*, 58
Robertson, Thomas, 34

Robespierre, Maximilien, 64
Robinson, David, 82–83, 87
Roebuck, John Arthur, 114
Rœderer, Pierre-Louis, 55, 62
Roland, 65
Roosevelt, Franklin D., 189
Roosevelt, Theodore, 145
Rosenthal, Jean-Laurent, 44
Ross, Edward A., 146
Rotteck, Karl von, 94–95
Rousseau, Jean-Jacques, 40, 47, 62, 68
  *Confessions*, 54
  *Contrat social*, 50, 52, 54, 56, 57
  'Économie politique', 55
  *Emile*, 52
  and the French Revolution, 54–55
  *Lettres écrites de la montagne*, 56
  and modern republicanism, 49–50,
    54–57, 64–65
  and physiocracy, 57–58, 61
  and political economy, 46, 52, 54–57, 69
Royal Dublin Society, 29–31, 32–34, 39,
  41
Rubinow, Isaac M., 146
Rudolph, L. I. and S. H., 210
rural history, *see* agricultural history
Ruskin, John, 16–17, 139–144
  culture-and-society tradition, 106
  environmentalism of, 105–106, 107,
    119–123
  and free trade, 122
  influence of Mill, J. S., on, 120–123
  influence of Smith, A., on, 124–125
  influence of Wordsworth, W., on,
    119–120
  influence of Xenophon on, 121
  and Malthus, T. R., 121
  and markets, 121–122
  and political economy, 123–128
  and religion, 115
  and socialism, 122–123
  *Unto This Last*, 105, 120

Sadler, Michael, 14
  *Law of Population*, 74, 77–78
Saint-Just, L. A. L. F. de, 64
Sale of Food and Drugs Act, 1875, 175
Sassen, Saskia, 11–12
Say, Jean-Baptiste, 2, 12–13, 18, 50–51
  and anglophobia, 67–69
  *Cours complet d'économie politique
    pratique*, 46
  and ethics, 66–68
  *La Décade philosophique, politique et
    littéraire*, 65, 66

Say, Jean-Baptiste (*cont.*)
  *Lettres à Malthus*, 47
  and liberalism, 66
  and physiocracy, 50
  on political economy, 46–47
  and religion, 66, 69
  and republicanism, 64–69
  *Traité d'économie politique*, 46, 47, 65
  *Traité de politique pratique*, 67
Schäfer, Axel R., 12, 14
Schlink, Frederick J. and Stuart Chase
  *Your Money's Worth*, 187
Schmoller, Gustav, 148, 150, 152, 153,
    157, 160, 161, 164
Schumpeter, Joseph, 153
Scotland
  agricultural history in, 25–26, 38–39
  agricultural societies in, 32
Scott, Walter, 82–83
Scruton, Roger
  *Dictionary of Political Thought*, 130
self, 136, 137
  *see also* person
self-government in Germany, 99–100
Sen, Amartya, 28
Senior, Nassau, 79
Seven Years War 1757–1763, 53
Shapin, Steven, 29, 35
Shaw, Albert, 151, 155
  *Contemporary Review*, 145, 147, 149
Shintô, 191
Sidney, Algernon
  *Discourses on Government*, 64
Sieyès, Emmanuel, 50
Sinclair, John, 34, 36
Sinha, Yashwant, 219–220
Sismondi, Sismond de, 92
Skinner, Quentin, 8
Small, Albion W., 146, 150–151, 152,
    160
  *American Journal of Sociology*, 150
Small, James, 38
Smith, Adam, 46, 48, 76, 79, 88, 94
  influence on John Ruskin, 124–125
  reinterpretation by progressives,
    151–152
  *Wealth of Nations*, 46, 61, 68, 75, 77, 133
Smith, Merrit Roe, 37
social connectivity, 11–12
  and global capital markets, 5, 236–238,
    245–246
  *see also* interconnectivity; networks;
    social co-ordination
social co-ordination, 1–2, 4–5, 10, 18–19,
    21–22

*see also* interconnectivity; networks;
    social connectivity
social history and governance, 9–10
socialism
  and Mill, J. S., 122–123
  and Ruskin, J., 122–123
  and Tönnies, F., 134–135, 144
social policy
  in United States, 165–168
  *see also* welfare
social protection, 4
Sombart, Werner, 3
Soros, George, 204
Sorty, Pierre, 36
Southey, Robert, 14, 75–76, 85, 87, 89,
    110, 114
  *Colloquies on the Progress and Future
    Prospects of Society*, 74, 75, 77, 78
  and Malthus, T. R., 77, 78–79
  and Mill, J. S., 117
  and political economy, 73–74
  *Quarterly Review*, 73, 79–80
standards in global capital market,
    243–244
state
  and civil society, 138–140
  and global capital market, 241–245
  and markets, 1–2, 6–8, 14
  theory of, 149
  and Tönnies, F., 138–140
state intervention, 145, 150, 160–161, 162
  *see also* consumer politics, protection and
    regulation; *laissez faire*; regulation
Stein, Burton, 206
Stephens, Dr, 32
Sterling, John, 114–115
Stiglitz, Joseph, 203
Stockholm Stock Exchange, 238
Storm, Theodor, 141
supply and demand, 224, 225–226
*swadeshi*, 15, 19, 20, 202
  definition of, 211–212
  and ethics, 220
  and Gandhi, M., 213–216
  and Mandal, 215–217
  and Mandir, 212–213, 214–215,
    217–221
  and markets, 217–223
  and Movement politics, 213
  and nuclear tests, 219–220
Swadeshi Jagran Manch (SJM), 212–213,
    217, 218, 221

Tagore, Rabindranath, 212
Tallin Stock Exchange, 238

Tatas, 221
taxonomy, 39–43
technology, agricultural, 37–39
technology, information, see digitization
    and the global capital market
Tennessee Valley Authority, 188
Thatcher, Margaret, 198
Theophilanthropy, 63
Third Way, 2
Thomson Financials, 239
Thoreau, Henry David, 106
Tönnies, Ferdinand, 2, 100
    and associations, 138–139
    contemporary relevance of, 143–144
    Gemeinschaft und Gesellschaft, 17–18,
        131–144
    and markets, 143–144
    on person, 136, 137
    personal life of, 141
    on self, 136, 137
    and socialism, 134–135, 144
    and state, 138–140
    on will, 135–137, 139–141
Toronto Stock Exchange, 238
Toryism, High
    and agriculture, 87
    and capitalism, 75
    and empire, 86
    and free trade, 13–14, 86–89
    and Malthus, T. R., 76–81
    and markets, 13–14, 74–78
    and monetary policy, 13–14, 81–84,
        85–86
    and political economy, 13–14, 73–89
    see also Conservative Party
traditions, 10–24
    and consumer politics, 170–181,
        200–201
    culture-and-society, 106
    and markets, 2–5, 18–19, 148, 202–205,
        211
    and modernity, 3–5, 11
    see also beliefs
transactions, 227–228, 232
Trentmann, Frank, 14–15
trust, 29, 30
Tugwell, Rexford, 164
Tull, Jethro, 34, 37
Turgot, Anne-Robert-Jacques, 48
Twentieth-Century Fund, 186

United Nations, 197
United States
    consumer politics, 177–179, 185–189,
        194–196, 200–201

progressivism, see progressivism,
    American
social policy, 165–168
welfare state, 146, 160–161, 165–168
Upadhyaya, Deendayal, 215
utilitarianism, see Mill, John Stuart

Vajpayee, Atal Behari, 209, 215
Vandermonde, Alexandre, 63
Veblen, Thorstein, 146, 152, 156, 162
Villeneuve-Bargemont, Comte de
    Économie politique chrétienne, 92
Voltaire, 62

Wade, Robert, 206
Wagner, Adolf, 148, 149, 150
Wagner, Robert, 188
Walpole, Sir Robert, 70
Watts, Frank, 184
Webb, Beatrice, 127
Webb, Sidney, 127
Weber, Max, 28, 164
welfare, 123–128, 146, 160–161, 165–168
    see also poor laws
Wesenwille, see will
Westminster Review, 88
Weyl, Walter, 163
Whatmore, Richard, 12–13
Whiggism, 70–71
will, 135–137, 139–141
Willetts, David
    Civic Conservatism, 130
Williams, Raymond, 106
Wilson, Woodrow, 145
Winch, Donald, 16–17, 80
Wise, M. Norton, 37
Wolinski, Louis, 93
women
    and consumer politics, 179
    and taxonomy, 42
    see also feminism
Women's Co-operative Guild (WCG),
    172, 173, 175, 181
Wordsworth, William, 73
    Description of the Scenery of the Lakes, 113
    influence on Mill, J. S., 112–117
    influence on Ruskin, J., 119–120
    and Malthus, T. R., 115–116
    Prelude, 112
World Bank, 203–204, 205
World Economic Forum, 241
Wrigley, E. A., 110

Xenophon
    influence on Ruskin, J., 121